# Investing in Closed-End Funds: Finding Value and Building Wealth

# Investing in Closed-End Funds: Finding Value and Building Wealth

## Albert J. Fredman
### and
## George Cole Scott

**New York Institute of Finance**
New York•London•Toronto•Sydney•Tokyo•Singapore

**Library of Congress Cataloging-in-Publication Data**

Fredman, Albert J.
   Investing in closed-end funds : finding value and building wealth
 / Albert J. Fredman and George Cole Scott.
     p.   cm.
   Includes index.
   ISBN 0–13–503491–4
    1. Closed-end funds.  2. Closed-end funds—United States.
   3. Closed-end funds—Directories.  I. Scott, George Cole.
   II. Title.  III. Title: Closed-end funds.
HG4530.F74   1991
332.63′27—dc20                   90–21030
                                 CIP

This publication is designed to provide accurate and authoritative information in regard to the subject matter covered. It is sold with the understanding that the publisher is not engaged in rendering legal, accounting, or other professional service. If legal advice or other expert assistance is required, the services of a competent professional person should be sought.

*From a Declaration of Principles*
*Jointly Adopted by*
*a Committee of the American Bar Association*
*and a Committee of Publishers and Associations*

10  9  8  7  6  5  4  3  2  1

# Dedication

To our wives, Kathleen L. and Leslie Jane, who tolerated our many hours of work

A.J.F. and G.C.S.


Authors' Disclaimer

While we feel the investment strategies presented in this book are sound and have generally proven profitable in the past, they are not guaranteed to produce profitable results in the future. Furthermore, the authors discuss many specific closed-end funds, but in no way are our discussions to be interpreted as recommendations for or against the purchase or sale of these funds. Also, the funds which aren't mentioned are not necessarily viewed by us as being any more or less desirable than those identified. The authors may own or may have owned some of the funds included in this book. Co-author, Scott is a member of the board of directors of a closed-end fund, which is disclosed. Finally, we have tried our best to ensure the accuracy of information presented but in no way can this be guaranteed.

# Contents

Foreword by Steven M. Cress                         xv
Preface                                             xvii
Acknowledgements                                    xxi
Introduction                                        xxv

## PART 1: OVERVIEW                                 1

## 1.  Investing in Closed-End Funds               3

Investment versus Speculation                       4
  Investment                              4
  Speculation                             5
Fund Basics                                         5
  Open- versus Closed-End Funds           5
Organizational Structure                            7
A Brief History                                     10
  Boom and Bust                           11
  Small Investors Return                  13
The Great Bull Market                               14
  Personality Funds                       16

Specialized Equity and Convertible
   Funds                                          16
The Bond Funds                                    17
Shareholder Reinvestment                          18
Advantages of All Funds                           20
   Diversification                              20
   Professional Management                      20
   Many Portfolio Choices                       21
   Economies of Scale                           21
   Record Keeping                               21
Unique CEF Advantages                             22
   Stability of Capital                         23
   Investment for Total Return                  24
   Trading Advantages                           24
Disadvantages of CEFs                             26
Types of CEFs                                     28
Conclusion                                        29

**2.   Discounts and Premiums                      31**

Computing Discounts or Premiums                   34
A Risk Factor                                     37
Advantages of the Discount                        39
   Leverage                                     39
   Higher Yield                                 39
Beware the Premium!                               40
Why the Discount?                                 42
   Fund Specific Factors                        45
   Sector Specific Factors                      46
   General Factors                              47
   Fund Type Affects the Discount               49
Narrowing the Gap                                 51
Studies of CEF Performance                        54
Will Discounts Persist?                           55
Conclusion                                        58

**3.   Analyzing a Fund                             61**

The Authors' Philosophy                           61
Standard Sources                                  63
   Media Coverage                               63
   Shareholder Reports                          64
   Visiting the Library                         65

Lipper Data                                              69
Advisory Letters                                        70
Brokers Who Specialize                                  71
Analyzing the Data                                      73
  Expense Analysis                                      73
  Distributions                                         78
  Analyzing Fund Distributions                          80
  Examining Performance                                 83
  Tracking Discounts                                    85
  Portfolio Turnover                                    87
  Unrealized Appreciation                               89
  Derivative Products                                   90
Conclusion                                              91
Appendix 3–1 Calculation of Total
  Return for a Multi-Year Holding
  Period: Closed- versus Open-End Fund                  92

**PART 2: EQUITY-ORIENTED FUNDS**

## 4. Investing in Stock Funds                          97

Stock Fund Differences                                  98
Diversified Versus Non-Diversified                      99
Advantages of Stock Funds                               100
  Superior Long-Term Performance                        100
  Time Diversification Lowers Risk                      102
  The Power of Compounding                              103
  Gifts to Minors                                       105
  Deeper Discounts                                      105
  Superstar Managers                                    106
Growth Versus Value                                     106
  Value Investing                                       107
  Approaches to Value                                   107
  Templeton's Principles                                108
  Growth Investing                                      109
Small Stocks                                            110
  When to Invest?                                       111
  Small Cap CEFs                                        112
Conclusion                                              116

## 5. Older Domestic Equity Funds                       117

Basic Data                                              118
Performance Records                                     118

Management Arrangement                             121
Fund Profiles                                      121
   Classic Funds                                   122
   Other Older Funds                               132
Can CEF Performance Be Measured
   in a Meaningful Way?                            138
Conclusion                                         140

**6.  The Personality Funds                        141**

Fund Features                                      143
Fund Profiles                                      144
Selection Guidelines                               159
Conclusion                                         164

**7.  Dual Purpose Funds                           165**

The Dual Fund Concept Was
   Dusted Off                                      166
Dual Fund Basics                                   166
   The Leverage Factor                             167
   Maturity Date                                   168
   Growth in Income                                170
Potential Pitfalls                                 171
Gauging Discounts and Premiums                     172
Dual Fund Analysis                                 172
Individual Funds                                   177
   Diversified Common Stock Funds                  177
   Specialized Dual Funds                          179
Conclusion                                         183

**8.  Sector Equity Funds                          185**

Sector Risk                                        186
Gold-oriented Funds                                187
Utility Funds                                      192
Financial Company Funds                            195
Other Sectors                                      198
Fund Selection                                     203
Consider Dollar Cost Averaging                     203
Conclusion                                         205

## 9. Global Investing                                            207

Cross-Border Investing Is Nothing New              208
Why Invest Internationally?                        208
    Diversification                               208
    More Opportunities                            213
    Better Opportunities                          214
    Protection Against a Falling Dollar           217
Risks of Investing Abroad                          217
    Currency Risk                                 218
    Political Risk                                219
The Investment Company Route                       219
    Returns to CEF Investors                      220
    Types of Funds                                221
Conclusion                                         222

## 10. Single- and Multi-Country Funds                           223

Single Country Funds                               223
What Attracts People to Country
    Funds?                                        227
Country Fund Profiles                              228
Country Fund Valuation                             232
    Country Funds as Growth Stocks                233
    1989 Country Fund Performance                 233
    1990 Country Fund Fall Out                    235
    Discounts Prevail in August 1990              236
    Premium-Discount Fluctuations                 237
    Should You Pay A Premium?                     237
    Funds at Large Discounts                      240
The Multi-Country Funds                            240
Fund Profiles                                      241
The Question of Expenses                           248
Conclusions                                        249

## 11. British and Canadian Funds                                251

The London Investment Trusts                       252
The Scottish Funds                                 259
Canadian Funds                                     261
Getting More Information                           262
Conclusion                                         262

PART 3: FIXED INCOME FUNDS

Introduction to Part 3 on Fixed Income Funds
By A. Michael Lipper

**12. Bond Fund Basics** 271

Closed- Versus Open-End Bond Funds 272
Bond Basics 274
Bond Types 274
Bond Risks 275
Bond Fund Basics 278
Analyzing a CEBF 280
Two Special Ratios 281
Income Dividends versus Income 281
Expense Analysis 283
Set Your Sights on Total Return,
Not Yield 284
Always Relate Turnover to Total
Return 285
Conclusion 285

**13. Older Bond Funds** 287

Past Performance 288
Older Investment Grade Fund Profiles 289
Direct Placement Funds 299
Conclusion 301

**14. Bond Fund Types
and Their Characteristics** 303

Bond Fund Categories 304
High-Yield Corporate Funds 305
U.S. Government Funds 307
Mortgage-Backed Securities Funds 308
Global and International Funds 311
Multi-Sector Funds 312
Flexible Portfolio Funds 316
Municipal Bond Funds 320
The Nuveen Funds 321
Choosing a Muni Fund 322
Loan Participation Funds 324

CEBF Selection Guidelines                      325
Conclusion                                     326

**15. Convertible Funds**                      **327**

The Basics of Convertibles                     327
    The Bond Value                       328
    The Conversion Value                 329
    A Closer Look at the Premiums        330
    Forcing Conversion                   330
Three Convertible Strategies                   332
The Convertible Funds                          334
Convertible Fund Profiles                      336
Conclusions                                    342

**PART 4: PUTTING IT ALL TOGETHER**

**16. Dealing with Your Broker**               **347**

Trading Basics                                 348
    Liquidity                            348
    Average Daily Volume                 349
    The Bid-Asked Spread                 350
    The "Size" in the Quote              351
Entering Orders-Timing is Important            351
    The Market Order                     352
    The Limit Order                      352
    Stop Orders                          354
    Do Not Reduce ("DNR") Orders         354
    All-or-None ("AON") Orders           355
    Discretionary Orders                 355
Watch out for the NAV Syndrome
   on Mondays                                356
Cash Versus Margin                             356
Stock Certificate Considerations               358
A Broker's Advice                              359
Conclusion                                     361

**17. Building Your Portfolio**                **363**

Let's Review our Philosophy                    364
Developing Your Investment Plan                365
The Risk-Return Trade-Off                      367

Risk—A Case Study                                    368
Diversifying Among Fund Types                        370
Time Diversification Makes Equity
  Investing Less Risky                               372
Use Dollar Cost Averaging                            372
Core CEF Holdings                                    373
Additional CEF Holdings                              374
Finding Value                                        374
When to Sell                                         377
Tax Considerations                                   377
Conclusions                                          380

**18.  Takeovers and Open-Ending                     381**

Takeover Basics                                      382
Advantages and Disadvantages
  of Open-Ending                                     386
What Attracts Arbitrageurs?                          387
Arbitrageurs Face Difficulties                       390
Schafer Value Trust: A Case Study                    392
Bergstrom Capital Corporation:
  A Case Study                                       393
Keeping the Discount Narrow                          395
Conclusions                                          396

**19.  A Final Word                                  399**

Funds Versus Ordinary Stocks                         400
Advantages of Open- and Closed-End
  Funds                                              400
Unique Advantages of Closed-End
  Funds                                              401
Recipe for Success                                   403
One Individual's Success Story                       404
Conclusions                                          405

**Glossary                                           407**
**Appendix 1—Directory of Closed-End Funds           431**
**Appendix 2—Directory of Closed-End Fund
  Information Sources and Services                   468**
**Appendix 3—Closed-End Funds Followed
  by *The Value Line Investment Survey*              475**
**Index                                              477**

# Foreword

Closed-end funds are one of the greatest investment vehicles available to the individual. This is a bold statement, but, after having read this book, you'll probably agree. If you don't agree, chances are you invested in a closed-end fund during the late 1980s; you lost money, and you think our assertion is all wet.

Our statement is based on the very reason why most investors purchase closed-end funds—for their attractive attributes. Closed-end funds offer features that other financial products do not possess. There are many reasons for this. The majority of U.S. closed-end funds trade on the New York Stock Exchange, can be bought and sold through any brokerage house, and offer investors the possibility to participate in a wide range of securities, including those from exotic countries. In fact, some country funds offer the only means to invest in foreign markets. Further, generous returns produced by many unreachable domestic sectors and foreign markets are easily attainable by the individual investor through closed-end funds. Also, fixed-income closed-end funds generally offer yields higher than similar mutual funds because leverage can be employed. Open-end funds are not permitted to utilize extensive leverage.

The most important quality that makes the closed-end fund an attractive investment vehicle is its inherent valuation barometer, the premium/discount level. Open-end funds and most other financial vehicles lack this trait. When a fund's current premium or discount is contrasted with its past levels or the levels of peer funds, the difference will likely indicate whether the fund is overvalued or undervalued. This built-in market sentiment barometer allows investors to minimize downside risk. Simply put, with closed-end funds, investors can allocate their assets to the financial sector of their choice and determine which fund offers the best value.

Investors are increasingly becoming aware that they should not be ignoring the benefits generated by closed-end funds. This book should enlighten readers about the features and characteristics of closed-end funds as well as enhance their opportunities to maximize returns and minimize risk.

Steven M. Cress
International Equities
Arnhold and S. Bleichroeder
New York, N.Y.

# Preface

Closed-end funds, both equity and bond funds, have come into their own in the early 1990s as the best investment vehicle for the thinking, value-conscious investor. There are more choices than ever before—perhaps too many—which make the authors' job more important than ever. *Investing in Closed-End Funds* is intended for all investors: large and small, successful and unsuccessful, old and young. It's also for professional investors, including investment advisers, financial planners, and a growing number of stockbrokers. We also believe that many mutual fund investors will recognize the advantages of moving a portion of their investments into the closed-end fund world.

Investors have increasingly become more sophisticated. They are learning that investment success is hard work but worth the effort. By following the principles and guidelines of this book, there is no reason why you can't build a large portfolio of closed-end funds and have the personal satisfaction of doing the job yourself. You may want to have other investments, but, after seeing how well carefully selected closed-end funds can perform, we think you will want to have the majority of your assets in this arena.

When picking a closed-end fund the investor has the opportunity to hire one or more of the world's best money managers. They are performing a real service for large as well as small investors and increasingly for institutions, looking for special expertise in sectors of the economy or in foreign markets. Buying these funds at a discount to their full or net asset value can yield a total return above that obtainable from an otherwise equivalent fund purchased at or above the net asset value. In addition, closed-end funds provide many advantages for which we here make a strong case.

The mission of this book is to demonstrate what you need to know to become a knowledgeable and successful closed-end fund investor. We provide the tools, but you will need to sow the seeds. By following our strategies and being conservative in your choices you should, in time, see your portfolio mature into a bountiful harvest. We are also bold enough to say that by picking the best funds and being careful and patient, you are less likely to face investment losses. But this success doesn't come to everyone. The investor needs to avoid speculative fads and apply the principles outlined in *Investing in Closed-End Funds* to make this happen. One of the co-authors has seen many of his clients build large portfolios by buying a top-performing fund and holding onto it for many years. It was this experience, in part, that led him to join an academician who recognized the vital and timely need for this book. Together, we have attempted to blend the academic and the real world of investment knowledge and insight into a comprehensive, well-documented, readable publication.

The 1980s was a period of explosive growth for both mutual funds and closed-end investment companies. The latter are still relatively unknown to the average investor in spite of extensive coverage in the financial press, particularly for country funds. The wide spectrum of choices available today makes closed-end funds more confusing to many people. We attempt to unravel this maze, clarify the misunderstandings, and point the way to successful closed-end fund investment. Closed-end funds still represent one of the last inefficiencies in the stock market in spite of a narrowing of discounts from time to time. We will show you how to recognize the values, and, if you are willing to work at it, to make consistently high returns.

The authors have interviewed, often face-to-face, many closed-end fund managers, Wall Street analysts, stockbrokers, investment advisers, and others who specialize in this area. Our travels have taken us to over ten cities—including three in the United Kingdom. Many of those we have interviewed have written short "Closed-End Insights" boxes for our book so you can see their points of view. The book contains nearly 30 "Insights" boxes. We consider these pieces to be extremely important, and we're sure they offer interesting reading.

Those who work with closed-end funds today, as managers or investment advisers, are among the best and brightest in the investment community. In an age when there is so much mediocrity in investment performance, the best of them are providing a valuable service for large as well as small investors from all walks of life.

The authors are generally risk-adverse and preservation-of-capital oriented. We search for the greatest value following the "get rich slowly" philosophy which has proven to be highly effective. If you are looking for a book on how to "get rich quick," this is not for you. But, if you are willing to be patient enough to learn about the values available in closed-end funds and what the concept of "total return" really means, this book will be a most valuable tool for achieving your investment goals. *Investing in Closed-End Funds* is the first comprehensive book published on the subject since 1980.

Finally, don't be discouraged if you're a small investor. You can purchase a round lot (100 shares) of many excellent closed-end funds for $1,000 or less. Their built-in diversification makes them a far safer investment than owning a few low-priced stocks.

# *Acknowledgements*

Many people have helped us to make *Investing in Closed-End Funds* a better, more complete book during our months of research and writing. Our greatest acknowledgement is to A. Michael Lipper, CFA, president, and Alling Woodruff, CFA, vice president, Lipper Analytical Services, Inc. Mr. Lipper gave us permission to use the Lipper data on closed-end funds extensively throughout our book. Messrs. Lipper and Woodruff helped us regularly by supplying useful data and analyses and both made helpful suggestions for improving the content of the manuscript.

Next, we thank J. Temple Bayliss of Manakin-Sabot, Virginia, for reading the entire manuscript. His comments and encouragement were very helpful. Steven M. Cress at Arnhold and S. Bleichroeder deserves special mention for sharing with us his viewpoints on closed-end funds.

We also wish to acknowledge our employers: Dr. John T. Emery, CFA, at California State University, Fullerton, and Thomas C. Robertson, CFA, and Donald H. Newlin at the Richmond and Fredericksburg, Virginia offices, re-

spectively, of Anderson & Strudwick, provided support
and encouragement.

The many knowledgeable people who wrote "Closed-
End Insights" boxes expressly for our book have provided
a great service and have certainly enriched our chapters.
Some have even prepared two "Insights" boxes. The authors are grateful for the contributions of the following individuals:

Roger Adams, S.G. Warburg Securities
Bruce C. Baughman and William J. Lippman, Franklin
    Advisers, Inc.
Erik E. Bergstrom, Bergstrom Capital Corporation
Alan G. Carr, H&Q Healthcare Investors
Gary N. Coburn, The Putnam Companies
Bryan G. Colbert, MoneyTrak, Inc.
John R. Cormey, CFA, The Blue Chip Value Fund
Thomas H. Dinsmore, CFA, Davis/Dinsmore Management
    Company
Barry H. Evans and James K. Ho, John Hancock Advisers,
    Inc.
Thomas J. Herzfeld, Thomas J. Herzfeld Advisors, Inc.
Jeffrey Hopson, CFA, A.G. Edwards & Sons, Inc.
Timothy P. Hurley, Delta Management Group, L.P.
Robert J.A. Irwin and Nina M. Arendt, Niagara Share Cor-
    poration
Robert S. Kapito, Blackstone Financial Management
Howard S. Marks, CFA, TCW Convertible Securities Fund,
    Inc.
Ronald G. Olin, Deep Discount Advisors
Charles M. Royce and Thomas R. Ebright, Royce Value
    Trust, Inc.
Steven Samuels, Samuels Asset Management
G. Peter Schieferdecker, Pilot Rock Investments
Robert A. Schwarzkopf, CFA, The Pilgrim Group
Richard J. Spletzer, CFA, Duff & Phelps Utilities Income
    Inc.
Robert H. Steers, Real Estate Securities Income Fund
Mary R. Stone, The Salomon Brothers Fund Inc
Barry Ziskin, The Z-Seven Fund, Inc.

Dr. Martin E. Zweig, The Zweig Total Return Advisors, Inc.

The following individuals helped us in various ways with our research:

David Alger, Fred Alger & Company Incorporated
Stanislaw Bednarski, deceased
Jonathan Clements, *The Wall Street Journal*
Tyler D. Davis, Warburg, Pincus Counsellors, Inc.
Georges L. de Montebello, Helvetia Capital Corp.
Eugene L. DeStaebler, Jr., General American Investors
Stephen J. Dunn and Richard E. Grayson, Current Income Shares
Kathleen M. Flanagan, John Nuveen & Co. Incorporated
Robert N. Gordon, Twenty-First Securities Corporation
Alex Hammond-Chambers, Ivory & Sime, plc
Edwin Anthony Heard, Excelsior Income Shares, Inc.
Frank E. Helsom, CFA, Templeton Investment Counsel, Inc.
Douglas W. Hitchlock, Midland Walwyn Capital Inc.
Mario Keller, Deutsche Bank Capital Corporation
Robert E. Kern, Jr., Morgan Grenfell SMALLCap Fund
Wilmot H. Kidd III, Central Securities Corporation
Sharon K. Kilmer, CFA, Transamerica Income Shares
Wayne D. Lyski, Alliance Capital
William L. McQueen, Bergstrom Capital Corporation
George Michaelis, Source Capital
Dr. J. Mark Mobius, Templeton Emerging Markets Fund, Inc.
Steven Norwitz, T. Rowe Price Associates, Inc.
Michael T. Porter, Smith Barney
William J. Reik III, Mitchell Hutchins
Richard M. Reilly, Quest for Value Advisors
Bradley A. Roberts, Lynch & Mayer, Inc.
Amy B. Rosenblum, Investment Company Institute
David K. Schafer, Schafer Capital Management, Inc.
Ronald T. Schroeder, J&W Seligman & Co. Incorporated
Adam Shapiro, Kayne, Anderson & Co., Inc.
William Silver, American Stock Exchange
Douglas Stone, Frank Russell Company

Paul E. Suckow, Oppenheimer Management Corporation
John M. Templeton, Templeton International
Norman Tepper, *The Value Line Investment Survey*
John S. Tobey, Liberty Asset Management
Ann-Margaret Ulrich, Templeton Funds Distributor, Inc.
John A. Weed, The Salomon Brothers Fund Inc
Glenn C. Weirick, TCW Convertible Securities Fund, Inc.
Patricia A. Zlotin, Massachusetts Financial Services

Kay Sullivan, a computer consultant at California
State University, Fullerton, helped with the graphics. Morgan Stanley Capital International and IDD Information Services provided useful data. The closed-end fund analysts at A.G. Edwards; Kidder, Peabody; PaineWebber; Prudential-Bache; Shearson Lehman Hutton; and Smith Barney shared their research reports with us.

Susan Barry, acquisitions editor; Sheck F. Cho, managing editor-production; and Philip R. Ruppel, associate publisher, all of the New York Institute of Finance, did an outstanding job working with us throughout the preparation of this manuscript. They helped make our job a pleasure.

# Investing in Closed-End Funds: Finding Value and Building Wealth Introduction

The closed-end (or publicly traded) fund is the original form of investment company. These funds played a major role in the speculative bubble of the late 1920s. Many investors in the newly created, highly leveraged trusts of the Roaring Twenties sustained staggering losses in the 1929 crash and closed-end funds quickly faded from the limelight, descending into relative obscurity where they remained for years. When individual investors did begin to re-enter the market after World War II, most chose open-end rather than closed-end funds.

Some interest developed in closed-end funds in the 1960s and 1970s. But the bull market of the 1980s turned out to be a major catalyst for the group. The growth in the number of individual closed-end funds as well as the total assets of closed-end funds in the United States skyrocketed. Their net assets surged from $8.1 billion at the end of 1985 to $60.9 billion at the end of June 1990, according to data published by Lipper Analytical Services.

Closed-end funds, which have attributes of stocks as well as mutual funds, to a large extent remain a relatively

specialized investment vehicle of interest to a more sophisticated group of investors. In fact, the amount invested in closed-end funds works out to be only about five
or six percent of the more than $1 trillion invested in
open-end funds.

Closed-end fund investors today have more choices
among fund types than ever but the funds themselves are
more complex. It also takes more knowledge to analyze
them. For instance, to take advantage of Europe 1992 as
well as the international diversification opportunities offered by the many funds which now invest overseas, one
must understand the risks and rewards of international
investing as well as how to analyze the funds themselves.
Further, more different types of bond funds exist today
than ever before. Sorting them out and analyzing them is
not always that easy.

We'll guide you through the maze of the closed-end
fund universe, pointing out the opportunities and pitfalls
along the way that exist in all the different types of funds,
including the more esoteric dual funds. We'll talk about
funds that range in size from the tiny $4 million Spectra
Fund, which trades in the over-the-counter "pink sheet"
market, to the grant $1.6 billion Nuveen Municipal Value
Fund. All together, we profile over 85 funds for illustrative
purposes. Our book will guide you step-by-step, helping
you to gain the knowledge to become a sophisticated
closed-end fund investor.

We go so far as to say that an investor would be foolish to purchase individual stocks, or open-end funds, at a
time when good closed-end funds are available at attractive discounts from the market values of their underlying
holdings. In fact, a number of these funds are managed
by investment superstars with brilliant long-term records.
Why pay full price when you may be able to find quality
merchandise at a discount?

Many who invest directly in stocks often lose considerable principal and sleep in the process. They become
greedy, fall into the speculation or gambling trap, act on
tips, do not analyze their stocks thoroughly on an ongoing
basis, invest in things they don't understand, and fail to
diversify properly. Mistakes like these can be devastating.

On the other hand, a number of value investors have made enormous profits from closed-end funds while at the same time taking on a relatively low level of risk. What became of the *efficient market hypothesis?* Closed-end funds are one of the best examples of the *inefficient* market. (In an efficient market stocks are presumed to sell at prices equal to their true values at all times. Thus, bargains don't exist as they could in an inefficient market).

Up front it should be understood that the authors advocate a conservative, long-term approach to value investing in closed-end funds. Basically, we'll show you how to buy sound dollar bills for 80 to 90 cents. Closed-end fund investing does not promise instant wealth. But, with the power of compound interest, investors can improve their returns a few percentage points a year which could amount to a considerably higher value of their investment portfolios years from now. This can be accomplished without the bouts of insomnia that often afflict stock speculators.

Our book is organized into four parts and 19 chapters. Part 1 consists of an overview of closed-end funds and covers fund basics, the history of closed-end funds, their advantages, and discounts and premiums. This section concludes with a thorough chapter on how to get information and use it to analyze a fund.

Part 2 focuses on equity-oriented funds. The advantages of common stock as an investment vehicle are explained. Old-line and newer stock funds are examined. More specialized funds like dual purpose funds and sector equity funds are also explained. Then we move on to global investing in Chapter 9, which contains a detailed discussion of the rewards and risks of investing in equity markets outside the United States. Chapter 10 takes a close look at closed-end funds based in the United States that invest in foreign markets. Country funds have experienced explosive growth since 1985 and were top performers in 1989. But the speculative bubble burst in early 1990. Funds that are top performers in one year seldom perform as well in a subsequent year. To round out Part 2, an overview of the British and Canadian closed-end fund markets is offered in Chapter 11. U.S. closed-end funds trace their ancestry to the British investment trust industry which began in the 1860s.

The burgeoning fixed-income funds are the focal point of Part 3. A huge assortment of diverse funds exists here. This part begins with an introduction by A. Michael Lipper, president of Lipper Analytical Services, Inc. The basics of fixed income securities and bond funds are covered in Chapter 12. We explain how to analyze a bond fund and how to spot the ones that are cannibalizing assets. Then we cover the older investment grade bond funds in Chapter 13. This group offers attractive opportunities for fixed income investors. Chapter 14 covers the gamut of bond fund types, including high-yield bond funds, government bond funds, mortgage-backed securities funds, multi-sector bond funds, municipal bond funds, and more. Chapter 15 examines convertible funds which perform like a balanced fund or a hybrid between stock and bond funds.

Part 4 ties things together and deals with important issues facing the closed-end fund industry. Chapter 16 contains a detailed discussion of what you need to know to get your closed-end fund transactions executed efficiently and at the most advantageous price. We offer an easy-to-use approach for determining the liquidity of individual funds as well as a discussion of the use of limit orders to get the best prices on New York Stock Exchange traded funds. Chapter 17 offers guidelines for structuring your overall investment portfolio with closed-end funds. Tax considerations facing fund investors are also examined. Chapter 18 takes a close look at closed-end fund takeovers and open-ending. It also identifies the factors that make funds vulnerable to raiders. Our concluding thoughts are contained in Chapter 19.

A glossary of commonly used terms and three appendixes, including a complete directory of closed-end funds are found at the end of the book.

Hopefully our guidance will help you find greater investment value and build more wealth.

# PART I

# Overview

CHAPTER 1

# Investing in Closed-End Funds

During the bear market of the early 1970s, Source Capital, a closed-end investment company, traded close to a 50% discount from the value of its underlying securities. The market's extreme undervaluation of Source in 1972 attracted Berkshire Hathaway chairman Warren Buffett and his partner Charles Munger who purchased 20% of its stock for companies they controlled.[1] Although we wonder why Buffett didn't take over the fund, George Michaelis, Source's president and a brilliant money manager himself, said it was never more than an investment. Buffett and Munger made a lot of money and sold Source's shares in a public offering through Prudential-Bache in July, 1977, netting sale proceeds of nearly $15.7 million.

Other investors have done quite well in closed-end funds, making them their specialty—and, of course, different investors have different approaches. Thomas J. Herzfeld of Miami, Florida, runs a brokerage firm under his name which specializes in closed-end funds.[2] An early pioneer, Herzfeld was attracted to the study of closed-end funds in the late 1960s. Ron Olin has a money manage-

3

ment firm called Deep Discount Advisors in Houston, Texas.[3] Olin, who deals exclusively in closed-end funds, employs a highly mathematical approach in analyzing them. The late Stanislaw Bednarski, a private investor, had great success in this area using approaches that emphasized an analysis of the discount.[4] Erik Bergstrom, chairman of Bergstrom Capital Corporation, has done very well as a long-term investor with his closed-end fund which he took over from Diebold Venture Capital in 1976. Bergstrom Capital has been the only closed-end fund on the *Forbes* honor roll for seven consecutive years.[5]

You don't have to be a highly sophisticated investor to do well in this area. Closed-end funds, or publicly traded investment companies, offer today's investors an opportunity to beat the market averages over long periods. This is true mainly because a number of these funds can be purchased at bargain prices by savvy investors who know how to capitalize on the opportunities, as Buffett and others did. It's like buying name brand merchandise at discounts of 10% or more at your favorite department store. And, as a special bonus, some portfolios are run by money managers who have compiled superior long-term results. Well-known investment professionals like Charles Allmon, Mario Gabelli, George Michaelis, John Neff, Charles Royce, John Templeton, and Martin Zweig run equity funds which are featured in this book.

Before we introduce closed-end funds we need to go over a few basic definitions.

## INVESTMENT VERSUS SPECULATION

First, a distinction must be made between the terms investment and speculation as used in this book.

### Investment

An investment is a *long-term* commitment to an asset which you expect to generate an adequate income flow while at the same time preserving your capital. The authors also feel that an investment should have long-term growth potential to provide inflation protection. Investing is a conservative process; you are building capital slowly and steadily as time passes. As will be demonstrated in Chapter 4, "Investing in Stock Funds," with a disciplined savings plan the power of compounding can do wonders for a conservative portfolio over the years. Investors maintain adequate diversification at all times; they never put all their eggs in one basket.

Our orientation favors the use of closed-end funds as an investment vehicle to build capital over the years. Specifically, the investor will do best by purchasing undervalued assets like closed-end funds at significant discounts and holding them for at least three years, as we'll explain.

## Speculation

A speculation is typically *short-term*–oriented, entails considerable risk, and often is undertaken with *unreasonable expectations of gain*—like turning $1,000 into $10,000 in a few weeks. An individual who, on the basis of a "hot tip," takes a big position in the stock of a small company which pays no dividends would be speculating. Traders of options and futures looking for quick profits are also speculating. The speculator faces the risk of losing considerable amounts of principal as well as sleep. Speculation can be detrimental to health as well as to wealth.

## FUND BASICS

Now let's make some basic distinctions between closed- and open-end funds.

### Open- versus Closed-End Funds

Closed-end funds, or CEFs, differ from their open-ended relatives in several respects. (Throughout the book the authors use the acronym CEF interchangeably with closed-end fund.) To understand the most important differences you must keep the meaning of the term net asset value (NAV) clearly in mind. The NAV of any fund is based on the sum of the market values of all the fund's security positions, plus its cash and minus its liabilities. The result, "net assets," is then divided by the number of fund shares outstanding to arrive at NAV. In equation form,

$$\text{Net Asset Value (NAV)} = \frac{\text{Total Assets } minus \text{ Liabilities}}{\text{Number of Fund Shares Outstanding}}$$

The more common open-end funds, or mutual funds, stand continuously ready to offer shares to incoming investors at the current NAV, plus any front-end load or sales charge, and to redeem investor shares at NAV, net of any redemption charge or back-end load. Investor money continually flows directly into and out of these funds. The important point is that the price of an open-end fund is directly tied to NAV. This gives the investor a certain assurance that is not present with closed-end funds.

CEFs, on the other hand, have relatively fixed capitalizations. These companies have an initial public offering (IPO) when they start. Assume that a fund issues 10 million shares and raises $100 million, ignoring underwriting fees. It then invests in a diversified portfolio of securities in accordance with its stated investment objectives. With some exceptions, like the Germany Fund and the Korea Fund which both had follow-on equity offerings, more shares would not be issued. Investor shares would not be redeemed unless the fund changes to an open-end structure. CEFs are often called "closed-end mutual funds" but by definition *they are not "mutual funds" as they do not redeem your shares.* This is a frequent error in terminology.

Most closed-end shares trade on the New York Stock Exchange (NYSE). A lesser number trade on the American Stock Exchange (Amex), and an even smaller number trade over-the-counter, mostly in the National Association of Securities Dealers Automated Quotation (NASDAQ) System. At this writing over 200 had shares listed on the NYSE and nearly 30 on the Amex.

The market prices of closed-end company shares are determined by supply and demand and are not directly tied to NAV. Prices of CEFs nearly always differ from NAV—sometimes dramatically as in the case of some single country funds that have traded at huge premiums to NAV. Many CEFs trade at market prices below NAV, or at a discount. To buy or sell the shares of a CEF you deal with your broker just as if you were buying 100 shares of IBM. The normal brokerage commission would apply. Large CEF investors usually can negotiate discounts like other stock buyers.

Although many closed-end funds were created in the 1980s, their number is still much smaller than the number of open-end funds. At this writing (September 1990), there were some 3,000 open-end funds with assets amounting to over $1 trillion. This compares with nearly 250 CEFs with assets of over $60 billion.

Closed-end funds are not to be confused with "closed-up funds." The closed-up fund is an open-end fund that has discontinued the sale of its shares to the general public but will still accept redemptions. Some open-end funds, like Vanguard's popular Windsor Fund which is managed by John Neff, will "close-up" when they do not want to accept more money because they feel that sufficient additional investment opportunities in their area of interest do not exist at the time. These funds can re-open when it again becomes appropriate for them to invest.

Incidentally, due to the increased attention being given to closed-end funds, **Franklin Balance Sheet Investment Fund,** an open-end fund, was recently introduced to invest about half its assets in CEFs. William Lippman the fund's president offers details in the Closed-End Insights box.

## Organizational Structure

The organizational structure is basically the same for open- and closed-end funds. Managed investment companies generally are organized as corporations so they will have a board of directors.[6] There is also an adviser and a portfolio manager. Let's take a closer look at this structure and the roles played by the different parties.

## AN OPEN-END FUND THAT INVESTS
## IN CEFS
### William J. Lippman
### Franklin Balance Sheet Investment Fund

The Franklin Group, which manages more than $42 billion of investment assets, has recently begun offering a uniquely different type of open-end fund, one that invests much of its portfolio in closed-end funds selling at a discount to net asset value. Franklin's management believes that a lack of investor interest and Wall Street sponsorship has left a great many high quality closed-end funds to sell at significant discounts to their net asset values. The Franklin Balance Sheet Investment Fund was formed to take advantage of these opportunities. Among the factors considered by Franklin Balance Sheet Investment Fund's managers in selecting closed-end funds are:

- The amount of the discount from net asset value.
- The range of the discount over varying market periods.
- The quality of the underlying portfolio.
- The capability of the closed-end fund manager.
- The use of leverage.
- Provision and timing to become open-end.
- Shares bought in open market for dividend reinvestment programs.

In addition to investing in closed-end funds, Balance Sheet Investment will also acquire non-fund companies that trade at a discount to book value. In either case the fund's objective will be to maximize total return by finding funds or companies whose intrinsic values are not currently reflected in the marketplace.

**Board of Directors.** The board of directors usually consists of five to ten members elected by the fund's stockholders. Board members serve terms of one to three years and are elected or reelected simultaneously unless there is a staggered board in which the voting on individual slots would rotate. For example, Fund A has six directors, two are elected each year for a three-year term. The staggered board is sometimes used as an anti-takeover measure. The board hires the adviser and performs a number of other duties including approving the fund's portfolio.

**Adviser.** The adviser is the money management unit hired by the fund to manage its assets for a fee. The adviser is responsible for investment research, portfolio management, and administrative matters. The adviser's contract must be reapproved by the board annually. A few CEFs are internally managed and therefore have no external adviser and no advisory fee, but there still would be investment related expenses to be passed along to the shareholders. The internal management arrangement will be explained in Chapter 5, "Older Domestic Equity Funds."

Some funds separate the management and administrative functions. For instance, the adviser for the Nicholas-Applegate Growth Equity Fund is Nicholas-Applegate Capital Management and the administrator is Prudential Mutual Fund Management.

The adviser's management fee generally is based on the amount of assets under management and is commonly set on a sliding scale where the percentage declines as total assets increase. Annual management fees could range between 0.3% to over 1.00%. Management fees may be linked to the performance of the portfolio under the adviser through an "incentive fee" arrangement. You should know what the advisory fee is for funds you invest in. This information can be found in the notes to the financial statements in the fund's annual and semi-annual shareholder reports or in Standard & Poor's *Stock Reports*.

**Portfolio manager.** The portfolio manager is an employee of the adviser. The authors feel that it is highly important for prospective investors to know who the portfolio manager is, his investment style, and his track rec-

ord. If you are uncertain about this information call the
fund.


## A BRIEF HISTORY

The earliest investment companies were of the closed-end
structure. In Brussels, Belgium in 1822, King William I
of the Netherlands created what is today generally recognized as being the first investment trust. It was initially
intended to make possible small investments in foreign
government loans.

Beginning in the 1860s similar investment trusts
were formed in England and Scotland. The London Financial Association and The International Financial Society
were believed to be the first British trusts. They were established in 1863. The Foreign and Colonial Investment
Trust, formed in London in 1868, is still going strong and
is covered in Chapter 11, "British and Canadian Funds."
The trusts slowly grew in popularity and number. In the
1880s there was renewed interest in the development of
British trusts. Many of them invested overseas in United
States securities to earn higher returns for their shareholders. From 1900 to 1914 it became increasingly popular for the managers of British trusts to invest in American
securities, especially those of the railroads.[7]

The British and Scottish investment trusts served as
a model for those subsequently formed here. The Boston
Personal Property Trust, the first CEF created in the
United States, was formed in 1893. The Railway and Light
Securities Fund was the first U.S. closed-end fund to employ leverage or borrowed funds to acquire securities. It
was formed in 1904. The oldest Canadian closed-end
funds originated in the early 1920s and were created by
people of English background.

The oldest U.S. CEF we have found to be still operating is General American Investors, organized by two investment firms, Lehman Brothers and Lazard Frères on
January 25, 1927. It immediately prospered and in 1928
its sponsors organized Second General American Investors; the two merged in September, 1929.

Like other publicly traded companies, CEFs are created in bull markets when existing funds are trading at high market valuations. Seasoned new issue investors know that the number of IPOs in a given year is directly related to the prevailing level of price-earnings ratios. Investor interest is obviously greatest at these times.

## Boom and Bust

During the 1920s, closed-end funds (or investment trusts as they were then known) had phenomenal growth in the United States; several hundred were formed, and they thrived in the seemingly endless boom. The large number of CEFs formed in the late 1920s to satisfy the speculative appetites of individuals typically had capital structures heavily laden with debt and preferred stock. This in turn exacerbated their problems.

A colorful discussion of the trusts in the late 1920s is contained in the following passage from Robert Sobel's book *Panic on Wall Street:*

By 1927, the leverage concept in corporate structure led to the creation of highly leveraged investment trusts. Generally speaking, the pre-World War trusts sold common stocks, but no bonds, and so were unleveraged. The new trusts of the late 1920s were highly leveraged. United States & Foreign Securities, for example, had three classes of stock (one common and two preferred) as well as a bond issue. Founded in 1924, U.S. & Foreign became the prototype for many of the 265 trusts formed in 1929 alone. The new trust companies of that year sold some $3 billion in securities to the public, and this money was almost immediately reinvested through stock purchases, many of them on margin. In mid-1929, an investor might purchase shares in an investment trust on margin, while the trust itself was using margin. It was conceivable that a buyer would put down $10 for $100 worth of stock, which itself represented $10 in equity and $90 in debt! In the early autumn of 1929, leveraged trusts were purchasing other leveraged trusts, compounding the situation still further.[8]

When the market crashed in October of 1929, the biggest losers were the highly leveraged funds which had borrowed more than their assets. Massive numbers of investors took a beating as they sold out at whatever price they could get. Premiums quickly vanished and turned to discounts. In the post-crash market the stronger funds purchased shares from the weaker ones. A handful of the pre-Depression funds, Adams Express, Central Securities, General American Investors, The Salomon Brothers Fund (formerly The Lehman Corporation), Niagara Share, Petroleum & Resources, and Tri-Continental, are in existence today. U.S. & Foreign Securities was liquidated in 1984. *Our First 50 Years,* the 50th anniversary brochure of General American Investors, told how their fund fared after the crash:

> Management's initial response to the stock market crash of 1929 was to buy more common stock at the newly reduced prices. Then as events in late 1929 and 1930 made it apparent that this was no ordinary shake out, the Company sold a number of equity issues at substantial losses, placed a larger proportion of its assets in high grade railroad bonds and in stocks of financial institutions, and purchased its own senior securities at prices below their par value. Following the Bank Holiday and with the emergence of the New Deal era, there came opportunities for new investment in stocks of petroleum and industrial corporations.
>
> By the end of this first very difficult decade [1936], not only was the value of the assets well ahead of the beginning but dividends on the Company's common began to be paid.[9]

The lesson to be learned from bear market periods like 1929–32, 1973–74, the October 1987 crash, and the 1990 sell-off which began in August, is that it is more prudent to be a buyer of bargains than a seller in panic situations.

Two major pieces of legislation were drafted on the heels of the 1929 Crash: the Securities Act of 1933 and the Securities Exchange Act of 1934. In 1934, the Securities and Exchange Commission (SEC) was created and stepped in to reform and regulate the abuses of the 1920s. Out of this came the Investment Company Act of 1940, the basis for regulation of both open- and closed-end funds, protection sadly needed before the Depression. Highly leveraged funds were prohibited; capital structures and dividends of funds were strictly regulated. Regulations were established for prudent portfolio diversification. The 1940 act requires investment companies to register with the SEC and to meet specific disclosure requirements. It also requires extensive SEC oversight of fund activities and their day-to-day operations.

The Investment Company Institute (ICI), the national association of the American investment company industry, was established in 1940. Its mission is to serve its members and monitor state and federal legislation. It also serves the investing public, news media, and government agencies as a clearinghouse for information about the industry. At this writing its membership includes over 3,000 open-end funds, over 200 closed-end funds, and 13 sponsors of unit investment trusts.

## Small Investors Return

After the widespread speculation and abuses of the 1920s, CEFs, with a few exceptions, became unpopular. Open-end funds developed as better stock markets appeared after World War II and the small investor returned to the market. Finally, in the 1960s as memories of the highly leveraged trusts grew dim, investors began to reexamine CEFs. The interest, however, was not nearly so great as that which had been developing for some time in their open-end cousins.

The Japan Fund, the first major closed-end country fund established in the United States, began operations in 1962. It experienced exceptional performance over the long term, reflecting the burgeoning Japanese economy. In fact, The Japan Fund earned the high distinction of a place on the *Forbes* honor roll seven times, the most recent being in 1984. It was converted to an open-end fund in 1987.

There were some closed-end equity fund offerings in the bull market years of the 1960s, including seven dual-purpose funds that appeared in 1967. Modeled after their English counterparts, these dual funds were the first to be marketed in this country. Among the new offerings were Gemini Fund, Putnam Duo-Fund, and Scudder Duo-Vest. The dual funds are a special type of CEF with income shares which receive all the investment income earned on the portfolio and capital shares which are entitled to all the capital appreciation (or depreciation). More than two dozen corporate bond funds, including several convertible bond funds, came to market in the early 1970s. But the number of closed-ends which came out in the 1960s and 1970s pales in comparison to those of the 1980s.

## THE GREAT BULL MARKET

The prolonged bull market of the 1980s proved to be a watershed for the closed-end fund industry as a great variety of different funds debuted—especially in the fixed income area as people were seeking dependable yields after the October 1987 crash. The considerable amount of money raised through these closed-end offerings in the 1980s, as well as the very limited availability of books on the subject, prompted the authors to write this book.[10]

Table 1–1 displays the number of CEF IPOs for the entire decade by year. (There were no CEF IPOs in 1980.) The amounts of money raised in each year are also reported. As seen, the really significant growth began in 1986. That year was definitely the turning point for the industry.

A Kidder, Peabody report indicated that CEF offerings in 1988 and 1989 represented 75 percent and 50 percent, respectively, of the new-issue volume for those years. A big year like 1988 when CEF offerings amounted to nearly $18 billion is not expected "anytime soon" adds the Kidder report.[11]

Another way to portray the growth of the closed-end fund universe is to see how dramatically the number of funds and their assets have surged since 1985. This is

**Table 1–1. Closed-End Fund IPOs**
**1/1/80 through 12/31/89**

| Year | Number of Issues | Amount Raised (Millions) |
|---|---|---|
| 1989 | 42 | $ 7,573.4 |
| 1988 | 62 | 17,761.6 |
| 1987 | 35 | 9,727.9 |
| 1986 | 26 | 4,162.1 |
| 1985 | 3 | 260.0 |
| | | |
| 1984 | 2 | 61.0 |
| 1983 | 3 | 28.8 |
| 1982 | 1 | 4.6 |
| 1981 | 1 | 60.0 |
| 1980 | 0 | 0.0 |
| | | |
| Total | 175 | $39,639.4 |

Source: IDD Information Services

clearly evident from the data in Table 1–2 which is based on all closed-end funds tracked by Lipper Analytical Services, Inc. As indicated by this data, the universe grew from 54 funds with about $8 billion in net assets at year-end 1985 to 209 funds with $56 billion in assets at the close of the decade. Incidentally, when Lipper initiated its coverage of closed-end funds in 1973 it reported total net assets of $5.5 billion for 66 funds. This again shows that the real growth took place since 1985.

**Table 1–2. Closed-End Fund Universe, 1985–1989**

| Year End | Number | Total Net Assets (Millions) |
|---|---|---|
| | All Closed-End Funds | |
| 1989 | 209 | $55,957.2 |
| 1988 | 175 | 42,862.5 |
| 1987 | 110 | 20,943.4 |
| 1986 | 81 | 14,533.9 |
| 1985 | 54 | 8,085.8 |

Source: Lipper Analytical Services, Inc.

## Personality Funds

Before the October 1987 crash there were a number of offerings of what have been called "personality funds" or "superstar funds." Their portfolios reflect the styles or personalities of their managers who have established reputations. In many instances the "star" investor's name appears in the fund name. Included here are Gabelli Equity Trust, Nicholas-Applegate Growth Equity Fund (named for two investors), Royce Value Trust, Schafer Value Trust (which liquidated in 1990), and The Zweig Fund.

Those personality funds whose names do not include the star manager's name include Growth Stock Outlook Trust (managed by Charles Allmon, founder of *Growth Stock Outlook*). Liberty All-Star Equity Fund (employs five different management organizations), and Z-Seven Fund (Barry Ziskin).

Even if the manager of the personality fund is not that well known, the investment style is still distinctive as will be seen in Chapter 6, "The Personality Funds."

## Specialized Equity and Convertible Funds

One of the biggest growth areas in the 1980s was in single country funds. The Mexico Fund which began in 1981 was the first country fund IPO of the decade. It was followed by the Korea Fund in 1984 and The First Australia Fund in 1985. There are now over 30 closed-end country funds compared with just one, The Japan Fund, at the end of 1980. More recent offerings include Future Germany Fund, The Indonesia Fund, Irish Investment Fund, Jakarta Growth Fund, Japan OTC Equity Fund, Mexico Equity & Income Fund, and Turkish Investment Fund.

There were also a number of sector equity fund offerings. These specialized funds invest in specific industries like financial companies and utilities. Duff & Phelps Utilities Income, H&Q Healthcare Investors, Pilgrim Regional Bank Shares, Real Estate Securities Income Fund, and Templeton Global Utilities are examples.

Several convertible bond funds were also offered in the 1980s. These include Ellsworth Convertible Growth &

Income Fund, Lincoln National Convertible Securities, Putnam High Income Convertible and Bond Fund, and TCW Convertible Securities Fund. The growth in Lipper's specialized equity and convertible funds category from 1985 to the close of the decade is seen in Table 1–3. Total net assets in this category increased from $1.9 billion at year-end 1985 to $8.4 billion at the end of the decade. The data in this table include country funds, sector funds, and convertible bond funds. The country funds accounted for the largest amount of growth in this category.

## The Bond Funds

In addition to the heady growth in the country fund area, a huge amount of money was raised by the new bond funds, the biggest growth area in terms of total funds raised. At year-end 1989, 127 bond funds with total net assets of about $39.2 billion were followed by Lipper compared with only 27 with assets of $2 billion at year-end 1979. Thus, the bond funds represented nearly 70 percent of the assets of the entire CEF industry at the end of the decade. The big surge in the growth in bond funds began in 1986 according to the Lipper data (Table 1–4). Many bond funds went public after the October 1987 crash to satisfy the demands of safety-conscious investors who were wary of equities.

A wider variety of fixed income funds also became available: for instance, U.S. government bond funds, mu-

**Table 1–3. Closed-End Specialized Equity and Convertible Fund Universe, 1985–89**

| | Specialized and Convertible Funds | |
| Year End | Number | Total Net Assets (Millions) |
| --- | --- | --- |
| 1989 | 51 | $8,428.4 |
| 1988 | 48 | 6,267.1 |
| 1987 | 38 | 4,716.9 |
| 1986 | 30 | 4,734.1 |
| 1985 | 16 | 1,945.5 |

Source: Lipper Analytical Services, Inc.

**Table 1–4. Closed-End Bond Fund Universe, 1985–89**

| | All Closed-End Bond Funds | |
|---|---|---|
| Year End | Number | Total Net Assets (Millions) |
| 1989 | 127 | $39,246.4 |
| 1988 | 98 | 30,072.1 |
| 1987 | 45 | 10,201.7 |
| 1986 | 30 | 4,223.6 |
| 1985 | 26 | 2,415.2 |

Source: Lipper Analytical Services, Inc.

nicipal bond funds, and global bond funds. Some of the offerings were quite large and new wrinkles were introduced. In June, 1987 the Nuveen Municipal Value Fund netted nearly $1.5 billion from its initial public offering. Here are some more highlights:

- In February, 1988 the Putnam Premier Income Trust netted proceeds of about $1.3 billion from its offering.
- In March, 1988 the MFS Intermediate Income Trust netted approximately $1.9 billion, making it the largest equity offering ever.
- That same month the Templeton Global Income Fund netted slightly over $1 billion.
- In May, 1988 Comstock Partners Strategy Fund netted nearly $1.2 billion.

Let's now take a close look at some of the special features and advantages of investment companies.

## SHAREHOLDER REINVESTMENT

Open-end funds pioneered a variety of shareholder services. With an open-end fund shareholders are allowed to reinvest dividend and capital gains distributions—net of management and administrative expenses borne by the shareholder—without charge, in full and fractional shares at the then current NAV. Most open-end fund shareholders reinvest distributions in this way.

In 1960 Tri-Continental was the first closed-end fund, and also the first NYSE-listed company, to offer an automatic dividend reinvestment service. Tri also offers an automatic cash withdrawal plan. Most CEFs today offer their shareholders dividend reinvestment plans. CEF investors can thus reinvest their dividend and/or capital gains distributions in additional fund shares.

However, instead of always being reinvested at NAV, as is the case with most open-end funds, CEF distributions are generally reinvested at the fund's per share market price when price is below NAV. For instance, if a CEF's market price is 9 and its NAV is 10, then the distribution would be reinvested in shares of the fund at 9. On the other hand, if the CEF trades at a premium, distributions would be reinvested at the greater of 95% of the market price or the NAV. Assume that the fund with the NAV of 10 is trading at a share price of 20, a 100% premium to NAV. Distributions would then be reinvested at 95% of market price or 19. It is important to be aware of this fact as some funds trade at huge premiums.

We strongly advise reinvesting dividends and capital gains distributions if possible. It is the best way to build up capital over the years through the power of compound interest, as we'll explain. Also, if the fund is trading at a discount, those shareholders who don't reinvest will experience a certain amount of dilution, since those who do reinvest will be acquiring fund shares below NAV.

A few of the CEFs, including Adams Express; Baker, Fentress; Blue Chip Value Fund; Petroleum & Resources; Salomon Brothers Fund; and Tri-Continental also have what are known as cash purchase plans. They allow shareholders to send in additional cash for investment in the fund's shares. This would be done in lieu of buying more shares through a broker. However, the authors prefer the latter as the investor would have more control over the timing of the trade and, consequently, over the price paid by dealing with the broker. This will be explained in more detail later.

## ADVANTAGES OF ALL FUNDS

Both open- and closed-end funds offer five basic advantages:

1. Diversification
2. Professional management
3. Many portfolio choices
4. Transaction cost economies
5. Shareholder record keeping

### Diversification

Diversification is an important advantage since many investors may not have enough money to acquire at least 10 or 12 different stock positions. Modern portfolio theory tells us this is necessary to eliminate most of the company specific risk from a portfolio. Of course, diversification does not eliminate the volatility inherent in the overall domestic equity market. In Chapter 9, "Global Investing," we'll explain how international diversification through CEFs can reduce the riskiness of a portfolio of domestic equities to some extent.

Many investors (in truth they're speculators) suffer huge losses simply because they fail to diversify properly; instead, they put all their eggs in one or a few baskets in the hopes of spectacular gains. But these potential gains come at the expense of considerable unnecessary risk. Further, individuals with brokerage accounts who trade stocks can and do succumb to the glamor of the quick riches potentially available through speculation. They can lose their life savings quickly buying a speculative stock or two. It is less likely that those who have an inherent speculative or gambling inclination will face the prospect of horrendous losses if they discipline themselves to stick with funds.[12]

### Professional Management

Professional management is important for those who don't have the time to do adequate research on their investments. Most people fall into that category. Many investors are busy with their careers and know that time is becoming an increasingly scarce resource. It's also nice to know that some highly successful money managers with long track records are managing the fund. Critics often point to the fact that academic studies indicate that on average all funds tend to underperform the market averages somewhat when transaction and management costs are considered. This is no doubt true, but if you buy a good closed-end fund at a discount you have a chance to outperform the market because of two inherent advantages you've gained: (1) the higher yield on your investment and (2) the potential for a narrowing of the discount. We'll provide specific examples of how this works in Chapter 2, "Discounts and Premiums."

## Many Portfolio Choices

Thanks in large part to the offerings of the 1980s, CEFs today offer a wide variety of different portfolios and different management styles. You can pick and choose a number of these funds, in whatever combination you like, to build your overall portfolio. And you can easily rearrange your portfolio as your needs change over the years. One of our major objectives is to guide you through the smorgasbord of fund-types.

## Economies of Scale

Economies of scale are especially important to smaller investors. Because the funds deal in large blocks of stock they are subject to lower transaction costs as a percentage of the dollar value invested than the individual investor would be. Lower transaction costs mean better performance.

## Record Keeping

The shareholder record keeping services offered by all funds are also helpful. For instance, by early February of each year the fund will send you IRS Form 1099-DIV (Statement for Recipients of Dividends and Distributions). Form 1099-DIV breaks down your taxable income and gains. This is quite useful in preparing your tax returns.

It is much simpler than keeping track of gains and losses and income on a portfolio of many individual securities. Presumably you own four or five funds at the most whereas you could hold dozens of stocks. Still record keeping for tax purposes on funds can be tricky. We'll cover it in detail in a later chapter.

## UNIQUE CEF ADVANTAGES

The fact that closed-end funds often sell at attractive discounts from their NAVs can be a major advantage for investors. This phenomenon will be explored in detail in Chapter 2, "Discounts and Premiums." For now, we'll simply say that when a fund is selling at a market price 20% below NAV, it's like buying a dollar's worth of earning assets for 80 cents. "Why pay a dollar for a dollar's worth of assets in Charles Royce's Pennsylvania Mutual Fund when at times you can buy the same dollar's worth of assets in his Royce Value Trust at a significant discount—paying, say, 87 cents on the dollar—and collect the dividends and capital gains on the full dollar's worth of assets while you wait for the discount to narrow," says Steven Samuels of Samuels Asset Management, a Sherman Oaks, California money management firm specializing in closed-end funds. "Even if the discount doesn't narrow it's still a better deal." As well as offering generous returns buying at a discount that is relatively wide can be a low-risk strategy.

Besides the discount, closed-end funds have a few special advantages which do not typically exist with open-end funds.

1. The most frequently cited advantage of the CEF structure is that it enables fund managers to perform better because they can work with a stable pool of capital. CEF managers do not face the prospect of huge inflows and outflows of investor money at the peak of a bull market and the nadir of a bear market, respectively, as open-end fund managers do.

2. CEF managers have more incentive to manage for high total return rather than high current yield. This is especially true in the case of bond funds.

3. Investors have greater control over the price at which they buy or sell fund shares.

## Stability of Capital

Probably the most important advantage of the closed-end structure is that the fund manager does not need to cope with large inflows or outflows of investor money at inopportune times. Remember, with open-end funds investors buy new shares directly from the fund. If a lot of investors pour money into the fund during a bull market period the fund managers are going to have to invest considerable amounts at potentially unattractive levels of stock prices. This is especially true for funds that follow a fully invested position all the time. Or, an open-end fund manager could be forced to unload fund shares at times when those prices are severely depressed; this might be the time when he should be buying more shares rather than selling out.

With a CEF, on the other hand, the manager does not have these headaches. If investors want to bail out they simply sell their shares in the open market; the manager doesn't have to touch the portfolio because lots of investors are unloading. The fund would probably go to a bigger discount but so what. This would provide investors with an opportunity to buy more shares, as explained in our section on "averaging down."

The closed-end structure is especially desirable for funds dealing in securities that are more volatile and thinly traded (like small cap stocks or stocks traded in emerging foreign markets) since massive investor withdrawals at the wrong time could be devastating with portfolios of less liquid securities in more volatile sectors. Also there may not be sufficient issues in an emerging foreign market to meet a huge inflow of new investor money. As the Investment Company Institute 1988 Annual Report states, "Closed-end funds can succeed in thinly traded markets because they need not search for additional in-

vestments to accommodate new purchases nor sell portfolio securities to meet redemptions."

## Investment for Total Return

In regard to the second advantage, CEF managers have
more of an incentive to manage their portfolios for total
return because with a closed-end fund the primary way
to build up assets under management is to increase total
return. The fund management usually earns a certain percentage of total assets under management. Consequently,
the greater the dollar amount of assets under management
the greater their dollar earnings. With an open-end fund, of
course, good management will attract an inflow of investor
dollars as Peter Lynch did with Fidelity Magellan Fund
which had $13 billion in assets when he resigned in 1990.
Closed-end stock funds will generally not get as large as
open-end stock funds. An exception is Tri-Continental, the
largest diversified equity closed-end fund, which has total
assets of about $1.6 billion.

Barry Ziskin who started the Z-Seven Fund in 1983,
the first of the personality funds introduced in the 1980s,
tells why he chose the closed-end fund format in the
Closed-End Insights box.

## Trading Advantages

The CEF investor generally deals through a broker and
should place limit orders to buy and sell shares at oppor-
tune times. Limit orders are given to a broker to buy or
sell a stock at a specific "limit" price or better, for example, buy 200 shares of Fund A at 12 or less. CEFs enable
the investor to take advantage, intraday, of today's more
volatile stock markets. And the funds themselves, unlike
mutual funds, exhibit a certain volatility as their discounts and premiums wax and wane.

Investors can get a number of up-to-the-minute quotes
from their brokers during the course of a trading day and
then place orders at what appears to be the best time. This
affords more control over the price at which the trade is
executed. Investors can also use a variety of orders. Most
importantly, they can use limit orders to buy and sell
closed-end shares at their price limit, or better—one can

## WHY ONE MONEY MANAGER CHOSE THE CLOSED-END STRUCTURE
### Barry Ziskin
### President, The Z-Seven Fund, Inc.

Why did I begin a closed-end fund instead of doing what was popular at that time? At the end of 1983 when Z-Seven was launched, closed-end fund offerings were few and far between as most investors were unfamiliar with them and preferred (open-end) mutual funds. Was it because I wanted to raise hundreds of millions of dollars under management to add to my advisory fee revenue? Actually, I prefer to stay small enough to be able to perform without the restriction of having too many dollars to invest in too few stocks. An investment manager who is flooded with money must either: a) choose investments which are below his/her standards in order to be fully invested; and/or b) concentrate so much money into those first investment selections that he/she drives the prices of those stocks up when buying and down when selling; and/ or c) keep cash or money market investments. Obviously, any of these, singularly or in combination with the other choices, will have a negative impact on performance. In this way, an investor who buys shares of an open-end fund is penalized for selecting a good manager with a proven track record because too much money winds up going into that fund.

never use limit orders with open-end funds. More on this appears in Chapter 16, "Dealing with Your Broker."

## AVERAGING DOWN

The authors want to stress that one's investment approach with CEFs should be radically different from the approach towards individual stocks. We would encourage averaging down because the fund won't go broke the way an individual stock might.

There are some compelling reasons for not averaging down on stock investments that have declined in price since they were purchased. Experts often advise investors to cut their losses and bail out before it's too late and price is down even further. Bad news tends to follow bad news, especially with smaller companies.[13] Stocks, particularly those of small, emerging growth companies, can fall precipitously and never come back; the company winds up in Chapter 7 bankruptcy proceedings, liquidates, and the stockholders, who are the last in line to receive a payment, often go away empty-handed. Even if the company does manage to survive through a Chapter 11 reorganization, the old stockholders' positions may be diluted to practically nothing.

CEFs do not go bankrupt, or fall to a share price of zero, however, because they virtually always hold a diversified stock portfolio and thus have little if any company risk. You can feel far safer averaging down with a CEF that has declined in price. It can also pay to average down with a CEF position when the discount from NAV has grown deeper because of investor pessimism. This is a doubly good practice at the nadir of a bear market, a time when most investors are fearful.

In sum, the patient, long-term investor in closed-end funds can watch for times to add to a position at bargain prices and need not worry about being wiped out by a single stock that will never recover.

## DISADVANTAGES OF CEFs

A good general rule is not to buy CEFs on their initial public offerings. This is because the funds are issued at a premium to NAV and their prices are supported for a while by the underwriters, but within three or four months the shares tend to slip to a discount.

This phenomenon has been well-documented by academic studies. A fairly recent study undertaken by Professor Kathleen Weiss, while she was a Research Economist at the Securities and Exchange Commission, was quite comprehensive.[14] Weiss examined the IPOs of 64 CEFs between 1985 and 1987. She also had a control sample of ordinary stock IPOs. On average, the aftermarket price performance of CEF IPOs was worse than that of other IPOs. Of the CEF IPOs, Weiss found that domestic equity and foreign equity funds experienced the worst performance during the 120 days following the offering. The price declines on bond funds were not as great as those of equity funds and were not statistically significant.

In any event, our strong advice is to wait until the fund has gone to a suitable discount before taking a position. A possible exception is a new offering of a country fund where you think the stock will go to a premium, but we definitely regard this as a speculation.

Another disadvantage brought out by closed-end critics is that you must pay a brokerage commission when buying or selling your shares. With pure no-load funds there would be no sales charges. However, there would be an effective sales charge with mutual funds which appear to be "no-load" but have 12b-1 plans. The 12b-1 plan allows a mutual fund adviser to reduce the NAV by a certain annual percentage (e.g., 0.5%) to cover the fund's marketing and distribution expenses including advertising, the printing and distribution of fund literature, and any trailing commissions to stockbrokers. The 12b-1 charge would be reflected in the fund's expense ratio. One estimate indicates about 1,650 mutual funds have 12b-1 charges.[15] Closed-end funds do not have 12b-1 plans.

In any event, when the favorable impact on the investor's performance of buying a CEF at a significant discount is appreciated, the brokerage commission which needs to be paid to trade its shares becomes trivial, especially for the long-term investor.

A final potential disadvantage of CEFs would certainly be pointed out by those who like switching among different funds within a family of open-end funds. This fund switching feature has become quite popular as a means of quickly and economically moving your assets around to different portfolios. It undoubtedly was a contributing factor to the large influx of money into open-end funds in recent decades. But, for longer-term investors, the absence of closed-end fund families should be unimportant. In fact, some, like closed-end fund expert Thomas Herzfeld, will trade closed-ends based on short-term fluctuations in discount and premium levels.

## TYPES OF CEFs

In the most basic sense there are two types of closed-end funds: bond funds and stock funds. But for practical purposes it is essential to make much finer distinctions since, as in open-end funds, there is a great deal of specialization in the closed-end area. This is especially true of the funds brought to market in the 1980s.

Our outline groups CEFs as follows:

I. Closed-end stock funds
- Old-line stock funds—those created prior to the bull market of the 1980s.
- The newer stock funds created in the 1980s and 1990s. This newer group also includes the dual funds of the 1980s and other funds which have pioneered innovations like multiple managers and performance-based management fees.
- Sector equity funds which invest in specific industries or sectors like banks, utilities, or health care companies.
- Global equity funds. The global funds invest anywhere in the world including their home country (the United States in our case).
- International equity funds. These invest exclusively in foreign securities. Investments may be spread across a dozen or more countries or restricted to a certain geographic area like the Pacific Basin, in which case the CEF would be known as a regional fund.
- The burgeoning single country funds like the Germany Fund and the Spain Fund.

II. Fixed-income funds.
- Investment grade bond funds
- Direct placement funds

- High-yield corporate bond funds
- U.S. government bond funds
- Mortgage-backed securities funds
- Global and international bond funds
- Multi-sector bond funds
- Flexible portfolio funds
- Municipal bond funds
- Loan participation funds
- Convertible funds

The authors will cover each of these kinds of funds in detail and profile one or more funds in each category.


## CONCLUSION

Closed-end funds offer superb investment opportunities for those willing to take a little time to understand them. As explained, they have certain advantages over open-end funds as they can present opportunities to buy at bargain prices. Chapter 2 will address the issue of discounts and premiums.

### Notes

[1]Jonathan Clements, "Compound interest machines," *Forbes*, August 21, 1989, p. 43.

[2]Julie Rohrer, "Open season for closed-end funds," *Institutional Investor*, February, 1989, pp. 117–119.

[3]Jonathan Clements, "Stocks on sale," *Forbes*, September 4, 1989, pp. 158 and 160.

[4]Jonathan Clements, "The almost-perfect-market thesis," *Forbes*, February 6, 1989, pp. 150–51.

[5]George Cole Scott is a member of the Board of Directors of Bergstrom Capital.

[6]A few of the closed-end funds are organized as Massachusetts business trusts. Examples are Hampton Utilities Trust, Liberty All-Star Equity Fund, the Massachusetts Financial Services (MFS) funds, and the Putnam funds. In the case of the Massachusetts business trust the fund has a board of trustees instead of a board of directors. However, from the fund shareholders' point of view the distinction between the Massachusetts business trust and the ordinary corporation is unimportant.

[7]These early historic facts were obtained from Theodore J. Grayson, *Investment Trusts, Their Origin, Development and Operation* (New York: John Wiley & Sons, Inc., 1928), p. 11–18.

[8]Robert Sobel, *Panic on Wall Street* (New York: Truman Talley Books/ E. P. Dutton, 1988), pp. 358–59.

[9]*Our First 50 Years* (New York: General American Investors Company, Inc., 1977), p. 8.

[10]To the authors' knowledge the only comprehensive book dealing with the subject is Thomas J. Herzfeld, *The Investor's Guide to Closed-End Funds* (New York: McGraw-Hill Book Company, 1980).

[11]Joseph P. McGowan, Thomas E. Bourque, and Ted Walsh, *Closed End Fund Review,* Winter 1990 (New York: Kidder, Peabody, Inc., February 1990), p. 1.

[12]Benjamin Graham, *The Intelligent Investor,* Fourth Revised Edition (New York: Harper & Row, Publishers, 1973), p. 118.

[13]James W. Broadfoot III, *Investing in Emerging Growth Stocks* (New York: John Wiley & Sons, Inc., 1989), pp. 151–53.

[14]Kathleen Weiss, "The Post-Offering Price Performance of Closed-End Funds," *Financial Management,* Autumn 1989, pp. 57–67.

[15]Kevin G. Salwen, "NASD Proposes Limit on Fees Set by Funds," *The Wall Street Journal,* April 18, 1990, p. C1.

CHAPTER 2

# Discounts and Premiums

Closed-end funds virtually always trade at either a discount or a premium to net asset value. On rare occasions they trade at NAV. Like the price-earnings (or P/E) ratio on an ordinary stock, the discount or premium on an individual CEF is a barometer of its popularity. As far as the level of discounts on funds in general is concerned, it can be said to reflect the market's sentiment at the time. For instance, if equities are out of favor the CEFs investing in them would tend to sell at wide discounts. Where you see large net redemptions with open-end funds you see wide discounts with closed-end funds.

A major point to remember is that CEFs are a potential bargain when purchased at relatively wide discounts to NAV. Benjamin Graham, in *The Intelligent Investor*, advised individuals to seek out the shares of CEFs selling at attractive discounts. "If you want to put money in investment funds, buy a group of closed-end shares at a discount of, say, 10% to 15% from asset value. . . ."[1] Chances are the investor will do better than buying a group of open-end funds with similar portfolios. We'll show why this is true later on but for now a brief explanation should suffice.

A CEF trading at a discount of 20% is like buying a dollar's worth of income producing assets for 80 cents. The discount becomes much more attractive if we learn that, on average, the fund has traded at a discount of only, say, 15%. In fact, CEFs represent a potential source of asset plays when trading at wide discounts and it appears that they will attract the attention of outside investors.[2] Some funds trade at premiums to NAV and are potentially overpriced. The risk is that the premiums will disappear and the fund will go to a discount.

Burton G. Malkiel, a professor of economics at Princeton University, wrote about the advantages of investing in undervalued CEFs in the 1973, 1975, and 1981 editions of his popular book *A Random Walk Down Wall Street.* Malkiel was a staunch advocate of the CEF and felt that inefficient pricing resulted in a number of unique bargains for investors. In his 1973 edition he wrote:

> I have spent considerable time discussing closed-end funds because I consider them unusually attractive investments at the present time. Nevertheless, I do not anticipate that such favorable discounts will always be available. Indeed, if this book achieves substantial readership and if the public acts on the suggestions I have made, I would anticipate that the discounts would narrow considerably.[3]

In the bull market of the 1980s heightened interest in CEFs developed. In fact, in his 1985 edition Malkiel reported that the discounts has just about disappeared and he felt closed-end funds were no longer a particularly attractive investment vehicle.[4] However, subsequent to the publication of Malkiel's 1985 edition discounts have widened somewhat making some of the funds more attractive buys. The discounts, therefore, are a recurring phenomenon! (Malkiel, however, failed to recognize this in his 1990 edition.[5])

Historic year-end average discounts are traced in Figure 2–1 based upon the Diversified Investment Company

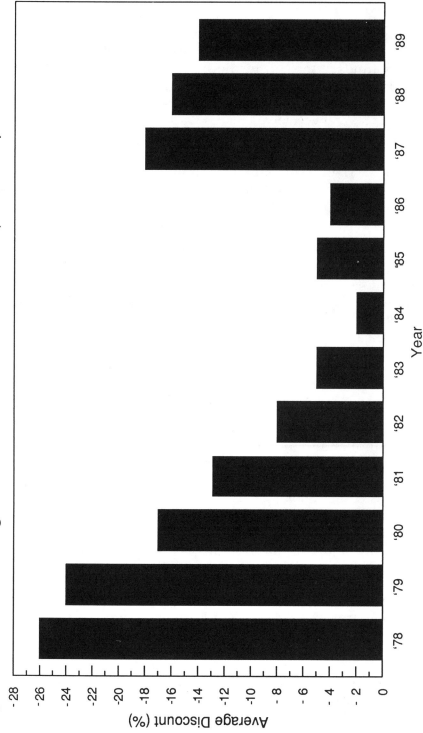

**Figure 2–1. Year-End Average Discounts on Closed-End Stock Funds (1978–1989)**

Average Discount (%)

Year

Source: Based on data from *Wiesenberger Investment Companies Service*

Average contained in *Wiesenberger Investment Compa-nies Service*. The average contains eight old-line domestic stock funds.[6] As seen in the bar chart, the discounts in the late 1970s were relatively wide as investor pessimism prevailed. In 1978 and 1979 the discounts stood at 26% and 24%, respectively. The discounts then narrowed dra-matically during the bull market years reaching a low of 2% in 1984. Investor skittishness during and after the Oc-tober 1987 crash resulted in some widening of the dis-counts. The discount was 18% at year-end 1987 and then narrowed to 14% at the end of 1989.

## COMPUTING DISCOUNTS OR PREMIUMS

A fund selling at a market price less than its NAV is said to be selling at a discount. Conversely, if market price is above NAV it is selling at a premium. The discount or pre-mium can be computed as follows:

$$\text{Discount or Premium} = \frac{\text{Share Price} - \text{NAV}}{\text{NAV}}$$

Using this equation a discount will appear as a nega-tive number and a premium as a positive value.

Suppose the XYZ CEF has an NAV of $10 and is trad-ing at a share price of 8–1/2. Its discount would be 15%, computed as follows: $-.15 = (8.5 - 10)/10$. If, instead, the fund were trading at 12 with an NAV of 10 it would be selling at a 20% premium. You may like to think of the discount or premium on a CEF in terms of a price/NAV ratio. This is explained in Figure 2–2.

You don't have to compute the discounts and pre-miums yourself as they are supplied weekly in the publicly-traded (or closed-end) funds columns which ap-pear in *Barron's*, the *Chicago Tribune*, *The New York Times*, and *The Wall Street Journal*. We'll explain how the information is reported in each publication, but be pa-tient as this tends to be rather confusing. You may notice that there have been some changes in reporting proce-

**Figure 2–2. The Price/NAV Ratio**
The price/NAV ratio is another way to look at premiums and discounts. For example, a fund trading at a price of 8 with an NAV of 10 would have a price/NAV ratio of 80%. If the fund trades at 12 with an NAV of 10 its price/NAV ratio would be 120%. If a country fund is trading at a premium of 100% this would represent a price/NAV ratio of 200%. In fact, the price/NAV ratio is essentially the same as the price/book value ratio used to value ordinary stocks. The only difference is that the NAV of a CEF is a much more precise gauge of value than the book value of the ordinary stock usually is.

dures or the CEF data may appear in additional financial publications by the time you read this book.

The complete Investment Company Institute (or ICI) List of closed-end funds, which includes over 50 bond funds, as well as nearly all equity funds, appears Mondays in *Barron's* (available at newsstands on Saturdays), Saturdays in *The New York Times*, and Mondays in the *Chicago Tribune*. The ICI List also appears Mondays in *The Wall Street Journal* but contains only a few of the bond funds so as not to duplicate those which will appear on their Wednesday Lipper Analytical Services List. The ICI List reports the data as of the previous Friday's market close. You may be interested to know that the ICI List is available Friday evenings (for that Friday) on the Dow Jones Capital Markets Wire. You can also call a fund to determine its NAV. Closed-end funds usually determine their NAVs weekly. But a few funds, like The Gabelli Equity Trust, H&Q Healthcare Investors, and Nicholas-Applegate Growth Equity Fund, have a telephone recording providing NAV on a daily basis.

The complete Lipper Analytical Services List of over 130 bond funds appears Wednesdays in the *Chicago Tribune, The New York Times*, and *The Wall Street Journal*. The Wednesday Lipper Lists contain bond fund data for the previous Friday. This is because the bond funds historically have needed additional time to calculate their NAVs because of the nature of their holdings. The Lipper List in

*Barron's* supplies bond fund data for the Friday prior to the immediately preceding Friday.

The weekly publicly-traded fund listings generally supply the following data for each fund covered:

1. Exchange where traded
2. Net asset value
3. Market price
4. Discount ( − ) or premium ( + )

For illustrative purposes the data on three closed-end funds taken from the ICI List in *Barron's* appear in Table 2–1. It should be clear that The Zweig Fund was trading at a premium and Adams Express and Baker Fentress were at a discount.

Let's take a closer look at what's available in *Barron's Market Week* in their Mutual Funds/Closed-End Funds section. The Lipper Analytical Services List gives data on bond funds separated into four categories: bond funds, convertible bond funds, international bond funds, and municipal bond funds. The Investment Company Institute List contains bond funds, diversified stock funds, flexible portfolio funds, loan participation funds (a unique kind of closed-end fund which buys bank loans), and specialized equity and convertible funds. All together these lists cover over 230 CEFs.

On the same page in *Barron's* there is a box that tracks CEFs. First, it contains the Herzfeld Closed-End Average, which measures the average price level of 18

**Table 2–1. Illustrative Weekly Closed-End Fund Data\*: Diversified Funds**

| Fund | Exchange | Net Asset Value (NAV) | Share Price | Percentage Discount ( − )/ Premium ( + ) |
|---|---|---|---|---|
| Adams Express | NYSE | 17.64 | 15 7/8 | − 10.01 |
| Baker Fentress | NYSE | 23.56 | 19 3/8 | − 17.76 |
| Zweig Fund | NYSE | 10.53 | 11 1/2 | + 9.21 |

\*Data as of April 20, 1990.
Source: Adapted from *Barron's*, April 23, 1990, p. 132.

equally weighted domestic equity CEFs. The Dow Industrials are graphed along with the Closed-End Average. Plotted in another chart are the weighted average NAV and the composite percent discount from NAV for these funds. The composite discount is useful as it gives the investor an idea of the current magnitude of discounts relative to their values during the past several quarters.


## A RISK FACTOR

The closed-end fund discount is really a component of extra risk to investors. With an open-end fund the basic risk is due to fluctuations in the value of the securities in the fund's portfolio as mirrored by fluctuations in NAV. But, with a closed-end fund there are two basic sources of uncertainty to investors:

1. Fluctuations in the value of the underlying portfolio (or NAV) as with the open-end fund.
2. Random variations in the discount or premium around NAV.

Thus, investors perceive CEFs as having more risk and pay a lower price for their shares to compensate for the added risk. This is one of the factors which contributes to the discount. But, don't worry! With a little homework you can use it to enhance your return. A discount is the flip side of buying a mutual fund with a front end load. With an 8% front-end load fund you get only $920 of the fund's securities for each $1,000 you invest. However, with a CEF you could be paying much less than NAV, perhaps getting $1,000 worth of securities for only $850 if the fund trades at a 15% discount.

There has been a tendency for funds to sell at relatively large discounts from NAV during bear market periods just as many stocks sell at low P/E ratios during such times. This is the ideal time to purchase CEF shares because you might find some at fire sale prices. For instance, at year-end 1973 and 1974, Wiesenberger's Diversified Investment Company Average discount stood at 25% and 24%, respectively.

Table 2–2 shows year-end discounts (or premiums) of eight old-line closed-end common stock funds at three different points in time: 1978, 1986, and 1989. At year-end 1978, when the discounts were especially wide, investor enthusiasm for stocks was at a low ebb. This would have been an ideal time to invest. Here you would be using the contrarian investment philosophy and buying what no one appears to want.

At year-end 1986 we were in the midst of a roaring bull market and investors were eager to purchase stocks and CEFs. As a result, you observe smaller discounts, and two of the funds have even gone to premiums. This could be a risky time to invest though. At the end of 1989 all of the discounts have widened and Source Capital is trading at a smaller premium than it did at the end of 1986.

Most investors know that at the peak of a bull market, when speculation is rampant, P/E ratios of stocks expand to excessive levels of overvaluation. At times like these discounts of CEFs shrink or turn to premiums. This is the best time for issuers to bring out new funds but the worst time to invest in them. Look at the chart of discounts at year-end 1986—less than ten months prior to the market crash in October 1987. This is a time when it is risky to

**Table 2–2. Selected Year-End CEF Discounts**

| | Discount (−)/Premium (+) | | |
| Fund | 1978 | 1986 | 1989 |
| --- | --- | --- | --- |
| Adams Express | − 22 | − 2 | − 15 |
| Baker, Fentress | − 38 | − 14 | − 15 |
| Central Securities | − 26 | − 9 | − 20 |
| General American Investors | − 27 | − 7 | − 15 |
| Niagara Share Corporation | − 24 | − 9 | − 17 |
| The Salomon Brothers Fund* | − 29 | − 2 | − 17 |
| Source Capital | − 20 | + 8 | + 1 |
| Tri-Continental Corporation | − 22 | + 3 | − 16 |
| Group Average | − 26 | − 4 | − 14 |

*Formerly The Lehman Corporation.
Source: *Wiesenberger Investment Companies Service.*

purchase the shares of CEFs and stocks in general. If a premium turns to a discount, or a small discount widens, the investor's return is adversely affected even if NAV increases.

## ADVANTAGES OF THE DISCOUNT

If a fund is purchased at a time when its discount is especially wide and the market in general is depressed, the investor could benefit in two ways when the market recovers:

1. From an increase in the fund's NAV as the value of its security holdings rises.
2. From the narrowing of the discount which would give an added boost to the stock price. Eventually the fund may even go to a premium, further accentuating performance. This is a form of leverage.

### Leverage

Buying a fund at a discount basically gives the buyer leverage free of charge since it can amplify profits, but the buyer need not pay for that leverage as in buying stocks on margin. In that case interest would be due on the borrowed funds. Suppose Fund A is purchased at a price of $9 per share when its NAV is $10—a 10% discount. The market advances over the next year and its NAV rises to $12 and the discount goes to zero so the stock price is $12. Thus the market price advanced 33% (from $9 to $12) when the NAV only advanced 20% (from $10 to $12). That's what favorable leverage is all about, as seen in Table 2–3.

### Higher Yield

But, even if the discount doesn't narrow, the CEF can offer an attractive buy at a wide discount since the return would be enhanced. This is true even if the fund's discount widens slightly after it's been purchased! Basically, if a fund is selling at a 20% discount investors enjoy the

**Table 2–3. Favorable Leverage**

|            | Beginning of Year | End of Year | Change |
|------------|-------------------|-------------|--------|
| NAV        | 10                | 12          | +20%   |
| Share price| 9                 | 12          | +33%   |
| Discount   | −10%              | 0%          | —      |

dividends and capital gains distributions on the full value of the portfolio because the free leverage is effectively working in their favor. Investors earn income and appreciation on a full dollar's worth of assets for an investment of 80 cents.

To illustrate the logic of the higher yield available from a CEF trading at a discount, suppose CDs go on special at your financial institution. Whereas normally you would need to invest $100,000 in a $100,000 CD to earn 10% interest over a 12-month period, today you are offered the opportunity to invest $80,000. But you will earn 10% interest on a full $100,000 CD for a year, at the end of which you will receive the $80,000 principal plus $10,000 interest. Thus, you are being offered a $100,000 CD at a 20% discount. The effective rate of interest would be 12.5%, or $10,000 annual interest divided by your $80,000 investment.

Assume now that the discount widened a bit and you got back just $79,000 of the $80,000 original investment at the end of the year. You still would net $9,000 ($10,000 interest less the $1,000 loss of principal) which would yield an 11.25% return on the $80,000 commitment. That's basically the way in which you earn a higher yield with a CEF trading at a discount.

**BEWARE THE PREMIUM!**

The risk of buying a CEF at a premium, at NAV, or even at a relatively narrow discount would be the disappearance of any premium and the widening of the discount. This would be analogous to the P/E contraction risk faced by individuals who buy stocks at overly inflated multiples only to see disappointing earnings. For example, if Fund A was purchased at $15 when its NAV was $12 (a 25% premium) and a year later its NAV had fallen to $10 and its price to $9 (a 10% discount), the price would have declined 40% when the NAV dropped only 17% as seen in Table 2–4.

Thus, if an investor buys a closed-end stock fund at a 5% premium during a bull market, then the market sinks and the fund goes to a 20% discount, losses would be considerably greater than they would have been with an open-end fund which would have no premiums or discounts. On November 10, 1989 the Spain Fund, one of the newer country funds, was trading at a 133.47% premium over its NAV of 13.76. On the same date the Korea Fund was trading at a 101.5% premium over its NAV of 18.61. Clearly premiums like this spell increased risk which will come back to haunt shareholders much of the time. In fact, by March, 1990 the share prices of these and other single country funds had dropped dramatically. As seen in Table 2–5, the prices of the Korea Fund and the Spain Fund plunged 39% and 42.4%, respectively, between November 10, 1989 and March 30, 1990.

If a fund is trading at a substantial premium it would be better to buy shares of some of the fund's major holdings instead of paying a premium for the fund. However, this is not always possible. For example, Korean government regulations have prevented U.S. investors from investing directly in shares traded on the Korean Stock Exchange. However, U.S. investors can buy individual Spanish stocks if they so choose.

If an equivalent no-load, open-end fund can be found at a time when CEFs are at premiums, the no-load fund would be the better investment. Just as buying a CEF at

**Table 2–4. Premium Turns to Discount**

|  | Beginning of Year | End of Year | Change |
|---|---|---|---|
| NAV | 12 | 10 | −17% |
| Share price | 15 | 9 | −40% |
| Prem. (+)/Disc. (−) | +25% | −10% | — |

**Table 2–5. Shrinking Premiums on Two Country Funds (Nov. 10, 1989 to Mar. 30, 1990)**

|  | Share Price (Premium) | | |
|---|---|---|---|
|  | 11-10-89 | 3-30-90 | Price Change |
| Korea Fund | 37 1/2 | 22 7/8 | −39.0% |
|  | (+101.5%) | (+31.77%) |  |
| Spain Fund | 32 1/8 | 18 1/2 | −42.4% |
|  | (+133.47%) | (+47.06%) |  |

Source: Based on data from *The Wall Street Journal,* November 13, 1989 and April 2, 1990.

a 20 percent discount is like buying a dollar's worth of assets for 80 cents, buying one at a 20 percent premium means you're paying $1.20 for a dollar's worth of assets.

If you buy a fund at a discount and it subsequently goes to a premium you may wish to consider selling it and investing the proceeds in another fund which represents better value. The authors recommend remaining fully invested most of the time in the best performing funds and holding them for many years unless they sell at large premiums. Our experience indicates that you should start taking profits at premiums of 10%. The same logic would apply to selling a stock. You'd want to consider selling when P/E ratios become excessive and you feel your stock has come to be overvalued.

Long-time closed-end fund analyst and trader Thomas Herzfeld explains how he takes advantage of the changing discount levels in the Closed-End Insights box.

## WHY THE DISCOUNT?

The discount has been regarded as somewhat of a mystery since no completely satisfactory explanation has ever been offered for its existence despite considerable sophisticated academic research. No mathematical equation can adequately explain the discount or premium on a fund. However, a variety of reasons have been put forth which help explain differences in discounts and premiums

# THE CLOSED-END FUND TRADING ADVANTAGE
## Thomas J. Herzfeld
### President
### Thomas J. Herzfeld Advisors, Inc.

Although closed-end funds offer a possibility to buy portfolios at a discount, this opportunity is of special value only if you can sell them at a narrower discount. If discounts remain the same, market price changes would occur only when the fund's portfolio changed in value. Fortunately, discounts do not stay the same, especially over intermediate to longer cycles. They tend to widen and narrow somewhat in predictable trends. This phenomenon is the key to obtaining greater profits than could be obtained only by changes in portfolio evaluation.

Under ideal conditions, I buy a fund when I believe:

- The market will rise.
- Its portfolio is concentrated in groups likely to demonstrate relative strength.
- Its discount from NAV is likely to narrow.

Conversely, I consider selling a fund when:

- A general market decline seems likely.
- The portfolio no longer appears concentrated in attractive areas.
- The discount from NAV is unlikely to narrow further.
  (It should be noted that, to trigger a buy or sell decision, not all conditions must be met.)

Generally, I try to buy a fund when it is trading at a discount to NAV that is at least five percentage points wider than its own average discount, based on a six month moving average. Under ideal circumstances, the shares should also be trading at a discount wider than the average for similar funds. We would buy a fund at a 20% discount if its average discount is 15% and the average discount of similar funds was less than 15%. This fund would be a candidate for sale if the discount narrowed to 10%.

In determining whether to buy, hold or sell, general shifts in the average discount of all closed-end funds have to be considered. When the average discount is narrowing, I buy at more aggressive discounts. For instance, if the average discount of the funds in the Herzfeld Closed-End Average (published in *Barron's* statistical section every week) slides by two percentage points, I would adjust my buy targets to more aggressive levels. The general narrowing and widening of closed-end discounts is akin to the expansion and contraction of price-earnings ratios on common stock.

Here is a good example. In 1989 the average discount to net asset value of Blue Chip Value Fund was 13%. In April the shares were trading at 6 1/8, an 18% discount to net asset value, 5 percentage points wider than average. The Herzfeld Closed-End Average was trading at an average 13% discount at the time. Six months later the net asset value per share of Blue Chip Value Fund had increased by approximately 15%, but its share price had increased by twice that amount, 30%, to 8 per share as the fund's discount narrowed to 6%.

among different funds as well as discounts and premiums on funds in general in different market environments.

In addition to being similar to mutual funds, CEFs are also stocks so, naturally, they behave like stocks. The authors like to think of the discount or premium on a fund as analogous to the P/E multiple on an ordinary stock and consequently affected by similar factors. These factors work together in a mysterious way to produce the final discount or premium on an individual fund. We group them into the following three categories:

1. Fund specific factors.
2. Sector specific factors.
3. General factors.

Let's examine each group of factors.

## Fund Specific Factors

1. Poor performance. A CEF which consistently underperforms its benchmark index and/or other similar funds would tend to have a wider discount.
2. High overhead. Funds which have higher management and administrative expenses (that is, higher expense ratios) than *comparable* ones should sell at wider discounts to offset the higher costs shareholders must bear.
3. Illiquid holdings. Funds which hold relatively illiquid stocks or bonds tend to sell at wider discounts. Illiquid securities, which have higher transaction costs if they are even marketable, are more difficult to value. A substantial price concession may be necessary to liquidate them. One example of a CEF with illiquid holdings would be a venture capital fund. Another would be a bond fund holding private placements.
4. Unrealized capital appreciation (or potential tax liabilities). Investors are wary of older funds with large unrealized capital gains on certain of their stocks which could have been held for many years. For example, the fund could have paid $2 per share for a stock in 1932 which now is trading at $300 per share. Thus, it has an unrealized gain of $298 per share! If the fund liquidates holdings like this you as a fund shareholder would have an immediate tax liability on your proportionate share of the distributions no matter how long you held shares in the fund. Like open-end funds, CEFs act as conduits passing along investment-related tax liabilities to their shareholders.

However, funds with larger amounts of unrealized appreciation may not sell at wider discounts because the unrealized appreciation factor could be offset by outstanding long-term fund performance.[7] The issue of unrealized capital appreciation will be discussed more fully in Chapter 3, "Analyzing a Fund."

5. Open-ending stipulations. Funds with provisions which would facilitate their open-ending, and thus the elimination of their discounts, would trade at narrower discounts. Many of the funds which went public in the 1980s have provisions to open-end starting in 1992, but this has to be approved by both the board of directors and the shareholders before it will happen. However, the board may prefer to keep the fund closed-end because it has illiquid investments.

6. Higher distributions. More generous shareholder distributions generally lead to narrower discounts.

7. Guaranteed annual distributions. As well as the amount, certainty of the distribution is important to investors. Funds which have elected to pay out, say, 10% of NAV annually experience a narrower discount. Funds which have this provision will be identified later on in the chapter.

8. Monthly distributions. Many shareholders prefer more frequent distributions, especially those in fixed income funds. Bond funds which have monthly distributions tend to sell at narrower discounts or at premiums.

9. Degree of diversification. Funds which have portfolios that are more widely diversified would generally be perceived by investors to have lower risk than those which have less diversified portfolios. Thus, a CEF which has 25% of its portfolio in one stock may sell at a wider discount than funds which are more fully diversified.

10. Random factors. CEFs as a group are relatively thinly traded. Thus, if one or a few big investors decide to buy a block of shares or liquidate holdings in a particular fund this could cause a sharp price swing leading to a change in the premium or discount.

**Sector Specific Factors**

For purposes of this discussion we define sector to encompass a specific industry, country, or type of security.

1. Sector sentiment. Funds that invest in the same sector could experience a widening of their discounts when problems or uncertainties develop in that sector. For instance, ASA Limited which invests in South African gold mining shares has seen its shares move from high premiums to wide discounts, based on the demand for gold on the one hand and racial tensions in South Africa on the other.

Some country funds trade at extraordinarily high premiums when others might be trading at huge discounts. The outlook for the particular country's economic growth, inflation, interest rates, stock market, and currency all play an important role in determining the level of the premium or discount.

2. New issues. If too many new funds are formed to invest in a popular sector premiums tend to narrow or discounts would widen on existing funds. This is based on the law of supply and demand. An illustration would be the formation of clone funds to invest in popular countries, such as Germany, in early 1990.

## General Factors

A variety of factors affect discounts on all funds.

1. CEF investors face an additional component of risk. As already explained, CEFs can be viewed as more risky than open-end funds since investors can't redeem their shares at NAV.

2. Lack of a marketing effort by the fund. After a CEF has gone public and the assets are locked up it generally does not promote itself, as open-end funds do to attract additional money. With a CEF it is not possible to sell more shares to incoming investors as open-end funds do. However, those funds which do promote themselves, like The Zweig Fund, tend to sell at narrower discounts or sometimes at premiums.

3. Less brokerage firm selling effort. Since institutional investor interest is generally not great in CEFs, brokerage houses, with few exceptions, do not actively research them. (However, this is changing as is shown in

the Closed-End Insights box in Chapter 3). Additionally, stockbrokers know that other products provide greater commission income.

4. Market sentiment. When investors are bullish, as they were during the late 1960s and the bull market of the 1980s, discounts on all funds tend to narrow and in some cases turn to premiums. These would also be times when a lot of investor money is flowing into open-end funds. Alternatively, when investors are pessimistic, as they were at various times during the 1970s and early 1980s, discounts can widen excessively. Also, at these times open-end funds would see a net outflow of investor money. Further, fear of a widening discount on funds with relatively narrow discounts during a bear market can cause them to widen.

The degree of investor uncertainty concerning the market outlook and future investment returns has been found to impact discounts. Greater discounts exist when uncertainty increases as evidenced by a mixed outlook and widely varying 12-month expectations.[8]

5. Year-end tax selling. This is especially pronounced during years of falling stock prices. Investors who have unrealized capital losses frequently want to realize them in November or December for tax purposes. A lot of selling forces shares to wide discounts. This is more evident in the funds that have done poorly during the year. And it is even more pronounced in smaller, thinly traded funds which would fall more in price under selling pressure. Your best bet is to buy these funds in December because they may rebound in January. This is known as the "January Effect" and it applies to other stocks as well as CEFs. Each year, in the December issue, *The Scott Letter* alerts its readers to bargains in CEFs created by tax-loss selling.

6. A market inefficiency. Perhaps the best way to look at the discount is as a market imperfection. This is particularly true because institutional interest and Wall Street research both run at low levels in the closed-end fund industry. This unique inefficiency in a relatively efficient marketplace offers sophisticated investors the opportunity to garner above-average long-term results.

Discounts and premiums on individual funds are thus

the result of a wide variety of factors working in combination. Accordingly, a fund's discount or premium can change when there is a change in one or more of the factors which impact its share price. However, investors may *overreact* to a negative or positive development resulting in an excessively deep discount or rich premium. This could present an opportunity to buy shares in a fund that is underpriced or to sell shares in a fund that has become overpriced.

## Fund Type Affects the Discount

At this point it should be clear that the type of fund affects the size of the discount. For instance, bond funds tend to trade at small discounts and often at premiums whereas the diversified and specialized equity funds have traded at discounts of 20% or 25% at times. See Figure 2–3, which compares historic discounts on bond and equity funds.

The discounts (or premiums) on bond funds compared to those on equity funds would be related to investor demand for stocks versus bonds among other things. The reason bond funds generally tend to sell at narrower discounts probably relates to the steadiness and predictability of the income and the lower risk of a bond portfolio. Another factor would be that many bond funds make monthly distributions.

The degree of diversification in the fund's portfolio would also be a factor. Funds that are broadly diversified would not go to premiums and discounts as extreme as the more specialized funds, since it is less likely that investors would feel extremely optimistic or pessimistic about all the different holdings in these broadly diversified fund portfolios. This explains why we see wider variations in discounts and premiums among country funds than among global equity funds that invest in a variety of different countries as well as in the United States.

The CEF investor should be well aware of these patterns. For instance, if you are buying a bond fund you might be happy to get it at a 6% discount whereas you would consider a 6% discount to be relatively narrow for an old-line, diversified common stock fund.

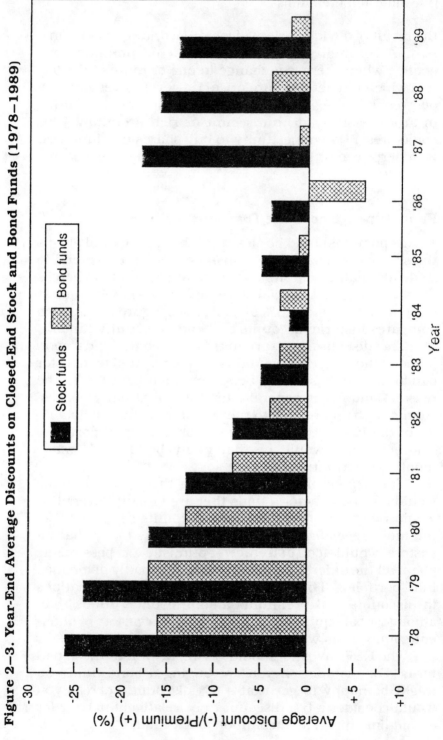

**Figure 2-3. Year-End Average Discounts on Closed-End Stock and Bond Funds (1978-1989)**

Source: Based on data from *Wiesenberger Investment Companies Service.*

50

Our viewpoint is that the equity funds offer investors the greatest advantage since they can sell at relatively wide discounts and, as we'll explain in Chapter 4, "Investing in Stock Funds," total returns over long periods of time could be expected to be much higher with stocks than with bonds. We will, accordingly, devote considerable attention to the equity group.


## NARROWING THE GAP

Closed-end fund managers are certainly conscious of the discount and prefer that it remain small since an excessive discount could instigate a raid on a fund with the intention of open-ending it. A number of strategies are used which could be expected to lead to narrower discounts.

A strategy which the authors favor is the fund's repurchase of shares trading at a discount. When a fund's share price falls substantially below NAV a repurchase of shares can increase NAV. Suppose a hypothetical fund's share price is $7.50 at a time when its NAV is $10. In theory you can see that the fund management could sell securities from the portfolio at their full market value, buy back some of the fund's outstanding shares at a discount, and increase the NAV in the process. Information on the share repurchase activities of a specific fund can be found in its shareholder reports or in the S&P *Stock Reports.* Fund share repurchases must be made in accordance with Rule 23c–1 of the Investment Company Act of 1940. Shares can be repurchased at the lower of the NAV or the market price. Usually this would be done when the shares trade at a discount.

Another alternative, adopted by many newer funds, would be to submit to shareholders the right to vote on whether or not to open-end a fund if it has been trading at a sufficiently large discount for a predetermined period of time. For example, starting January 1, 1991, shareholders of the Nicholas-Applegate Growth Equity Fund will be able to vote on whether or not to open-end if the shares were selling at an average discount of more than 5% from NAV during 1990. Starting in late 1990 H&Q Healthcare has the option each year to open-end. But Alan Carr, H&Q's president, told us that opening-ending would materially change the character of the fund.

Still another possibility, which has become quite popular with equity fund managers, is to institute a constant annual payout of 10% of net asset value. This was first used by George Michaelis at Source Capital in 1976. Michaelis felt that Source was capable of generating a total return (net income plus appreciation) in excess of 10 percent per annum. Thus, he could pay out 10 percent of NAV annually and that payout could be sustained over the years. If Michaelis produces more than a 10 percent total return Source's NAV would tend to increase. The 10 percent payout can result in a predictable return for shareholders who want to be able to plan on receiving regular cash distributions.[9]

The funds which employ the 10 percent annual payout tend to trade at narrower discounts. The mechanics of the 10% distribution policy are explained by George Michaelis, president of Source Capital, Inc., in its 1989 Annual Report and reprinted here in Figure 2–4.

Incidentally, Source Capital has been an outstanding long-term performer and this undoubtedly contributed to the success of its 10% distribution policy in narrowing the discount. The problem with this tactic is that it could force fund managers to liquidate portfolio holdings during a severe bear market in order to be able to meet the target payout. Those funds which, to our knowledge, adhere to a 10% payout policy (or some other fixed target amount as indicated) are identified in Figure 2–5. More could be following the policy by the time this book is published. To determine whether or not a particular fund follows the policy, check in the "Dividend Data" section of the S&P *Stock Reports* or contact the fund.

Finally, it should be mentioned that some of the funds feel it is important for them to market themselves, while others do not. Funds that do a good job of keeping the lines of communication open to brokers and shareholders should sell at narrower discounts. Martin Zweig feels very strongly about the importance of marketing for CEFs. It's

**Figure 2–4. Source Capital's Distribution Policy**

> Source Capital has a Common Stock Distribution Policy which provides for cash distributions of approximately 10% of the ongoing net asset value of its Common shares. Only a portion of such distributions is paid from net investment income. The remainder is paid from any net realized capital gains and/or paid-in capital, as determined by each year's results. To the extent the Company realizes net long-term gains for any year which are not distributed to shareholders under the Company's distribution policy, the Company designates such gains as undistributed and, accordingly, pays the capital gains tax (presently 34%) thereon, which payment is available as a tax credit to Common shareholders of record on the last day of the Company's year. Distributions to Common shareholders have been paid quarterly with periodic adjustments to maintain the indicated annual rate at approximately 10% of net asset value. This policy is designed to allow Common shareholders to benefit not only from income, but a portion of the capital appreciation which has resulted to date. The taxable status of the distributions varies from year to year and is not determinable until the end of each year.

Michaelis adds that the 10% distribution policy has worked out very well for Source:

> Since the policy was adopted in June 1976, at an initial annual rate of $1.40 per share, continued increases in net asset value, despite payments from capital, have permitted 15 subsequent increases to the current rate of $3.60. Maintenance of the current $3.60 annualized rate is dependent upon achieving a total return on the Common Stock from both income and appreciation of at least 10 percent.

Source: Source Capital, Inc., 1989 Annual Report, p. 1.

**Figure 2–5. CEFs which Distribute 10% of NAV Annually**

Baker, Fentress & Co.[1]
Blue Chip Value Fund
The Europe Fund[2]
Gabelli Equity Trust
Inefficient-Market Fund
Liberty All-Star Equity Fund
Pilgrim Regional Bank Shares
Source Capital
TCW Convertible Securities Fund[3]
Worldwide Value Fund
The Zweig Fund
The Zweig Total Return Fund

[1]Distributes 8% of NAV.
[2]Distributes 7% of NAV.
[3]Distributes $0.21 quarterly.

something that he feels most haven't done well. He feels it's their responsibility to shareholders to do so.

## STUDIES OF CEF PERFORMANCE

Academic research indicates that CEF shares are inefficiently priced and thus afford the potential for better than average performance even though their managers, by and large, would be expected to achieve investment results which are no better or worse than the results achieved by those who manage open-end funds.

Professor Rex Thompson analyzed the performance of a sample of 23 CEFs over the period January 1940 to December 1975. Thompson observed discounts above 20% frequently and also noted that discounts above 30% and 40% were not uncommon. High premiums were also observed on occasion. Thompson summarized his research as follows: "It is found that discounted fund shares, adjusted for risk, tended to outperform the market in the period 1940 to 1975. Funds selling at a premium appear to have been bad investments over the same time period."[10]

Professors R. Malcolm Richards, Don R. Fraser, and John C. Groth analyzed weekly data over the period 1970 to 1976 for a sample of 18 closed-end equity funds.[11] Both diversified and specialized funds were included in the group. The stock market exhibited extreme fluctuations during this period. The researchers tested certain trading rules which called for buying funds below a predetermined discount level (say 20%) and selling them when the discount had narrowed (say to 10%). They concluded that these trading rules resulted in risk-adjusted returns exceeding those resulting from the use of a simple buy and hold strategy with the funds. They also found that the specialized funds produced better results than the diversified funds.

In a more recent study, Professor Seth Copeland Anderson analyzed three time periods ranging from July 1965 to August 1984, using a slightly different sample of CEFs than Richards, Fraser, and Groth had employed. Anderson sought to strengthen the findings of the earlier researchers by applying their trading rules to different data. From his analysis of weekly data on 17 closed-end equity funds, Anderson concluded that there appear to be opportunities for earning above-normal returns in closed-end shares through the use of certain trading rules. These essentially involve buying CEFs at a discount and selling them when the discount narrows. Anderson concluded that the best strategy would be to buy funds at a discount that exceeds 20% and sell them when the average narrows to 15%. These are the same buy-and-sell points that Richards, Fraser, and Groth found to work best.[12]

Of course, there is no guarantee that results observed in the past will be repeated in the future.

## WILL DISCOUNTS PERSIST?

In our viewpoint no one really knows the answer to this question. You can't predict the market. Hopefully, discounts will persist for our readers to take advantage of them for many years in the future. There is always the argument that discounts will narrow as the market for CEFs becomes more efficient. It is our feeling, however, that discounts will probably continue to exist, as they are the closed-end fund equivalent to investor redemptions on open-end funds. We still see how the inefficiencies of the market continue to create discounts wide enough to provide value as well as downside protection to the investor in declining markets. Just as P/E ratios and dividend yields fluctuate, the level of premiums and discounts will fluctuate in accordance with changes in investor sentiment. We think Steve Samuels' viewpoints on this question in the Closed-End Insights box will prove particularly interesting.

---

### STEVE SAMUELS' VIEWPOINTS ON THE DISCOUNT
#### Steven Samuels
#### Samuels Asset Management

**WHY DO DISCOUNTS PERSIST?**

A couple of questions must first be addressed. Why discounts persist, will they continue to exist, and, if they will, in what investment areas?

It is my opinion that the single greatest reason that discounts persist is that securities are sold, not bought. Because it is not in the best financial interest of the brokerage community, closed-end funds are not recommended to their clients. It is only when these funds trade at substantial discounts that investment professionals take an interest.

It is important to understand why recommending closed-end funds it is not in the best interest of the brokerage community. First of all, closed-end funds offer high compensation only on the offering. Therefore, after the offering, closed-end funds will trade on an exchange and the compensation is reduced dramatically. Secondly, investors tend to hold funds far longer than individual securities, which of course is not appealing to brokers. And lastly, it is a difficult task for brokers and advisers who "pride" themselves on their investment wisdom to then invest in funds managed by other professionals. It is a tough sell.

## WILL DISCOUNTS CONTINUE TO EXIST?

Lately there have been frequent closed-end fund liquidations and open-endings. It poses the question of how long discounts will continue to be found.

Closed-end funds have a very distinct pattern. First a bull market begins and funds come public, creating new supply. Next the investment climate changes, and investors become disenchanted and sell the funds, creating discounts and, I might add, opportunities. (We are currently in this phase.) Then, when the funds are at large discounts, provisions like 10% payout policies that reduce discounts are created or outside raiders try to force open-endings or liquidations. Again, this is a cycle that has been seen many times and it will be no different this time. The important thing is to be able to take advantage of it.

## IN WHAT AREAS WILL DISCOUNTS CONTINUE TO BE FOUND?

As with the patterns of closed-end funds in general, within the different investment types there arc patterns of discounts and premiums. For example, during the bull market in 1986 and 1987, equity funds came public in record numbers. After the crash in 1987, investors sold off equity funds and bought the new bond funds, first buying higher quality governments and corporates and eventually lower rated "junk" bonds.

It is my opinion that the bond funds will shortly provide opportunities as their discounts widen. This will occur as current yields are reduced once again causing frustration for investors in those funds.

## CONCLUSIONS

Discounts persist because investments are sold and not bought. As long as it is in the best interest of the brokerage community to ignore closed-end funds after

> the initial offering, discounts will continue to exist.
> Within the area of closed-end funds, discounts will be
> determined by the current popularity of that invest-
> ment group—for example, bond funds, equity funds,
> and convertible funds.

## CONCLUSION

Discounts and premiums are fascinating phenomena and
their nature, risks, rewards, and possible causes should
be thoroughly understood by closed-end fund investors. A
myriad of factors impact discounts and premiums in general, although identifiable factors can be pointed to in particular instances.

Perhaps the best analogy would be between the
discount/premium on a closed-end fund and the price-
earnings ratio or price-book value ratio on an ordinary
stock. Stocks with low P/E ratios are rather like funds trading at discounts. Stocks with excessively high P/E ratios
resemble funds trading at a premium. Just like high P/Es,
high premiums spell increased risk. Of course, the analogy is not perfect but it does go a long way towards showing that market sentiment as well as factors unique to the
particular security and sector are driving forces.

### Notes

[1]Benjamin Graham, *The Intelligent Investor*, Fourth Revised Edition
(New York: Harper & Row, Publishers, 1973), p. 127.

[2]New York Institute of Finance Editorial Staff, *Asset Plays: Profiting
from Undervalued Stocks* (New York: New York Institute of Finance,
1988), pp. 65–67.

[3]Burton G. Malkiel, *A Random Walk Down Wall Street* (New York:
W.W. Norton & Company, Inc., 1973), p. 225.

[4]*Ibid.*, 1985 edition, pp. 346–48.

[5]*Ibid.*, 1990 edition, pp. 388–91.

[6]They are Adams Express Co., Baker, Fentress & Co., Central Securi-
ties, General American Investors, Niagara Share Corp., The Salomon
Brothers Fund (formerly The Lehman Corp.), Source Capital, and Tri-
Continental Corp.

[7]Thomas J. Herzfeld, *The Investor's Guide to Closed-End Funds* (New
York: McGraw-Hill Book Company, 1980), p. 10.

[8]Seth C. Anderson and Jeffery A. Born, "Closed-end funds: What causes the discounts?" *AAII Journal*, July 1987, pp. 9–12.

[9]*Outstanding Investor Digest*, June 23, 1989, p. 27.

[10]Rex Thompson, "The information content of discounts and premiums on closed-end fund shares," *Journal of Financial Economics*, June/September, 1978, p. 151.

[11]R. Malcolm Richards, Don R. Fraser, and John C. Groth. "Winning strategies for closed-end funds," *The Journal of Portfolio Management*, Fall 1980, pp. 50–55.

[12]Seth Copeland Anderson, "Closed-end funds versus market efficiency," *The Journal of Portfolio Management*, Fall 1986, pp. 63–65.

# CHAPTER 3

# *Analyzing a Fund*

Analyzing a closed-end fund may be a bit easier than analyzing an ordinary common stock. Still, one needs to do a thorough job and to avoid the pitfalls facing the unwary. The first priority is to be acquainted with the customary sources of information. But, before covering that, we, the authors, want to discuss our investment philosophy.

## THE AUTHORS' PHILOSOPHY

The authors believe in the philosophy of "get rich slowly"; accumulate your wealth over many years and you will be more likely to keep it. Locating undervalued funds, that is, those trading at attractive discounts, is the key. Then plan on holding them for many years. Make them the core around which you build your portfolio. There are sound reasons to have an entire portfolio in CEFs. But most investors would probably choose to hold a portion in CEFs and the balance in mutual funds, stocks, bonds, or other investment assets. We want to emphasize that once you are a dedicated closed-end fund investor, you may want to hold nothing else. In any event, we suggest they become your core holdings. When individual funds become over-valued sell them and go into others that appear under-priced. Our 10 percent rule states that you should sell your funds at a premium of 10 percent over NAV. Some analysts recommend selling before that point, say when the discount shrinks to a predetermined value.

Our investment views are summarized as follows:

1. Don't expect to get rich overnight. Leave this for the speculators and in-and-out traders who inevitably lose money. Be a patient value investor. Get rich slowly but steadily; this should be your goal.

2. Don't try to time the market. Market timers will dispute this, but we feel they nearly always underperform and incur large commissions from their frequent trading. Market timing is in conflict with our views that you cannot predict the future. Instead, keep your eyes open for value in individual funds at all times. Wait for the discount to widen—this is the best kind of market timing.

3. Don't jump in and out of funds. This results in high transaction costs and lowers your odds for good solid long-run performance. It also makes record keeping and tax return preparation more complicated.

4. Don't expect last year's hottest fund to repeat its dramatic performance for you this year. The best per-formers for the year are usually specialized funds which are highly volatile. A recent example would be the stellar performance of some single country funds in 1989. But, like risky stocks, these funds plunge as fast as they soar, especially when they reach heady premiums.

5. Aim for long-term compound annual returns which are slightly above the market averages. Buying shares at a discount greater than the fund's past average discount as well as greater than the discounts of other comparable funds increases the odds of beating the market.

6. It is best to choose funds which have a history of performing well and operating efficiently. By operating ef-ficiently, we mean they have low expenses as reflected by their expense ratios.

7. The reputation and track record of the management is very important. Although others may disagree, we think it's the most important factor. The bottom line is to look for good management, then keep your eyes open for an opportunity to buy at a discount.

Let's now go over the sources of information you'll need to work with.

## STANDARD SOURCES

You already know that closed-end corporations are publicly traded stocks. This means that you would be able to consult the usual sources of investment information like Standard & Poor's, Moody's, and Value Line. Daily prices and trading volumes are printed in the stock tables of newspapers for nearly all of the funds just as they are for ordinary stocks. Except for the fact that there is no P/E ratio for a CEF, the information on them in the stock tables is the same as that for any stock. For instance, if your fund trades on the New York Stock Exchange you would simply consult that table. You can get intra-day prices and other trading statistics from your broker. Computer users who are interested in keeping attuned to recent news or just having access to basic data on different funds should consider the investor services available on Dow Jones News/Retrieval.®

Our coverage of sources of information is broken down as follows:

1. Media coverage
2. Shareholder reports
3. Library sources
4. Lipper data
5. Closed-end advisories
6. Brokerage research

### Media Coverage

Closed-end fund investors should keep up with the various articles on the subject. *The Wall Street Journal* regularly publishes articles of general interest as well as on specific

64 Overview

funds. Check the "Index to Businesses" found in the "Marketplace" section of *The Wall Street Journal* to see if there are any articles on the funds you are following. From time to time *Forbes* has articles on closed-end funds. *Barron's* has at least one article on closed-end funds in its quarterly mutual fund survey issue, which is generally written by Thomas Herzfeld. Other business publications also have occasional articles on closed-end funds. However, closed-end fund coverage is not as widespread as that of open-end funds since there is more money and greater investor interest in the latter.

## Shareholder Reports

The most basic, direct kind of information on closed-end funds would be the customary shareholder reports. However, there are some differences between the reports supplied by closed-end funds and those of the ordinary publicly traded company. At the minimum, closed-end funds have to supply stockholders with an annual and semiannual report. Most report quarterly.

The fund's shareholder reports allow you to study the portfolio composition and portfolio changes. You can see how many and what securities the fund holds, its cash position, how the assets are diversified across different industries, the biggest positions, and major changes in security holdings. For a bond fund you would be interested in such things as the ratings of individual bonds held in the portfolio as well as the portfolio's average maturity.

Unlike other publicly traded companies, closed-end funds are not required to file a Form 10-K with the Securities Exchange Commission. However, they do file a Form N-SAR semiannually with the SEC. Also, unlike open-end funds which continually offer new shares to the public and therefore always have a ready prospectus for interested shareholders, closed-end funds may not have a prospectus available, especially if the fund is relatively old. However, you should always attempt to get the prospectus on a CEF you want to invest in since it may be available.

The proxy statement also contains useful information. Closed-end funds send proxy statements to their shareholders prior to the annual meeting. Information you'll want to look for in the proxy includes the number of shares of the company owned by its officers and directors as well as by other principal holders of the stock. These outside investors are required to file a Schedule 13D with the SEC when their holdings amount to 5% or more of the company's outstanding stock. Officers and directors must file a Form 4 with the SEC when they buy or sell their fund's shares.

In general, we like to see closed-end funds that have relatively high ownership by the officers and directors, as this indicates their commitment and confidence in the fund's future performance. It also gives greater assurance that their interests coincide with those of the shareholders.

## Visiting the Library

Standard & Poor's has three basic sources of information which would be of interest to the closed-end fund investor: the *Stock Reports, Security Owner's Stock Guide,* and *Corporation Records.* We'll examine each in turn. Of the three, you'll probably find the *Stock Reports* most useful.

If you are interested in getting an overview of a particular closed-end fund, your best bet is to consult an S&P *Stock Report* first. One for Tri-Continental appears in Figure 3–1. S&P's *Stock Reports* are available on virtually all the closed-end funds you would want to invest in and they provide considerable detailed information. Of course, the smaller, thinly traded over-the-counter funds may not be included. But you are probably better advised to stay away from these, unless they offer special value.

To get further information call or write the funds you are most interested in. The addresses and phone numbers of the funds are found in the *Stock Reports* and they also appear in the CEF directory in Appendix I at the back of this book. Of course new funds are introduced and you need to know where to go to find their addresses and phone numbers. Again, the S&P *Stock Reports* would probably be the best place to start. But the fund may not be there if it's very new or obscure. The Investment Com-

## Figure 3–1. Sample Page from Standard & Poor's Stock Reports

# Tri-Continental Corp.   2256

NYSE Symbol TY Options on Phila (Mar-Jun-Sep-Dec)

| NAV | Price | % Difference | Dividend | Yield | S&P Ranking | Beta |
|---|---|---|---|---|---|---|
| May 4'90 | May 4'90 | | | | | |
| 27.03 | 22⁷/₈ | -15.4% | ¹0.84 | ¹3.7% | NR | NA |

### Summary

Tri-Continental is a publicly traded (closed-end) investment company. With the bulk of investments in a broadly diversified list of common stocks, it offers participation in a high-grade portfolio under professional management. Recent emphasis has been on communications, consumer goods, industrial equipment, energy, and drugs and health care.

### Business Summary

Tri-Continental Corp. is a diversified publicly traded investment company that invests primarily for the longer term with the objective of producing future growth of both capital and income while providing reasonable current income. Funds are invested in established and better-known securities.

At December 31, 1989 investments aggregated $1.61 billion (at market; 98.1% of total assets). Net assets at December 31, 1989 and December 31, 1988 were divided as follows:

| | 12/89 | 12/88 |
|---|---|---|
| Common stock: | | |
| Communications ............ | 13.5% | 8.3% |
| Consumer goods............ | 9.6% | 11.6% |
| Industrial equipment........ | 9.1% | 10.8% |
| Energy........................ | 8.3% | 6.3% |
| Computers & services..... | 1.8% | 5.8% |
| Chemicals ................... | 2.4% | 5.3% |
| Drugs & health care ....... | 7.1% | 5.3% |
| Printing & publishing ...... | 1.4% | 4.7% |
| Retail trade .................. | 5.0% | 4.4% |
| Special holdings............ | 1.9% | 3.7% |
| Transportation.............. | 3.0% | 3.7% |
| Other ......................... | 24.7% | 14.4% |
| Total common stock .......... | 87.8% | 84.3% |
| U.S. Gov't securities.......... | 7.5% | 12.1% |
| Short-term holdings .......... | 2.3% | 2.7% |
| Corporate debt................. | 1.0% | Nil |
| Cash & other (Net)............. | 1.4% | 0.9% |

At December 31, 1989 the 10 largest holdings (representing 27.6% of common stock investments) were AT&T, General Electric, Capital Cities, PepsiCo, Walt Disney, United Telecommunications, GTE, Schering-Plough, Boeing, and CPC International.

Management and administrative services are provided by J. & W. Seligman & Co. For its services Seligman receives 0.45% of the first $1.25 billion of the fee base ranging down to 0.225% of the fee base over $3.25 billion. The management fee was

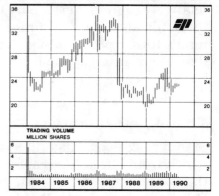

TRADING VOLUME MILLION SHARES

1984 | 1985 | 1986 | 1987 | 1988 | 1989 | 1990

$5,125,878 in 1989, versus $4,505,682 in the prior year.

The company offers a dividend reinvestment plan whereby all or part of distributions may be reinvested in additional shares. TY reports audited statements of operations and changes in net investment income on a semi-annual basis only.

### Important Developments

**Jan. '90—** During the 1989 fourth quarter TY made initial investments in Alexander & Alexander Services, American International Group, Baker Hughes, Commonwealth Edison Co., Laidlaw Transportation, Pfizer, Philip Morris, and Wellman Inc., while additional investments were made in BankAmerica Corp. and Fluor Corp. Eliminated from the portfolio were Barnett Banks of Florida, Giant Food Inc. Class A, IBM, Kellogg, and Pitney Bowes, while reductions were made in AMR Corp., Honeywell, Mead Corp., and Sundstrand Corp.

**Next earnings report expected in mid-May.**

### Per Share Data ($)

| Yr. End Dec. 31 | 1989 | 1988 | 1987 | 1986 | 1985 | 1984 | 1983 | 1982 | 1981 | 1980 |
|---|---|---|---|---|---|---|---|---|---|---|
| Net Asset Value² | 27.44 | 23.55 | 23.94 | 27.94 | 29.78 | 25.36 | 30.82 | 29.08 | 26.08 | 31.55 |
| Yr. End Prices | 23 | 19¹/₄ | 20⁵/₈ | 28⁵/₈ | 29³/₈ | 24⁷/₈ | 29³/₈ | 26⁷/₈ | 20³/₄ | 23⁵/₈ |
| % Difference | -16.2% | -18.3% | -13.8% | +2.5% | -1.3% | -1.9% | -4.7% | -7.6% | -20.4% | -25.1% |
| Dividends— | | | | | | | | | | |
| Invest. Inc. | 0.84 | 0.81 | 0.89 | 0.97 | 1.04 | 1.13 | 1.09 | 1.08 | 1.15 | 1.14 |
| Capital Gains | 2.55 | 1.25 | 3.73 | 4.34 | 2.62 | 2.40 | 4.46 | 1.48 | 2.72 | 1.64 |
| Portfolio Turned | 60% | 67% | 79% | 51% | 61% | 72% | 44% | 40% | 36% | 41% |

Data as orig. reptd. 1. Paid in the past 12 mos. from invest. inc.; excl. 2.55 from capital gains. 2. Bef. dilution from exercise of wts. NA-Not Available.

**May 11, 1990**
Standard & Poor's Corp.
25 Broadway, NY, NY 10004

Source: Standard & Poor's Corporation

**Figure 3–1. (continued)**

# 2256

## Tri-Continental Corporation

### Income Data (Million $)

| Year Ended Dec. 31 | Total Invest Inc. | —Net Invest Income— Total | —Net Invest Income— Per Share | Realized Cap. Gains Total | Realized Cap. Gains Per Sh. | [1]% Net Inv. Inc./ Net Assets | —% Expenses To— [1]Net Assets | —% Expenses To— [1] Invest. Inc. | Price Range Com. Stk. HI | Price Range Com. Stk. LO |
|---|---|---|---|---|---|---|---|---|---|---|
| 1989 | 56.1 | 47.8 | 0.84 | 137 | 2.36 | 3.2 | 0.6 | 14.8 | 25³/₄ | 19¹/₈ |
| 1988 | 50.8 | 43.3 | 0.80 | 61 | 1.13 | 3.3 | 0.6 | 14.7 | 22⁷/₈ | 19¹/₈ |
| 1987 | 48.0 | 40.1 | 0.82 | 178 | 3.45 | 2.7 | 0.5 | 16.6 | 34 | 20¹/₂ |
| 1986 | 49.7 | 42.6 | 0.98 | 181 | 3.94 | 3.1 | 0.5 | 14.4 | 34¹/₂ | 26¹/₂ |
| 1985 | 48.4 | 42.7 | 1.05 | 102 | 2.62 | 4.6 | 0.6 | 11.9 | 29³/₄ | 24 |
| 1984 | 47.9 | 42.9 | 1.14 | 87 | 2.43 | 4.5 | 0.6 | 10.4 | 31 | 21⁵/₈ |
| 1983 | 41.7 | 36.4 | 1.08 | 142 | 4.46 | 3.6 | 0.5 | 12.9 | 29³/₄ | 24³/₈ |
| 1982 | 39.4 | 35.0 | 1.08 | 46 | 1.49 | 4.5 | 0.6 | 11.2 | 27⁵/₈ | 17⁵/₈ |
| 1981 | 38.3 | 33.9 | 1.15 | 75 | 2.69 | 4.7 | 0.5 | 11.5 | 24¹/₂ | 18¹/₂ |
| 1980 | 35.4 | 32.3 | 1.14 | 43 | 1.60 | 4.2 | 0.4 | 8.7 | 24 | 16⁷/₈ |

### Balance Sheet Data (Million $)

| Dec. 31 | Net Assets | % Change NAV | % Change [2]S&P 500 | Bonds AAA | Investments Cost | Investments Market | % Net Asset Distribution Net Cash | % Net Asset Distribution ST Oblig. | Bonds & Notes | Com. Stk. | Other Invest. |
|---|---|---|---|---|---|---|---|---|---|---|---|
| 1989 | 1,632 | +26.5 | +27.3 | +8.1 | 1,247 | 1,610 | 1.4 | 2.3 | 8.5 | 87.8 | Nil |
| 1988 | 1,301 | +3.4 | +12.4 | -0.3 | 1,158 | 1,290 | 0.9 | 2.7 | 12.1 | 84.3 | Nil |
| 1987 | 1,275 | -2.4 | +2.0 | -8.9 | 1,116 | 1,257 | 1.4 | 3.9 | 10.2 | 84.5 | Nil |
| 1986 | 1,317 | +14.6 | +14.6 | +8.9 | 1,032 | 1,349 | d2.4 | 4.6 | 9.8 | 88.0 | Nil |
| 1985 | 1,194 | +26.2 | +26.3 | +19.1 | 980 | 1,271 | d6.4 | 10.9 | 6.3 | 89.2 | Nil |
| 1984 | 949 | -4.9 | +1.4 | +3.6 | 890 | 1,022 | d7.8 | 11.7 | 13.6 | 82.5 | Nil |
| 1983 | 1,019 | +10.9 | +17.3 | -10.2 | 769 | 1,013 | 0.6 | 7.5 | 12.5 | 79.4 | Nil |
| 1982 | 929 | +21.1 | +14.8 | +34.0 | 694 | 974 | d4.8 | 9.1 | 12.2 | 83.5 | Nil |
| 1981 | 767 | -12.4 | -9.7 | -16.7 | 626 | 762 | 0.7 | 8.9 | 16.7 | 73.7 | Nil |
| 1980 | 876 | +27.0 | +25.8 | -15.6 | 573 | 878 | d0.2 | 6.0 | 2.0 | 92.2 | Nil |

Data as orig. reptd. 1. As reptd. by co. 2. Bef. reinvestment of dividends. d-Deficit.

### Net Asset Value Per Com. Sh. ($)

| As of: | 1989 | 1988 | 1987 | 1986 |
|---|---|---|---|---|
| Mar. 31 | 24.62 | ... | 32.68 | 31.91 |
| Jun. 30 | 26.90 | 25.30 | 33.69 | 34.26 |
| Sep. 30 | 29.66 | ... | 35.11 | 31.21 |
| Dec. 31 | 27.44 | 23.55 | 23.94 | 27.94 |

In the 12 months ended December 31, 1989 net asset value per share (adjusted for capital gains distributions) advanced 27.3%. In the same period the Standard & Poor's 500 Stock Index also rose 27.3%.

Investment income for 1989 rose 10% from that of 1988, primarily reflecting increased investment income. Following an 11% rise in expenses, net investment income was also up 10%. After preferred dividends, per-share income was $0.84 on 8.2% more shares, versus $0.80. There were net realized and unrealized gains on investments of $6.78 and $1.01 a share in the respective years.

### Net Invest. Inc. Per Com. Sh. ($)

| Quarter: | 1989 | 1988 | 1987 | 1986 |
|---|---|---|---|---|
| Mar. 31 | 0.20 | 0.18 | 0.22 | 0.23 |
| Jun. 30 | 0.22 | 0.19 | 0.21 | 0.23 |
| Sep. 30 | 0.22 | 0.22 | 0.19 | 0.25 |
| Dec. 31 | 0.20 | 0.21 | 0.20 | 0.27 |
| | 0.84 | 0.80 | 0.82 | 0.98 |

### Dividend Data

Virtually all net investment income is paid out to shareholders. Realized capital gains are distributed each year before year-end. Dividends have been paid since 1945. A dividend reinvestment plan is available.

| Amt. of Divd. $ | Date Decl. | Ex-divd. Date | Stock of Record | Payment Date |
|---|---|---|---|---|
| 0.20 | Jun. 8 | Jun. 15 | Jun. 21 | Jul. 1'89 |
| 0.22 | Sep. 14 | Sep. 19 | Sep. 25 | Oct. 1'89 |
| *2.55 | Nov. 22 | Nov. 30 | Dec. 6 | Dec. 29'89 |
| 0.23 | Dec. 14 | Dec. 18 | Dec. 22 | Dec. 29'89 |
| 0.19 | Mar. 13 | Mar. 19 | Mar.23 | Apr. 1'90 |

*Capital gains: 2.40 long-term; 0.15 short-term; in cash or stock.

### Capitalization

**Long Term Debt:** None.

**$2.50 Cum. Preferred Stock:** 752,740 shs. ($50 par); red. at $55.

**Common Stock:** 58,089,221 shs. ($0.50 par). Institutions hold about 3.5%. Shareholders of record: About 50,000.

**Warrants:** 25,171, ea. to purchase 8.81 com. shs. at $2.55 a sh.

Office—130 Liberty St., New York, N.Y. 10006. Tel—(212) 432-4100. Chrmn—W. C. Morris. Pres—R. T. Schroeder. Secy—C. J. White. Treas—K. J. Blanchfield. Dirs—F. E. Brown, S. R. Currie, L. A. Lapham, W. B. Marshall, B. S. Michel, W. C. Morris, J. C. Pitney, W. M. Rees, J. Q. Riordan, H. J. Schmidt. Transfer Agent—Union Data Service Center, Inc., NYC. Incorporated in Maryland in 1929.

Information has been obtained from sources believed to be reliable, but its accuracy and completeness are not guaranteed. Adam J. Penn pany Institute can serve as another source of information for CEF investors. The ICI may be able to help you locate information on newer or more obscure funds. The ICI's address and phone number can be found in Appendix II.

The S&P *Security Owner's Stock Guide* is published monthly and is a compact source of information. You'll learn a few of the basics about the fund, such as its ticker symbol, where it trades, and some information on recent dividend payments, past prices, and net asset values. You can also determine its average daily trading volume by dividing the past month's volume by 20 (the usual number of trading days in a month). As will be explained in Chapter 16, "Dealing with Your Broker," it's important to know the fund's average daily trading volume before placing an order to buy or sell its shares—especially if you're planning on placing a relatively large order. Basically, the higher the average daily trading volume the more liquid the fund and the easier it is to buy (or sell) its shares without raising (or lowering) the price with your transaction.

The *Stock Guide* also provides data on the amount of institutional holdings of each fund's shares. With few exceptions, like some single country funds, institutional holdings are low as closed-end shares are held mainly by individual investors.

Standard & Poor's *Corporation Records* contain detailed information which may be useful to the closed-end fund analyst. Generally, however, we feel that the S&P *Stock Reports* are the place to look first.

*Wiesenberger Investment Companies Service* is a major publication dealing with mutual funds. It is published annually in late summer in hardback form and contains closed-end as well as open-end fund profiles. Its statistical survey includes basic data on over 230 closed-end funds. Detailed profiles are not available on all closed-end funds though. For instance, the 1990 volume has detailed descriptions of nine CEFs and short descriptions of approximately 50 others. A few of the chapters contain useful general background information on closed-end funds.

Wiesenberger also reports annual total returns for each of the past ten years. In addition, cumulative returns

for periods ranging from two through ten years are presented as well as volatility statistics. These performance
data are presented for some 60 established CEFs. You'll
find the data useful. Wiesenberger expects to continue to
expand its CEF coverage in 1991.

   *The Value Line Investment Survey* covers over 40
closed-end funds separated into domestic equity, foreign,
and bond fund (income) categories. The fund profiles are
updated every 13 weeks. A table listing the funds covered
by *Value Line* can be found in Appendix III. Norman Tepper has been covering CEFs for Value Line since 1968.
Tepper also writes general commentary about the closed-
end fund industry and offers useful guidance for analyzing
a fund. The address and phone number of *Value Line* is
in Appendix II.

## Lipper Data

Lipper Analytical Services, Inc. publishes a comprehensive pair of monthly services (*Lipper Closed-End Bond
Funds Analysis* and *Lipper Closed-End Equity Funds
Analysis*) which provide data on the entire universe of domestic closed-end funds. (For the address and phone number of publisher see Appendix II). These publications provide extensive descriptive and historical data, including
investment performance, yields and market price histo-
ries. Both the bond and equity fund universes are separated into a large number of different categories.

   Subscriptions to these Lipper services are limited to
professional investors. However, much of the Lipper performance data on closed-end funds appears regularly in
the financial press. For instance, "Mutual Fund Scorecard," which appears daily in the third section of *The Wall
Street Journal* often displays groups of top and bottom
performers in various closed-end fund categories. Each
Wednesday a complete tabulation of closed-end bond fund
values, showing premiums and discounts is also provided.
This also appears each week in *Barron's*.

   Much of the data in this book has been taken from the
Lipper services described above as well as from a prede-

cessor service, *Lipper Annuity & Closed-End Survey*
(LACES), which commenced publication in 1973.


**Advisory Letters**

There are several advisories that concentrate exclusively
on closed-end funds. They are as follows:

1. *Closed-End Fund Analyst* is a technical analysis
of about 50 closed-end funds published monthly by the
Worden Brothers. It includes charts of all of the funds covered—principally equity funds.

2. *Frank Cappiello's Closed-End Fund Digest* is published monthly and includes an annually updated book
available to subscribers as well as to the general public at
bookstores.[1]

3. *The Investor's Guide to Closed-End Funds* is published by Thomas J. Herzfeld Advisors, Inc. This monthly
research report provides basic information for analyzing
and trading closed-end funds.

For those who want a detailed reference work on
closed-end funds we recommend *The Thomas J. Herzfeld
Encyclopedia of Closed-End Funds* which covers some
225 closed-end funds. This book is published annually in
the summer.

4. *The Scott Letter: Closed-End Fund Report* has
been published monthly (except August) by co-author
Scott since April 1988. *The Scott Letter* emphasizes in-
depth interviews with the managers of selected closed-end
funds. Each issue contains two or more of these interviews. There are also tables of data on closed-end stock
and bond funds, buy and sell recommendations for certain
funds, and a variety of news items of interest to CEF investors. There is also a telephone Hot Line, which is updated
weekly.

Some mutual fund advisory services may also cover
closed-end funds. For instance, *Mutual Fund Forecaster*
includes one-year profit projections and risk ratings as
well as past performance data on nearly 60 closed-end
funds.

Addresses and phone numbers of each of the above
advisory services appear in Appendix II.

## BROKERS WHO SPECIALIZE

Thomas J. Herzfeld & Co., Inc., a Miami, Florida stock brokerage firm specializes exclusively in closed-end funds. For many years Herzfeld has been recognized as the leading authority on closed-end funds and has been quoted extensively on the subject. In addition to his work with domestic CEFs, he is an expert on those in the London market. Herzfeld advocates trading closed-end funds based on short-term changes in their discount/premium levels.

A number of brokerage firms provide research on closed-end funds. Included are A.G. Edwards & Sons, Kidder Peabody, PaineWebber, Prudential-Bache, Shearson Lehman Hutton, Smith Barney, and Dean Witter. Jeffrey Hopson at A.G. Edwards publishes a quarterly report on closed-end funds. Dean Eberling and Anthony Maltese at Shearson have been analyzing closed-end funds since 1987. Andrew Davis at PaineWebber specializes in bond funds. Michael Porter at Smith Barney tracks over 30 country funds. Joseph McGowan, Thomas Bourque, and Ted Walsh at Kidder Peabody put out a quarterly survey of closed-end funds.

Analyst Jeff Hopson discusses Wall Street coverage of CEFs in the Closed-End Insights box.

---

**WALL STREET COVERAGE OF CEFs**
**Jeffrey Hopson, CFA**
**Research Analyst**
**A.G. Edwards & Sons, Inc.**


Like the dramatic increase in popularity of closed-end funds in the past several years, there has been a significant increase in Wall Street coverage of closed-end funds during this time period. This increase in coverage primarily reflects the fact that this sector is now of legitimate size and interest to justify the dedication of resources. Back in September of 1986, there were just 38 equity funds traded and 27 bond funds traded, many of which were small and thinly traded. At that time, there was no serious degree of Wall Street coverage, but there were a few specialists following the group who otherwise existed in relative obscurity. Today, there are approximately 94 equity funds and 139 bond funds traded, representing billions of dollars of net worth. There is coverage by at least six major investment firms, a sprinkling of regional firms, and several newsletters dedicated to this cause. This increased coverage came over time and can be viewed at various stages.

The initial push to increase coverage of closed-end funds was precipitated by the increase in initial public offerings. Once the products were sold, clients and brokers needed a source of information and support. At this stage in the process, coverage was primarily reactive and information oriented. Initial obstacles to legitimate research were a lack of historical data and information, a lack of true understanding by investors, and insufficient experience of the analysts themselves.

In the middle stage of the process, after a couple years of sporadic coverage, Wall Street realized that the actual size of investment in closed-end funds was substantial and that the public awareness of this investment sector had rapidly improved. Most people familiar with this industry then realized that it was here to stay and deserved attention. At that point, the research effort was given more serious consideration and it became reactive in nature and much more sophisticated. Several firms began publishing regular reports that included performance data, portfolio descriptions, and specific recommendations.

In the final stage, which is still developing, investors will see more action-oriented buy/hold/sell recommendations and more complete performance data. Investment firms have a captive audience in clients who already own shares of closed-end funds. Therefore, firms have a responsibility to serve them and an interest in providing ongoing investment advice.

## ANALYZING THE DATA

Next we turn our attention to certain ratios and other measures which closed-end fund analysts always look at. They are as follows:

1. Expense analysis.
2. Shareholder distributions.
3. Performance evaluation.
4. Analysis of the discount.
5. Portfolio turnover.
6. Unrealized appreciation.

Ideally, you want a fund which operates efficiently (at low cost), performs well, and is relatively undervalued.

### Expense Analysis

A commonly used measure, known as the expense ratio, indicates how well the fund is controlling its costs. It is computed by dividing the annual expenses of operating the fund by the average net assets. The expense portion of the ratio includes various administrative, investment management, and interest costs (if the fund uses leverage or borrows to buy its securities). Management fees usually comprise the major portion of the expenses.

A few of the equity funds which came out in the 1980s, like Royce Value Trust and Z-Seven Fund, have management fees which are linked to performance. Thus, the management fees could be relatively high when performance is good and may be zero when the fund lags the market averages by a predetermined amount. In the case of Z-Seven there is even a penalty fee which must be paid by management for poor performance. We explain how it works in Figure 3-2.

Occasionally an equity fund will have legal fees incurred in fighting off a takeover attempt which would become part of the expense ratio. The detailed breakdown of expenses for a particular fund can be found in its annual report in the statement of operations which is essentially

**Figure 3–2. Z-Seven's Bonus/Penalty Fee Structure**

Z-Seven's quarterly bonus or penalty ranges from zero to 2.5% and is based upon the fund's performance relative to the S&P 500 for trailing 12 month periods. The adviser must outperform the S&P 500 by 10 percentage points for a given year to earn the minimum quarterly bonus of 0.25%. An example would be a 12 month period where the fund returns 20% versus 10% for the S&P 500. In order to earn the maximum quarterly bonus of 2.5% the fund's performance must exceed the S&P 500's by at least 100 percentage points. This would be difficult. For example, if the return for the S&P 500 is 10% Z-Seven would have to earn 110%! If the fund underperforms the S&P 500 the adviser would pay the shareholders a penalty fee based on the same schedule.

Z-Seven's base management fee is 1.25% per annum. It would be increased or decreased by the amount of any bonus or penalty. Thus, if the fund's trailing 12 month performance falls within plus or minus 10 percentage points of the S&P 500 the total management fee would simply be 1.25%. For 1989 the base management fee was $255,056 and the adviser's penalty was $477,139 for underperformance. The penalty can exceed the base fee, as in 1989, where the adviser actually lost money. In contrast, in 1986 the adviser's bonus was $411,354 for outperforming the S&P.

an income statement. The operating expenses portion of the 1989 statement of operations of Tri-Continental Corp. appears in Table 3–1.

Brokerage commissions paid by a fund *do not* enter into the expense ratio. Rather, they are a part of the cost basis of securities purchased and are deducted from the gross proceeds of securities sold. Thus, brokerage commissions are reflected by a direct reduction in NAV. Some funds report the total brokerage commissions they paid during the past year in their annual reports.

When analyzing expense ratios we should compare funds of the same size and nature. For example, it would be logical to compare the expense ratios of different country funds which are of approximately the same size. Country funds tend to have significantly higher expense ratios

**Table 3–1. Operating Expenses of Tri-Continental Corp. For the Year Ended December 31, 1989**

| Expenses | |
|---|---:|
| General expenses: | |
| Management fee | $5,125,878 |
| Stockholder account, transfer, and registrar services | 2,197,940 |
| Stockholder reports and communications | 367,396 |
| Auditing and legal fees | 130,912 |
| Directors' fees and expenses | 127,414 |
| Stockholders' meeting | 118,319 |
| Corporate data processing | 53,364 |
| Payment of dividends | 21,081 |
| Miscellaneous | 88,013 |
| | $8,230,317 |
| Registration—Securities Act of 1933 | 59,640 |
| Total expenses | $8,289,957 |

Source: Adapted from Tri-Continental Corporation, 60th Annual Report 1989, p. 17.

than average because of their somewhat smaller sizes and the greater expenses associated with overseas investing.

Small funds have higher expense ratios than larger funds since the larger ones can benefit from economies of scale. If a fund has a very high expense ratio it may have incurred interest expense to buy its securities on credit. Watch for this especially in leveraged bond funds.

Naturally, the lower the expense ratio the better. Look at the fund's past expense ratios for comparison purposes. The more years you can examine the better feel you gain for expenses. The expense ratios for the past five years (or less for newer funds) are found in a table of comparative per share data and ratios near the back of the fund's annual and semiannual shareholder reports with a heading like "supplementary information." This table is especially useful as it contains a variety of historic data you'll need to analyze your funds. The supplementary information table from the 1989 Annual Report of Adams Express Company is found in Table 3–2. Expense ratios of Adams Express

**Table 3-2. Supplementary Information Table for Adams Express Co.**

| | Year Ended December 31 | | | | |
|---|---|---|---|---|---|
| | 1989 | 1988 | 1987 | 1986 | 1985 |
| Per Share Data* | | | | | |
| (1) Investment income | $ .79 | $ .63 | $ .67 | $ .72 | $ .80 |
| (2) Expenses | (.09) | (.09) | (.10) | (.11) | (.10) |
| (3) Net investment income | .70 | .54 | .57 | .61 | .70 |
| (4) Dividends from net investment income | (.70) | (.50) | (.78) | (.71) | (.72) |
| (5) Net realized gain and change in unrealized appreciation and other changes | 3.60 | 1.47 | (.72) | 2.81 | 3.80 |
| (6) Distribution from net realized gains | (1.36) | (1.32) | (2.66) | (3.74) | (1.20) |

| | | | | | |
|---|---|---|---|---|---|
| (7) Net increase (decrease) in net asset value | 2.24 | .19 | (3.59) | (1.03) | 2.58 |
| Net asset value: | | | | | |
| (8) Beginning of year | 16.11 | 15.92 | 19.51 | 20.54 | 17.96 |
| (9) End of year | $18.35 | $16.11 | $15.92 | $19.51 | $20.54 |
| (10) Market price at end of year | $15.625 | $14.75 | $14.875 | $19.125 | $19.375 |
| Ratios | | | | | |
| (11) Ratio of expenses to average net assets | 0.51% | 0.55% | 0.48% | 0.53% | 0.54% |
| (12) Ratio of net investment income to average net assets | 3.87% | 3.20% | 2.68% | 2.81% | 3.81% |
| (13) Portfolio turnover | 26.04% | 18.00% | 27.58% | 34.52% | 30.71% |
| (14) Number of shares outstanding at end of year (in 000's) | 29.983 | 28.296 | 26.834 | 24.005 | 21.313 |

*Selected data for each share of common stock outstanding throughout each year.
Source: The Adams Express Company 1989 Annual Report, page 10.

77

for each of the years from 1985 to 1989 appear on Line 11. These data facilitate a year-by-year analysis of the level and trend of the expense ratio.

Past expense ratios from seven different equity funds are contained in Table 3–3. This table shows you some extremes in expense ratios and fund sizes. Bigger funds like Adams ($550 million in assets), Salomon Brothers ($1 billion), General American ($382 million) and Tri ($1.6 billion) tend to have much lower expense ratios than far smaller funds like Engex ($14 million), Spectra ($4 million) and Z-Seven ($18 million). Also, General American is not as big as Salomon Brothers or Tri so one would expect its expense ratio to be somewhat above their numbers as it is. The expense ratio for Adams appears to be quite low considering its size.

In any event, extraordinarily high expense ratios should be investigated before you invest. The best source of information on expenses would be the statement of operations in the annual report. See which expenses, if any, are out of line and why. Do you feel comfortable with the reasons? Engex's high expense ratios in 1986 (4.04 percent) and 1987 (6.68 percent) appear to be due to high levels of interest expense in those years as seen in its statements of operations. The fluctuations in Z-Seven's expense ratio (from a low of 1.16 percent in 1989 to a high of 4.42 percent in 1986) are probably due in large part to the fact that its management fees are tied to performance. Its performance was exceptionally good in 1985 and 1986. Thus, the high management fees in those years appear justified.

## Distributions

Distributions are important to fund shareholders and funds which make high, relatively dependable distributions are sought after. The funds that have the highest distributions tend to trade at narrow discounts or at premiums. Like most open-end funds, closed-end funds can make two basic types of shareholder distributions: income distributions which consist of quarterly dividend payments (net of expenses) and capital gains distributions

**Table 3–3. Expenses to Average Net Assets**

| Fiscal Year-End | Adams Express | Engex | General American Investors | Salomon Brothers | Spectra | Tri-Continental | Z-Seven |
|---|---|---|---|---|---|---|---|
| 1989 | 0.51% | 2.25% | 1.04% | 0.44% | 4.09% | 0.55% | 1.16% |
| 1988 | 0.55 | 2.31 | 1.14 | 0.47 | 3.05 | 0.57 | 2.73 |
| 1987 | 0.48 | 6.68 | 1.19 | 0.44 | 2.39 | 0.53 | 3.23 |
| 1986 | 0.53 | 4.04 | 1.10 | 0.43 | 2.25 | 0.53 | 4.42 |
| 1985 | 0.54 | 1.34 | 1.29 | 0.47 | 2.70 | 0.55 | 3.50 |
| **AVG.** | **0.52** | **3.32** | **1.15** | **0.45** | **2.90** | **0.55** | **3.00** |

Source: 1989 annual reports of the individual funds.

which are typically made once a year. The Internal Revenue Code essentially requires a "regulated investment
company" (RIC) which has taxable income to distribute at
least 98 percent of that income on an annual basis to avoid
paying an excise tax on retained income. However, some
funds elect to retain their realized capital gains. Figure
3-3 contains the information you need to know if your
fund does this.

## Analyzing Fund Distributions

Obviously, the relative importance of income versus realized gains distributions will depend on the type of fund
you own. Generally, successful equity funds which stress
growth would have larger capital gains distributions than
income funds. It is useful for an investor to analyze the
distributions which have been made by a fund over
the past several years. The necessary data can be found
in the table of supplementary information contained near
the back of the fund's annual or semi-annual report.

Let's use the data contained in the table of supplementary information for Adams Express (Table 3-2). The

## Figure 3-3. Some Funds May Retain Realized Gains

A regulated investment company can either retain or pay out
realized capital gains. Most elect to pay capital gains distributions to shareholders rather than retain them. Funds that elect
to retain their realized gains do so in order to build up their
assets. A given fund may retain its realized gains just in certain
years, like those in which it has especially large gains. Others
may follow the practice consistently. Examples of funds which
have retained capital gains are Baker Fentress, Bergstrom Capital, Gabelli Equity Trust, and Z-Seven.

If the fund retains the realized capital gains, in order to
build its portfolio, it must pay the tax on them at the corporate
capital gain tax rates on behalf of its shareholders. Since corporate tax rates often exceed the corresponding individual
rates you may be entitled to receive the difference. Your tax
status would determine how you are affected.

The procedures can appear confusing at first so bear with
us as we explain.

1. If you are a taxpaying shareholder:

a. You include your share of the realized, but undistributed, gains in your gross income and pay federal taxes on them based upon your personal tax rate. This information would be contained in your IRS Form 2439 (Notice to Shareholder of Undistributed Long-Term Capital Gains). Form 2439 would be issued to you in February or March by the fund; it would be issued by your broker if your stock is held in street name.

b. You then file an IRS Form 2439 with your federal tax return to receive a tax credit for your proportionate share of the federal taxes paid by the fund on your behalf.

c. Finally, you increase the year-end cost basis of all your shares by the net retained amount. This is because you are deemed to have reinvested the amount retained by the fund net of tax. For example, if the fund retained $1.00 per share and paid taxes of 34 cents the cost basis of each share you held as of December 31 should be increased by 66 cents. If your cost basis is $10 per share it would be increased by 66 cents to $10.66. This increase in your cost basis will lessen your taxable gain (or increase your tax deductible loss) in the future when you sell your shares.

2. Tax-exempt investors (like those with IRAs or Keogh Plans) are entitled to receive a full cash refund for their proportionate share of taxes paid by the fund. These investors would take the information on Form 2439 and use it to complete IRS Form 990 T. The two forms should then be sent in together to the IRS for a federal tax refund.

The Z-Seven Fund has retained its realized capital gains since the 1986 calendar year. Let's illustrate how the procedures work using Z-Seven data.

a. For 1989 Z-Seven paid 18 cents per share in taxes on capital gains of 54 cents per share, leaving 36 cents for a year-end cost basis write-up by shareholders.

b. Taxpaying shareholders should file Form 2439 with their tax returns to receive a tax credit of 18 cents per share. They would include their share of the gains in gross income and pay taxes on them based on their personal tax rate. Finally, they would write-up the year-end tax basis of their shares by 36 cents.

c. Non-tax paying shareholders are entitled to a full refund of 18 cents per share. They must file Form 990-T along with their Form 2439 for the refund.

necessary data have been placed in Table 3–4. It contains end of year net asset values (taken from Line 9 in Table 3–2), dividends from net investment income (Line 4), and distributions from net realized gains (Line 6).

Using the data in Table 3–4 two useful calculations can be made:

1. The ratio of average total distributions to average NAV.

2. The ratio of average net investment income distributions to average total distributions.

The average total distribution of $2.74 divided by average NAV of 18.09 equals 15.15%. This is relatively favorable. In general, funds that distribute 8 to 10% or more of their NAV each year would tend to sell at relatively narrow discounts. This is the reason for the implementation of the 10% payout policy which was first instituted by George Michaelis at Source Capital in 1976. Adams Express doesn't have the 10% payout policy and in 1985 it paid out slightly less than 10%. Although the authors are not necessarily in favor of it, it should be recognized that the 10% payout policy leads to a more stable total payout provided the fund does sufficiently well over time to sustain that target level of distributions.

The ratio of average income distributions to average total distributions is 24.82% ($0.68 divided by $2.74).

## Table 3–4. Distributions on Adams Express Company Shares

|  |  | Annual Distributions (per share) | | |
| Year End | NAV | Income | Capital Gains | Total |
| --- | --- | --- | --- | --- |
| 1989 | 18.35 | .70 | 1.36 | 2.06 |
| 1988 | 16.11 | .50 | 1.32 | 1.82 |
| 1987 | 15.92 | .78 | 2.66 | 3.44 |
| 1986 | 19.51 | .71 | 3.74 | 4.45 |
| 1985 | 20.54 | .72 | 1.20 | 1.92 |
| **AVERAGES** | **18.09** | **.68** | **2.06** | **2.74** |

Source: The Adams Express Company, 1989 Annual Report.

This statistic gives you an idea of how stable your future distributions can be expected to be. This ratio varies from 0 to 100%. The higher the value the more income-oriented the fund and the more likely that the distribution will be maintained. However, capital gains are relatively unpredictable and a fund with a high capital gains distribution for the last few years and little or no income (a very low ratio) may not be able to sustain that distribution. Past data on distributions could be obtained from your fund's annual (or semiannual) report or S&P's *Stock Reports.* Of course, funds that have been in existence for just a year or so do not lend themselves to this sort of analysis.

Looking at the fund's yield as indicated in the stock table of the newspaper can be very misleading, especially when it is quite high, like 14 to 16%. Don't buy a fund just because it has a high yield. The high ratio is typically due to large capital gains distributions which cannot be counted on as a regular source of return.

## Examining Performance

*Total Return.* As far as the closed-end fund investor is concerned there are three basic sources of return:

1. Dividend distributions
2. Capital gains distributions
3. Changes in the market price of the fund's shares

The simple example in Figure 3–4 will illustrate how these three sources contribute to the total return.

To be meaningful the performance of a closed-end fund, like the performance of any professionally managed portfolio, must be examined over a relatively long period of time. This is easy to do in the case of funds that have been in existence for many years, but you have to look at the track records of the managers in the case of the newer ones. For instance, Charles Royce, president of Quest Advisory and manager of Royce Value Trust, which went public in 1986, has established an enviable long-term record as evidenced by his performance with the Pennsylvania Mutual Fund, an open-end fund he has managed since

**Figure 3–4. Computing Your Total Return**

Assume that an investor pays $8 per share for the XYZ Growth Equity Fund when it is selling at a 20% discount from its $10 NAV and holds it for one year. At the end of the year its NAV has risen to $10.50 and the discount has narrowed and the fund is trading at $9.50 per share. The important point to remember when we compute the total return is that the investor's price has increased by $1.50 (or $9.50 less the $8.00 cost). Also assume that total income distributions for the year (INC in our equation) amount to $0.20 per share and capital gains distributions (CAP GAIN) are $0.80 per share. The following formula can be used to compute your total return (TR):

TR = (INC + CAP GAIN + CHANGE IN PRICE)/
INITIAL PRICE
TR = (.20 + .80 + 1.50)/8.00 = 2.50/8.00 = 31.25%

The narrowing of the discount from the initial 20% to 9.5% at the end of the year made an important contribution to your total return. If we calculate TR on the basis of NAV and its change it would work out to just 15% (.20 + .80 + .50)/ 10.00. The 15% would reflect the performance of the fund manager, but the 31.25% return would indicate your performance. For simplicity, we've ignored taxes and transaction costs.

The TR formula would be appropriate if the fund is held for one year or less. If the fund is held for less than a year the return obtained from the formula would have to be annualized. If the fund is held for longer than a year a finance calculator should be used as illustrated in the Appendix to Chapter 3.

1973. Be sure to obtain some evidence of the manager's performance before you invest in newer funds.

For funds that have been in existence for some time a good source of data can be found in *Forbes* Annual Fund Ratings—covering both open- and closed-end funds— which appear in early September. *Forbes* also includes the newer funds, but of course, there isn't as much data available on them.

*Forbes* uses a rating system including grades of "A" through "F" for a fund's performance in up and down markets. Funds that have done exceptionally well over time have a shot at the prestigious honor roll, which is very difficult to make. *Forbes* rates funds over three market cycles. To be rated a fund must have been in existence for at least two of the three cycles.

*Wiesenberger Investment Companies Service* also contains useful performance data. They give annual performance figures for different funds so you can track performance from year to year.

The performance of a closed-end fund is typically gauged in terms of its net asset value rather than the market price in published performance data. This is because NAV-based total returns represent the fairest way to evaluate the performance of management. In this regard the fund's performance should be compared to that of a representative market index and to other funds with similar objectives. For instance, the performance of the Germany Fund should be compared with an index of German stock prices, not with the Standard & Poor's 500.

An individual investor can determine his performance with a finance calculator by looking at the price paid for the fund, the annual distributions received, and the recent stock price. This method was illustrated in Figure 3–4 for a one year holding period and in the Appendix to Chapter 3 for a longer holding period. The Appendix also shows how the total return for a closed-end fund would differ from that for an open-end fund with an equivalent portfolio.

If you buy a fund at a discount and sell it when the discount narrows significantly or turns to a premium your performance would be better than the net asset value performance customarily reported in sources like *Forbes*. Of course, your performance could be worse if you buy at a premium and the shares subsequently go to a discount.

## Tracking Discounts

We have stated many times that the discount is a very important consideration for closed-end fund investors—perhaps the most important. The discount/premium should be studied in two separate ways:

1.  The long-term discount pattern.
2.  Weekly discount patterns over the past several months.

**Long-Term Patterns.**  Our advice is to study the discount/premium behavior of a fund you plan to invest in over a period of at least 10 years, preferably longer. Tri-Continental's year-end discounts serve as an interesting case study (Table 3–5). For the 13 year period 1973–85 Tri's average discount was 14.5%. Suppose an investor is thinking of buying Tri at the end of 1986 when it was selling at a 3% premium. This would have been dangerous since: (1) there is always risk when buying a closed-end fund at a premium and (2) its discount had averaged 14.5% over the past 13 years. We can see that in 1987 Tri's shares turn to a discount. Thus, it would not have been a good idea to buy at the premium of 3% at year-end 1986. However, it would have been a good idea to buy at

## Table 3–5. Tracking Tri-Continental's Discount

| Year-End | Market Price | Discount (−)/ Premium (+) |
|---|---|---|
| 1989 | 23 | −16% |
| 1988 | 19-1/4 | −18 |
| 1987 | 20-5/8 | −14 |
| 1986 | 28-5/8 | + 3 |
| 1985 | 29-3/8 | − 1 |
| 1984 | 24-7/8 | − 2 |
| 1983 | 29-3/8 | − 5 |
| 1982 | 26-7/8 | − 8 |
| 1981 | 20-3/4 | −20 |
| 1980 | 23-5/8 | −25 |
| 1979 | 19-7/8 | −23 |
| 1978 | 17-5/8 | −22 |
| 1977 | 20-5/8 | −12 |
| 1976 | 22 | −21 |
| 1975 | 18-1/2 | −22 |
| 1974 | 15-7/8 | −14 |
| 1973 | 25-5/8 | −13 |

Source: *Wiesenberger Investment Companies Service.*

discounts of 20% or greater during the late 1970s and early 1980s and then sell when the discount narrowed or turned to a premium between 1983 and 1986.

*Near-Term Patterns.* In addition to tracking a fund's discount over the years as illustrated for Tri-Continental, shorter-term fluctuations in discounts and premiums should also be followed, certainly by those who are more oriented towards short-term trading. As was pointed out, the discounts and premiums on individual funds appear weekly in *Barron's*, the *Chicago Tribune*, *The New York Times*, and *The Wall Street Journal*. Investors should have a feel for how discounts and premiums have been acting recently on funds they are interested in buying or selling. They can collect the weekly discount/ premium tabulations and keep records which will allow them to spot important changes in the magnitudes of discounts and premiums. If they intend to follow a fairly large number of funds it is a good practice to enter this data into a computerized spreadsheet.

## Portfolio Turnover

Portfolio turnover is defined as the lesser of the value of a fund's security purchases or sales for a given year divided by its average net assets for that year. A turnover of 100% would mean that on average the fund holds its securities for one year. A turnover of 50% would imply an average two year holding period and a turnover of 200% would mean that the fund holds its securities for only about six months. Higher turnover ratios mean higher transaction costs which are absorbed by the investor.

Historic turnover ratios are readily available from S&P's *Stock Reports*, Wiesenberger, and the fund's annual and semiannual shareholder reports. If you have the fund's report look in the back for its table of supplemental information. As seen in Table 3–2 the portfolio turnover numbers for Adams Express for 1985–1989 appear on Line 13. Value investors prefer a fund with a lower turnover, other things equal, since true value investors are patient and have a long-term view. Table 3–6 contains past turnover ratios of several different funds.

**Table 3–6. Turnover Ratios**

| Year | Adams Express | Baker, Fentress | Bergstrom Capital | General American Investors | Spectra | Z-Seven |
|------|--------|---------|-----------|-----------|---------|---------|
| 1989 | 26.04% | 35.47% | 35.58% | 27.00% | 139.94% | 87.29% |
| 1988 | 18.00 | 53.23 | 16.12 | 19.00 | 139.59 | 4.73 |
| 1987 | 27.58 | 28.58 | 25.14 | 30.00 | 127.30 | 23.34 |
| 1986 | 34.52 | 15.13 | 44.15 | 31.00 | 122.00 | 30.56 |
| 1985 | 30.71 | 9.00 | 11.54 | 26.00 | 106.00 | 24.22 |
| **AVG.** | **27.37** | **28.28** | **26.51** | **26.60** | **126.97** | **34.03** |

Source: 1989 annual reports for the individual funds.

88

The data in this table bring up several important facts. First, one must study turnover figures over a number of years since some funds, like Baker, Fentress; Bergstrom Capital; and Z-Seven, can have turnover numbers which vary widely over time. Don't make a judgment based on the turnover statistic for a single year. Second, consider the fund's objectives when studying turnover. For example, comparing turnover ratios of a bond fund that does short-term trading of debt securities with old-line stock funds, like Adams Express, would be meaningless. Spectra Fund, a small equity oriented fund, apparently does more buying and selling of stocks than the other equity funds included in the table. Of course smaller funds are more nimble than very large funds so they may have a tendency to do more trading.

## Unrealized Appreciation

It is important for equity fund investors to consider the amount of unrealized appreciation on stocks in the fund's portfolio. This information could be found in the fund's shareholder reports or in S&P's *Stock Reports* and other sources like Wiesenberger and Value Line. The information can appear in different places in the shareholder reports of different funds so you have to search for it. As explained in Chapter 2, older funds with large amounts of unrealized appreciation may sell at wider discounts because if the gains were realized fund investors would face an immediate tax liability on their proportionate share, no matter how long they were shareholders.

Investors concerned about the amount of unrealized appreciation in a particular fund's portfolio but who like that fund as an investment would be shielded from Uncle Sam by including it in a tax-sheltered retirement plan like an IRA, since even if the appreciation were realized it wouldn't result in a tax liability.

In order to compare the unrealized appreciations of individual funds we suggest taking total unrealized appreciation and dividing it by the fund's total assets. This would facilitate the direct comparison of unrealized appreciation of funds of varying sizes. Some funds report unrealized appreciation in individual positions. We like this additional information and hope to see a larger number of funds adopt this practice in the future. Bergstrom Capital, Royce Value Trust, Salomon Brothers Fund, and Source Capital are examples of funds providing this important information. We strongly approve of this kind of disclosure presentation and wish that all funds would do it. Co-author Scott encourages all funds he visits to supply this stock-by-stock disclosure, but finds very few willing to do it.

## Derivative Products

A number of funds are able to use options and futures (derivative products) to alter the risk-reward characteristics of their portfolios. This is especially evident in some of the newer funds. Quite a number of the newer bond funds use options and futures to varying degrees.

There are several reasons why funds use options and futures. First, they may want to protect the portfolio during an anticipated bear market. This could be done by shorting stock index futures or purchasing index puts. Of course, the hedge will work out fine if it is always instituted at the correct time. But things don't necessarily work out that way. We feel that it is very difficult if not impossible to accurately predict future market movements. A stock index futures hedge could wind up costing the portfolio its upside performance if the market quickly rebounds. The purchase of index puts always involves the payment of a put premium and transaction costs. Our argument is that if the portfolio is being held as a long-term investment it is best to not try to hedge as this strategy could well reduce the long-run compound return for two reasons. First, it interferes with portfolio appreciation and, second, it results in increased transaction costs.

Try to ascertain to what extent your fund uses options and futures. If a fund plans to use these products it would be set forth in its prospectus. Funds which have the ability to use options and futures don't always use them, however, or may use them only in very special circumstances.

The uses of options and futures by certain funds will be discussed in subsequent chapters.

## CONCLUSION

This chapter has presented the basic information one would need to analyze a closed-end fund. It has also shown how to use that information to make inferences about the fund's future performance. Future chapters will go into some detail about the more specific considerations dealt with in analyzing different kinds of funds: domestic equity funds, dual funds, country funds, bond funds, and so on.

## Note

[1]Frank Cappiello, W. Douglas Dent, and Peter W. Madlem, *The Complete Guide to Closed-End Funds: Finding Value in Today's Stock Market*, Second Edition (Chicago: International Publishing Corporation, 1990).

# APPENDIX 3–1

# *Calculation of Total Return for a Multi-Year Holding Period: Closed- versus Open-End Fund*

A CEF purchased at a relatively large discount would benefit the investor greatly since the total return would be enhanced. This is especially true if the fund is held for a long period of time. As shown in our illustration, the discount can even widen and the investor is still better off than with an equivalent open-end fund. Co-author Fredman has his investments students work through problems like the one in this appendix with their finance calculators. It provides them with a better understanding of how the discount can lead to higher total returns.

## ASSUMPTIONS:

1. An investor purchases shares in a no-load, open-end fund at its NAV of $10.
2. The investor also purchases shares in a CEF at $8, a 20% discount from its NAV of $10.

3. The two funds have identical portfolios and management.

4. Each fund is held for 5 years during which $1.00 is distributed to fund shareholders annually.

5. At the end of the 5 years the NAV of each fund has increased to $12. The investor redeems his open-shares at NAV and sells his closed-end shares in the secondary market.

**RESULTS:**

|                                          | Compound Annual Return |
|------------------------------------------|:----------------------:|
| 1. Open-end fund                         | 13.08%                 |
| 2. CEF terminal price (and discount):    |                        |
|    a) $12 (0% discount)   | 19.31                  |
|    b) $9.60 (20% discount)| 15.44                  |
|    c) $9 (25% discount)   | 14.38                  |
|    d) $8.40 (30% discount)| 13.27                  |
|    e) $8 (33% discount)   | 12.50                  |

**DISCUSSION:**

The point of this illustration is that investors can earn higher compound annual returns with a CEF selling at a discount than with an equivalent open-end fund even if the discount remains the same or widens somewhat.

The reason is that the investor gets a higher initial yield on his CEF: 12.5% on his purchase price of $8 as opposed to 10% on the NAV of $10 on the open-end fund. The yield is computed by dividing the $1 annual fund distribution by the price paid for the fund—$8 for the CEF and $10 for the open-end fund.

If the discount disappears at the end of the 5 years the investor earns 19.31% compounded annually on the CEF versus 13.08% on the open-end fund.

If the discount remains the same at 20%, he earns

15.44% per annum—considerably above the 13.08% on the open-end fund.

Even if the discount widens from 20% to 30%, the investor earns 13.27% on the CEF still slightly above the return on the open-end fund. Only when the discount widens to 33% does the investor earn less per annum on the CEF.

# PART II

# Equity-Oriented Funds

# CHAPTER 4

# *Investing in Stock Funds*

The most basic question to confront when deciding how to allocate your resources is how much of your savings should be invested in stocks? You will also need to think about your individual risk tolerance. What was your previous experience as an investor? Are you a long-term investor or are you trying to make a quick killing? Are closed-end funds really for you or would you rather have the excitement (and higher risk) of picking your own stocks?

These are basic and vital questions any investor must answer before investing in closed-end funds. The authors obviously have their biases; our experiences for a combined total of about sixty years have led us to closed-end funds for low risk, high total return investing. Coauthor Scott has helped his clients do extremely well with closed-end funds since 1975 when he started buying them. We hope the soundness of our philosophy will be evident by the time this book reaches its conclusion.

Whether they buy stocks or stock funds, investors must have an equity component in their portfolios. A care-

97

fully selected and monitored stock portfolio has been proven to result in favorable long-term growth of invested capital for patient investors. The results should more than offset the ravages of inflation after the payment of taxes on income and realized capital gains.

Stock funds move in tandem with the stocks they hold. This is the most basic way in which individual stock funds differ from one another.

## STOCK FUND DIFFERENCES

There are four general areas in which you see differences.

1.  The kinds of stocks and other securities in the portfolio and the relative emphasis accorded growth (or capital appreciation) and income. Some funds hold medium size or smaller companies, others large "blue chip" companies. Different funds weight different industries or sectors differently. Some CEFs hold a certain proportion of foreign stocks in addition to their domestic holdings. Stock funds may hold some convertible bonds as a part of their investment strategy.

2.  The extent to which the fund diversifies. Some funds hold several hundred stocks, others may hold 25 or fewer. Sector equity funds hold the securities of companies in a single sector like banks or utilities. At the extreme, global equity funds can invest anywhere in the world.

3.  Whether the fund remains fully invested or whether it can move significant amounts of its portfolio into cash equivalents when its management feels a defensive position is warranted. Some funds with a greater tolerance for risk use leverage or borrowing to further increase their equity exposure.

4.  Whether the management can use options and futures as a part of their investment strategy. If they can, you would want to determine the extent to which they actually use these derivative instruments to manage risk and return.

## DIVERSIFIED VERSUS NON-DIVERSIFIED

Some funds are classified as "diversified" and others as "non-diversified" as defined by the Investment Company Act of 1940. The distinction is important as it could have implications for the fund's risk and return since diversified companies would be expected to be less risky than non-diversified ones.

To be diversified a fund must satisfy the following guidelines:

1.  It must invest 75% or more of its total assets in a diversified manner.

2.  Within the diversified 75% of the portfolio (a) no single issuer's securities may exceed 5% of the portfolio's assets, and (b) the fund may not own in excess of 10% of the voting shares of any one issuer. There is no limitation on holdings of cash, cash items (including receivables), and government securities.

After the above criteria have been met, the balance of the portfolio can be invested in any way the fund chooses; for example, it could hold more than 10% of the voting shares of one or more companies. This would enable the fund to hold some small companies if it so chooses.

A fund which chooses not to adhere to the above guidelines would be classified as non-diversified.[1] One might therefore think that a non-diversified fund could invest in just one or two stocks. Not so. Under the Internal Revenue Code all regulated investment companies (non-diversified as well as diversified) are required to have the same kind of diversification within 50% of their assets that diversified funds need for 75% of their assets. Additionally, the Code requires that not more than 25% of the assets be invested in any one company. The implications are that non-diversified funds are usually fairly well diversified.

Non-diversified funds may experience greater volatility in their investment returns than diversified funds, however, since their performances could be heavily affected by big positions in one or a few stocks. Of course, non-diversified funds differ in the degree to which they actually do diversify. Some may be highly diversified. To determine this, study the individual fund's portfolio composition.

Both diversified and non-diversified stock funds differ in the extent to which they hold cash. Some could be 80% or more in cash equivalents at times whereas others maintain a policy of being nearly fully invested all the time. Those that can alternate between a large cash position and a fully invested stock position obviously try to time the market (although they don't always admit it). An example is Charles Allmon's Growth Stock Outlook Trust, which, at this writing, was nearly 80% in cash equivalents as Allmon waits for better values before he buys stocks again. He is an example of a super-cautious investor.

## ADVANTAGES OF STOCK FUNDS

The stock funds are our favorite in the closed-end universe for several reasons.

### Superior Long-Term Performance

First, as a long-term investment, total returns from small and large company stocks clearly outdistance those from various categories of fixed income securities as seen by the Ibbotson and Sinquefield data on annualized total returns over the period 1926–1989 (Table 4–1).

The common stock series is represented by the S&P Composite Index which currently includes 500 domestic stocks with the largest market capitalizations (price per share times number of shares outstanding). The small company stocks series prior to 1982 is represented by those equities traded on the NYSE which rank in the bottom 20 percent in market capitalization. Starting in 1982 the series is represented by the performance of the Dimensional Fund Advisors Small Company Fund.

## Table 4–1. Basic Long-Term Total Returns, 1926–1989

| Series | Geometric Mean Annual Return | Standard Deviation of Annual Returns |
|---|---|---|
| Common stocks | 10.3% | 20.9% |
| Small company stocks | 12.2 | 35.3 |
| Long-term corporate bonds | 5.2 | 8.5 |
| Long-term government bonds | 4.6 | 8.6 |
| Intermediate-term government bonds | 4.9 | 5.5 |
| U.S. T-bills | 3.6 | 3.4 |
| Inflation rate | 3.1 | 4.8 |

Source: Ibbotson, Roger G. and Rex A. Sinquefield, *Stocks, Bonds, Bills and Inflation* (SBBI), 1989, updated in *Stocks, Bonds, Bills and Inflation 1990 Yearbook,*™ Ibbotson Associates, Chicago. All rights reserved.

These data indicate that common stocks are by far the best performing long-term security investment. The words "long-term" must be emphasized here, however. This is because there can be long stretches of time, even a decade or more, where stocks perform miserably. Take, for example, the period from the beginning of 1929 to the end of 1941 when Ibbotson and Sinquefield data report stock returns of a negative 2.4% compounded annually. Or the more recent period from the beginning of 1969 to the end of 1974 when stocks returned a negative 3.4%, according to Ibbotson and Sinquefield data. The fact that stocks are riskier than fixed income securities is evident from their higher standard deviations which indicate the greater volatility of returns. Higher return and greater risk go hand in hand.

During a recent 15-year period, diversified closed-end equity funds outperformed closed-end bond funds by a wide margin according to Lipper data. The diversified equity funds had a 15.73% compound annual total return as opposed to 10.58% compounded annually for the bond funds (Table 4–2). As you can see in the table, the equity fund returns are also above the S&P 500 yardstick. The

**Table 4–2. Performance of Closed-End Stock and Bond Funds (3/31/75 to 3/31/90)**

|                                        | Returns* |
|----------------------------------------|----------|
| Diversified equity funds               | 15.73%   |
| Specialized equity & convertible funds | 16.25    |
| Bond funds                             | 10.58    |
| S&P 500 reinvested                     | 14.80    |

*Returns reflect compound average annual changes in NAV including reinvestment of all distributions.
Source: Adapted from data provided by Lipper Analytical Services, Inc.

best performing group over the 15 years was the specialized equity and convertible funds.

## Time Diversification Lowers Risk

In order to do well with stocks you must be patient and practice "time diversification"; that is, you must stay in the market for as many years as possible so that the performance in bad years (like the 1973–74 bear market) will be averaged out with the good years (like the bull market of the 1980s) and you will realize overall appreciation in your portfolio. The longer the time horizon the closer your returns will correspond to the long-term returns on equities. Time diversification leads to significant risk reduction and adds an important dimension to the portfolio diversification process.[2]

Thus, if the aim is to park your money for a relatively short period, fixed income securities have proven to be the best since a stock portfolio could be down when you need the money. However, many investors are in a position to invest a significant portion of their savings with the long term in mind. It should be evident from the data in Table 4–1 that bonds—and especially T-bills—are not nearly as good a long-term investment as equities. This is especially evident after the impacts of taxes and inflation are factored in. For instance, it's not too soon for a 25- or 30-year old to start thinking about retirement. The power of compounding interest and dividends is perhaps the first and most important thing to learn about investing. With that

firmly in mind, you'll be well on your way to a successful
investment program.

## The Power of Compounding

Relatively small amounts set aside annually can grow to
considerable sums over the decades through the power of
compounding. In Table 4–3 one can see how $2,000 in-
vested yearly grows over time at compound annual returns of 5, 10, and 12%. For simplicity, taxes and transaction costs are ignored. In this example it is assumed that
a person invests $2,000 at the beginning of each year. At
the end of 41 years (the year 2030) our investor has accumulated $268,464 at 5% compounded annually. This is
how one might do if the money were invested in bonds
through a tax-sheltered retirement plan. On the other
hand, at a rate of 10% the money amounts to over $1 mil-
lion in 2030 whereas at 12% it adds up to over $1.9 mil-
lion! These two figures correspond roughly to how one
would do if investing at the historic rates of return earned
on diversified portfolios of common stocks and small company stocks, respectively, which appear in Table 4–1. Of
course these past rates are not necessarily representative
of the future but they do show that diversified stock portfolios increase the odds of accumulating greater wealth
than bonds would over the years.

  As seen in Table 4–3 the power of compounding becomes even greater in more distant years as the amount
of money invested builds up to ever increasing amounts.
The absolute annual increases in your portfolio value become much larger even though only $2,000 per year is
being invested. For instance, at 12 percent portfolio value
would increase by more than $200,000 between the years
2029 and 2030!

  Of course taxes and transaction costs were ignored in
our example. Still one may be able to achieve results similar to these through a tax deferred savings plan like an
IRA. The real key to success is to have the patience and
discipline to unfailingly follow the savings plan for many
years. One must resist the temptation to withdraw the
money along the way and use it for speculative purposes

**Table 4–3. The Power of Compound Interest**

| Year | Investment | Future Values at Rates of: | | |
|------|-----------|--------|--------|--------|
|      |           | 5% | 10% | 12% |
| 1990 | 2,000 | 2,100 | 2,200 | 2,240 |
| 1991 | 2,000 | 4,305 | 4,620 | 4,749 |
| 1992 | 2,000 | 6,620 | 7,282 | 7,559 |
| 1993 | 2,000 | 9,051 | 10,210 | 10,706 |
| 1994 | 2,000 | 11,604 | 13,431 | 14,230 |
| 1995 | 2,000 | 14,284 | 16,974 | 18,178 |
| 1996 | 2,000 | 17,098 | 20,872 | 22,599 |
| 1997 | 2,000 | 20,053 | 25,159 | 27,551 |
| 1998 | 2,000 | 23,156 | 29,875 | 33,097 |
| 1999 | 2,000 | 26,414 | 35,062 | 39,309 |
| 2000 | 2,000 | 29,834 | 40,769 | 46,266 |
| 2001 | 2,000 | 33,426 | 47,045 | 54,058 |
| 2002 | 2,000 | 37,197 | 53,950 | 62,785 |
| 2003 | 2,000 | 41,157 | 61,545 | 72,559 |
| 2004 | 2,000 | 45,315 | 69,899 | 83,507 |
| 2005 | 2,000 | 49,681 | 79,089 | 95,767 |
| 2006 | 2,000 | 54,265 | 89,198 | 109,499 |
| 2007 | 2,000 | 59,078 | 100,318 | 124,879 |
| 2008 | 2,000 | 64,132 | 112,550 | 142,105 |
| 2009 | 2,000 | 69,439 | 126,005 | 161,397 |
| 2010 | 2,000 | 75,010 | 140,805 | 183,005 |
| 2011 | 2,000 | 80,861 | 157,086 | 207,206 |
| 2012 | 2,000 | 87,004 | 174,995 | 234,310 |
| 2013 | 2,000 | 93,454 | 194,694 | 264,668 |
| 2014 | 2,000 | 100,227 | 216,364 | 298,668 |
| 2015 | 2,000 | 107,338 | 240,200 | 336,748 |
| 2016 | 2,000 | 114,805 | 266,420 | 379,398 |
| 2017 | 2,000 | 122,645 | 295,262 | 427,166 |
| 2018 | 2,000 | 130,878 | 326,988 | 480,665 |
| 2019 | 2,000 | 139,522 | 361,887 | 540,585 |
| 2020 | 2,000 | 148,598 | 400,276 | 607,695 |
| 2021 | 2,000 | 158,128 | 442,503 | 682,859 |
| 2022 | 2,000 | 168,134 | 488,953 | 767,042 |
| 2023 | 2,000 | 178,641 | 540,049 | 861,327 |
| 2024 | 2,000 | 189,673 | 596,254 | 966,926 |
| 2025 | 2,000 | 201,256 | 658,079 | 1,085,197 |
| 2026 | 2,000 | 213,419 | 726,087 | 1,217,661 |
| 2027 | 2,000 | 226,190 | 800,896 | 1,366,020 |
| 2028 | 2,000 | 239,600 | 883,185 | 1,532,183 |
| 2029 | 2,000 | 253,680 | 973,704 | 1,718,285 |
| 2030 | 2,000 | 268,464 | 1,073,274 | 1,926,719 |

or unwise consumption. That could quickly destroy a large, growing nest egg.

## Gifts to Minors

Stock funds could also be wise investments for parents who are saving for a minor's college education under the Uniform Gifts to Minors Act. It is best to start the program as early in the child's life as possible, to provide the maximum power of compound returns. Parents should not be discouraged from following this program by tax law changes which place children under age 14 with more than $1,000 of annual income in their parents' or guardians' tax bracket. *Following this program with dedication will reap large rewards at college time.*

Under the tax laws in effect in early 1990, if assets are placed in the name of a child who is under 14, the first $500 of income is tax free and the next $500 is taxed at 15%. Thus, the tax amounts to only $75 on the first $1,000 of income. But, income over that would be taxed at the parents' marginal rate, usually 28% or 33%. Beginning at age 14, however, income and gains are taxed at the child's rate, rather than the parents'. The assets can then accumulate with a lower tax bite.

Of course, older individuals would generally want to have a greater portion of their portfolios invested in fixed income securities. We'll talk about those options in Part 3 on bond funds when we explore fixed income funds and the different philosophies regarding bond and equity investing.

## Deeper Discounts

Another reason we favor stock funds over bond funds is that they tend to sell at wider discounts than the bond funds (which typically sell either at premiums or narrow discounts). Thus, stock funds offer the two primary CEF advantages—the free leverage and the higher total return—to a potentially greater degree. The stock funds can also experience wide variations in discount levels over time and thus allow one to diversify advantageously across time by adding to one's position at times when the discount is particularly wide; for instance, after sharp market declines or during the end-of-year tax loss selling season.

## Superstar Managers

Many stock funds are managed by well-known, talented individuals. These "superstar" managers have their own special criteria they use to select stocks. Typically, their approaches are based on either the "growth investing" or "value investing" philosophy or some combination thereof. Many managers follow a "bottom-up" approach. They focus primarily on a thorough analysis of the individual company and place lesser emphasis (or even no emphasis) on the outlook for the market and the economy. Dr. Martin Zweig is an exception as he places primary emphasis on market timing through the use of his indicators.

Before we get into specific approaches we'll look in general at the characteristics of the growth investing and value investing philosophies.

## GROWTH VERSUS VALUE

The terms "growth investing" and "value investing" are encountered frequently in discussions of professional managers' investment styles. A clear distinction should be made between these philosophies. Of course things are not always black and white. Virtually all managers incorporate elements of each of these approaches to varying degrees.

Both philosophies have their roots in fundamental analysis, characterized by the study of balance sheets, income statements, management, economic and industry conditions, and other factors. Fundamental analysts often go out and "kick the tires." They may visit the company's headquarters so as to size up the people who run the company and their plans. They may also talk to its competitors, suppliers, and customers. A good example of this kind of analyst is Mario Gabelli, who spends most of his time out of his office.

## Value Investing

Value investing really began with the publication of the classic *Security Analysis* by Benjamin Graham and David Dodd in 1934. Graham was the first to apply logic to the investment process and to emphasize a quantitative approach to company analysis. Value investors search for market inefficiencies. They are bargain hunters trying to buy a dollar's worth of assets for significantly less than a dollar.

This is basically the same approach followed by experienced closed-end fund investors when they look for good funds at wide discounts from NAV. You double your odds for above average performance if you find a discounted CEF managed by a value investor. Charles Allmon, Erik Bergstrom, Mario Gabelli, George Michaelis, John Neff, Charles Royce, and John Templeton are respected value investors managing CEFs.

The concept of value investing is well illustrated by the following passage from the 1989 Annual Report for The Gabelli Equity Trust:

> Transactions in the art world illustrate the value of irreplaceable assets. For example, Van Gogh's "Irises" recently changed hands for $53.9 million, more than 50 times the $1 million it fetched in 1979. We focus our research on uncovering a collection of "Industrial Irises", that is companies with franchises that are likely to be sought by highly liquid domestic and international corporate entities seeking synergistic benefits from or entry into fundamentally attractive businesses. Short term returns and the short term market perspective on these companies are not paramount. They are unique stores of value. These values will be recognized as the world's abundant capital flows to companies capable of delivering superior long term returns.

## Approaches to Value

Value investors want to buy assets or earning power at a discount. Some value investors might be looking for "asset plays" where the true value of the assets, perhaps real estate, is understated on the balance sheet, and the stock is cheap. Others, like George Michaelis of Source Capital, focus on yardsticks of earning power like return on equity (ROE). "There are all kinds of different approaches to value," Michaelis told us. "Basically, I'm looking for companies that have high profitability. Somebody else might be looking for stocks where he can buy assets real cheap. Those companies are not going to have high ROE in all likelihood. They're probably going to have relatively low ROE. It's a different parameter of value that attracts different value investors. Ben Graham was almost totally an asset-dominated investor. Warren Buffett, in looking for the business franchise, has been a profitability-oriented investor."

## Templeton's Principles

Let's examine the criteria used by one closed-end fund manager. We are convinced the industry has attracted some of the best minds in the field of money management. John Templeton, a pure value investor and pioneer in worldwide investing, has developed a set of common sense principles that underlie the work being done by portfolio managers such as Dr. Mark Mobius at Templeton International.

Born in Tennessee in 1912, Templeton has been managing money since 1940. For many years now he has lived in the Bahamas, far from the action on Wall Street. His loyal open-end fund investors have done extremely well, as evidenced by the performance of the Templeton Growth Fund which started in 1954. Ten thousand dollars invested at the inception of the fund would have grown to nearly $1.3 million at December 31, 1989. That translates into a 14.8% total return compounded annually.

Templeton feels that the investor must think independently and not be afraid to go against the crowd in order to find the best bargains. He feels one should buy what others are selling since people often overreact to negative developments, driving prices down to bargain levels. As with closed-end funds, the prices of ordinary stocks fluctuate more widely than their values. Templeton emphasizes the importance of diversification. He firmly believes one must search worldwide for the best bargains available and invest most heavily in those countries where the greatest value exists. For instance, following World War II he invested heavily in Europe. He focused on Canada in the mid-1950s, and on Japan in the early 1970s. Most people don't realize how hard it is to achieve good long-term investment results, says Templeton.

In February, 1987, Templeton International started its first closed-end fund, the Templeton Emerging Markets Fund, which holds stocks from dozens of emerging countries in its portfolio. This fund illustrates another of Templeton's investment principles, "the broaden-your-knowledge rule."[3] Templeton believes that one should become an expert on any country where a bargain exists or hire someone to help make investments there. The Templeton organization also manages open- and closed-end funds based in other countries, including Australia, Great Britain, Canada, and Hong Kong, for people who reside in those countries.

## Growth Investing

Growth stock investors are concerned primarily with the growth rate in earnings. The late T. Rowe Price, founder of the mutual fund group which bears his name, was a strong proponent of growth investing. Price looked for "fertile fields for growth." Growth stock investors start by analyzing a company's past growth in earnings and sales. Then they look for clues as to what the future growth rate might be. The profit margin is an important variable which growth investors track. It is defined as net income after taxes divided by total revenues. Ideally, growth investors want companies with revenues that are projected to grow at an above-average rate and a profit margin which is expected to increase—the expanding profit margin will leverage up the growth rate in earnings per share.

Growth investors certainly look at the company's balance sheet and its financial health, but they differ from the value investors in that they don't mind paying a relatively high P/E where a company is expected to continue growing at an above average rate. Of course, the P/E is still important to growth investors but not as important to them as it would be to the value investors.

Closed-end funds employing the growth stock philosophy include Baker, Fentress; General American Investors; Morgan Grenfell SMALLCap Fund; Nicholas-Applegate Growth Equity Fund; and Tri-Continental.


## SMALL STOCKS

Academic studies have shown that small companies have outperformed their larger counterparts over long periods of time.[4] These companies typically focus on a single product or service and often have managers who invest heavily in their own firms. Smaller companies can grow at a faster rate than larger firms since the former are compounding off a smaller base. For instance, it's far easier for a firm with $25 million of annual revenues to double its revenues in a year or two than for a firm with $5 billion of revenues.

But the investor who picks a few small stocks could easily get wiped out because of the volatility or riskiness of these companies. Small companies often face difficulties obtaining financing, experience erratic growth in revenues, have inexperienced managements, and face devastating competition from larger companies. The low prices of their stocks can be deceptive—they don't necessarily represent bargains as they may be overpriced at a few dollars a share. Further, small companies frequently are illiquid and tend to have wider spreads between their bid and asked prices than larger companies do. So it's important to be well diversified if you do buy small companies.

The big advantage of investing in small companies is that you can earn higher returns over a relatively long period of time, as indicated by the Ibbotson and Sinquefield data in Table 4–1. These data indicate that small company stocks returned 12.2% per annum over the period 1926–89 as opposed to 10.3% for big cap stocks. Of course, these higher long-run returns on small stock portfolios come at the expense of greater volatility as indicated by the standard deviation of 35.3% for small stocks compared with 20.9% for common stocks.

## When to Invest?

Timing is important when investing in small cap companies as the sector moves in clearly-defined cycles relative to the big cap market. The T. Rowe Price New Horizons Fund is a large open-end fund, with assets of nearly $1 billion, which has been investing in emerging growth stocks since it was started in 1960. The average (unweighted) P/E ratio of the New Horizons Fund portfolio of some 200 stocks relative to the S&P 500 P/E is a useful valuation indicator. (Both P/Es are calculated using earnings per share estimates for the next 12 months). The relative P/E is frequently published in the New Horizons Fund quarterly shareholder reports. Typically the market pays more for emerging growth companies than it does for stodgy, big cap slow growers. But, just how much more the market will pay for growth is subject to wide variations over time.

Suppose the P/E for the New Horizons Fund is 15 and the multiple for the S&P 500 is 10. That would put the relative P/E at 1.5. The relative P/E tells you whether or not you can get good value in small companies. The median relative P/E over the history of the fund has tended to be around 1.4 or 1.5, explains Steven Norwitz, vice president, T. Rowe Price Associates, Inc. This is the normal valuation relationship; the further below this the relative P/E is the more extreme the undervaluation and the further above it the greater the overvaluation of the small cap sector.

As seen in Figure 4–1, it has generally varied between 1.0 to slightly above 2.0 since 1961. The ratio was at a low point of 0.94 in March 1977 and at a high of 2.17 in June 1983. At the end of 1989 it stood at 1.01. When the indicator gets close to 1.0 small stocks represent especially good value. If it were 1.10, for instance, that would indicate that small stocks are trading at a 10% premium to the overall market. This means that you can buy growth cheaply. On the other hand, as the relative P/E climbs to near 2.0, one should consider cutting back on small cap holdings. The higher the relative P/E the greater the risk of multiple contraction and consequent poor performance.[5]

Norwitz doesn't encourage people to use the relative P/E as a short-term timing indicator since, for example, a ratio of 1.00 can stay at that level for years even though it typically doesn't. But it definitely is a good long-term timing indicator. T. Rowe Price has done studies indicating that when the ratio is at 1.0 the performance of the New Horizons Fund will beat the market averages over the next five years, whereas if the ratio is at 2.0 the fund will underperform the market over the ensuing five years.

The New Horizons' relative P/E can be a good guide for investing in small cap CEFs. Just as you want to buy CEFs at a discount, you also want to buy emerging growth stocks when they are cheap. By combining a low relative P/E with a small cap CEF trading at a discount you have the odds for success on your side.

## Small Cap CEFs

Closed-end funds because of their diversified nature and professional management offer individuals an ideal means for investing in small stocks. A major advantage of closed-end funds (as opposed to open-end funds) is that the managers do not need to deal with shareholder redemptions. Thus, the relatively illiquid small stock portfolio would not be disturbed due to shareholder redemptions.

Two closed-end funds which invest exclusively in the stocks of smaller companies are Morgan Grenfell SMALL-Cap Fund and Royce Value Trust. The Morgan Grenfell SMALLCap Fund invests in companies with market caps of $50 million to $500 million. The Royce Value Trust invests in small and medium sized stocks with market caps generally under $300 million. Growth Stock Outlook Trust also has a small stock orientation although there were a few larger companies in its portfolio at this writing. Some CEFs emphasize medium size and smaller companies but still hold larger companies. We'll identify them later on. We would like to see more CEFs formed which invest in small companies. By contrast, 83 open-end funds explicitly focused on small firms at this writing.[6] However,

# Figure 4–1. T. Rowe Price New Horizons Fund
## P/E Ratio of the Fund's Portfolio Securities Relative
## to the S&P "500" P/E Ratio (12 Months Forward)

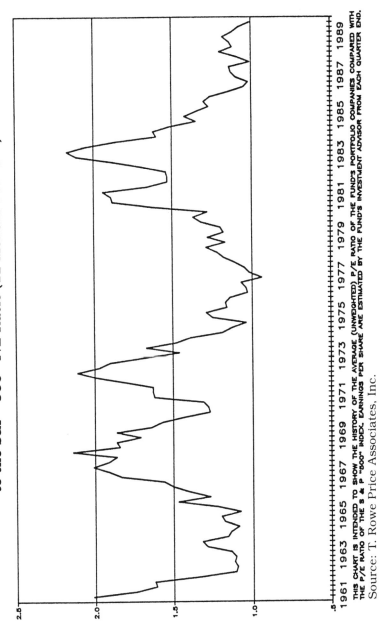

1.01

THIS CHART IS INTENDED TO SHOW THE HISTORY OF THE AVERAGE (UNWEIGHTED) P/E RATIO OF THE FUND'S PORTFOLIO COMPANIES COMPARED WITH
THE P/E RATIO OF THE S & P "500" INDEX. EARNINGS PER SHARE ARE ESTIMATED BY THE FUND'S INVESTMENT ADVISOR FROM EACH QUARTER END.

Source: T. Rowe Price Associates, Inc.

113

if small stocks start to perform well relative to large caps we might see a number of small cap CEF IPOs. Nothing sells funds better than a bull market!

Charles Royce, president and treasurer of Royce Value Trust, has established an enviable long-term record as a highly successful money manager. This is evidenced by the excellent long-term performance of Pennsylvania Mutual Fund which he manages. It has had a compound annual total return of 18.72% since Royce took over the fund in the third quarter of 1973 up to the end of 1989. Charles Royce and his associate Thomas Ebright explain the philosophy of Royce Value Trust in the Closed-End Insights box.

---

### ROYCE VALUE TRUST PHILOSOPHY
### Charles M. Royce and Thomas R. Ebright
### President and Vice President, respectively
### Royce Value Trust, Inc.

For the past 20 years we (at Quest Advisory) have invested exclusively in small capitalization companies. Our attraction to small company stocks stems from what many people refer to as the "small company effect." That is, the availability of higher long-term returns in the small company universe (of 5,000 to 10,000 companies). There is a higher probability of inefficiently priced stocks here, the result of a general lack of information, research, and institutional support for these issues. Combined with this is the difficulty of working in this marketplace; the buying and selling of small company stocks requires extra time and patience and is usually more expensive. And finally, small companies are often better companies in that they offer higher growth rates and the potential for higher internal returns than their large company counterparts. For all these reasons we have built our portfolios around small-cap stocks.

The majority of the small company work we see

being done in the U.S. uses a growth approach, not unlike that which was popularized by the legendary investor, T. Rowe Price. In our opinion, growth approaches are difficult to implement and the least productive within this market sector. The inherent problem with these approaches is the assumption that superior growth over time will compensate for the tendency of a growth stock to be overpriced at the time of purchase. The reality of small growth companies is more a tendency for their growth to diminish, be interrupted and generally not be sustaining, thus negating emerging growth's basic premise. The challenge is to avoid overpaying for unsustainable growth and this challenge is best answered, in our opinion, by the more disciplined tenets of a value approach.

Our value-oriented work with small-company stocks at Quest Advisory Corp. has been categorized as an updated version of similar value work popularized by Graham and Dodd but applied primarily to large companies. We value businesses (in the form of stocks) looking for discrepancies between market and appraisal value (or positive worth). We work from the assumption that any business, regardless of its growth rate, is attractive, but only at a specific price level. The price we pay for a given set of "financial characteristics" is critical to our *value approach*. We constantly attempt to seek out the best companies in our universe based on their returns on assets, growth rates, and balance sheet quality, but are careful to avoid the pitfall of over-paying for any characteristic. Over time, the normal "ebb and flow" of the market gives us the opportunity to buy almost any stock at "our" price. It is this pricing discipline applied to the "best small companies" that separates our work from that of our peers and has delivered our long-term returns.

We apply our value principles to small-cap from year to year, and attempt to avoid the opportunistic and fashionable investment styles of any given moment. We believe that this disciplined method, which emphasizes patience and value, comes the closest to an all-weather strategy in delivering long-term (three years and beyond) returns from the small company sector.

## CONCLUSION

The domestic stock funds should form the cornerstone of a portfolio since equities can be expected to deliver long run returns considerably above those of debt securities. This is reflected by both the Ibbotson and Sinquefield data and the Lipper data on the performance of diversified equity funds versus bond funds. The authors advocate a long-term buy and hold strategy with the domestic stock funds selecting well-managed funds with attractive discounts wherever possible. In Chapters 5 and 6, which are essentially a continuation of this chapter, we'll guide you through the domestic equity fund universe.

## Notes

[1]Under Section 12 of the Investment Company Act of 1940, investment companies face several percentage limitations in terms of what they can invest in other investment companies. This is designed to prevent undue "pyramiding" of investment companies. These percentage limits exist no matter whether a fund is diversified or non-diversified. The overall limitation is that an investment company cannot hold positions in investment companies (including its own) having an aggregate value in excess of 10% of its total assets.

[2]William P. Lloyd and Richard L. Haney, Jr., "Time diversification: Surest route to lower risk," *The Journal of Portfolio Management*, Spring 1980, pp. 5–9.

[3]Norman Berryessa and Eric Kirzner *Global Investing: The Templeton Way* (Homewood, Illinois: Dow Jones-Irwin, 1988), pp. 138–39.

[4]See Rolf W. Banz, "The Relationship between Return and Market Value of Common Stocks," *Journal of Financial Economics*, March 1981, pp. 3–18.

[5]A good discussion of the New Horizons' relative P/E is contained in James W. Broadfoot III, *Investing in Emerging Growth Stocks* (New York: John Wiley & Sons, Inc., 1989), Chapter 2.

[6]This was the number of small company growth mutual funds tracked by Lipper Analytical Services in mid-October, 1990.

# CHAPTER 5

# *Older Domestic Equity Funds*

The domestic equity investor has a wide variety of CEFs to choose from. This chapter introduces you to the older ones. Chapter 6 covers the personality funds of the 1980s. The older funds can be separated into the following two groups:

1. *Classic Funds.* This small group contains the old-line, plain vanilla common stock funds, most of which were formed as closed-end funds in 1929. Included here are the two largest domestic stock CEFs—Tri-Continental and The Salomon Brothers Fund. The classic funds have tended to have low expense ratios (an expense ratio under 1 percent is considered low) and trade at wider discounts than funds in the other groups at this writing.

2. *Other Older Funds.* Most of the companies in this small group began operations as closed-end funds in the late 1960s or early 1970s. Two of these which, coincidentally, both started in 1968, have stellar long-term performance records—Bergstrom Capital and Source Capital.[1]

## BASIC DATA

Some basic data on these funds appear in Table 5–1. The funds range in size from Tri-Continental with assets of over $1.6 billion down to the tiny Spectra Fund with assets of only $4 million. An average of expense ratios over a five year period is also included in the table for each fund. As explained in Chapter 3, larger funds have dramatically lower expense ratios than smaller ones. Observe that Tri's average expense ratio is 0.55% whereas Spectra's is 2.90%.

The data on institutional holdings reflect the fact that CEF shares are generally held mainly by individual investors rather than institutions. Baker, Fentress has the highest institutional holdings in the group of older funds. Institutional ownership of less than 10 percent of a company's shares is considered low. Note that the institutional holdings are very low for the three largest CEFs in the table: Adams Express, The Salomon Brothers Fund, and Tri-Continental Corporation.

The CEFs in Table 5–1 are diversified under the Investment Company Act of 1940 definition set forth in Chapter 4 with the exceptions of Baker, Fentress; Bergstrom Capital; Central Securities; Engex; and Spectra Fund.

## PERFORMANCE RECORDS

A fund's performance is most meaningful when examined over long periods of time relative to other comparable funds and performance benchmarks. In examining the Lipper performance data on the older stock funds we will separate them into diversified and non-diversified categories for purposes of analysis. The non-diversified equity funds are part of Lipper's specialized equity and convertible funds category. The ten older funds for which data are available for recent 10- and 15-year periods appear in Table 5–2. These performance figures represent total compound annual returns including reinvested distributions.[2]

**Table 5–1. Selected Data on Older Domestic Common Stock Funds**

| Classic Funds | Began as CEF | Net Assets (Millions) | Past Avg. Expense Ratio | Institutional Holdings |
|---|---|---|---|---|
| Adams Express | 1929 | $ 550 | 0.52% | 1.0% |
| Central Securities | 1929 | 129 | 0.89 | 3.6 |
| General American Investors | 1927 | 382 | 1.15 | 7.1 |
| Niagara Share Corp. | 1929 | 230 | 1.10 | 3.7 |
| The Salomon Brothers Fund | 1929 | 1,027 | 0.45 | 3.4 |
| Tri-Continental Corp. | 1929 | 1,632 | 0.55 | 3.5 |
| | | | | |
| Other Older Funds | | | | |
| Baker, Fentress & Co. | 1970 | 456 | 0.59 | 18.2 |
| Bergstrom Capital Corp. | 1968 | 66 | 1.02 | 0.4 |
| Engex | 1975 | 14 | 3.32 | 6.7 |
| Source Capital | 1968 | 314 | 0.97 | 1.0 |
| Spectra Fund | 1978 | 4 | 2.90 | n.a. |

n.a.: Not available

Source: Net assets and expense ratios provided by individual funds. Net assets as of year end 1989 or end of fund's 1989 fiscal year; expense ratios represent averages of 5 years through fiscal year 1989. Institutional holdings represent the percentage of the fund's common shares held by institutions. The number is based on data in S&P's *Security Owner's Stock Guide*, April 1990.

**Table 5-2. Long-Term Performance of Older Stock Funds\***

|  | 10-Year Period | | 15-Year Period | |
|---|---|---|---|---|
|  | Return | Rank | Return | Rank |
| Diversified Equity Funds | | | | |
| Adams Express Company | 15.53% | 5 | 14.60% | 3 |
| General American Investors | 17.62 | 2 | 16.61 | 2 |
| Niagara Share Corp. | 12.96 | 6 | 13.17 | 6 |
| Salomon Brothers Fund | 15.64 | 4 | 13.82 | 5 |
| Source Capital | 19.26 | 1 | 19.82 | 1 |
| Tri-Continental Corp. | 16.67 | 3 | 14.41 | 4 |
| Non-Diversified Equity Funds | | | | |
| Baker, Fentress & Co. | 15.26% | 3 | 15.04% | 3 |
| Bergstrom Capital Corp. | 20.34 | 1 | 21.39 | 1 |
| Engex, Inc. | 11.49 | 4 | n.a. | |
| Spectra Fund | 17.49 | 2 | 18.81 | 2 |
| Performance Benchmarks | | | | |
| Diversified equity funds | 16.42% | | 15.73% | |
| Specialized equity | | | | |
| & convertible funds | 14.98 | | 16.25 | |
| Lipper Growth Fund Index | 15.55 | | 13.53 | |
| S&P 500 reinvested | 17.69 | | 14.80 | |

\*Returns reflect compound average annual changes in NAV incuding reinvestment of all distributions. Both periods end March 31, 1990.
n.a.: Not available.
Source: Adapted from data provided by Lipper Analytical Services, Inc.

The performances of the funds are also ranked within each category for each time period.

The older stock funds lend themselves well to performance analysis since they have a long track record. The performances of these funds can be judged relative to the S&P 500, the Lipper Growth Fund Index, and the performance benchmark for the respective category. (The performances of the non-diversified funds should be compared with the average for specialized equity and convertible funds.) The first- and second-best performing of all funds over both periods were Bergstrom and Source, respectively. Their performances were superior to the averages for their respective categories, the Lipper Growth Fund Index, and the S&P 500.

The real key to long-term investment success is to avoid losing money in down markets. Erik Bergstrom and George Michaelis, the managers of the two best performing funds, are both very risk averse and feel strongly about the importance of preserving capital in down markets. Charles Allmon, Warren Buffett, and Martin Zweig are also good examples of highly risk averse investors.

Naturally, past performance is not necessarily an indicator of future results. The data presented here are intended merely to show how results can vary among funds over given time horizons.

## MANAGEMENT ARRANGEMENT

A relatively small number of CEFs are internally managed, with no advisory fee; namely, Adams Express; Baker, Fentress; Central Securities; General American Investors; Niagara Share; and Petroleum & Resources Corp. (a sector fund). With an internally managed fund, the officers and directors attend to all administrative and investment operations. Like an operating company, an internally managed investment company pays the salaries and business expenses directly.

Most funds are managed by an external investment adviser. Externally managed CEFs establish a relationship with an external investment adviser, who provides the investment management function for the fund. The external adviser charges a management fee which is usually based upon a percentage of total net assets of the fund. The usual sources of investment information on closed-end funds will name the investment adviser and indicate the fee arrangement.

## FUND PROFILES

A profile of each of the eleven older funds beginning with the classic funds is presented. These profiles are intended as introductions to the funds. We generally do not cover details such as the companies and sectors represented in the fund portfolios as well as other facts which you could locate in the fund's shareholder reports. These details are subject to change and the most recent shareholder reports are your best source of information. Further, our discussions are not meant to be recommendations to buy or not to buy the shares in any fund. You must investigate them further.

For more information, consult the S&P *Stock Reports* or contact the individual funds and request their shareholder reports. (Addresses and telephone numbers of all CEFs which appear weekly in the publicly-traded funds box—and a few smaller ones which do not—are found in our directory in Appendix I).

## Classic Funds

**Adams Express Co. (NYSE Symbol: ADX).** Adams Express, headquartered in Baltimore, became a closed-end fund in 1929. The original company of the same name was organized in 1854 and operated as a leading express company for many years. Today, as an investment company, its principal objective is preservation of capital. ADX is one of the few funds we have found utilizing preservation of capital as a primary objective. Its secondary objectives are reasonable income and capital appreciation. ADX's philosophy is implemented through the purchase of stocks with defensive characteristics like health care. The fund may use put and call options. In practice, they keep the use of options simple and may employ them when attempting to buy or sell certain securities.

ADX has a 9% interest in **Petroleum & Resources Corp. (NYSE: PEO),** an affiliated closed-end sector fund which will be discussed in Chapter 8. ADX has a low expense ratio, low portfolio turnover and, as was just noted, is internally managed. With $550 million in assets and some 43,000 shareholders, it is one of the bigger diversified stock funds. ADX has a cash payments plan along with its dividend reinvestment plan.

**Central Securities (Amex: CET).** Central Securities is the least known of the older funds. CET was started in

1929 as Central Illinois Securities by the securities affiliate of the Central Bank & Trust Company of Chicago. It was highly leveraged with a lot of preferred stock and didn't do well in its earlier years. The $15 million fund dropped to about $4 million by 1936. After World War II it had less than $5 million in assets and the common stock was "under water." However, it had a resurgence, experiencing phenomenal growth in the 1950s. Its assets had surged to $44 million at year-end 1961. Central Securities traded at premiums to NAV during a good part of the 1960s. In fact, at year-end 1968 and 1969 it sold at premiums of 31 and 58 percent, respectively.

About 1950 the fund was moved to New York after the late C.A. Johnson became its president. Its present name was adopted in 1959. CET is one of the few closed-end funds controlled by management and its affiliates. The C.A. Johnson Endeavor Foundation holds 35% of the voting shares. CET has a convertible preferred issue in its capital structure as well as the common. The primary objective of the $129 million fund is long-term growth; income is secondary.

Over the years this non-diversified fund has concentrated much of its portfolio in a relatively few issues, some of which are restricted securities, (that is, their resale is restricted by the SEC). The fund has half its portfolio invested in about 10 stocks. According to academic studies of portfolio diversification, you eliminate about 94 percent of company-specific risk with the first ten stocks, explains Wilmot Kidd, CET's president. "Our theory has always been to have a few significant positions with the balance invested in a broad general market portfolio. It would be ideal if you could have positions of such quality that you never want to sell them and you could continue to compound your growth without paying capital gains taxes." Overall, CET's portfolio contains about 50 stocks generally consisting of medium-sized companies coupled with positions in some smaller companies.

Kidd is a patient, long-term investor and Central's portfolio turnover averages well under 25%. He does not believe in using options or futures. "Our theory is that it complicates an already infinitely complex business. We view our investments as investments in businesses rather than as pieces of paper. In an overall sense, I am not sure options and futures provide any benefit to our capital markets. They are certainly not productive investments in an economic sense." CET appeared on the *Forbes* honor roll in 1984. The fund has been buying in its own shares, a practice we encourage. In 1989, when about 700,000 shares traded in the open market, CET bought in over 200,000 shares.

**General American Investors (NYSE: GAM)** Founded in 1927, General American (with assets of $382 million) invests mostly in medium-sized companies and has an objective of long-term capital appreciation with less emphasis on income. Management selects stocks using a bottom-up approach and does not try to time the market. William Gedale, president and portfolio manager of GAM visits as many companies as he can. Gedale has been with General American since 1969. Normally, a substantial, fully invested position in stocks is maintained. Each of the stocks selected by General American management is expected to meet a clearly defined portfolio objective using a three-year time horizon.

General American has been internally managed since its founding. However, in 1987 it filed an application with the SEC which, if approved, would allow it to convert (subject to shareholder approval) to the much more common external management arrangement. GAM feels that having a management company will give it greater investment flexibility and, thus, benefit shareholders. We are not completely in agreement with this position.

General American has performed well in the past and appeared on *Forbes* honor roll five times. Its most recent appearance was in 1984. GAM's performance ranked it second among the six diversified funds for both our 10- and 15-year periods (Table 5–2).

Like other older funds, GAM has gradually changed the relative weightings given to the different sectors, or industries, where it invests. This can be seen in Table 5–3 which is reproduced from General American's 1989

Annual Report. This table displays the percentage distribution of GAM's net assets by industry at the end of 1989 in comparison with the breakdowns for 1988, 1979, and 1969. Over the 20 year period there was a major reduction in emphasis given to oil and natural gas, metals and mining, and data handling. On the other hand, increases in relative weighting occurred in the retail trade, health care, and finance, insurance, and real estate groups. Retail trade (29.9%) and health care (22.9%) were by far its largest sectors at year-end 1989.

**Niagara Share Corp. (NYSE: NGS)** Niagara was founded in Buffalo in 1929 from a previous holding company founded in 1925 to buy electric utility stocks on the Niagara Frontier. It became a diversified investment company in 1952. The emphasis is on long-term growth with income secondary. Recent conversations with management, however, indicate that income will be given more emphasis than previously.

Niagara has been investing overseas since the 1950s, making it the most globally-oriented of the classic funds. "We look for opportunities throughout the world without limitation," says Robert J.A. Irwin, Niagara's president and portfolio manager. Between 20% and 35% of its portfolio has been invested overseas for a number of years. NGS is one of the few funds in which officers and directors own a substantial portion of the company. According to a recent proxy statement, their ownership was 16%, much of it by the founding Schoellkopf family. An ownership interest this high is not common but is highly positive, it shows a strong commitment and we commend them for it. Niagara's portfolio contains some 80 issues, primarily of small and medium-size companies. NGS particularly likes to invest in companies which have a dominant market share and are out of favor on Wall Street. Niagara also has a long history of investing in mining and precious metals companies to offset the ravages of inflation.

Although Niagara Share's performance over the 10- and 15-year periods ended March 31, 1990 was below average (Table 5–2), it did perform well in earlier periods. It made the *Forbes* honor roll three times and appeared

## Table 5–3. Distribution of General American Investor's Net Assets by Industry over Time

DIVERSIFICATION OF INVESTMENT ASSETS

The diversification of the net assets of the Company by industrial groups at December 31, 1989 is shown in the following table which also indicates the percentage distribution of the Company's net assets in these industries at the end of 1989 in comparison with that at the end of 1988, 1979, and 1969.

During the twenty-year period, there was a major reduction in emphasis in oil and natural gas, in metals and mining, and in data handling. The principal increases in relative importance occurred in the retail trade, health care, and finance, insurance and real estate industries.

| STOCKS | Cost (000's) | Market Value (000's) | Percentage of Net Assets December 31, | | | |
|---|---|---|---|---|---|---|
| | | | 1989 | 1988 | 1979 | 1969 |
| Aerospace (Including Components) | $ 5,737 | $ 7,228 | 1.9% | 2.3% | — | — |
| Chemical (Incuding Instrumentation) | — | — | — | 0.7 | 7.1% | 6.1% |
| Consumer Products and Services | 20,953 | 33,870 | 8.9 | 8.5 | 3.2 | 4.2 |
| Data Handling | — | — | — | 1.5 | 3.7 | 10.2 |
| Data Information and Services | 2,763 | 8,266 | 2.1 | 2.8 | — | — |
| Electronics | 3,641 | 4,874 | 1.3 | 6.0 | 11.3 | 4.1 |
| Environmental Control (Including Services) | 10,024 | 11,946 | 3.1 | — | — | — |

| | | | | | | |
|---|---|---|---|---|---|---|
| Finance, Insurance and Real Estate | 22,197 | 34,661 | 9.1 | 9.8 | 9.6 | 4.4 |
| Forest Products | — | — | — | — | — | 7.1 |
| Glass | — | — | — | — | — | 5.8 |
| Health Care (Including Instrumentation) | 64,470 | 87,358 | 22.9 | 17.8 | 7.7 | 1.7 |
| Industrial (Manufacturing) | 10,635 | 11,291 | 3.0 | — | — | — |
| Machinery and Equipment | 2,955 | 2,761 | 0.7 | — | 2.7 | 1.7 |
| Metals and Mining | — | — | — | — | 1.8 | 12.3 |
| Miscellaneous | 9,498 | 11,662 | 3.1 | 4.8 | 3.3 | 8.6 |
| Oil and Natural Gas (Including Services) | — | — | — | 1.1 | 15.3 | 15.6 |
| Publishing and Broadcasting | 3,661 | 16,147 | 4.2 | 4.2 | 9.3 | 2.4 |
| Retail Trade | 40,900 | 114,531 | 29.9 | 26.6 | 8.6 | 4.5 |
| Special Holdings | 5,625 | 6,417 | 1.7 | 1.9 | — | — |
| Transportation | 2,764 | 2,616 | 0.7 | 1.9 | 2.4 | 2.5 |
| Wholesale and Distribution | 1,036 | 7,795 | 2.0 | 1.9 | 5.6 | — |
| Total Stocks | $206,859 | 361,423 | 94.6 | 91.8 | 91.6 | 91.2 |
| Short-Term Securities, Cash and Other Assets, Less Liabilities | | 20,510 | 5.4 | 8.2 | 8.4 | 8.8 |
| Total Net Assets | | $381,933 | 100.0% | 100.0% | 100.0% | 100.0% |

Source: General American Investors Company, Inc., Annual Report 1989, p. 14.

there last in 1980. Its performance during a good part of the 1980s was unfavorably impacted by the fact that it holds medium-sized and smaller companies which lagged the big cap sector of the market. Further, Niagara also holds gold and other mining issues which underperformed the market in the 1980s. During the first nine months of 1990 NGS outperformed the S&P 500.

**The Salomon Brothers Fund Inc (NYSE: SBF)** The Salomon Brothers Fund invests primarily in large capitalization companies. With assets of over $1 billion and approximately 70,000 shareholders, SBF is the second largest diversified stock fund. In addition to being traded on domestic exchanges, SBF's shares also trade on the Geneva Stock Exchange and the Paris Bourse. The primary objective is long-term capital appreciation with income as a secondary consideration.

Formerly The Lehman Corporation, its name was recently changed to The Salomon Brothers Fund Inc. The Lehman Management Company, the fund's previous adviser, was purchased by Salomon Brothers and the new adviser is Salomon Brothers Asset Management Inc. SBF is being run by the same people who had been running it under its former adviser.

The portfolio is fully diversified and divided into sectors but stocks are purchased for their individual values rather than to fill a particular category. SBF has always been a conservative, value-oriented fund, and the management buys stocks which it believes offer above-average growth prospects at a reasonable price-earnings ratio. Visiting managements of the companies SBF invests in is an important element of its style of fundamental analysis. The adviser doesn't try to time the market and generally remains fully invested in equities. Salomon Brothers Fund's expense ratio has averaged 0.45% over the past five years, and is the lowest within the classic fund group, as seen in Table 5–1. SBF has a cash purchase plan along with its dividend reinvestment plan.

Mary Stone, corporate secretary, provides some interesting background history on the fund in the Closed-End Insights box.

## SHORT HISTORY OF A CLASSIC FUND
### Mary R. Stone
### Corporate Secretary
### The Salomon Brothers Fund Inc

To delve into the background of The Lehman Corporation one must start with the rich history of the prestigious investment banking firm of Lehman Brothers.
Founded in 1806 in Montgomery Alabama, Lehman
Brothers moved to New York just prior to the Civil
War, and by 1906, Robert Lehman and his partners
had brought the firm from its turn-of-the-century position as a commodities house specializing in cotton to
the status of a major financial adviser, a leader in the
business of underwriting securities, and the preferred
investment banker to leading companies of the times.

On September 11, 1929, the first meeting of the
incorporators was held for the largest and most successful investment trust offering of its time. Of the
eight original members of the board of directors of The
Lehman Corporation, five were Lehmans. Philip was
elected chairman; Arthur, president; and Allan, Har-
old and Robert, vice presidents. The Lehman Corporation operated under direct Lehman family guidance
until the death of Robert in 1969.

One of the most crucial periods of the Corporation's life was its fortunate beginning. On September
14, 1929, after selling one million shares in the public
offering of The Lehman Corporation in only three
days, the firm was not prepared to start investing the
$100 million they had raised. The rapid success of the
offering had caught them by surprise, and until such
time as their investment policies were securely in
place, Lehman Brothers negotiated bank call loans for
the majority of the money. Luck was with the Lehmans, and on Black Tuesday, October 29, 1929, The
Lehman Corporation held over $57 million of the origi-
nal $100 million in cash and bank call loans. Where
other investment companies had been fully invested

at that time and lost almost everything, Lehman Brothers had been cautious and had retained their reputation for "action predicated by knowledge."

Besides cotton, some of the early investments made by The Lehman Corporation were initial public offerings of such famous corporations as American Cyanamid, Coty, Deere & Co., Great Lakes Corporation, Marine Midland, Gimbel Brothers, R.H. Macy & Co., and May Department Stores. Other early investments included Union Carbide, Archer Daniels, American Telephone and Telegraph, General Electric, American Can, Western Union, Dupont, Standard Oil, and Eastman Kodak. The Corporation also held mortgages for some of the most valuable property in Manhattan.

The Lehman Corporation evolved into solely an equity fund in the 1940s and has continued to prosper as an equity investment company. During its sixty year history, the Corporation has survived the Great Depression, three wars, two stock market crashes, nine bear markets, and countless periods of economic and political instability. Although the same commitment to excellence and fundamental principles of conservative, value-oriented management that guided the Corporation in its first sixty years continue to guide the investment decisions today, the history books have closed on the Lehman name. On March 14, 1990, the investment adviser to the Corporation, Lehman Management Co., was sold to Salomon Brothers Asset Management Inc. and on April 30, 1990, the shareholders of the Corporation approved a new management contract with Salomon Brothers Asset Management and changed the name of the Corporation to "The Salomon Brothers Fund Inc." The legacy will now continue, combining the unique blend of knowledge and experience of Lehman and the financial power of the house of Salomon.

**Tri-Continental (NYSE: TY)** Tri-Continental is a member of the J. & W. Seligman group of investment companies, which consists of a number of open-end funds. With a $1.6 billion portfolio, TY is the largest diversified closed-end equity fund. Organized in 1929, it now has about 75,000 common shareholders.

The name Tri-Continental was given the fund since it initially intended to invest in the stocks of companies located on three continents—North and South America and Europe.[3] It did in fact do this for a relatively short time, but subsequent to the 1929 Crash it has concentrated its investments in the United States. "When the outlook was obscured by conditions abroad," declares Tri-Continental's annual report for 1931, "foreign holdings were sold, and the Corporation has concentrated its investments in the securities of American companies ever since."[4]

In addition to being traded on domestic exchanges, its shares trade on the London Stock Exchange. Besides its common stock, the capital structure includes preferred stock and perpetual warrants. At one time CEF warrants were a popular trading vehicle. But, today TY is the only fund in the U.S. that has them outstanding. The number of TY's outstanding warrants has declined considerably due to investor exercise.

TY invests in a broadly-diversified, high-grade portfolio of well-known securities. The management prefers superior companies: those characterized by high profit margins and high returns on equity. The objective is long-term growth in capital and growth in income. Its expense ratio is low because of its size and its dividends are above average for an equity fund.

Tri-Continental focuses more heavily on its shareholder interests than most funds. It was one of the first investment companies to take its annual meetings around the country. These meetings are well attended by loyal shareholders. TY has a dividend reinvestment and cash purchase plan. Shareholders can also arrange for checks to be drawn on their checking account in a fixed monthly amount for investment in new shares. There is also an automatic cash withdrawal plan, whereby owners of shares worth $5,000 or more may receive a fixed amount of income at regular intervals.

Both Tri-Continental and Salomon Brothers Fund have listed put and call options which trade on the Philadelphia Stock Exchange. The options could be of interest to those who like to write covered calls for additional income or to write puts with the hope of being able to purchase a stock below its current market price. For example, if you hold Salomon Brothers Fund you could write covered calls against it. It should be noted that this strategy—as well as writing puts—has an opportunity cost if the stock market advances sharply. Further, the options on SBF and TY do not trade that actively.

## OTHER OLDER FUNDS

**Baker, Fentress & Co. (NYSE: BKF).** BKF was established as a partnership in 1891, became a closed-end corporation in 1907, and converted to a closed-end investment company in 1970. The non-diversified fund's objective is capital appreciation. Baker has held some of its positions more than 20 years and consequently it has large unrealized capital gains. For this reason, it has traded at wide discounts for much of its history. In fact, at year-end 1973 and 1974 its discounts stood at 54 and 58%, respectively. Its year-end discounts averaged 23% for the 12 years ended December 31, 1989. The discount has narrowed since the fund instituted an 8% annual dividend in 1987. In 1989 BKF instituted a new dividend reinvestment plan, providing for optional quarterly cash purchases by shareholders. Insiders own about 17% of BKF's shares.

The following excerpt from BKF's *Fact Book* gives good insight into its investment philosophy as a non-diversified fund.

> As a closed-end fund, Baker, Fentress & Company does not have the liquidity requirements typical of open-end funds. Accordingly, we are able to make investments which because of size, or method of purchase, or required holding period, might not be appropriate for other types of funds.
>
> By plan, our ten largest individual holdings typically account for about 60% of total net asset value. In the course of pursuing an investment strategy which

commits major funds to relatively few individual issues, we purchase securities in a variety of ways, for
a number of different reasons.

The largest single holding is Consolidated-
Tomoka Land Co. [CTLC] and we own approximately
80% of that company's outstanding shares. This
Florida-based company's operations are based upon
the utilization and conversion of its land assets. Principal revenue sources are citrus operations, real estate
development, property leasing, resort operations, and
forestry.

As of September 30, 1990, CTLC was 15% of BKF's
$360 million portfolio. The cost of its 2.5 million share po-
sition in CTLC, most of which was acquired in the 1930s,
was just $5 million. Its recent value on BKF's balance
sheet was $55 million. BKF appeared on the *Forbes* honor
roll in 1984. BKF also holds large positions in Barnett
Banks in Florida and MCI.

**Bergstrom Capital (Amex: BEM).** BEM is non-
diversified and was founded in 1968 as Diebold Venture
Capital Corp. by John Diebold, a computer consultant. In
1976, after a proxy contest with The Bergstrom Group
which held 35% of the shares, the investment contract
was transferred to Bergstrom Advisers. The company was
moved to Seattle and was renamed Claremont Capital,
after Claremont Graduate School where Bergstrom earned
his MA degree.

BEM is unusual as it hired two sub-advisers to assist
in managing two-thirds of its portfolio. This occurred
when it converted from a venture capital to a growth fund.
BEM hired a venture capitalist to assist the adviser in selling most of that portion of the portfolio. Bergstrom also
hired Stewart and Patten of San Francisco to advise him
for another part of the portfolio. Its manager, Frank Branson, did a good job. When Branson left Stewart and Patten
to found his own investment advisory firm, he remained
as sub-adviser. BEM decided to hire RCM Capital Management for another portion of the portfolio. At this writing,
Frank Branson and RCM, a subsidiary of Primerica Corporation, are each a sub-adviser for about one-third of the

portfolio. The final portion is managed exclusively by Bergstrom Advisers.

Erik Bergstrom explains why he chose the sub-adviser system in the Closed-End Insights box.

---

### THE SUB-ADVISER SYSTEM
### Erik E. Bergstrom
### Chairman
### Bergstrom Capital Corporation

I have used four firms as sub-advisers to assist me in managing portions of the portfolio since I began in 1976 to manage the assets of Bergstrom Capital Corporation (BEM). In each case I have been able to obtain the services of excellent investment managers that I would not have been able to hire as employees of my investment advisory firm. Excellent investment managers often either want to have their own firm or to join in a partnership to manage substantial assets. Since my family and I together with our foundation own almost one-third of BEM, I wanted to obtain the very best help I could in managing the assets of BEM. But I did not want to become part of a larger firm, managing assets where I did not have an ownership interest.

---

BEM is also one of two CEFs which made the 1990 *Forbes* honor roll (the other was Source Capital). It also has the distinction of having been chosen for the honor roll for seven consecutive years. In November 1988, its name was changed to Bergstrom Capital Corporation. About 31% of the outstanding shares are held by Erik Bergstrom, his family and the Bergstrom Foundation. The directors and their families are also large shareholders.

**Engex (Amex: EGX)** A non-diversified fund, EGX started in 1968 as an open-end fund named The Emerging Securities Fund. In 1975 it was converted to a closed-end fund. It invests in "the emerging smaller companies or the non-blue chips," as stated in its 1989 fiscal year shareholder report. At that time its portfolio contained 36 common stocks. Its assets of $14 million place it near the bottom of the size range.

Engex's 1986 Annual Report noted that for the 10 years ending September 30, 1986 its performance would rank it second among all domestic equity funds with a total appreciation of about 1000 percent over that decade. But, more recently, its performance has fallen off. According to Lipper data, its performance over the 5 years ended March 31, 1990 was about −1% compounded annually. EGX's volatile year-to-year record and high past average expense ratio of 3.32% (Table 5–1) no doubt have contributed to its extraordinarily wide discounts: 36% at year-end 1988 and 22.5% at the end of 1989.

We are aware, however, that some sophisticated investors like Engex's large discount and have purchased its shares. Stanislaw Bednarski (a highly successful CEF investor profiled in Chapter 19 "A Final Word") held 8 percent of its shares according a recent proxy statement. J. Morton Davis, EGX's president, holds about 12 percent of the shares; about 17 percent are held by Rivkalex, Inc. (all of whose shares are held by Mrs. Morton Davis). D.H. Blair Advisors, Inc., a wholly-owned subsidiary of D.H. Blair & Co., Inc., serves as adviser to EGX.

**Source Capital (NYSE: SOR)** Source was formed as a private placement fund in 1968 and was originally managed by Fred Carr who included highly speculative go-go companies in the portfolio. Then, in 1971, George Michaelis, a conservative and talented investment manager with a background in venture capital, took over and had the job of cleaning out the illiquid letter stock and other private placement issues and replacing these with high quality stocks.

Michaelis became president in 1977 and has turned in a truly remarkable performance record with SOR. Portfolio decisions are based on fundamental analysis in choosing individual securities rather than economic or stock market forecasts. He likes companies with low debt ratios and consistently high returns on equity. Basically, he likes to buy sustainable earning power at a discount. Michaelis looks for stable businesses that make sense to him.

The excellent long-term performance of SOR is attributable in large part to the high returns on equity generated by the companies it holds. It is quite revealing to examine the average annual returns on equity of SOR's portfolio versus the figures for the S&P 400 Industrials over a number of years. As seen in Table 5–4, the return on equity for the SOR companies has exceeded that of the S&P 400 by a wide margin in all years except the last three when SOR's numbers have been fairly close to the S&P's. The return on equity on the S&P 400 shot up dramatically in the last several years because the profitability of large parts of corporate America has improved dramatically. According to Michaelis this reflects a cyclical above-average profitability and it is now going to reverse. Michaelis wants high returns on equity on companies which are not vulnerable to the cycle.

Source made the 1990 *Forbes* honor roll and was

**Table 5–4. Return on Equity Source Capital versus S&P 400 Industrials**

| Year | Source Portfolio | S&P 400 |
|------|------------------|---------|
| 1978 | 24.9% | 15.9% |
| 1979 | 25.4 | 18.2 |
| 1980 | 22.3 | 16.3 |
| 1981 | 21.2 | 15.5 |
| 1982 | 19.9 | 11.2 |
| 1983 | 18.0 | 12.5 |
| 1984 | 18.2 | 13.5 |
| 1985 | 20.0 | 12.8 |
| 1986 | 17.0 | 11.9 |
| 1987 | 17.0 | 16.3 |
| 1988 | 19.0 | 19.5 |
| 1989 | 18.0 | 17.0 |

Source: SOURCE CAPITAL Investment Philosophy Historical Review 1985–87, p. 4; figures subsequent to 1985 from Source Capital Annual Reports.

awarded an A+ rating in down markets. It also appeared on the honor roll in 1989 and 1984. Michaelis also had the distinction of being included as one of eight talented investors in John Train's book *The New Money Masters.*[5] Michaelis expresses his current views from time to time in publications like *Barron's, Forbes,* and *Fortune.* His shareholder reports are well written and thorough providing detailed fundamental and valuation data on all stocks contained in SOR's portfolio. For instance, his 10-year growth analysis presents a 10-year growth rate as well as the number of years earnings per share declined on a company-by-company basis. The fund's excellent performance has certainly played a role in the narrowing of its discount which has averaged just 6% in the 12 years ended December 31, 1989. This is less than half the 13% year-end average discount for the eight funds in Wiesenberger's Diversified Investment Company Average over the 12 years. Source's capital structure includes a $2.40 cumulative preferred issue in addition to the common.

**Spectra Fund**—a tiny, non-diversified fund traded exclusively on the "pink sheets," Spectra has assets of about $4 million and approximately 1,200 shareholders. The fund invests in small and large cap growth stocks with the objective of capital appreciation. It was originally offered as an open-end fund in August 1969 and became closed-end in June 1978. Spectra's above-average long-term performance ranked it second in our non-diversified CEF category over both the 10- and 15-year periods (Table 5–2). The fund holds some 30 common stocks representing a variety of different industries. Fred Alger Management, Inc. in New York City is the adviser. David Alger is primarily responsible for the management of its portfolio. The market makers are Carr Securities Corp. in New York and Perkins Smith, Inc. in Tampa, Florida. According to these market makers the fund hardly ever trades and has a wide bid-asked spread.

Collectively, all insiders including Fred Alger & Co., Inc. own 104,000 of Spectra's 257,000 outstanding shares. Spectra does not appear in the weekly publicly traded funds box. Inquiries about Spectra can be addressed to the management.

## CAN CEF PERFORMANCE BE MEASURED
## IN A MEANINGFUL WAY?

Measuring closed-end fund performance in a meaningful way is a real challenge according to Robert Irwin, president of Niagara Share. Irwin and his administrative assistant Nina Arendt explain why in the Closed-End Insights box.

---

### THE CHALLENGE OF CLOSED-END FUND
### PERFORMANCE ANALYSIS
### Robert J.A. Irwin and Nina M. Arendt
### President and Administrative Assistant
### to the President, respectively
### Niagara Share Corporation

One would think that calculating investment results for closed-end funds would be fairly straightforward. This, however, is not the case.

Should performance be calculated based on net asset value or on market value? The Securities and Exchange Commission has proposed that total return be calculated for reporting purposes using market prices with appropriate adjustment for distributions. Stockholders are naturally interested in the movement of the adjusted market price as this influences their actual investment experience. Portfolio managers, however, argue that the fund's market price is not subject to their control. They argue they should be judged by the investment results of the assets under their management.

There is no one generally accepted method of measuring the investment results of a closed-end fund. Methods currently in use result in significantly divergent results. The Closed-End Fund Committee of the Investment Company Institute in Washington, D.C. has been working to develop a methodology for measuring investment results which could lead to more uniformity within the industry and make results reasonably comparable to those of mutual funds. Such a methodology would include appropriate yet practical methods of adjusting for the reinvestment of capital gains and income distributions and, where applicable, the payment by funds of Federal income taxes on retained capital gains. There are also other factors that can affect the results of individual funds; however, it is difficult to provide for all such factors in a single comprehensive methodology.

What are some of these other factors that complicate the measurement of closed-end fund investment results?

The price obtained by shareholders who accept their distributions in stock is referred to as the "reinvestment price" and is usually the lower of net asset value or market value. In order to make calculations of closed-end fund performance reasonably comparable with those of mutual funds it is necessary to assume reinvestment of distributions at, or at some approximation of, actual reinvestment price. This "reinvestment price" is difficult to obtain and normally has to be supplied by each individual fund. This has caused some popular services to calculate closed-end fund performance assuming reinvestment at asset value, a method which accurately expresses what happens in an open-end fund but which understates results experienced by the shareholder of a closed-end fund if the reinvestment price is lower than the net asset value.

In addition, all shareholders experience a reduction or "dilution" in the net asset value per share of their shares because of the issuance of new shares at less than net asset value to those who receive their distributions in shares. This dilution is offset, more or less, for those shareholders who accept their distributions in stock at a discount.

Another complicating factor in calculating investment results is the measurement of the benefit a fund derives from the buyback of its own shares at a discount. Repurchasing shares at a discount enhances the net asset value per share and helps to offset the dilution effect of issuing shares at a discount. Thus, the performance experienced by a shareholder can be affected by these several factors not related to the performance of the fund's investments.

## CONCLUSION

This concludes our discussion of the older domestic equity funds. For investors who are new to closed-end funds the bigger older funds are the best way to get started—and to build your portfolio. They have loyal shareholders and have withstood the test of time. In Chapter 6 you will be introduced to the personality funds of the 1980s.

### Notes

[1]George Cole Scott is a member of the Board of Directors of Bergstrom Capital.

[2]In studying the performance data of closed-end funds it is important to understand that the numbers reflect portfolio performance and do not consider discounts and premiums (or market prices). The closed-end fund data published by Lipper Analytical Services, Inc. report on the performance of the fund's portfolio from the viewpoint of the disinterested director, rather than the experience of individual shareholders. Therefore, the performance figures shown reflect the change in net asset value including the reinvestment of all income dividends and capital gains distributions at net asset value, *on the fund's ex-dividend date*. Reinvestment of distributions at market value below NAV produces higher returns than shown.

[3]Ross L. Muir and Carl J. White, *Over the Long Term . . . the story of J. & W. Seligman & Co.* (New York: J. & W. Seligman & Co., 1964), p. 135.

[4]*Ibid*, p. 139.

[5]John Train, *The New Money Masters* (New York: Harper & Row, Publishers, 1989), Chapter 6.

# CHAPTER 6

# *The Personality Funds*

The newer domestic stock funds which debuted in the 1980s were in large part personality funds or superstar funds. Many of them are managed by well known individuals who have their own special philosophies. Even in the few cases where the managers aren't that well-known, the style still has distinctive features which tend to set that fund apart from others. The personality funds are identified in Table 6–1 which contains some basic data.[1]

All CEFs in Table 6–1 are diversified with the exceptions of Cypress Fund, Gabelli Equity Trust, The Inefficient-Market Fund, and Z-Seven which are non-diversified. We don't present performance data on the newer funds as we did with the older ones since we feel it is more meaningful to study performance over longer periods. The best way to address the performance issue with newer funds is to see what kind of track record the management has had with their other investment vehicles, like open-end funds, if they have some with longer records.

**Table 6-1. Selected Data on Personality Funds**

| Fund | Began | Net Assets (Millions) | Expense Ratio 1989 | Expense Ratio 1988 | Inst. Holdings |
|------|-------|----------------------|------|------|------|
| Blue Chip Value Fund | 2/87 | $ 73 | 1.98%* | 2.22%* | 6.8% |
| Cypress Fund | 10/86 | 75 | 3.35† | 1.28 | 5.7 |
| Gabelli Equity Trust | 8/86 | 590 | 1.18 | 1.25 | 3.4 |
| Growth Stock Outlook Trust | 3/86 | 124 | 1.43 | 1.46 | 1.4 |
| The Inefficient-Market Fund | 1/90 | n.a. | n.a. | n.a. | n.a. |
| Liberty All-Star Equity Fund | 11/86 | 514 | 1.25 | 1.33 | 23.3 |
| Morgan Grenfell SMALLCap Fund | 5/87 | 54 | 2.13* | 2.56* | 13.1 |
| Nicholas-Applegate Growth Equity Fund | 4/87 | 108 | 4.55* | 4.60* | 20.8 |
| Royce Value Trust | 11/86 | 131 | 0.95 | 1.09 | 12.7 |
| Z-Seven Fund | 12/83 | 18 | 1.16 | 2.73 | 2.2 |
| The Zweig Fund | 10/86 | 409 | 1.31 | 1.39 | 0.4 |

*Includes interest
†Includes extraordinary costs resulting from NAV Partners' attempt to open-end fund.
n.a.: Not available or not meaningful.
Source: Data provided by individual funds. Net assets as of year end 1989 or end of fund's 1989 fiscal year. Institutional holdings are based on data from S&P's *Security Owner's Stock Guide*, April 1990.

## FUND FEATURES

Features which some of the personality funds might have
include the following:

1. The capability of using options and futures. These
products experienced phenomenal growth in the 1980s
with the introduction of stock index futures and index options. Thus, it would seem natural for the newer funds to
consider them. Some funds use them, others don't. Some
funds have tried them and decided they don't like them.
Others like to have the capability of using options and futures but don't make a practice of using them on a regular
basis. The best way to find out to what extent a particular
fund uses them is to contact the fund itself.

2. The possibility for shareholders to vote to open-
end the fund if its discount drops below a certain level. Or
the fund may submit to shareholders the proposal to vote
to open-end the fund at a predetermined future time.
These features would tend to lead to narrower discounts.

3. Management fees which are related to performance. Z-Seven Fund was the first to introduce this feature
in 1983. The idea is simply that better performance results in higher management fees. In general there is a
tendency for management fees, and consequently, expense ratios to be higher on the newer funds. Thus, the
expense ratio warrants a close look when evaluating a
newer fund.

4. The 10% annual payout. Many newer funds have
this feature. A positive aspect of the policy is that it reflects management's confidence that the fund will be able
to perform well enough on average to support the payout.
Since shareholders like distributions, this guaranteed payout tends to lead to a narrower discount. However, during
a prolonged bear market it could result in a shrinkage of
fund assets, since the manager may be forced to return
capital to meet the target payment.

5. Multiple investment managers. Liberty All-Star
Equity Fund is the only one to employ multiple managers.
This will be discussed in our profile of that fund.

6. The use of leverage. Closed-end funds differ from
open-end funds in that some can use leverage of borrow-

ing as appropriate. A few of these CEFs, like Nicholas-Applegate Growth Equity Fund, can use leverage.

Let's take a look at the individual philosophies of the personality funds.

## FUND PROFILES

**Blue Chip Value Fund (NYSE: BLU)** BLU uses what Denver Investment Advisors (the adviser) calls its Modern Value Investing® Approach. BLU's approach to value investing is described by portfolio manager John Cormey in the Closed-End Insights box. The fund instituted a target payout of a minimum of 10% of NAV annually. This policy has resulted in a narrowing of the discount from an average of 17% in 1988 to 6% in the last several months of 1989 where it remains at this writing. BLU has a cash purchase plan along with its dividend reinvestment plan and a shareholder hot line for recorded weekly updates.

In late 1989, John Levin & Co. started buying BLU's shares when the discount was greater than 10% and as we go to press held about 5% of the shares, according to Securities and Exchange Commission filings. The authors address the issue of various groups which have tried to open-end CEFs in Chapter 18 "Takeovers and Open-Ending."

**Cypress Fund (Amex: WJR)** This is a non-diversified fund whose objective is long-term capital appreciation using a specialized strategy: ownership of a limited number of family controlled, consumer-oriented companies possessing strong market positions. Mitchell Hutchins Asset Management, the fund's adviser, is a subsidiary of PaineWebber.

William J. Reik, Jr. the vice president and portfolio manager, invests in companies that meet the following criteria: little or no debt, a significant equity ownership by the company's founders or management, a strong market position or franchise, and little institutional ownership.[2] According to its prospectus, WJR expects to invest in a limited number of issues—not less than 12 but usually not more than 22. Because the fund concentrates its assets

## MODERN VALUE INVESTING®
### John R. Cormey, CFA
### Vice President
### Portfolio Manager for
### The Blue Chip Value Fund

The Modern Value Investing® approach used to manage Blue Chip Value Fund consists of a multi-factor valuation model and a set of portfolio rules which are designed to control the diversification of the portfolio. All of our valuation work is applied to a universe (established annually) which consists of the 300 largest (based on revenues) companies headquartered in the United States that currently pay a dividend.

The multi-factor model comprises three sub-models which are weighted equally to arrive at a composite score. Those factors or sub-models are: (1) A dividend discount model driven by consensus estimates; (2) A price momentum model; and (3) A measure which combines earnings estimate revisions and earnings surprises. Each month we rank all 300 companies using this multi-factor model.

The portfolio comprises 50 stocks at all times, and holdings are approximately equally weighted (2% in each). This acts as a sell discipline since whenever we buy a new stock, a less attractive one must be sold. We begin with the top 50 stocks, and then make adjustments based on our portfolio rules. We will generally control our industry weightings in accordance with industry weightings defined by the S&P 500. We will also continue to hold a stock which ranks between 50 and 90 (that is in the top three deciles) even if another stock not owned ranks in the top 50.

The resulting portfolios have several consistent characteristics which are typical of value investing. We have an average Price/Earnings ratio lower than the S&P 500, a higher dividend yield, and generally a lower Price/Book Value ratio.

in a limited number of companies with low institutional ownership, its performance could be expected to deviate significantly from proxies for the "big cap" market, like the S&P 500.

In early January 1989 WJR's wide discount attracted Robert Gordon, president of Twenty-First Securities. Working through NAV Partners, Gordon attempted to open-end WJR by obtaining 35% of its shares prior to the 1989 annual meeting. The fund was able to prevail at the meeting by agreeing to open-end in June 1991. But Gordon told the authors that he would continue to buy shares, hoping to open-end it prior to that time. He said he was prepared to buy as much as 50.1% of the shares.

**Gabelli Equity Trust (NYSE: GAB)** Mario Gabelli's bottom-up style has its foundation in the philosophies of Ben Graham and Warren Buffett. Like Graham, Gabelli searches for companies selling at prices below intrinsic value and like Buffett he wants to take substantial positions in companies he likes.[3]

GAB is the largest non-diversified domestic equity fund ($590 million) and has a primary objective of long-term capital appreciation. Gabelli is a very talented analyst with a superior record. He frequently expresses his views in *Barron's* and other prominent publications. Gabelli selects investments on the basis of fundamental value, that is, priced lower than justified by their assets. GAB also invests in securities that it sees as special situations such as mergers, possible liquidations, reorganizations, and possible changes in management.

Gabelli, who just buys domestic stocks, is good at spotting unfolding trends early and takes big positions in stocks he likes. Gabelli's goal is to have his stocks appreciate 50% in two years. GAB follows the set 10% payout of NAV each year. When examining his fund's portfolio of about 100 stocks you'll see that he holds a few positions in other closed-end funds including Growth Stock Outlook Trust, Morgan Grenfell SMALLCap Fund and Royce Value Trust. By dialing an 800 number you can obtain a daily NAV and share price on GAB.

**Growth Stock Outlook Trust (NYSE: GSO)** This fund is run by Charles Allmon, founder of Growth Stock

Outlook, a newsletter started in 1965 specializing in small, lesser-known companies. Allmon, who describes himself as "a contrarian, value-oriented investor" held a few large cap companies at this writing because, in addition to being positive on their outlook, he is concerned about liquidity. Since 1987 Allmon has been looking for a downswing in the market; the 1987 crash wasn't deep enough nor did it last long enough for him.

Allmon's conservative philosophy is evident from the following passages in his 1988 Annual Report:

> Warren Buffet, whom I consider the finest investor of the past 30 years, reportedly has two cardinal rules for successful investing. Rule number one: Don't lose any money. Rule number two: Don't forget rule number one. It is easy enough to lose your capital in an investment of almost any kind. For many years I have stated that the most important aspect of successful long-term investing is not how much you make in a bull market, but how much you avoid losing in a bear market.
>
> Let me give you a startling example. Many investors lost 15% of their capital in 1987. Therefore they must gain 17.6% in 1988 simply to get even. Let's assume that they wanted to see a modest 9% return on their capital for both 1987 and 1988. What must happen in 1988? They must gain 40% in one year to realize that two-year 9% rate of return. That simply is not in the cards, unless you are a riverboat gambler and roll dice on full margin, or play the options/futures crapshoot. Neither is a reasonable choice for thinking investors.

At this writing Allmon's portfolio remains nearly 80 percent in cash although he is bullish for the 1990s. The balance of the portfolio consists of over 80 companies, the majority of which are small, over-the-counter stocks. GSO can invest up to 15% of net assets in foreign securities and is expanding its foreign holdings. "Just as the 1980s was the decade of the Pacific Rim countries, the 1990s could be the decade of Europe," wrote Allmon in GSO's 1989 Annual Report.

GSO has repurchased a considerable amount of its

own shares in the open market because Allmon feels they represent good value. Allmon, who owns a substantial proportion of GSO shares himself, feels that too few managers have significant ownership positions in their funds. They should share the risks and rewards of the fund along with the investors.

**The Inefficient-Market Fund (Amex: IMF)** The newest of the personality funds, IMF went public in January, 1990 with a relatively small offering of 1 million shares at $12 each. Smith Barney is the adviser. To our knowledge, IMF was the first personality fund to come out since the 1987 crash.

IMF is non-diversified and has long-term capital appreciation as its objective. Most good money managers presumably are constantly on the lookout for market inefficiencies or undervalued securities. That's the name of the game! This fund apparently makes a special effort in that regard. According to its prospectus, IMF invests in companies with market caps of less than $500 million which it feels are mispriced. The adviser looks for stocks with relatively low price/earnings or price/cash flow ratios which are neglected—that is, underowned by institutions and underfollowed by analysts. IMF could use leverage, short selling, and options and futures, although it expects to use these techniques to a limited degree if at all. Starting in 1991 it will follow the popular 10% payout policy.

**Liberty All-Star Equity Fund (NYSE: USA)** Liberty All-Star of Boston with offices in Westport, Connecticut, is headed by Richard Roberts. It is managed by five outside advisers in what is known as a "multi-manager" or "All-Star" concept of portfolio management. This is common practice among pension fund managers, but is new to the investment company industry.

Multi-management is a total return concept according to which the fund hires more than one adviser, in this case five, to utilize various investment styles. All-Star has three value managers—Cooke & Bieler, Newbold's Asset Management, and Oppenheimer Capital—and two growth stock firms—Phoenix Investment Counsel, and Provident Investment Counsel. Each manages one-fifth (at this writing about $100 million) of the total portfolio. Cooke &

Bieler invest in stocks of small and medium-sized companies; Newbold's invests in larger companies. Oppenheimer Capital recently replaced Dreman Value Management. Based upon a group effort, Oppenheimer seeks companies it feels are undervalued because they are out-of-favor or overlooked. In the growth area, Phoenix likes moderate-size, moderately-priced companies while Provident seeks faster growing companies with smaller capitalizations.

Professor J. Peter Williamson of Dartmouth College's Amos Tuck School of Business Administration has conducted a study which confirms the advantages of multi-management. Williamson comments on his study in All-Star's 1989 Annual Report. Here are excerpts:

> The most obvious argument for multiple management is the same as the argument for including more than one stock in a portfolio: the risk reduction from diversification almost always outweighs the expected benefit from choosing the apparently best stock and betting 100% on it.
>
> The argument, essentially, says that entrusting the fund to a single manager, no matter how carefully that manager is chosen, is simply too risky.
>
> My examination of the performances one might expect from different styles of management, and the performances one might expect of different managers within a single style, suggested significant opportunities for diversification benefits when more than one manager is selected to take charge of an actively managed equity fund.

All-Star's portfolio is periodically "rebalanced." The process entails reallocating funds among managers so as to maintain equality in the amount of assets managed by each, irrespective of their performances. During the first six months of 1993 a meeting of shareholders will be called to vote on whether or not to convert All-Star to an open-end fund. A simple majority would be required to open-end the fund at that time.

Critics feel that the multi-management system leads to high expenses for an investment company and that the individual would be better served by investing in different funds managed by individuals with different styles.[4] Our viewpoint is that even though a fund may have a relatively high expense ratio it can still be a good buy if the discount is wide enough, you like the concept, and its performance has been good. All-Star's expense ratio has declined steadily since inception—it was 1.25% in 1989 versus 1.92% in 1987. All-Star makes cash distributions at the annual rate of 10% of NAV. Over 23% of its shares are held by institutions (Table 6-1).

**Morgan Grenfell SMALLCap Fund (NYSE: MGC)** is a diversified fund seeking capital appreciation through investments in companies with market capitalizations of $50 million to $500 million. Morgan Grenfell Capital Management, Inc., the adviser, is a U.S. subsidiary of London-based Morgan Grenfell Group PLC. Deutsche Bank AG, the largest bank in Germany, recently became the parent of Morgan Grenfell Group PLC.

Companies in an early stage of their growth cycles are sought. Robert Kern, president of MGC, finds his investments by screening a universe of 1,700 U.S. companies and narrows the field to 500 stocks to be monitored and followed closely by his team of five analysts/portfolio managers who specialize by economic sector. From this larger group, investments in about 60 companies are made. Kern stresses that each of his managers has a significant stake in the fund. He believes that the historic higher rates of return achieved by investing in small companies will allow MGC to outperform the large cap universe over the long term. According to a recent proxy statement, Yale University holds over 12 percent of the outstanding shares of MGC.

MGC has a relatively high expense ratio (Table 6-1) but, as can be seen in the statement of operations in its annual reports, interest on the loan from its adviser to cover its underwriting discount has a significant impact on the expense ratio. The $3,625,000 loan in May 1987 enabled MGC to invest the full $50 million gross proceeds of the offering.

**Nicholas-Applegate Growth Equity Fund (NYSE: GEF)** GEF is a diversified fund with the objective of capital appreciation. GEF's investment adviser is Nicholas-

Applegate Capital Management, a California limited partnership, which manages about $2 billion in assets. Arthur Nicholas is the principal architect of the adviser's growth equity management approach.

This fund invests in growth stocks the earnings and prices of which its adviser expects to grow at a rate in excess of the rate of the S&P 500. GEF invests in companies with market caps over $500 million and it may invest in convertible securities and foreign securities. "We utilize a bottom-up investment approach seeking 30 to 50 companies that are generating strong earnings gains and exhibiting strong relative price strength," says Fred Applegate, GEF's president.

The fund's investment approach may result in greater risk and a relatively high portfolio turnover. For the years ended December 31, 1988 and 1989 the turnover numbers were 183% and 120%, respectively. Management fees are based on performance and can range between 0.5% to 1.00% per annum depending on GEF's performance relative to the S&P 500. The fund also uses leverage and the resulting interest cost increases the expense ratio. In 1989 the ratio of total expenses to net assets was 4.55% whereas the ratio before interest and loan fees was 1.14%. GEF offers shareholders daily recorded phone messages reporting its NAV, share price, industry concentrations, and the extent, if any, to which it is leveraged. GEF had a shareholder rights offering in 1990. Over 20% of GEF's shares are held by institutions (Table 6–1).

**Royce Value Trust (NYSE: RVT)** This is a diversified fund holding close to 300 issues. Its objective is long-term capital appreciation through investment in the common stocks of small and medium-sized companies using a value approach. Charles Royce buys companies whose market capitalizations are between $15 million and $300 million. His value philosophy was explained in the Closed-End Insights box in Chapter 4. RVT has repurchased its shares from time to time, especially when the discount has widened. We like this policy.

Quest Advisory is the fund's adviser. Established in 1967 by Charles Royce, Quest manages over $1 billion for pension funds, endowments, and two open-end funds. The organization's philosophy for all its accounts is value oriented, focusing on the small company sector.

Royce does not like the idea of the 10% payout which has become so popular among newer CEFs. You should pay out what you earn, not just an amount dictated by a formula, Royce told us. He feels that the 10% payout policy has gained more popularity than it deserves. Royce also told us that he does not believe in anti takeover provisions and, consequently, RVT has no built-in takeover impediments.

Royce has a dividend distribution policy which is different from the usual CEF plan. Essentially, new shares are issued to those reinvesting rather than shares which have previously been repurchased by the fund in the open market. According to Royce, the purpose of issuing new rather than repurchased shares is to encourage shareholders to participate in the dividend reinvestment plan, thereby compounding their returns over the years. Royce told us that 85% of the shareholders reinvest their distributions in RVT shares. Since not all shareholders reinvest, however, RVT's policy may result in a small amount of dilution to those who take their dividends in cash, as explained in a Dominick & Dominick research report. However, the dilution has been less than 1% since RVT's inception.[5]

In August 1989 RVT offered its shareholders the right to subscribe to additional common shares of the fund through a rights offering. The purpose of the rights offering was to give the long-term shareholder the right to purchase additional shares at a price below market value. It served as a dollar cost averaging tool for the shareholder, an option typically not afforded the traditional one-time buyer of a closed-end fund.

RVT has an incentive fee formula. The base management fee is 1% per annum. Subject to two conditions the fee can be increased (to 1.5%) or decreased (to 0.5%) based on the fund's performance relative to the S&P 500. The formula is explained in detail in a note in RVT's annual and semi-annual reports. The fee will be waived if the fund shows absolute negative returns over any performance period.

**Z-Seven Fund (NASDAQ: ZSEV; Pacific Stock Exchange: ZSE)** Introduced in late 1983 by Barry Ziskin, Z-Seven was the first of the personality funds of the 1980s. Ziskin has received a lot of coverage in the financial press.[6] His annual reports go into considerable detail about Z-Seven, its philosophy and current holdings. The fund is now headquartered in Ziskin's home in Mesa, Arizona.

Ziskin has a bottom-up approach incorporating both value and growth investment philosophies. He uses seven criteria in selecting stocks. The most important of these, he feels, deals with the company's accounting procedures. "Companies must not defer operating expenses or prematurely realize revenues and must have an auditor's report on financial statements that is unqualified in all material respects," states Ziskin in Z-Seven's 1989 Annual Report.

Ziskin has applied his criteria since 1973. Finding stocks which satisfy all seven criteria can be difficult. Ziskin analyzes more than 14,000 companies throughout the developed world in search for those which meet the criteria. At this writing, he sees value in the United Kingdom and, accordingly, has deployed a large percentage of his assets in that area. Z-Seven is really a global fund since it can invest anywhere, although in its earlier years it invested mainly in domestic equities. Its foreign holdings increased dramatically in 1989 and it holds nearly 50 positions in Europe.

As Z-Seven is the oldest of the personality funds we will examine its yearly performance relative to the S&P 500 without dividends (see Table 6–2). Z-Seven experienced superior performance in 1985 and, especially, in 1986 but since has lagged the market. Ziskin feels confident its performance will improve with its portfolio of recently acquired foreign stocks.

The fund is small, with $18 million in assets, and has a unique bonus/penalty management fee structure as explained in Chapter 3. Ziskin owns about 22% of its outstanding shares. ZSEV repurchases its own shares in the

**Table 6–2. Z-Seven Performance Relative to S&P 500**

| Year | Z-Seven NAV* | S&P 500 |
|------|--------------|---------|
| 1984 | − 5.70% | + 1.40% |
| 1985 | +37.13 | +26.33 |
| 1986 | +41.40 | +14.62 |
| 1987 | − 2.60 | + 2.03 |
| 1988 | + 1.01 | +13.59 |
| 1989 | − 4.33 | +25.91 |

*NAV adjusted for tax credit/refund 1986-present and distributions in 1989.
Source: The Z-Seven Fund, Inc.

open market from time to time. The fund tends to trade close to NAV or at a premium. Ziskin feels that closed-end funds that are well managed should sell at premiums. Not all would agree, of course.[7] His views are expressed in the Closed-End Insights box.

---

**BARRY ZISKIN'S VIEWS
ON CEF VALUATION
Barry Ziskin
President
The Z-Seven Fund, Inc.**

Most people who, over recent years, have been developing a better understanding of publicly-traded investment companies, have been focusing in on the investment company aspect and relating it to buying "mutual funds" (which this vehicle is not). What all too often is forgotten is the publicly-traded aspect of this hybrid vehicle. Like all companies listed on the NYSE (and traded elsewhere), publicly-traded investment companies shares go up or down depending upon supply and demand. In this way, the shareholder of a publicly-traded investment company benefits doubly by good performance from the portfolio manager much the same way as would a shareholder of any public company in any other industry. Good management in any industry increases the underlying value of the assets and profits and, by so doing, makes its limited supply of shares more attractive to investors. Thus, the double play. Any company, regardless of whether it makes widgets, or furniture, or jet engines, or investments that can offer a high return on assets over the long-term, justifies a share price which reflects this ability to grow. That's just common investment sense.

Today, all too many individuals and institutions are short-term traders. Long-term investors in Berkshire Hathaway, however, have had the last laugh . . . all the way to the bank. The shares of this truly great investment/holding company have risen from $12 apiece to over $8,000 over the past twenty or so years. While Mario Gabelli, Erik Bergstrom, Nick Bratt, Charles Royce, John Templeton, George Michaelis, Charles Allmon, John Neff, myself, and others may have to take a back seat to Warren Buffett, the greatest investor of the past quarter century, we still represent some of the best potential for growth through the next several years. Yet, somehow, investors today would rather pay 2 1/2 times NAV (book value) for a stodgy group of Dow Industrials than to pay NAV or slightly higher for some of the best managed publicly-traded companies in any business around today. Obviously, over time, this inefficient disparity will be resolved by the marketplace. Long-term investors with vision will be particularly well-rewarded.

**The Zweig Fund (NYSE: ZF)** The Zweig Fund and its sister fund **The Zweig Total Return Fund (NYSE: ZTR)** are personality funds managed by Dr. Martin Zweig, the well-known investment adviser and publisher of *The Zweig Forecast*. Zweig has an outstanding long-term performance record which has been well documented by publications such as *The Hulbert Financial Digest*. In 1989 Martin Zweig acquired a family of open-end funds which he now also manages.

The Zweig Fund, an equity fund that dabbles in bonds, has an objective of capital appreciation consistent with capital preservation and elimination of unnecessary risk. The Zweig Total Return Fund is a combination bond and equity fund and will be described in Chapter 14 "Bond Fund Types and Their Characteristics." ZF was the first CEF to establish a telephone hotline for investors. A prerecorded message provides NAV, share price, current portfolio highlights, and other information updated weekly.

ZF can use hedging vehicles, such as stock index futures, options, and short sales of stock to help it achieve its objectives. "I want all the tools so that we can always move towards liquidity or, if we're sitting with a lot of cash, so we can get in the market," Zweig told us. He uses stock index futures fairly often. Being able to short S&P stock index futures was vitally important to Zweig in the crash of 1987. ZF almost always has some short sales in individual stocks the adviser doesn't like. Its 1989 Annual Report reflected short positions in 14 stocks (about 3.2 percent of net assets).

Unlike many other CEF managers, Zweig's major concern is not what stocks to buy, but, rather, to what extent he should be invested in the market. The Fund diversifies widely in order to participate in market movements—25 sectors were represented in its portfolio at year-end 1989. ZF has a high portfolio turnover rate; it averaged over 200% per year for the three years ended December 31, 1989.

The fund traded at discounts to NAV during its earlier years but more recently has traded at significant premiums. Zweig attributes this change in valuation in part to his active marketing efforts which include conference calls with brokerage firms, seminars, the weekly telephone hotline, and newspaper adds. Zweig feels that you need the marketing for closed-end as well as open-end funds. He adds that lack of communication with shareholders and the brokerage community could result in a wide discount and having to fend off raiders.

Another factor which contributed to the narrowing of ZF's discount was the institution of the policy of distributing 10% of NAV annually (paid quarterly) to shareholders. By the spring of 1987 the discount got as wide as 17 percent but within a week after the policy was started it had narrowed to single digits said Zweig. Finally, ZF may repurchase its shares in the open market when the discount is 10 percent or greater.

Zweig explains his risk-averse investment philosophy in the Closed-End Insights box.

---

## DR. ZWEIG'S INVESTMENT PHILOSOPHY
### Dr. Martin E. Zweig
### President
### The Zweig Total Return Advisors, Inc.

My basic investment philosophy is to be risk averse. To my way of thinking, the most important investment decision is not necessarily which stocks or bonds to buy but whether or not to be invested in the markets and, if so, to what extent.

Market timing is the key. Here I employ stock and bond market-timing techniques that I have developed over a period of 28 years and continue to refine to meet changing market conditions. I measure risk by examining four main factors.

The first covers monetary conditions, to which I give the most weight (50%). Here I track the trend of interest rates, monetary policy, and loan demand. I look for the level of liquidity in the overall system. When that liquidity is low, when the Federal Reserve is tightening, it is usually a period of high risk in the stock and bond markets. When rates are low and the Fed is loosening, it is usually a low-risk period.

My second concern is with sentiment indicators, which get 25% weight. These measure crowd psychology and, ultimately, liquidity in the stock market itself. The aim there is to discover where investors have their cash. If most investors are bearish, it means that they have already done their selling and that cash has been built up on the sidelines, which usually points to low risk. If people are too optimistic and have already committed their cash reserves, it usually means low liquidity and high risk.

The third area, to which I give 10% weight, covers valuation in the market, where I look at price/earnings ratios, book value, and similar financial data. Obviously, cheaper markets have lower risk than markets that are overpriced.

Finally, for stocks and bonds I look at the momentum of the market itself, which gets the remaining 15% weight. Believing that "the trend is your friend," I like to stay in gear with the direction of the market. The risk I take is that I might get "whipsawed" if short-term trends change quickly. But by riding with the long-term trend, I actually lower my risk because I am forced to cut back if the market itself starts to behave poorly.

As investment manager, my primary objective is to preserve capital. Small losses are manageable, large losses can be insurmountable. It is a matter of simple arithmetic. Should you lose 20% on a stock, you must earn 25% to recoup. Should you lose 50%, you must make 100% to break even. But if you were to lose 90%, say by riding a stock down from 100 to 10, you would require a tenfold increase, and that is almost impossible.

I don't like to lose money so I try to be very protective in bear markets. If I am going to make a mistake, I would prefer that it be made by holding too much cash and watching the market go up, rather than holding too much stock and seeing the market go down.

To my mind, the only consistent way to beat the market in the long run is to cut losses, run with profits, and never fight the "tape." I move assets from stocks and/or bonds to money market securities or other cash equivalents as my market-timing models indicate a rising level of risk. When my indicators point to declining risk, I increase exposure to stocks and/or bonds.

Summing up, by making a reasonable return during bull markets and holding onto the bulk of the money during bear markets, I hope to achieve above average results for investors over the long term—and with less risk.

## SELECTION GUIDELINES

When selecting a stock fund it is well to bear in mind the following guidelines:

1.  Avoid buying new CEFs. It has been documented that closed-end equity funds bought at a premium to NAV during an initial public offering experience poor performance relative to the overall equity market and to seasoned funds.[8] Basically, the shares move from a premium over NAV to a discount.[9] Our advice is to be patient. Wait and buy at a discount.

2.  Look for funds that have attractive discounts first. But don't just buy because of the discount; there is always a reason and the deeper discounts may reflect poor performance. With well-run funds, discounts of 12% or more can give your returns a significant boost. At this writing the classic older funds have the widest discounts among the domestic equity funds, ranging as high as 20%.

3.  The best time of the year to buy funds is always in December. During tax-selling season investors, particularly in new funds, are dumping at any price. It is the best bargain hunting time of the year. Other excellent times for bargain hunting would be in bear markets or after sizeable market declines, the best recent examples being October, 1987 and during the last half of 1990. The large market declines do not occur that often but when they do they offer fantastic opportunities for value hunters.

4.  Determine who the fund manager is. To what extent is this person involved in the day-to-day decisions of managing the portfolio? If the management is new you would want to see a record of past performance. Make sure the fund manager's philosophy agrees with your own— particularly regarding the degree of risk he is willing to assume. Management's capability is especially important with non-diversified funds since they can be more volatile because of concentrated positions.

5.  Study the manager's thinking process as revealed by his discussion in the annual report. The annual reports of some CEFs are especially detailed and well prepared. Examples are those written by George Michaelis of Source Capital and Charles Allmon of Growth Stock Outlook

Trust. Of course, a brief annual report cannot be interpreted as a bad sign.

6. Examine the fund's portfolio. Determine the percentages it has invested in different industries. Look at its
ten largest positions. Are there any non-U.S. investments?
Make sure you like the industries and stocks the fund
manager invests in.

7. Past performance, although not necessarily indicative of future performance, is most important. But, there
is one problem. It is hard to find funds with outstanding
records that trade at discounts. CEFs with superb histo-
ries like Bergstrom and Source tend to trade at premiums.

In any event, look at the fund's past performance in
different market environments and relative to other comparable funds. Particularly helpful in this regard are the
*Forbes* ratings of fund performance during up and down
markets. Also study the annual performance data contained in Wiesenberger for as many years as it is available.
This way you can tell how consistent a fund's performance has been.

Performance data may not be available on all the
CEFs you are interested in. Generally, the larger and older
the CEF the easier it is to find performance data. You can
keep track of virtually all CEFs in which you are interested, however, by tracking the most recent year's performance reported in *Forbes* each year. For older funds
you will find long-term performance data there as well.

Professional investors who subscribe to the *Lipper
Closed-End Bond Funds Analysis* and *Lipper Closed-End
Equity Funds Analysis* know that they are the most comprehensive, timely sources of performance data on closed-
end funds. These publications provide net asset value as
well as market value performance data over various periods. We find Lipper's extensive performance data very
useful.

8. The authors like funds that repurchase their own
shares, other things equal. This information can be found
in the fund's shareholder reports. We also like funds
where the management holds a significant percentage of
the outstanding stock. Insider ownership can be found in
a recent proxy statement or by asking the fund.

9. Look carefully before investing in funds with excessive expense ratios relative to their peers. High expenses deplete your returns. Funds with high expense ratios may be acceptable though, if the discount is wide enough to compensate for the higher costs. Study the fund's expense ratio over several years using S&P *Stock Reports.*

10. Look carefully before investing in funds with excessive portfolio turnover relative to their peers. High turnover translates into high transaction costs which are borne by fund shareholders. Again, study the fund's turnover over several years using S&P's *Stock Reports.*

11. One last note for sophisticated bargain hunters willing to do some extra digging: Don't forget that the discount is all important, but not a tail that wags the dog. But in some cases an excessively wide discount could represent an opportunity even though the CEF may have had problems like a volatile past performance or high expenses.

Ron Olin, president of Deep Discount Advisors, which specializes in quantitative analysis of closed-end funds, feels that the discount is the *most important* variable closed-end investors have to work with. According to Olin, it is even more important than a fund's management and past performance. Olin is very good at selecting funds which later open-end and takes this possibility into consideration when choosing funds. He offers his views in the Closed-End Insights box.

---

### DISCOUNTS VERSUS NAV PERFORMANCE
### Ronald G. Olin
### President
### Deep Discount Advisors

The primary characteristic that distinguishes closed-end funds from their open-end counterparts is the existence of premiums and discounts. If that factor were removed, purchase and sale decisions would be based on the same considerations as for regular mutual funds: expected NAV performance and expenses. The relative importance of the discount in overall investment returns is crucial to analysis of closed-end funds.

## REALITIES OF PROJECTING PERFORMANCE

Most people believe that if you are smart enough, you can pick stocks or bonds that will perform better than the overall markets. Many also believe that smart people can time their purchases and sales so as to outperform a simple buy-and-hold approach. This follows naturally from our experience in most aspects of life, and seems logical. However, an impressive body of evidence suggests that for most investment professionals the expenses of research and transaction costs more than eliminate any small advantage their specialized knowledge may give them over the markets. Year after year, the indexes outperform all but a few of the professionals. Over long periods of time, professional money managers who can outperform the appropriate indexes, adjusted for risk, are very rare indeed. Furthermore, the degree by which the best beat the market can be measured in the range of 2% to 4% a year compounded. This is a very impressive accomplishment, but is much less in magnitude than generally believed. Added difficulty arises in that it is only after the fact that we know which money managers were the best. Past performance is not necessarily indicative of future returns.

Picking closed-end funds based on past performance is no better or worse than picking open-end funds or individual stocks or market sectors based on past performance. That is to say, as much fun as it is, it is of questionable economic value. It certainly is not a reason to focus on closed-end funds as an investment vehicle of choice.

## WHAT DO DISCOUNTS BUY YOU?

Discounts in closed-end funds present a unique opportunity in the investment markets. If you buy a fund at a 20% discount and never sell it, the dividends and capital gains distributions will be 25% higher than an identical open-end fund or managed portfolio. Unless the investment performance or expenses are extremely unreasonable, in the long run you will do better than a similar investment in an index with no expenses. Furthermore, if the discount narrows or disappears and you sell it to buy another discounted fund, you will do even better. These combined effects have been shown conclusively in a number of studies to provide one of the few bona fide ways of beating the markets. Historical evidence has shown the added returns that are available to be in excess of the 2% to 4% reward for having the ability to pick the Warren Buffett, John Neff, or Peter Lynch of the next generation.

The rewards for focusing on discounts and discount reduction in closed-end funds are so important that the added effects of trying to project performance are not worthwhile. Such projections are so unreliable that their use will cost more in missed discount opportunities than they will add in extra NAV performance.

## FUTURE VERSUS PAST DISCOUNTS

With the added focus on closed-end funds in recent years, the era of plentiful 20% to 30% discounts may be behind us forever. While this may spell reduced opportunity for some of the more simple approaches in exploiting discounts, the vast increase in quantity and variety of closed-end funds in recent years has actually increased opportunities. Sophisticated approaches to exploiting discounts rely more on the timing and nature of discount reduction than on the simple magnitude of the discount. Over time, it is far more valuable to exploit a 5% or so discount reduction in the several months before a fund liquidates or open-ends than it is to buy a fund at a 20% discount and wait for the discount to narrow by some unknown time in the future. Various discount reduction provisions in a large number of the newer funds provide the greatest set of opportunities yet available in closed-ends.

## CONCLUSION

The personality funds can be especially attractive if you're able to get them at discounts of 10% or more. Buying them at or near NAV does not offer you any value. In that case you're essentially betting that the fund manager will continue to deliver superior performance.

You may wish to select several domestic equity funds so as to diversify among managers and management styles—this is especially true if you want to include some non-diversified funds in your portfolio. This will help you hedge against the risk of picking a fund that turns out to be the worst performer in its group. But, don't overdiversify.

### Notes

[1]Dual purpose equity funds and sector equity funds which came to market in the 1980s will be identified in their respective chapters.

[2]See Ellen Benoit, "The Family that Buys Families," *Financial World*, June 30, 1987, pp. 24–28.

[3]Julie Rohrer, "What makes Mario run?," *Institutional Investor*, March 1989, p. 101.

[4]Benjamin J. Stein, "Throwing Shareholders a Curve: Why One Closed-End Fund Was No Big Hit With Investors," *Barron's*, March 7, 1988, p. 42.

[5]Dan O'Neill, Tony Russ, and Whitney George, "Royce Value Trust," Dominick & Dominick, 90 Broad Street, New York, New York 10004. September 11, 1989, pp. 3–4.

[6]See, e.g., Stephen Taub, "The Odyssey of Barry Ziskin," *Financial World*, August 5, 1986, pp. 100–101.

[7]David Schiff, "The Z-Seven Fund: Promises, Promises, Promises," *Barron's*, February 13, 1989, pp. 65–67.

[8]See John W. Peavy III, "Closed-End Fund IPOs: Caveat Emptor," *Financial Analysts Journal*, May–June, 1989, pp. 71–75. We also refer the reader to the Weiss article cited in Chapter 1 (footnote 14).

[9]Exceptions are some of the highly popular country funds.

# CHAPTER 7

# *Dual Purpose Funds*

During the "go-go" years on Wall Street, which began in the mid-1960s, investor interest was running high in equities and mutual funds were chalking up dramatic performances. In 1967 seven dual purpose funds (or dual funds) were offered: American DualVest, Gemini Fund, Hemisphere Fund, Income and Capital Shares, Leverage Fund of Boston, Putnam Duofund, and Scudder Duo-Vest. This seemed logical at a point when people were looking for high appreciation since dual funds offer plenty of leverage. These funds, which are a special type of CEF, were eventually redeemed in the late 1970s and early 1980s.

Although dual funds are somewhat esoteric and don't have the wide investor appeal of the conventional CEF, no book on the subject would be complete without addressing them. This is the most technical chapter in the book due to the somewhat greater complexity of this small group of CEFs.

## THE DUAL FUND CONCEPT
## WAS DUSTED OFF

Since there was considerable interest in closed-end funds
in the 1980s, the dual fund concept was dusted off and six
of them were offered beginning with Gemini II in 1985.
One of these, Global Growth and Income Fund (managed
by First Boston Asset Management Corporation) was liquidated in the summer of 1989 at the request of its largest
shareholder, Nikko Securities Co. Nikko and its Japanese clients were dissatisfied with the performance of
the fund's capital shares versus the income shares and
wanted to liquidate their ownership position at a minimum loss. Nikko, which held about 83% of the capital
shares, felt that the fund's portfolio favored the income
shares over the capital shares.

   We'll introduce the individual funds after examining
the characteristics of dual funds in general beginning with
a description of the underlying logic.


## DUAL FUND BASICS

Dual funds were originally conceived as a means to split
the attributes of equity investing between the objectives
of income on the one hand and capital appreciation on the
other. Basically, a traditional dual fund has two classes of
stock:

   1. **Income (or preferred) shares** carry a cumula-
      tive dividend and are entitled to 100% of the in-
      come earned on the entire portfolio but do not
      share in any of the fund's capital appreciation.
      The income shares are redeemed at a predeter-
      mined future date. All fund expenses are passed
      on to the income shares.

   2. **Capital (or common) shares** receive all capital
      appreciation or depreciation. The amount, if
      any, to which the capital shares are entitled

would be determined when the income shares are redeemed. The capital shareholders do not receive any income but bear none of the fund's expenses.

The total market value of the fund equals the sum of the market values of the income and the capital shares.

Dual fund portfolios are generally similar to those of ordinary closed- and open-end funds and contain many familiar securities. But, in all cases the portfolio of a dual fund is made up of securities with both income and growth potential geared to meeting the requirements of both groups of shareholders. The fund is managed to achieve its dual investment objectives—not to maximize either capital appreciation or income growth.

## The Leverage Factor

By splitting a common stock portfolio into both income and capital components, both kinds of shares become leveraged. Dual funds usually begin with a 2 to 1 leverage factor. Effectively, this puts twice as much money to work for the income or capital shareholder as was initially invested by that class of shareholder. The leverage will change over time as the underlying share prices and NAVs change. Assume a new fund raises $100 million net of underwriting fees. It issues 5 million income shares at $10 for a total of $50 million and 5 million capital shares at $10 for a second $50 million. The leverage factor is expressed as follows:

$$\text{Leverage} = \frac{\text{Value of Fund}}{\text{Value of Capital Shares}}$$

$$\text{Leverage} = \frac{\$100 \text{ million}}{\$50 \text{ million}} = 2$$

If the $100 million portfolio yields 4% the income shares would earn 8% because they benefit from 2:1 leverage. The arithmetic works out as follows: 4% of the $100 million portfolio yields $4 million. Divide this by the $50 million value of the income component and you get 8%. Following the same logic, if the portfolio advances 10% the capital shares would gain 20%. If the portfolio drops 10% in value the capital shares would fall 20%.

## Maturity Date

The income shares of all dual funds mature on a specific date, usually ten to twelve years after the initial offering. At that time they would be entitled to their NAV which is usually the same as, or very near, the NAV at the offering date. The NAV of the income shares at any time is equal to the lesser of the following two amounts:

1.  Their initial NAV plus accumulated and unpaid net income. This is the value which would normally be appropriate.

2.  The total net assets of the CEF divided by the number of income shares outstanding. This second number would be the relevant one only if there has been a drastic decline in the value of the fund's portfolio.

The income shares will generally have 200% asset coverage at the CEF's inception, that is, total assets will then equal two times their redemption value. Thus, they are virtually guaranteed a return of principal unless the market value of the portfolio drops by more than 50%. However, should the fund's assets be insufficient to pay the income shares, the proceeds to which they are entitled, the total net assets would be distributed pro-rata to the income shareholders.

The capital shares would be entitled to what's left over after the income shares are satisfied. The NAV of the capital shares is equal to the net assets of the fund minus net assets attributable to the income shares, divided by the number of capital shares outstanding. This is illustrated in Table 7–1 where it is assumed that the initial

**Table 7–1. Dual Fund Values at Termination**

| Net Assets of Fund (Millions) | Net Assets of Income Shares (Millions) | Net Assets of Capital Shares (Millions) | NAV of Capital Shares |
|---|---|---|---|
| $ 40 | $40 | $ 0 | $ 0 |
| 50 | 50 | 0 | 0 |
| 75 | 50 | 25 | 5 |
| 100 | 50 | 50 | 10 |
| 150 | 50 | 100 | 20 |
| 200 | 50 | 150 | 30 |

assets of the fund were $100 million ($50 million income plus $50 million capital shares). There are 5 million income shares and 5 million capital shares.

As seen in Table 7–1, the income shareholders collectively receive $40 million if the net assets of the fund are $40 million. This translates into a per share value of $8 ($40 million divided by 5 million shares). Thus, they don't get their original investment back since the portfolio value of the fund has declined by 60% from its original $100 million. On the other hand, if the total value of the fund at termination is $50 million the income shareholders will get back their NAV of $10 per share. This is the most they can receive no matter how high the portfolio value of the fund is.

If the value of the fund exceeds the $50 million to which the income shareholders are entitled the balance goes to the capital shares as seen in Table 7–1. For instance, if the value of the fund equals $150 million the capital shareholders would be entitled to $100 million or an NAV of $20 based on their 5 million shares.

At the time of redemption of the income shares the fund may either be liquidated, converted to an open-end fund, or continue as an ordinary CEF. Because of the known maturity date on the income shares and the potential for the capital shares to liquidate or open-end the fund, any discount to NAV will ultimately disappear. This is an advantage that the dual fund structure offers and any discount will tend to lessen or turn to a premium as maturity nears.

## Growth in Income

The income shares resemble an intermediate-term bond since they have a specific maturity date and a known redemption price. These shares also have a fixed minimum annual dividend payment, but if the fund earns more than that minimum they would receive the excess—so there is potential for growth in income. This is what the prospective income shareholder would be looking for. The income shares should be evaluated on an expected yield to maturity (YTM) basis rather than on a current yield basis (which would simply be the indicated annual dividend divided by the present market price as reported by the financial press).

Thus, a major difference between the dividends from the income shares of a dual fund and the interest payments from a bond is that the former may experience growth. This is because the fund management could invest in common stocks with yields of, say, 3% or 4%, where the dividends would be expected to increase over the years. Even though a bond might yield more, say, 8%, there would be no growth in income. The proper evaluation of a dual fund would involve an analysis of various possible yields to maturity resulting from different assumed growth rates in the dividend stream. An example of this appears in Table 7-2.

In this illustration it is assumed that the income shares of a dual fund with ten years till redemption trade at a price equal to their NAV of 10. The dividend starts out at 80 cents and dividends are paid once a year. Various dividend growth rates ranging from 0% to 10% are used. The NAV at the redemption date of the income shares is also 10. If the dividend stays constant at 80 cents (0% growth rate) the investor would realize a YTM of 8%. The higher the dividend growth rate, the higher the potential YTM. Thus, if dividends grow at 10% per annum the YTM works out to 12.77%. Of course, the price paid for the income shares will also have an impact on the YTM. If the income shares are purchased at a discount the YTM would be higher.

**Table 7–2. Prospective Income Share Returns**

| Dividend Growth | YTM |
|---|---|
| 0% | 8.00% |
| 2 | 8.81 |
| 4 | 9.70 |
| 6 | 10.65 |
| 8 | 10.86 |
| 10 | 12.77 |

Assumptions:
1. Initial NAV = 10
2. Time horizon = 10 years
3. Initial dividend = 80 cents
4. Redemption price = 10

## POTENTIAL PITFALLS

One of the criticisms of the dual fund structure is that the portfolio has to meet the separate needs of two distinct types of investors: those looking for capital appreciation, and those looking for investment income. Thus, the fund is going to have to hold securities which simultaneously satisfy the needs of both groups of investors. ". . . dual-purpose funds are a fine but sad example of jacks-of-all-trades who are masters of none," wrote Thomas Herzfeld.[1] In a sense, the portfolio of a dual fund represents a compromise. However, despite this potential drawback, John Neff has managed to deliver stellar performance with the dual fund structure as you'll see.

One of the problems that dual funds tend to experience is that their capital shares can trade at excessively deep discounts. There are two reasons for this:

1. The capital shares of a traditional dual fund pay no dividend from investment income. Thus, there is considerably greater uncertainty associated with the distributions to the capital shares.

2.  The leverage of the capital shares introduces risk which could be considerable in a rapidly falling market.

## GAUGING DISCOUNTS AND PREMIUMS

The discounts and premiums for dual purpose funds appear along with the other publicly traded funds weekly. In most instances you would have a separate discount or premium for each class of stock. If one class of the stock didn't trade that week, however, its discount or premium would not be displayed.

There is some concern about the meaningfulness of the discount and premium data as reported. A *Forbes* article written by William Baldwin argued that reported discounts and premiums on dual fund income and capital shares assume that the fund will be liquidated tomorrow. "The capital shareholders don't own outright the property that is assigned to them in this calculation," wrote Baldwin. "They own only a remainderman's interest."[2]

For meaningful information, Baldwin and others recommend summing the NAVs and the prices of the income and capital shares and then calculating a discount (or premium) on the total fund. This figure is comparable to a reported discount or premium on an ordinary CEF.

## DUAL FUND ANALYSIS

A dual fund's discount and leverage can be analyzed weekly using data from the publicly-traded funds box. This is illustrated in Table 7–3 with data from the closed-end funds box in *Barron's* for Convertible Holdings, Gemini II, and Quest for Value Dual Purpose Fund.

As seen in Table 7–3, Convertible Holdings and Quest for Value sold at overall discounts of 12.96% and 9.11%, respectively. Gemini II sold at a premium of 5.52%. These numbers tell you how the fund is valued overall. Our preference is to give the most weight to the total discount or premium of a dual fund but to also be aware of the historic

**Table 7–3. Discount/Premium and Leverage Analysis**

| Fund | NAV | Price | Discount/ Premium | Leverage |
|------|-----|-------|-------------------|----------|
| **Convertible Holdings:** | | | | |
| Capital shares | $ 9.64 | $ 5.125 | −46.84% | **1.98** |
| Income shares | 9.46 | 11.500 | +21.56 | **2.02** |
| **Total fund** | **19.10** | **16.625** | **−12.96** | |
| **Gemini II:** | | | | |
| Capital shares | 15.33 | 13.375 | −12.75 | **1.61** |
| Income shares | 9.31 | 12.625 | +35.61 | **2.65** |
| **Total fund** | **24.64** | **26.000** | **+ 5.52** | |
| **Quest for Value:** | | | | |
| Capital shares | 17.21 | 13.25 | −23.01 | **1.68** |
| Income shares | 11.67 | 13.00 | +11.40 | **2.47** |
| **Total fund** | **28.88** | **26.25** | **− 9.11** | |

Source: NAVs and prices from *Barron's*, February 12, 1990, p. 170.

ranges of the individual discounts and premiums on the income and capital shares.

Of course, you should try to buy dual funds at overall discounts which are at historically wide levels since this will enhance leverage and reduce risk. The ideal time to purchase the capital shares would be at the nadir of a bear market, especially if the overall fund is trading at a wide discount. During the ensuing bull market the capital shareholder would benefit from two forms of leverage: the leverage from the deep discount and the leverage from the dual fund structure.

You can also use the figures in Table 7–3 to calculate the leverage ratios for both the capital and income shares. For example, the leverage factor for the Gemini II capital shares is 1.61 (24.64 NAV of total fund divided by 15.33 NAV of capital shares) and for the Gemini II income shares it is 2.65 (24.64 divided by 9.31 NAV of income shares). All our computations assume an equal number of income and capital shares outstanding which was the case for the three funds analyzed here.

Ron Olin, president of Deep Discount Advisors, offers some important observations on dual fund evaluation in the Closed-End Insights box.

# DUAL PURPOSE FUND ANALYSIS
## Ronald G. Olin
## President
## Deep Discount Advisors

Arguably, the most complicated type of closed-end fund is the *Dual Purpose Fund.*

The Net Asset Value (NAV) reported for capital and income shares of dual purpose funds is the redemption or liquidation value that would be received if the fund were terminated today. Since the yields received by the income shareholder derive from the entire capitalization of the fund, they are generally much higher than one could receive from any equivalent risk investment of the reported income shareholder NAV. Therefore the redemption value which will be received many years in the future far understates the *current* investment value of the income share. Any added investment value which correspondingly accrues to the income share will detract from the investment value of the capital share, since the sum of any investment should not be greater than its parts. To say that a premium of 20% or 30% reported for an income share in the paper means it *is not* a good investment or that a 40% to 50% discount for the corresponding capital share *is* a good investment, for that reason alone, is just plain wrong!

Throughout their history, most income shares of dual funds have traded at significant premiums to their redemption value and most capital shares have traded at large discounts.

## OPTION THEORY

One of the most creditable approaches to dual fund analysis involves the recognition that the capital shares represent an option to buy the entire fund portfolio by redeeming the income shares at their fixed redemption price at a distinct time in the future. Established option formulas exist for evaluating such assets based on assumptions regarding portfolio volatility, interest rates, and future dividend payments. After using this approach to establish a value for the capital shares, the remaining value of the fund may be assigned to the income shares. This has been done in the past on a previous generation of dual funds and is currently being done by a few knowledgeable individuals today. The results fly in the face of conventional wisdom. They show that the large discounts on capital shares commonly observed and bemoaned by most observers of closed-end funds should generally be *much larger!* Correspondingly, the analysis shows the income shares to be largely underpriced most of the time, in spite of their premiums. Aside from factoring such important factors as interest rates and redemption timing into the analysis, this approach also implicitly takes the higher risk levels of the capital shares into consideration.

**PRESENT VALUE ANALYSIS**

Whereas the option analysis approach starts with capital share evaluation, another very creditable approach attempts to evaluate the net present value of the future cash stream of the income shares. This is similar to standard yield-to-maturity type analysis for bonds with the addition of a factor for dividend growth. Risk analysis is included in determining the rate at which one discounts back the future cash flows to arrive at present value. Once a fair value is established for the income shares, the remaining value of the fund can be used to get the investment value of the capital shares. Although it has not been publicized, a major brokerage firm used this technique to prepare an early redemption proposal for a dual purpose fund they manage. Refinements to this approach include provision for taxes paid on behalf of the capital shareholders and future anticipated portfolio shifts. Again, the results are surprising to some. They indicate the income shares to be largely underpriced by the market place and, by extrapolation, the discounts generally seen in the capital shares are shown to be *not large enough!*

The state of the art in dual fund analysis encompasses a combination of the option theory and present value approaches, together with important refinements which have not yet been published.

## THE HISTORICAL RECORD

In general, conventional wisdom would have one buy discounted capital shares and stay away from income shares. More sophisticated analysis suggests the income shares may be better investments.

From their inception around 1967 until their redemption in the late 1970s and early 1980s, seven dual purpose funds traded in the United States. This period spanned both strong and weak markets and the different dual funds used a wide range of valuation and stock selection approaches. In every single case, the total return to the income shareholders was superior to the total return to the capital shareholders. This was true even before making an adjustment for the much higher risk profile of the capital shares. This was also true even after reinvesting the tax payments made on behalf of the capital shareholders in new, discounted capital shares and reinvesting the dividends received by the income shareholders in additional income shares, largely at premiums.

This relative difference in performance between the income and capital shares has been equally as true in recent times. Performance of the capital shares of the four true dual purpose funds begun in recent years has ranged from passable to dismal, while the corresponding income shares have produced total returns ranging from very good to extraordinary. In all cases, the income shares have outperformed their capital brethren whenever sufficient time has passed to include reasonable and inevitable market corrections.

Let's turn to an examination of the individual dual purpose funds.

## INDIVIDUAL FUNDS

The dual funds currently in existence are identified in Table 7–4. Two of these, Gemini II and Quest for Value Dual Purpose Fund, are diversified common stock funds. The others are specialized.

### Diversified Common Stock Funds

**Gemini II [NYSE: GMI** (capital shares), **GMI PR** (preferred shares)] At its offering, GMI issued 10 million capital shares and an equal number of income shares. Net of the underwriting discount, the initial NAV for both income and capital shares was $9.30. This is the amount at which the income shares will be redeemed in 1997. A member of the Vanguard Group, Gemini II was the first dual fund to be offered in 18 years. Under normal conditions Gemini II will be at least 80% invested in common stocks.

The first Gemini Fund was brought to market in March, 1967 and terminated its dual fund structure at year-end 1984, when all income shares were redeemed. In September, 1986 the capital shares of Gemini were merged into the existing open-end Windsor Fund, also of the Vanguard Group. Wellington Management Co. served as investment adviser for the first Gemini and now is adviser for Gemini II and Windsor. Wellington had over $38 billion of assets under management as of year-end 1989.

John Neff, a managing partner at Wellington, managed the original Gemini and now oversees the second one. Neff is a highly visible, successful value investor who likes unloved, misunderstood stocks with low P/E ratios and good solid dividends. He has the honor of being one of eight money masters profiled in John Train's book *The New Money Masters.*[3] The original Gemini returned 15% compounded annually over the 1967–84 period, far in excess of the 8% annualized return for the market.[4] Neff has also managed the open-end Windsor Fund since 1964 which has been on the *Forbes* honor roll six times. Wind-

**Table 7–4. Dual Fund Information**

| Fund | Began | Redemption Date | Net Assets (Millions) | Expense Ratio 1989 | Expense Ratio 1988 |
|---|---|---|---|---|---|
| Convertible Holdings | 7/85 | 7/97 | $264 | 0.80% | 0.79% |
| Counsellors Tandem Securities Fund | 10/86 | 10/96* | 108 | 1.08 | 1.34 |
| Gemini II | 2/85 | 1/97 | 306 | 0.61 | 0.71 |
| Hampton Utilities Trust | 3/88 | 3/94 | 23 | 1.45 | 1.14† |
| Quest for Value Dual Purpose Fund | 2/87 | 1/97 | 534 | 0.83 | 0.86 |

*Latest possible redemption date.
†Annualized.
Source: Data provided by individual funds. Net assets as of year-end 1989 or end of fund's 1989 fiscal year.

sor now has assets of about $8 billion making it one of the largest open-end funds.

**Quest for Value Dual Purpose Fund (NYSE: KFV, KFV PR)** The largest of the dual funds, KFV initially issued 18 million capital shares and an equal number of income shares. KFV invests in what it feels are undervalued common shares of domestic and foreign issuers. It also invests in debt securities. Quest for Value Advisors, Inc., a subsidiary of Oppenheimer Capital, serves as the fund's adviser. Oppenheimer Capital has $19 billion in total assets under management.

Quest for Value can use options and futures to hedge its portfolio. It originally did so but was not pleased with the results. KFV's reason for using options and futures relates to the experience of the earlier group of dual funds which began in the 1960s. Their capital shares went to big discounts which caused concern about the attractiveness of the structure. In an attempt to ease the widening of the discount on their capital shares KFV employed portfolio insurance which helped it substantially during the October 1987 crash. However, portfolio insurance really carried a very high cost, Richard M. Reilly, former president of Quest for Value Advisors told us: "The benefit we realized on October 16 and 19 was not worth the cost of having carried these positions through the summer."

Since the latter part of 1987 KFV has made very little use of options and futures. Coincidentally, its performance improved dramatically, said Reilly. "I think that a lot of professional managers feel that they can manage their way through different cycles with good stock selection or good basic asset allocation, and the additional ingredient of options and futures may not add that much," he commented. The authors fully agree with this viewpoint.

## Specialized Dual Funds

Each dual fund is unique and must be analyzed separately. The remaining three have specialized portfolios.

**Convertible Holdings (NYSE: CNV, CNV PR)** As its name implies, Convertible Holdings (formerly ML Convertible Securities) invests mainly in convertible bonds and preferred stock. Merrill Lynch Asset Management serves as investment adviser. The capital shares contributed 42.5% of the initial assets and the income shares contributed the balance. Even though CNV has a specialized portfolio we still consider it to be a traditional dual fund. The remaining two dual funds, however, are structured differently from the other three as we'll now explain.

Both **Counsellors Tandem Securities Fund (NYSE: CTF, CTF PR)** and **Hampton Utilities Trust (Amex: HU, HU PR)** have portfolios that consist largely of utility equities, and have a preferred share that pays out a fixed dividend, appealing to institutions that want the 70% dividends-received deduction.[5]

Since the preferred shares pay a fixed dividend compared to those on traditional dual funds that afford growth potential, they would be of little or no interest to individual investors. However, the capital shares would be of interest for those looking for a leveraged investment vehicle in utilities.

The capital shares of Counsellors and Hampton are also unique in that they pay a residual income dividend after the dividend has been met on the preferred. However, these funds can't make any distribution to the capital shareholders if after the distribution the coverage of the preferred is not two to one. That is, the total net assets of the fund have to be at least twice the liquidation value of the preferred subsequent to any distribution to the capital shares.

Utility equities are ideal securities for a dual fund portfolio according to Bruce Baughman and William Lippman, Hampton's portfolio manager and president, respectively. They explain why in the Closed-End Insights box.

## UTILITIES ARE THE IDEAL ENGINE FOR A DUAL FUND
### Bruce C. Baughman and William J. Lippman
### Portfolio Manager and President, respectively
### Hampton Utilities Trust

Let's invent the perfect investment. First, it should be an investment, not a speculation. But it will have significant growth potential. It also must offer current income—wait, current income that will increase while we hold it. And, if we can't start out with a high yield, let's at least have the stability we associate with companies that are able to pay generous dividends. How about being able to borrow money to put into this great investment? Only please, no margin calls or other early demands for repayment. And let's borrow at a very cheap rate—close to where Uncle Sam does, at the Treasury rate.

The preceding describes the capital shares of Hampton Utilities Trust. The fund had its genesis in the summer of 1987, when an investment banker at L.F. Rothschild approached us, then in Rothschild's mutual fund group, and asked us to come up with a high quality, fixed income investment of six years maturity that small banks and thrifts could use in the place of municipal bonds, some of whose tax advantages to banks had been taken away by the Tax Reform Act of 1986. The idea that eventually took shape was an answer for the banks and a dream stock for equity investors. The key was using utility stocks to power an intermediate term dual fund.

Hampton is a dual fund of six years duration (from its inception) that pays a fixed dividend to preferred shareholders, who put up half the money. The six-year preferred is rated A because of the protection afforded by 2-to-1 asset coverage and the quality of the fund's portfolio. The payments are tax advantaged to corporations (banks, thrifts, and so on), so the rate

paid is low, only 50 to 85 basis points over 5 to 7 year
Treasuries. Though technically an equity stock, the
preferred investment works like a very cheap borrowing for the capital investors. The money is invested in
common stocks of better quality utilities that generate
more than enough income to pay the preferred dividends and the fund's expenses. The remainder goes
to the capital shareholders at the end of each year.
This last wrinkle is a departure from the original dual
purpose fund, where all investment income goes to
the so-called "income shares."

Leverage can be dangerous, and even defensive
utility stocks are capable of going down. But over time
the record for market appreciation has been good, especially among those companies with good managements operating in good areas. The 2-to-1 leverage
doubles those good returns for the capital shareholders. Even when the equity markets are weak, utilities
will often hold their ground well thanks to their yields
and relative insensitivity to the economy. Electric utilities are at some risk when major capital expansion is
underway, but it's easy enough to build a diversified
portfolio and still avoid situations where rate treatment is uncertain.

For various reasons, Hampton was not presented
to investors until March of 1988, by which time L.F.
Rothschild was impaired financially, and could not
mount an effective underwriting. We went ahead any-
way, raising $20 million, including $10 million from
preferred investors, since even a small fund would be
able to demonstrate the investment merit of the idea.
In the meantime, we discovered that Warburg, Pincus
Counsellors had hit on the same idea. They brought
their Counsellors Tandem Securities Fund to market
in late 1986. The timing was excellent from the standpoint of funding the preferred, which pays only 7-1/
4%. By comparison, Hampton's preferred costs the
common shareholders 8%, still a nice rate to pay for
six years of leverage.

At this writing (April 1990) Hampton, which we
still manage, but at Franklin Resources, has passed its
second birthday. The investment potential of Hampton's capital shares is not only intact, but on sale at a
discount.

## CONCLUSION

Dual purpose funds are a specialized type of CEF which may have appeal for more sophisticated investors who know how to do their homework and spot value when it exists. Like the ordinary CEF, the dual fund can represent good value if purchased at a sufficiently wide discount. Be certain to examine the discount of the total fund since it is the most meaningful indicator of under- or overvaluation.

One final thought. For those who want both income and appreciation there is nothing wrong with purchasing both income and capital shares of the traditional dual funds (Convertible Holdings, Gemini II, and Quest for Value) in whatever relative proportions suit your preferences.

### Notes

[1]Thomas J. Herzfeld, *The Investor's Guide to Closed-End Funds* (New York: McGraw-Hill Book Company, 1980), p. 138.

[2]William Baldwin, "The unload funds," *Forbes*, September 5, 1988, p. 160.

[3]John Train, *The New Money Masters* (New York: Harper & Row, Publishers, 1989), Chapter 7.

[4]Baldwin, p. 158.

[5]Some have questioned whether Counsellors Tandem should be placed in the dual fund category. They may also raise this question about Hampton since its structure is so similar to that of Counsellors'. However, based upon discussions with the managements of both funds the authors feel that they definitely are dual funds.

# CHAPTER 8

# *Sector Equity Funds*

In a broad sense sector equity funds are members of the "specialty funds" family. Specialty funds are designed to enable investors to meet specific objectives. Examples would be funds with portfolios tailored to a specific industry or geographic area. These funds require specialized investor analysis and familiarity with the area in which they invest. The largest and fastest growing category of specialty funds consists of the single country funds to be covered in Chapter 10.

Sector equity funds invest in a certain industry or group of industries which make up the target sector. An example would be a fund investing in the industries which comprise the health care sector, such as biotechnology, diagnostics, health services, managed care, medical supplies, and pharmaceuticals. Other sector funds invest in certain commodities like gold and silver bullion.

Sector funds may be well diversified within their particular area but are risky in the sense that they will do poorly if the sector does. On the other hand, if their sector turns out to be the hottest performer of the year, they could far outdistance more broadly based portfolios. It is not uncommon to see some specialty funds listed among both the best and worst performing funds for a given year. Thus, they could be expected to be more volatile performers than the typical diversified domestic equity fund.

Not all specialized funds are equally volatile, however. A few of them, while they do invest primarily in the utility sector, focus chiefly on producing high current income rather than capital appreciation. They also pay monthly dividends. In these cases the emphasis is on the income. These funds could normally be expected to be considerably more stable than a fund holding gold and silver bullion that pays no interest or dividends. But by no means are they risk free. Since the high current income funds would behave more like bond funds their prices (and any premiums to NAV) could drop substantially if there was a sharp rise in inflation and interest rates. Thus, they would be subject to *interest rate risk* as will be explained in Chapter 12 "Bond Fund Basics."

## SECTOR RISK

By itself, no sector (or specialized) fund is suitable for a complete investment program (as a diversified domestic equity fund might be) since industry or sector risk is present. The funds advise prospective investors of this "sector risk" in their prospectuses. The following statement which appeared in the prospectus for the Global Utility Fund is typical:

> The Fund is not intended to be a complete investment program. Because, under normal conditions, the Fund will invest at least 65% of its assets in securities of domestic and foreign companies in the utility industries, the Fund's assets will be especially affected by developments in the utility industries and may be subject to greater risk than the assets of an investment company whose portfolio is not similarly concentrated.

The prospectus details the specific risks. Investors in a particular sector fund should be well aware of them.

However, the funds still have the advantages of diversification and professional management. Thus, they have considerably less risk than holding one or two stocks in that sector.

The majority of the CEF sector equity funds are identified in Table 8–1. These and six other sector funds are included in our directory in Appendix I.

We'll take a look at the different sectors and their funds next.

## Gold-Oriented Funds

The price of gold is highly volatile and subject to dramatic upward and downward price movements over short periods. Consequently, it is very difficult to predict the metal's price. However, having a small portion of your assets in gold would broaden your diversification and, thus, from a portfolio theory standpoint, would appear justified. Gold may perform well in economic environments that are unfavorable for stocks and bonds. This certainly was true in the inflationary environment of the late 1970s; gold took off reaching a peak of $875 an ounce in January, 1980. Thus, some gold holdings could be beneficial to your portfolio if inflation gets out of control.

There are four gold-oriented CEFs for those who wish to have some exposure to the metal. Silver may also be represented in the fund's portfolio. In comparison to direct holdings of bullion, the gold and precious metals funds offer a convenient economical means for the small investor to diversify into the sector. However, each of the four differs significantly from the others in terms of its portfolio composition. The funds also have different philosophies with respect to timing the market. If you're interested in the area you should get the shareholder reports from each of the four funds and carefully compare them. We'll introduce the funds here. As with other CEFs, the key to success is to buy at wide discounts.

**ASA Limited (NYSE Symbol: ASA)** The largest and oldest of the gold-oriented funds, ASA is incorporated in the Republic of South Africa. It invests over half its assets in the shares of South African gold mining company equi-

**Table 8-1. Sector Equity Funds**

| Category and Fund | Began | Net Assets (Millions) | Expense 1989 | Ratio 1988 |
|---|---|---|---|---|
| **Gold** | | | | |
| ASA Limited | 6/58 | $ 672 | 0.51% | 0.52% |
| BGR Precious Metals | 10/83 | 71 | n.a. | n.a. |
| Central Fund of Canada | 11/61 | 86 | n.a. | n.a. |
| Meeschaert Gold & Currency | 10/86 | 39 | 1.17 | 1.25 |
| **Utility** | | | | |
| Counsellors Tandem Securities Fund | 10/86 | 108 | 1.08 | 1.34 |
| Duff & Phelps Utilities Income | 1/87 | 1,728 | 1.33 | 1.59 |
| Global Utility Fund | 12/89 | 171 | n.a. | n.a. |
| Hampton Utilities Trust | 3/88 | 23 | 1.45 | 1.14* |
| Patriot Premium Dividend Fund | 10/88 | 206 | 1.39* | n.a. |
| Patriot Premium Dividend Fund II | 12/89 | 300 | n.a. | n.a. |
| **Financial** | | | | |
| Dover Regional Financial Shares | 9/86 | 6 | 1.96 | 1.99 |
| First Financial Fund | 5/86 | 83 | 1.45 | 1.46 |
| Pilgrim Regional Bank Shares | 1/86 | 103 | 1.26 | 1.18 |
| Southeastern Savings Institutions Fund | 8/89 | 19 | n.a. | n.a. |
| **Other** | | | | |
| H&Q Healthcare Investors | 4/87 | 59 | 1.89 | 1.98 |
| Petroleum & Resources | 1/29 | 353 | 0.66 | 0.68 |
| Real Estate Securities Income Fund | 8/88 | 21 | 1.29 | 2.90* |

n.a.: Not available or not meaningful.
* Annualized.
Source: Data provided by individual funds. Net assets as of year-end 1989 or end of fund's 1989 fiscal year.

ties, and most of the remainder in other South African companies. The shares of nearly all the companies it invests in are traded on the Johannesburg Stock Exchange. Social unrest in South Africa has had an adverse effect on the market for all South African shares.

ASA's net asset values are computed in terms of rand, the currency of the Republic of South Africa, and then converted into U.S. dollars. Thus, the fund has a currency risk as fluctuating exchange rates are reflected in changes in the NAV in dollars of ASA's shares.

ASA was on the *Forbes* honor roll five times having last appeared in 1983, at which time it had an A rating for both up and down market performance. In contrast, in the 1990 *Forbes* "Fund Ratings" it had D ratings in both up and down markets. At year-end 1984 ASA shares sold at a 10 percent premium—a sharp contrast to their 49 percent discount at the end of 1986. Going back even earlier in its long history, it sold at a premium of 77 percent at year-end 1967. This reinforces the fact that sector funds can be volatile and are risky if held by themselves without other equity exposure.

ASA's expense ratio and portfolio turnover are both very low. In fact, its turnover, which has averaged less than 2% since 1979, is the lowest of any fund we've encountered. ASA has listed options that trade on the Amex. The fund has some U.S. directors and officers. Robert J. A. Irwin, president of Niagara Share (Chapter 5), is an ASA director. A shareholder representative is located in Florham Park, New Jersey. See Appendix I for the address and phone number.

**BGR Precious Metals (TOR: BPT.A)** BGR is a Toronto based fund with the objectives of capital appreciation and a hedge against inflation. Using a flexible asset mix policy it invests in the equities of North American and non-North American precious metals companies as well as directly in precious metals. It may use options and futures. Its shares are listed on both the Toronto and Montreal Exchanges and can be purchased through major U.S. brokers.

BGR Management Ltd., a wholly-owned subsidiary of

Dynamic Capital Corporation, manages the portfolio. The manager is advised by three advisers: Beutel, Goodman & Co. Ltd., Toronto, on North American precious metals equities; Guardian Trustco International Inc., of Toronto, on precious metals bullion; and N.M. Rothschild Asset Management Ltd., London, England, on non-North American precious metals equities.

At this writing BGR is emphasizing senior North American producers. Its biggest position is in American Barrick Resources Corporation, a North American gold producer with interests in seven mines. BGR is not included in S&P's *Stock Guide* as it is a Canadian fund; contact the fund directly for information.

**Central Fund of Canada Limited (Amex: CEF)** CEF, a closed-end Canadian investment holding company, began operations in 1961 and changed its strategy in 1983 to one of holding gold and silver bullion. Its shares are listed on both the American and Toronto Stock Exchanges and a large proportion of its investors reside in the U.S. Institutions hold about 21% of its outstanding shares. Its objectives are capital appreciation and protection against inflation. A unique fund, it normally has at least 90% of its assets invested in gold and silver bullion. Its investments primarily are long-term; it does not speculate on short-term gold and silver price changes.

Recently, it had 59% in gold bullion (about 129,000 ounces), 39% in silver bullion (6 million ounces), and the remainder in cash. The bullion is stored on a segregated basis in the underground vaults of the Canadian Imperial Bank of Commerce and is fully insured by Lloyd's of London. Although CEF is a Canadian company, it is *not* a currency play as gold and silver bullion are priced worldwide in U.S. dollars. CEF is subject to the regulation and reporting requirements of the U.S. Securities and Exchange Commission and various Canadian Provincial regulatory authorities.

CEF's discounts and premiums vary over time. Its highest premium was 23.6% (4/10/87) and its largest discount was 28.5% (12/13/84). Investing in CEF's shares would have important advantages over holding bullion directly especially when they can be purchased at a wide discount. CEF incurs annual charges of about 1% of NAV for storage and other costs associated with the bullion.[1] Since bullion pays no interest or dividends CEF has reported losses in recent years. Further, the price of CEF's shares depends solely on the prices of these two commodities which, in turn, depend heavily on factors like inflationary expectations and investor sentiment.

During the 5 years ended March 31, 1990 CEF's compound annual return was − 1.54% according to Lipper. That contrasts with 13.04% for ASA, and 18.82% for Lipper's closed-end specialized equity and convertible funds category. More information on CEF can be found in S&P's *Stock Guide.*

**Meeschaert Gold and Currency Trust (MWST: GCT)** A non-diversified fund set up as a Massachusetts business trust, Meeschaert trades on the Midwest Stock Exchange. Its objectives are long-term appreciation and preservation of purchasing power. Its adviser is Meeschaert Investment Management Corporation located in St. Johnsbury, Vermont. The adviser is affiliated with the Meeschaert organization in France.

Timing is an important part of GCT's strategy. During periods of actual or anticipated inflation it will invest at least 65% of its portfolio in precious metal-related assets including gold bullion, gold certificates, silver bullion, gold mining company stocks, and coins. At such times it will also invest up to 35% in short-term debt like Treasury bills and foreign currency contracts.

During periods of deflation GCT will invest mainly in fixed income securities. As stated in its prospectus: "The success of the Trust's investment program will be dependent to a high degree on the Investment Adviser's ability to anticipate the onset and termination of inflationary and deflationary cycles."

At year-end 1989 Meeschaert had about 22% of its assets in common stocks (mostly gold mining), 46% in precious metals (mainly gold bullion), and 29% in Treasury bills. GCT is not included in S&P's *Stock Guide;* contact the fund directly for information.

**Utility Funds**

Traditionally utility stocks have been regarded as safe havens for widows and orphans. They have been characterized as low beta (low volatility) equities with generous, dependable dividend yields. The demand for heat and light is relatively stable and predictable, and we're all going to need these services even during depressions.

However, investors in utility stocks have received several shocks during the past couple of decades. For instance, General Public Utilities fell by more than 80 percent from its 1979 high to a low of 3-3/8 in 1980 following the March 1979 Three Mile Island nuclear plant breakdown. Investing in utilities is more complex today with issues like nuclear power, acid rain, and nonutility diversification.[2] It follows that the diversification and professional management of a fund are highly important in the utility industry as in other sectors.

CEFs specializing in the utility sector include **Counsellors Tandem Securities Fund** and **Hampton Utilities Trust** which were introduced in Chapter 7 as they are dual funds. Their capital shares provide a way to take a leveraged position in the utility sector. Counsellors Tandem holds at least 65% of its portfolio in utility stocks but also invests up to 35% in equities outside the sector.

**Global Utility Fund (NYSE: GL)** GL invests in the stocks and bonds of domestic and foreign utilities: electric, telecommunications, gas, or water. Its objective is to provide total return without incurring undue risk. Less than 25% of the portfolio would generally be invested in fixed income securities—it's basically an equity fund. At this writing about 40% of GL's portfolio is invested in foreign securities. The fund can invest up to 35% of its assets in securities of issuers outside the utility sector. GL's adviser is Wellington Management Company.

**Duff & Phelps Utilities Income (NYSE: DNP)** As a balanced fund, DNP holds utility bonds as well as stocks in its large portfolio. Its primary objectives are current income and long-term growth of income; capital appreciation is secondary. DNP came to market in January, 1987 raising $1.2 billion, at that time the largest initial public offering ever. DNP's adviser is Duff & Phelps Investment Management Co., a subsidiary of Duff & Phelps, Inc., a major rating agency that has also provided research to institutions that invest in utilities since its founding in 1932.

Richard Spletzer, who provides some facts on DNP in the Closed-End Insights box, headed the utility research division at Duff & Phelps from 1981 through 1986. Subsequently he has been the chief investment officer at DNP.

---

**FACTS ON DUFF & PHELPS
UTILITIES INCOME
Richard J. Spletzer, CFA
Senior Vice President
and Chief Investment Officer
Duff & Phelps Utilities Income**

DNP's shareholders are mainly individuals and IRA's; institutional holders own less than 2% of the 140 million common shares outstanding. Dividends are paid monthly. An estimated one-third of the approximately 240,000 common shareholders are enrolled in the dividend reinvestment plan. The plan is rather unique, inasmuch as if the market price of the Fund is equal to or exceeds net asset value, new shares for the dividend reinvestment program are *issued* at the greater of either 95% of market price or net asset value. If the market price is less than net asset value, shares for the plan are *purchased* in the open market.

To best achieve its stated investment objectives, DNP was designed as a balanced fund. Bonds helped to increase the portfolio yield and lower the risk level in terms of market fluctuations. The utility common stock investments provide growth in income and capital appreciation potential. At year-end 1989, about 48% of total investments were in utility common stocks and 51% in utility bonds.

During 1988, DNP shareholders voted overwhelmingly in favor of a proposal to further leverage the Fund by selling up to $500 million of remarketed preferred stock. A total of five issues of $100 million each was sold to institutional investors during the fourth quarter of 1988. Each issue is remarketed at the end of 49 days. [Essentially, this means that the dividend rate on DNP's preferred could increase or decrease every 49 days based on the going level of interest rates]. As expected, the preferred stock program had a positive impact on the Fund's earnings in 1989.

The selection of the Fund's fixed income investments is based on identification of value and avoidance of credit risk while maintaining adequate liquidity. The weighted average quality of the Fund's fixed income investments at the end of 1989 was single-A.

On the equity side, the Fund's selections are based on ongoing detailed analysis of qualitative factors (primarily the regulatory environment and management) as well as of quantitative factors such as prospective growth in dividends relative to price, yield, and risk. Because of the Fund's emphasis on income, the equity selections are geared largely to the higher-yielding electric companies as compared with gas companies or the faster growing telecommunication companies.

The leverage provided by DNP's remarketed preferred should lead to a higher level of earnings and, consequently, dividends for common shareholders. The idea is that the yields realized by DNP from its portfolio of utility securities should normally be in excess of the fluctuating dividend rate on the preferred. The wider this spread the more favorable the effect of the leverage on the common stock. Of course, leverage adds risk and, if interest rates increase sharply, the common stock could be adversely affected. DNP tends to trade close to its NAV as it is an income fund and pays monthly dividends.

**Patriot Premium Dividend Fund (NYSE: PDF)** and **Patriot Premium Dividend Fund II (NYSE: PDT)** The objective of both PDF and PDT (which are nearly identical) is to generate high income as well as modest capital growth. The funds are specialized more as income funds

and not so much as sector funds. They hold mainly investment grade or comparable quality utility common and
preferred stock and pay monthly dividends. Patriot Premium Dividend II was brought out to meet continued demand for this type of fund. PDT can also invest in bonds.

In an effort to enhance yield to common shareholders
they have leveraged with investment grade Dutch auction
preferred stock issues (or DARTS) paying dividends that
vary with the level of interest rates. The DARTS are held
by corporate investors willing to accept a low dividend
rate because the income qualifies for their 70% dividends
received deduction (that is, 70% of the dividends are ex-
cludable from their income). Options and futures strategies are not implemented by either fund. Patriot Advisors
in Boston manages both funds. Both PDF and PDT have
always traded at premiums to NAV.

## Financial Company Funds

The financial company sector includes banks and savings
and loans. Like the utility equities, their shares are interest sensitive. Banks differ widely in size. At the top you
have the big money center banks, then you go down to the
super-regionals, the regionals, and finally the community
banks. Four CEFs invest in the financial company sector.
All have capital appreciation as a primary objective with
investment income being secondary. However, each has
its own personality and one who wishes exposure to this
sector should carefully compare the portfolios, management philosophies, and other characteristics, of the four
before investing in any one of them. A brief description of
each follows.

**Dover Regional Financial Shares (NASDAQ:
DVRFS)** A small fund with assets of $6.3 million, Dover
invests primarily in equity securities of smaller regional
banks and thrifts located mainly on the Eastern seaboard.
It can invest up to 20% of its assets in restricted securities
(as defined by the Securities Act of 1933). Dover's discount or premium to NAV does not appear in the weekly
publicly-traded funds listing. However, a weekly NAV can
be obtained from the adviser, Dover Financial Manage-

ment, located in Philadelphia. Dover's shares trade over-the-counter in NASDAQ with a relatively wide bid-asked spread implying low liquidity. Its portfolio turnover is low—it was only 3.4% in 1989. DVRFS is not included in S&P's *Stock Guide;* contact the fund directly for information.

**First Financial Fund (NYSE: FF)** FF invests primarily in equity securities of small to medium-sized savings and banking institutions and their holding companies. FF's portfolio is geographically dispersed. The deposits of the institutions FF invests in are insured by the FSLIC or the FDIC, as the case may be. The fund's adviser is Wellington Management Co. Institutions hold a large percentage of FF's shares, about 45% at this writing.

**Pilgrim Regional Bank Shares (NYSE: PBS)** PBS basically lives up to its name. About 71% of its assets were invested in regional banks, 20% in community banks, and 5% in thrifts at this writing. The deposits of the banks the fund invests in are insured. PBS pays out 10% of its NAV annually, a policy it instituted in early 1989 in order to reduce its discount, which it has. Institutions hold about 21% of its outstanding shares. Robert A. Schwarzkopf, portfolio manager of PBS, discusses the investment opportunities in banks and how PBS takes advantage of them in the Closed-End Insights box.

---

**OPPORTUNITIES IN BANK STOCKS**
**Robert A. Schwarzkopf, CFA**
**Portfolio Manager**
**The Pilgrim Group**

The banking industry provides a unique opportunity to investors. That opportunity results from the fragmented and diverse nature of the industry. The banking industry and the automobile industry stand at extremes in terms of fragmentation versus concentration. An investor in auto stocks finds only three potential candidates: General Motors, Ford, and Chrysler. Not surprisingly, "Wall Street" does an excellent job of researching these companies and efficiently pricing their securities. The banking industry, on the other hand, consists of 13,000 commercial banks.

Although Wall Street does a good job of researching the 100 largest banks and efficiently pricing their securities, there are thousands of smaller banks that Wall Street doesn't research at all. This provides the opportunity of an inefficient market for bank stocks. We find that bank stocks are priced much more homogeneously than they should be when consideration is given to their wide divergences in loan quality, leverage, profitability, and growth prospects. Perhaps investors have drawn the conclusion that since their products are very similar (deposit accounts, loans, and so on), their investment merits are also similar. Nothing could be further from the truth. Pilgrim Regional Bank Shares was formed to take advantage of this opportunity. The Fund concentrates on buying the nation's best quality banks at price/earnings and price/book value multiples of average quality banks.

The average bank stock currently trades at price/earnings and price/book value multiples that approximate 50% of the S&P 400 Index multiples. The reason for the severe discounting is clear. After years of bad news from banks due to a surge in bank failures, troubled loans to less developed countries, dramatic losses on energy loans that were syndicated across the nation, and so on, investors don't believe that bank earnings and equity are real. We agree that poor business practices and poor corporate reporting exist in the banking industry. However, there are also many banks that don't make loans to foreign countries, don't participate in out-of-area lending, and account for their earnings and equity very conservatively. The banks in Pilgrim Regional Bank Shares, on average, maintain a reserve for future loan losses that exceeds troubled loans by 30%, have 50% more capital behind every dollar of assets than the average bank, have a history of growing earnings as fast as the S&P 400 with less earnings cyclicality and, because of lumping the good with the bad, sell at price/earnings and price/

book value ratios of approximately 50% of the S&P 400 Index multiples—about the same multiples as the average bank in the nation.

This environment provides the opportunity for finding exceptionally attractively priced securities in exceptionally high quality companies with less than average earnings, balance sheet, and price risk, provided that the investor is willing to commit the substantial time and effort needed to find these companies without the help of Wall Street. This is what Pilgrim Regional Bank Shares is structured to do.

**Southeastern Savings Institutions Fund (NAS-DAQ: SSIF)** A relatively new fund with about $19 million in assets, SSIF invests primarily in small to medium-sized savings and loans, as well as their holding companies, chiefly in the Southeastern United States. Interstate Asset Management, Inc. in Charlotte, North Carolina is the adviser. The fund's primary objective is long-term appreciation; income is secondary.

SSIF intends to dissolve on June 30, 1994, extendible for up to three years. It may be disadvantageous for the fund to dissolve should the market value of its securities be below their cost. Prior to any dissolution the board of directors will submit to shareholders the questions of whether to dissolve the fund or to convert it to an open-end fund. If shareholders vote to convert it to an open-end company it would have perpetual existence.

### Other Sectors

The three remaining sectors represented are healthcare, petroleum and natural resources, and real estate.

**H&Q Healthcare Investors (NYSE: HQH)** HQH seeks long-term appreciation by investing in small emerging growth companies in the healthcare field, with emphasis on the pharmaceutical, biotechnology, and medical specialty groups. Many of the companies it holds trade over-the-counter. HQH may invest up to one quarter of its assets in venture capital or other restricted securities.

Hambrecht and Quist Capital Management Inc. is the adviser. HQH should be in a good position to benefit from demographic forces, a better outlook for government funding, and continued above-average growth in its sector.

Alan Carr, president of H&Q, discusses the venture capital investments of the fund in the Closed-End Insights box.

---

### VENTURE CAPITAL INVESTMENT BY H&Q
### HEALTHCARE INVESTORS
### Alan G. Carr
### President
### H&Q Healthcare Investors

Six hundred billion dollars a year is currently being spent for healthcare in the United States and over a thousand publicly held companies participate. More than half of them have healthcare as their principal activity. We are sometimes asked, given that opportunity, why did we provide that up to 25% of the assets of the Fund can be invested in private companies or restricted securities of public companies?

The broadly defined healthcare industry continues to grow at a rate substantially greater than the general economy and is generally immune to broad economic cycles. That growth, in addition to being propelled by demographic factors, is driven by new technologies and innovative providers of service. Much of this new technology and innovation is provided by a myriad of new companies providing an abundance of investment alternatives. Participation in the early growth phase of these companies through venture capital investment provides an opportunity to enhance long-term investment returns for our shareholders.

There are other benefits from this activity. Particularly in the area of technology, the pace of develop-

ment is extremely rapid. Through its venture investment activity, Fund management has the opportunity
to observe changes which may have an increasingly
rapid impact on the publicly traded companies in the
industry. This opportunity enhances the process of investment research and security selection in our publicly traded investments in a way not generally available to other investors.

Additionally, healthcare investment at the venture capital stage is somewhat different from private
investment in other sectors. The major publicly
traded companies in the industry have very extensive
distribution networks. They often also suffer from disappointment within their own research and development programs. As a result, they are unable to provide
a continuing flow of new products for their marketing
and sales groups. Consequently, these large companies frequently choose to augment their product
portfolios through acquisition of smaller companies
developing new innovative products. Often these acquisitions are made at premium valuations and before
these venture-backed enterprises have matured to the
point where they would be able to have their initial
public offerings. These opportunities for "exit" from
H&Q's portfolio holdings may, over time, have a very
favorable impact on long-term performance.

We believe that our investment strategy is particularly appropriate for the long-term investment focus
of a closed-end fund and could prove to be of material
benefit to our shareholders.

## Petroleum & Resources Corporation (NYSE: PEO)

The oldest sector fund in existence today, PEO began in
January 1929 as Petroleum Corporation of America. Its
name was changed to Petroleum & Resources Corp. in
1977. Since 1944 Adams Express (Chapter 5) has owned
a percentage of PEO's outstanding stock. The two funds
work closely together, operating out of the same Baltimore
office.

PEO is an equity fund with the objectives of capital

preservation, income, and an opportunity for capital appreciation. PEO holds a diversified portfolio of energy securities, including equities of international and domestic oil companies, natural gas distributors, oil and gas producers, and oil service companies. Its capital structure includes preferred as well as common stock.

PEO has performed well in the past in sync with its sector and made the *Forbes* honor roll six times, last appearing there in 1982. Its expense ratio and portfolio turnover are both low.

**Real Estate Securities Income Fund (Amex: RIF)**
RIF is the only CEF which invests in the real estate area today. This non-diversified fund seeks high income through investment in publicly-traded real estate securities. Capital appreciation is secondary. Its adviser is Cohen & Steers Capital Management in New York.

A relatively small fund, RIF would normally have at least 65% of its assets invested in real estate equity securities; up to 35% could be invested in debt securities of real estate companies. RIF primarily holds positions in a variety of Real Estate Investment Trusts (REITs). At this writing its bigger REIT holdings included BRE Properties, Universal Health Realty Income Trust, and Koger Equity. RIF also invests in publicly traded master limited partnerships as well as other securities of real estate companies.

REITs themselves are like closed-end funds in that they use professional managers to supervise a portfolio of real estate holdings.[3] However, it takes special expertise to analyze REITs, and it is also important to have diversification among different REITs as they may concentrate in different areas of the country and specialize in different kinds of properties. RIF is subject to risks associated with investment in real estate generally as pointed out in its prospectus. The prospectus also indicates that RIF shareholders bear their proportionate share of expenses of the fund but also, indirectly, bear similar expenses of the underlying REITs. Robert Steers of Cohen & Steers Capital Management discusses the issue of fund investor costs in REIT and other equity funds in the Closed-End Insights box.

## INVESTOR COSTS ASSOCIATED WITH FUNDS HOLDING REITs
### Robert H. Steers
### Chairman
### Real Estate Securities Income Fund

Investors in funds owning real estate investment trusts (REITs) incur no greater costs or fees than a general equity fund.

REITs are corporations like any others except that qualifying and filing tax returns as a REIT permit them to avoid taxation at the corporate level. Importantly, REITs that are actively managed by experienced real estate professionals have historically provided consistently higher returns than passive or unmanaged equities. Not unlike corporate America, to attract successful real estate managers REITs must offer competitive performance-based compensation arrangements. Management of a REIT requires expertise in all aspects of real estate, including acquisitions, leasing, property management, and financing. Although it is preferable that management be directly employed by the REIT, the trustees of smaller entities may find it to be more economic to employ an outside real estate management firm on an advisory basis. In either event, management typically is compensated with a small percentage of the fund's assets annually plus a potential bonus based upon growth in cash flow.

Equity funds, whether or not investing in REITs, pay an adviser an investment management fee to structure and actively manage the fund. If REITs are owned in the portfolio there is no extra layer of management expenses not found in other corporations. Moreover, unlike most corporations a REIT's management expense is limited and typically a function of the size and performance of the portfolio, which may be the preferred arrangement.

In short, corporate managements, whether of REITs or other entities, do not work for free. Further,

REIT management compensation, either direct or through an advisory contract, is typically denominated at a base level with a bonus determined by corporate performance. This is well in line with the practice throughout corporate America.

After January 1, 1993, RIF may convert to an open-end fund with the affirmative vote of two-thirds of the outstanding shares. RIF's discount has tended to be relatively low which is probably due to the fact that it pays fairly large dividends from income. It acts like a hybrid of a bond and equity fund even though it holds primarily equities.

## FUND SELECTION

Four key considerations when selecting a sector fund are:

1.  The economic outlook for the sector itself and investor sentiment towards companies in that sector.
2.  Investor valuation of the sector in terms of conventional yardsticks including price-earnings ratios, price book value ratios, and dividend yields.
3.  The particular sector fund's diversification strategy, its management philosophy, and its track record.
4.  The discount. Because of the potentially greater volatility in the NAVs of sector funds, like ASA for example, you may see greater fluctuations in discount and premium levels and thus more opportunities.

## CONSIDER DOLLAR COST AVERAGING

Uncertain about the future? Perhaps you like the idea of investing in a sector but feel you aren't able to predict its near-term performance. (The authors maintain it's very difficult to predict the near-term performance of *any* portfolio.) You have a conviction that your sector will do well long-term. As we've explained, sector equity funds have a potentially greater volatility than more broadly diversified equity funds. One thing is certain about the stock market—it will continue to fluctuate. Thus, sector CEF investors may wish to consider taking their positions, in particular funds gradually through a systematic program of dollar cost averaging. This takes out a lot of the guess work.

With dollar cost averaging a fixed amount of money is invested at specific time intervals, like $500 every month or $800 every other month, regardless of the level of security prices. In this way more shares will be purchased at lower prices and fewer shares at higher prices. This will mean that the average cost per share will be below the simple average of market prices on the purchase dates. If followed rigorously over many years, this program is a form of time diversification and improves the odds of obtaining superior returns with low risk.

The strategy is doubly good with a CEF because its discipline will help you to buy more shares when pessimism prevails and discounts are deep. You don't have fluctuating discounts with open-end funds or individual stocks. This is a key advantage that comes with buying closed-end funds.

Dollar cost averaging works especially well with the most volatile funds—like ASA or the capital shares of dual purpose funds (Chapter 7) such as Counsellors Tandem and Hampton Utilities Trust. Investors would be able to acquire a bigger share position at times when the price is quite low. The mechanics are illustrated in Table 8–2. Here it is assumed one invests $3,000 at the end of every third month in a volatile sector fund.

Our extreme example is an ideal case for the strategy. For instance, you were able to purchase twice as many shares when the price was 5 than when it was 10. Your average cost per share of $7.79 is below the $8.50 simple average of market prices. Further, if you had invested the entire $15,000 initially at the January month-end price of $10 you would only have been able to purchase 1,500 shares in contrast to the 1,925 acquired with the program.

**Table 8–2. Dollar Cost Averaging Illustration**

| Month End | Share Price | Shares Purchased | Total Cost |
|-----------|-------------|------------------|------------|
| Jan.      | $10.00      | 300              | $3,000     |
| Apr.      | 7.50        | 400              | 3,000      |
| July      | 5.00        | 600              | 3,000      |
| Oct.      | 8.00        | 375              | 3,000      |
| Jan.      | 12.00       | 250              | 3,000      |
| **Totals** | **$42.50** | **1,925**        | **$15,000** |

Average cost per share ($15,000/1,925) = $7.79
Simple average of prices ($42.50/5)     = $8.50

Of course, the long-term trend in prices must be up for dollar cost averaging to be a success. This is why it is far safer to use this strategy with funds than with ordinary stocks. As we've said before, some ordinary stocks may go down and never recover. Specialty funds tend to come back eventually as their sectors return to favor.

The investor using dollar cost averaging must be disciplined and not afraid to buy when prices are depressed and discounts are wide, since, according to Templeton and other value investors, that is when you get the best bargains. This is the hardest part about following the program.

The authors add one caveat: It is important for the shares to sell at a discount when you are making your purchases. If the fund goes to a premium consider discontinuing your purchases and possibly selling out (if the premium is 10 percent or greater) or holding on until the shares go back to a discount and then resuming your buying. In this way we advise those who use the strategy with CEFs to depart from the pure, or traditional, formula. We'll have more to say about dollar cost averaging with CEFs in Chapter 17 "Building Your Portfolio."

## CONCLUSION

Sector equity funds are useful for investors who want direct exposure to a particular industry or investment area like gold. But, as stated in fund prospectuses, they do not represent complete investment programs by themselves. They are riskier than diversified domestic equity funds and require more knowledge on your part.

In addition to sector considerations, the usual factors which are important to CEF investors (like expense ratios) also apply. Before making your selection be sure to compare all the funds within a sector. Consider open-end funds if the CEFs in a particular sector are at a premium. A thorough study of their current shareholder reports is vital as portfolios change over time.

## Notes

[1]Stanley W. Angrist, "Central Fund of Canada Is Viewed by Some As Convenient Substitute for Owning Bullion" (Heard on the Street), *The Wall Street Journal*, April 18, 1990, p. C2.

[2]Albert J. Fredman, "Rate Expectations," *Personal Investor*, May 1990, pp. 49–54.

[3]For an excellent discussion of REITs see *Real Estate Investment Trusts* (New York: New York Institute of Finance, 1988).

# CHAPTER 9

# *Global Investing*

Sophisticated CEF investors should become accustomed to allocating their assets throughout the world as well as in sectors of the U.S. economy. Global asset allocation is more important now than ever since international (or "cross-border") opportunities have become too great to ignore. New closed-end funds are being turned out to meet strong investor demand, especially for equities of companies expected to benefit from "1992" and the important developments in Western and Eastern Europe. Recent IPOs include The Europe Fund, G.T. Greater Europe Fund, The Latin America Investment Fund, and Scudder New Europe Fund.

This chapter covers the basics of international investing. The single country and multi-country funds are covered in Chapter 10.

## CROSS-BORDER INVESTING IS NOTHING NEW

International investing has appealed to Europeans for well over a century. The earliest investment trust, formed in Belgium in 1822 by King William I of the Netherlands, "was intended to facilitate small investments in foreign government loans which then offered more security and returns than home industry."[1] The investment trusts which were formed in Great Britain beginning in the 1860s invested in overseas markets for better returns. The interest in foreign investing as a means of obtaining higher returns grew over the decades with the growing need for capital in the United States.

In recent years cross-border investing has grown in popularity with U.S. investors for good reasons. Many internationally oriented open- and closed-end funds were introduced in the 1980s and continue to be offered as we go to press. The planned unification of Europe's markets in 1992 as well as opportunities in the changing "eastern bloc" have generated considerable investor interest and enthusiasm.

## WHY INVEST INTERNATIONALLY?

There are several motivating factors for investing on an international level. Specifically, it can offer:

More complete diversification.
More investment opportunities.
The opportunity for better performance.
Protection against a decline in the dollar.

### Diversification

International investing allows the investor to add an additional dimension of diversification to a domestic stock portfolio. The authors feel that this is the most important of the advantages listed above. You don't want to put all your eggs in one basket. As we've already explained, the

investor who buys stock in only one company faces substantial risk. While a diversified portfolio of domestic equities, or a domestic CEF, would be far less risky than investing in a single company you would still be subject to
the risk of your home stock market.

The concept of international diversification is
straightforward. To take a simple example, assume you
invest equal amounts of money in two countries. The
stock market in one of them might decline 20% in a given
year while the other advances 20%. Holding currency exchange rates constant you would break even for the year.

Diversifying internationally spreads the risks across
different economies and stock markets. This is the way to
avoid having all your money in the one market that turns
out to be the worst performer—like the one that declined
20% in our example. Being well-diversified internationally
means being invested in at least a half dozen markets besides your own. Multi-country funds offer an efficient way
for individual investors of modest means to diversify into
many different stock markets.

The best way to visualize the diversification benefits
of multi-country investing is in terms of the correlation of
price movements between the U.S. market and different
foreign markets. The correlation coefficient ranges from
$+1$ to $-1$. A correlation of $+1$ would imply that prices (or
total returns) in the two markets always move precisely in
tandem. If one market was up 10% last year the other
would also be up 10%. A correlation of $-1$ would mean
that prices always move in opposite directions. If the first
market was up 10% the second would decline by 10%. A
correlation of zero would imply that price movements in
the two markets were completely unrelated. The correlation coefficient is usually not equal to its extremes of $-1$
and $+1$. In the case of movements between a pair of stock
markets the coefficient generally lies somewhere between
zero and $+1$—like 0.5.

Usually, correlations of returns between pairs of stock
markets are positive over periods of five or more years.
However, the lower the value the better. The best diversification benefits are found by investing in markets which
have the lowest correlation of price movements to the U.S.

market. This has been true of the Spanish market. The least beneficial diversification would be obtained by investing in markets like the Canadian which have been more highly correlated with our own.

The correlation of price movements between the U.S. market and different foreign markets can and does change over time. There is evidence that the world's economies and equity markets have become more closely integrated. This implies that there might be less benefit from international diversification since the correlation coefficients between markets may be greater.

For instance, an article in the May 1988 issue of the *AAII Journal* on international mutual funds by Professors Kenneth Jessell and Jeff Madura states:

> If the U.S. economy influences foreign economies, non-U.S. stocks may behave very much like U.S. stocks. Consequently, an internationally diversified portfolio may still be highly exposed to the U.S. economy. The worldwide recession in 1982 provided evidence that economies are becoming well integrated. In addition, the stock market crash in October 1987 affected most stock markets around the world.[2]

The authors found that the U.S. stock market impacts the performances of international funds to varying degrees.[3] But, if the funds have U.S. as well as foreign stocks in their portfolios (that is, they are global funds) the impact of the U.S. market would obviously be greater.

However, the findings of a definitive study undertaken by David Brunette and Douglas Stone of the Frank Russell Company make a compelling case for international diversification today.[4] The researchers examined the correlations between the total returns on the U.S. stock market (represented by the Russell 3000 Index) and eight foreign stock market indexes. They also examined the correlation between the Russell 3000 and three composite indexes: the Pacific Basin Index, the Europe Index, and the Europe, Australia, and Far East (EAFE) Index. Brunette and Stone tell us that generally correlation coefficients under about 0.75 indicate a weak relationship between a given pair of stock markets. The results for the period January 1980 through March 1988 (separated into halves) appear in Table 9–1.

Brunette and Stone conclude that the low correlations they observed reflect attractive opportunities for risk reduction through international diversification. They also conclude that the case for international diversification of an equities portfolio has not been diminished by events preceding and including October 1987. On October 19th, when U.S. stocks plunged nearly 23 percent, markets worldwide were affected. However, this was a unique phenomenon occurring during a relatively short period and thus does not weaken the argument for international diversification as a long-term portfolio strategy.

International diversification plays an important role in an asset allocation program. In Chapter 8 we discussed the use of sector funds which also fit into an asset allocation portfolio. The idea here is that you're spreading the risk across the securities markets in different countries, allocating your assets more heavily to those markets offering the greater values. G. Peter Schieferdecker, a member of the board of directors of the Clemente Global Growth Fund and a consultant to fund investors, offers some ob-

## Table 9–1. World Market Correlations

|  | Correlations* | |
| --- | --- | --- |
| U.S. Versus: | Jan. '80–Dec. '83 | Jan. '84–Mar. '88 |
| Australia | .51 | .46 |
| Canada | .75 | .81 |
| France | .37 | .49 |
| Germany | .40 | .38 |
| Hong Kong | .15 | .53 |
| Japan | .27 | .26 |
| Switzerland | .52 | .56 |
| United Kingdom | .51 | .62 |
| Pacific Basin Index | .36 | .32 |
| Europe Index | .60 | .63 |
| EAFE Index | .53 | .50 |

*Correlations are based on U.S. dollar adjusted monthly total returns.
Source: WORLD MARKET CORRELATIONS by David L. Brunette and Douglas Stone, Frank Russell Company, May 18, 1988.

servations on asset allocation in the Closed-End Insights box.

## ASSET ALLOCATION
## WITH CLOSED-END FUNDS
### G. Peter Schieferdecker
### Pilot Rock Investments

There really is no investment that does not involve some form of risk. The best way to deal with risk is to accept it as a challenge and to use portfolio diversification to reduce its impact. A disciplined asset allocation program offers a time-tested tool to reduce risk and increase rewards.

Two important concepts should guide the structuring of an asset allocation plan: *first*—knowledge of an investor's risk tolerance, and *second*—awareness that the deployment of assets within a portfolio should be regularly reviewed and adapted to the constantly changing investment scene. Mutual funds, especially closed-end funds, are excellent vehicles for investors who know their own risk tolerance and want to structure an asset allocation program to match it. Since all funds must adhere to a specific investment policy, investors can deploy assets among several investment styles, industry groups, or geographic areas and be reasonably certain that the fund manager will stick to his knitting. Anybody who reviews the history of financial markets will agree that there have been many changes in volatility and direction that, over time, necessitated often quite drastic course corrections. These changes can most efficiently be implemented through funds.

Closed-end funds, particularly those that trade at a discount from net asset value, offer an excellent opportunity to use the new global investment opportunities that have broadened our investment horizon. Many new funds have been introduced that invest in countries that have become important economic powers in the last forty years or are showing above average growth. For instance, recent political developments and the emergence of new economic powers, particularly in Asia, have presented attractive opportunities for global investment. It is in this area that closed-end funds are now playing an increasingly important role.

As markets all over the world began to grow, our own markets became less dominant. In 1980, U.S. stock markets represented 50% of the world's total market capitalization. In 1989 this figure had declined to 31%. In the same period the weight of Japan's markets increased from 15% to 39%. Other markets in Europe and Asia have also grown, broadening investment opportunities in the "global village."

The year 1989 brought a record number of public offerings of new closed-end country funds. These funds can be seen as similar to ADRs (American Depositary Receipts which represent holdings in a foreign company). Country funds enable a U.S. investor to diversify worldwide through a representative portfolio invested in one country, without having to cope with foreign markets and security settlements in other currencies. Recently, more sophisticated global funds have been introduced that invest worldwide in broadly defined security groups, such as small growth companies or specific industries. They are the real asset allocation tools of the future because they select the best companies in a specific sector and, at the same time, emphasize the most promising markets to invest in.

## More Opportunities

By investing on an international scale you have many more investment opportunities open to you. Today, nearly two-thirds of the market value of publicly traded companies exists outside the United States. So if you invest only stateside you are eliminating nearly two-thirds of the possible investment opportunities. An extreme analogy would be a resident of Florida investing only in companies headquartered there.

There are tens of thousands of different companies traded in over three dozen stock markets located around the globe. These markets are growing in importance and more U.S. money managers are investigating them. Portfolios consisting of only U.S. stocks ignore many of the largest companies in the world, like Switzerland's Nestle and Italy's Olivetti. To be well diversified we suggest that you consider having a minimum of 10 to 20% of the value of your investments in foreign securities. As you gain some familiarity and experience with foreign stock CEFs you may want to raise this allocation. More importantly, if your choices and timing are good, you will gradually see the rewards of global investing.

Much investor enthusiasm has been shown for the 1992 unification of Europe's markets and the gradual disappearance of the Iron Curtain. Europe is on the verge of a transformation that has been likened to the Industrial Revolution that began in England in the 18th Century. The large single market and the likely benefits of Soviet *perestroika* promise change and opportunity.

The key elements of Europe 1992 are *integration* and *liberalization*, according to Jon Woronoff, publisher of *International Fund Monitor*. Woronoff illustrates this in a discussion in his publication reproduced in Figure 9–1. (The address and phone number of *International Fund Monitor*, which is quite useful for investors in non-U.S. markets, can be found in Appendix II.)

## Better Opportunities

The performance of foreign equity markets is often far ahead of that of the U.S. market. Morgan Stanley Capital International data showing the annualized total returns of equities in 12 different stock markets, the U.S. market, and the World Index for the past 20 years as well as the past 10 years appear in Table 9–2.

There are more markets that could have been included in this tabulation but the data are sufficient to show that foreign markets can far outperform our own. Of course, others, like Australia in this table, can underperform ours. Further, the past performance of any market is

**Figure 9–1. What is European Integration?**

As of 1992, or thereabouts, for most sectors, it should be possible for a company in one country to cover not only its national market as today but the whole common market of over 200 million customers, the second biggest in the world. Not only should it be easier to distribute goods and services beyond its border, it should also be easier to open branches and subsidiaries abroad or to buy up foreign enterprises. This is already quite an advantage. But it is enhanced by the second aspect which is less often mentioned, namely liberalization. Even within its home market, as well as in other countries, it should be much easier to do business without encountering bureaucratic regulations and red tape.

This opens various opportunities for enterprising businessmen. Most obviously, a company with a particularly good product or service, or one that can be sold cheaper, or one that uses more advanced technologies or is covered by proprietary rights, should be able to boost sales considerably because it can operate in the larger market. It should also be able to bring down costs because it can produce on a larger scale. Moreover, a multinational which already covers several markets will no longer have to maintain factories and offices in all of them, a costly and complicated practice. It can work out of the cheapest or most efficient facilities and close down the rest.

For a dynamic company which wants to expand or diversify, it will no longer be as necessary to operate a local branch, slowly acquire personnel, and gradually make its products or services known. It can, quite simply, assuming it has the money, buy up other companies in the desired sectors. Or it can enter into alliances, tie-ups, or mergers to share production capabilities, technologies, or costs.

Source: Jon Woronoff, *International Fund Monitor*, December 1989, pp. 1–2.

not necessarily indicative of its future performance. A good case in point is Japan. Even though the Japanese market was the top performer for the past 20 years in our table, we should recall that the bear market in Japan which hit in early 1990 led to a plunge of over 25% in the Nikkei stock averages in the first quarter. The point is simply that cross-border investing can lead to better returns at the same time that it provides greater diversification.

**Table 9–2. Annualized Total Returns from Selected World Markets**

|                     | Compound Annual Total Returns* | |
|---------------------|:----------------:|:-------------:|
|                     | Past 20 Years    | Past 10 Years |
| Australia           | 7.53%            | 12.44%        |
| Belgium             | 15.90            | 19.62         |
| Canada              | 10.58            | 10.78         |
| France              | 12.44            | 16.42         |
| Germany             | 12.25            | 15.44         |
| Hong Kong           | 18.85            | 13.64         |
| Italy               | 6.89             | 21.96         |
| Japan               | 22.40            | 28.36         |
| Norway              | 14.61            | 11.90         |
| Singapore/Malaysia  | 16.36            | 12.90         |
| Sweden              | 16.27            | 28.43         |
| United Kingdom      | 12.02            | 18.18         |
| United States       | 9.29             | 15.58         |
| World Index         | 12.04            | 18.80         |

*In U.S. dollars with dividend net of foreign tax. Both the 20- and 10-year periods end 12/31/89.
Source: Morgan Stanley Capital International.

Perhaps the best indicator of this is the Morgan Stanley World Index which significantly outperformed the U.S. market in both the past 20 and 10 years.

There are several reasons for the superior performance of certain foreign equity markets. First, a number of countries have experienced a higher real growth in gross national product than we have. A number of countries also have higher personal savings rates which, in turn, facilitate a higher degree of capital formation. Additionally, for some time now certain foreign countries have been extremely competitive in producing and marketing a number of traditional U.S. products. The automobile and consumer electronic products are common illustrations.

It is not surprising that open- and closed-end funds which concentrate their assets in foreign equity markets were among the best performing funds of the 1980s. This was especially evident in 1989 when many country funds far outperformed other stocks as we'll see in the next chapter. Some of the older funds investing in non-U.S. equities have compiled impressive records over longer periods. For the five years ended June 30, 1990 The Korea Fund and The Mexico Fund had compound annual total returns of 40.91% and 45.61%, respectively, based on Lipper Analytical Service's data. In contrast, Lipper's diversified equity funds group (which invest mainly in U.S. equities) had a 14.83% compound annual total return over that same period.

## Protection Against a Falling Dollar

Currency fluctuations can represent gains as well as losses to foreign investors. For instance, investing abroad at a time when the U.S. dollar is at a high value relative to foreign currencies could provide significant gains if the dollar should decline as it did beginning in 1985. This is the reason some people invest in foreign securities—to hedge themselves against a decline in the value of the dollar. Currency fluctuations are a double-edged sword, however, and present a risk to overseas investors.

## RISKS OF INVESTING ABROAD

The cross-border investor faces the usual kinds of company-specific, industry-specific, stock market, and economy-wide risks that domestic investors do. However, the stock market and economic risk factors could be greater in many countries than they are in the United States. For instance, the stock markets in developing countries are often more volatile and less liquid than ours. Furthermore, these markets may not be as strictly regulated. Or a foreign economy may be experiencing uncontrollable hyperinflation or have huge foreign debt obligations.

One who invests in foreign markets must be concerned about converting income and principal from those investments (which would be payable in foreign currency) into the currency of their own country. This gives rise to two risk factors that are unique to international investing: currency (or exchange) risk and political risk.

## Currency Risk

The thing to remember about currency risk is that when the U.S. dollar strengthens or gains in value relative to a foreign currency you would be adversely affected if you have investments in that country. If the opposite were true and the foreign currency gained relative to the dollar you would benefit. An illustration of the effect of currency fluctuations on investment returns appears in Figure 9–2.

### Figure 9–2. Effect of Currency Fluctuations on Investment Returns

Assume you made an investment in a publicly-traded French company. Your investment would be affected by the investment performance of that company as well as by the fluctuations in the French franc relative to the U.S. dollar.

Suppose your French security costs 10,000 francs. If the exchange rate is five francs for the dollar the cost in U.S. currency would be $2,000. Let's look at several possible outcomes.

1. The security price stays the same in francs but the franc grows stronger relative to the dollar. The exchange rate is now four francs to the dollar. Whereas before each franc was worth 20 cents it is now worth 25 cents. Your security is still worth 10,000 francs but this now translates into $2,500. In this case you benefited from a decline in the value of the dollar relative to the franc.

2. Suppose instead that the security has increased in value to 12,000 francs but the franc has declined in value. The exchange rate is now six francs to the dollar. Even though your investment has increased 20 percent in francs it is still worth $2,000, your original cost, since the value of the franc relative to the dollar has decreased by nearly 17 percent. The increase in the value of the dollar relative to the franc adversely affected your return.

Naturally, other possibilities exist. The idea is that currency exchange rates fluctuate as well as security prices, introducing an additional element of risk. Some fund managers attempt to limit this risk through the use of currency futures. But, this doesn't always work since the timing of the currency hedge could be off.

## Political Risk

Political risk is a problem in politically unstable or vulnerable countries. From a U.S. investor's point of view, political risk is defined as any uncertainty about the ability to convert a particular foreign currency into U.S. dollars.[5] Examples are foreign exchange controls that block the investor from repatriating income and principal or (at the extreme) total expropriation of the U.S. investor's foreign holdings. Nationalization of a certain economic sector in a particular country would be another illustration. However, recent trends evident in the 1980s have been away from nationalization towards privatization, as in the case of the United Kingdom. Thus, nationalization is less of a problem now than it was in the 1950s and 1960s.

By diversifying across many different foreign markets an individual is able to lessen significantly the risks of international investing. For this reason the authors favor multicountry CEFs as they facilitate maximum diversification.

Additionally, foreign market funds generally have the ability to move their assets defensively into money market instruments, including U.S. and non-U.S. government securities, if a market they invest in is affected by negative factors. Information on a particular fund's defensive asset allocation policies can be determined from its prospectus or by talking to a shareholder representative. Make sure the funds you plan to invest in have the ability to move their assets defensively should the need arise. Let's now look at your fund options for cross-border investing.

## THE INVESTMENT COMPANY ROUTE

The increasing numbers of open- and closed-end funds which invest abroad offer a sensible way for individuals to broaden their diversification to include foreign equities. The fund concept is more important for investing in foreign equities than in domestic.

There are a number of obstacles and pitfalls which confront people who try to invest overseas via the direct route by purchasing stock on a foreign market. Stateside investors face difficulties such as obtaining timely, meaningful investment information and getting stock transactions executed in distant foreign markets. One could choose to invest in American Depositary Receipts (ADRs) which are traded domestically and represent an ownership interest in a foreign company. This simplifies the process but ADRs are not available on many foreign companies; they are created mainly for bigger companies of greater investor interest. ADRs on more issues have become available, however, and even more should be introduced in the future according to a recent *Barron's* article indicating that ADRs exist on over 750 issues.[6] The authors feel that ADRs are most appropriate for larger, sophisticated investors who have considerable knowledge about international investing and the companies which underlie the ADRs.

Even if you are hesitant about using investment companies for your domestic investments because you like having the freedom of being able to pick your own stocks you still should consider CEFs for your foreign equity holdings, provided you can get them at a discount.

## Returns to CEF Investors

The return to the investor in CEFs which hold foreign equities would be affected by several factors:

1.  A change in the fund's discount or premium to NAV. As the authors emphasized in earlier chapters, your objective as a value investor is to find a good fund trading at a discount. Things are no different when the fund deals in foreign equities.

2.  The performance of the foreign market or markets represented in the fund's portfolio.

3.  The skill of the portfolio manager in selecting stocks which perform well relative to their respective stock market benchmarks.

4.  Changes in the exchange rate of the U.S dollar relative to the currencies represented in the fund's portfolio. Some funds may try to hedge

against adverse currency fluctuations. If the fund manager follows a policy of hedging the success as well as the cost of the program would further impact performance.

## Types of Funds

Since our primary topic is closed-end funds the authors will focus on the use of these funds to diversify internationally. The funds which invest overseas (both open- and closed-end) can be divided into four general categories:

**Global funds** These funds can invest in the host country as well as in a wide range of different foreign countries.

**International funds** The international funds invest exclusively in different foreign countries, holding no domestic equity positions.

**Regional funds** The regional funds restrict their investing to a particular region of the globe like the Pacific Basin or Europe.

**Country funds** Single country funds confine their activities to investing in a specific country like Germany, Indonesia, or Switzerland.

The global funds have the greatest diversification potential and the country funds have the least. It follows that global funds would have the lowest risk. The global fund manager decides how to allocate assets among the different nations based on the fund's investment philosophy. Investors who already have substantial holdings of domestic stocks or domestic funds may want to select an international fund rather than a global fund.

Regional funds are somewhat riskier than international funds since they have less global diversification. The single-country funds have the least diversification and therefore, by themselves, entail the greatest risk. However, investors who hold shares in a number of different country funds could achieve homemade international diversification.

## CONCLUSIONS

Frank Russell Company research as well as a number of academic studies present convincing evidence of the risk-reducing benefits of international diversification. Foreign markets also offer investors the chance for superior long-run returns as evident by their past performances and the favorable outlook for certain regions of the world. In the next chapter we'll examine the closed-end funds investing in non-U.S. equities.

### Notes

[1]Theodore J. Grayson, *Investment Trusts, Their Origin, Development, and Operation* (New York: John Wiley & Sons, Inc., 1928), p. 11.

[2]Kenneth Jessell and Jeff Madura, "What Affects International Fund Returns?" *AAII Journal,* May 1988, p. 10.

[3]*Ibid.,* p. 11.

[4]David L. Brunette and Douglas Stone, *World Market Correlations,* Frank Russell Company, Tacoma, WA, May 18, 1988.

[5]Gordon J. Alexander and William F. Sharpe, *Fundamentals of Investments* (Englewood Cliffs, NJ: Prentice-Hall, Inc., 1989), p. 628.

[6]Anna Merjos, "Lure of Faraway Places: ADRs Grow in Numbers and Popularity," *Barron's,* April 16, 1990, pp. 27–29 and 31.

# CHAPTER 10

# *Single- and Multi-Country Funds*

There are some three dozen equity markets throughout the world which perform differently in each year for different reasons. Over the past two decades many foreign markets have had more generous returns than the United States, in spite of domestic stock market indexes reaching record levels (Chapter 9, Table 9–2). Non-U.S. equity market capitalization has now risen to about two-thirds of the world's total. Economic growth rates for many Pacific Basin countries have exceeded the U.S. growth rate over the past two decades. These facts mean that you must consider investing a portion of your portfolio in non-U.S. equities. In this chapter we examine the best vehicles for doing so: the single- and multi-country CEFs.

## SINGLE-COUNTRY FUNDS

In the late 1980s and early 1990s single-country funds clearly captured the most interest and excitement within the whole spectrum of closed-end funds. This is because

223

if you buy one, such as those investing in Germany, Spain, Korea, Taiwan, Mexico, or Turkey, you are participating in the excitement of what's happening in a particular nation. If you buy them right, you can make a lot of money in a short time as many have.

But buyer beware! Volatility is the key word here. Some country funds can be as volatile as OTC glamour stocks, if not more so. Since many of these funds are more volatile and therefore riskier than the more broadly diversified global and international funds, those who have poor timing lose a bundle. This occurred in early 1990 when many investors who had followed the 1989 rainbow of forever higher prices and premiums suddenly found the markets collapsing around them. Substantial amounts of capital were lost in the early 1990s because investors didn't do their homework. It was a classic speculative bubble with speculators chasing after stocks trading at overly inflated prices. We want our readers to avoid "tulip crazes" like this. Whether you participated in this speculative bubble or not, we will take you through the maze of the country fund phenomena so if you do decide to invest, you will at least have done your homework.

Most people who invest in country funds pick one which invests in a single country rather than a regional or cross-border fund such as The Europe Fund, The Latin America Investment Fund, or Scudder New Asia Fund, which capitalize on economies or events of countries in a particular region. Broadly speaking, regional funds also fall under the general heading of "country funds." But regional funds offer an additional dimension of professional management since the proportionate asset allocation to each country in the region is determined by the fund's adviser. The Templeton Emerging Markets Fund is an international fund under our multi-country fund definition, but it buys securities of companies in specific emerging markets. It is really a collection of country funds; the risks of investing in any one of the emerging nations would be considerable.

Nearly all single-country funds are closed-end. As many of them invest in illiquid markets, large redemptions in an open-ended structure could prove disastrous for the fund manager who should be long-term oriented.

Closed-end fund managers have a better record of taking a longer view, but open-ending activity may change this.

The historic evolution of the country fund, beginning in the early 1950s with the Israel Development Corp. and the open-end Canadian Fund, is traced in Figure 10–1. You notice that not many country funds were introduced until the latter half of the 1980s. Note also that in 1989 four of the best performers on the NYSE were country funds. These funds have produced fat underwriting fees for a brokerage industry still suffering from the after-effects of the 1987 crash. In 1990 investor interest shifted more towards the regional or cross-border funds. This was partly a function of availability: there simply aren't that many countries left and investors wanted more funds.

## Figure 10–1. Historic Evolution of Country Funds in the U.S.

- In 1951 the Israel Development Corp. (IDC) was offered. To our knowledge it was the first single-country CEF underwritten in the U.S. A small fund with net assets under $20 million, IDC invested in a diversified group of Israeli firms; in 1978 it was merged into Ampal-American Israel Corp.

- In 1952 the open-end Canadian Fund began offering its shares. As its name implies it invests in Canadian equities. Still in existence as an open-end fund, it is now a member of the Alliance fund group.

- The Japan Fund, the first U.S. closed-end single country fund of major significance was offered in 1962. Its excellent performance mirrored the burgeoning Japanese economy. The fund appeared on the *Forbes* honor roll seven times. It open-ended in 1987.

- The Mexico Fund, offered in June 1981, was the first single-country CEF underwritten in the 1980s. It is now one of five Latin American funds.

- The Korea Fund, offered in August 1984, has always traded at a premium as direct foreign investment in South Korean companies is restricted.

- The First Australia fund was underwritten in December 1985.

- Single-country CEFs investing in Europe first appeared in 1986. The Italy Fund, offered in February, was the

**Figure 10–1. Continued**

first. It was followed by the France Fund (which subsequently open-ended) and The Germany Fund. The Taiwan Fund was offered towards the end of the year.

- In 1987 country funds of the regional variety began to appear. Asia Pacific Fund and Scudder New Asia Fund were offered. The Templeton Emerging Markets Fund also went public. Single-country fund IPOs in 1987 were Malaysia Fund, Swiss Helvetia Fund, and The United Kingdom Fund.

- 1988 country fund IPOs were Brazil Fund, First Iberian Fund (which invests in Spain, and to a lesser extent, Portugal), India Growth Fund, Spain Fund, and Thai Fund.

- 1989 offerings were Austria Fund, Chile Fund, First Philippine Fund, Portugal Fund, ROC Taiwan Fund (in conjunction with the reorganization of a predecessor fund), and The Turkish Investment Fund.

- 1989 was a banner year for country fund performance. Four of the NYSE's ten best performing issues were country funds: Spain Fund (#1), up 198.8%; Asia Pacific Fund (#4), 178.4%; Thai Fund (#5), 174.5%; and Germany Fund (#10), 156.7%.*

- In January 1990 New Germany Fund raised $375 million, the largest single-country equity fund IPO in U.S. history. During 1990 twelve single-country funds had been underwritten by mid-August: France Growth Fund, Emerging Germany Fund, Future Germany Fund, New Germany Fund, Indonesia Fund, Irish Investment Fund, Jakarta Growth Fund, Japan OTC Fund, Mexico Equity & Income Fund, Singapore Fund, Growth Fund of Spain, and Thai Capital Fund. Additionally, Austria Fund and Taiwan Fund offered more shares.

- 1990 was a big year for European regional funds reflecting investor interest in 1992. Alliance New Europe Fund, The Europe Fund, European Warrant Fund, GT Greater Europe Fund, Pacific-European Growth Fund, and Scudder New Europe Fund had been issued by August 1. The Latin America Investment Fund went public in July.

*Richard Karp, "The home-run hitters," *Institutional Investor*, March 1990, p. 52.

Many of the newer CEFs, aware that so many investors have been burned by new issues going quickly to discounts, have built-in provisions to keep discounts narrow and discourage raiders. These provisions could also discourage those of us seeking the value offered by the discount, however. In spite of some open-ending activity, we see plenty of opportunities presented by so many new funds many of which still can't generate enough demand to remain at prices near NAV.

## WHAT ATTRACTS PEOPLE TO COUNTRY FUNDS?

A number of things. There is the emotional attraction— to invest in a specific country such as in the land of your forebearers. Some may want to participate in the exciting events of 1992 or the reunification of Germany. In each case, we'll assume you don't want to buy the securities directly. Even if American Depositary Receipts (ADRs) are available you probably want diversification. A single-country fund may be the answer. Virtually all of them are listed on the New York Stock Exchange. Just two trade on the American at this writing: First Australian Fund, and First Iberian Fund. Thus, they provide the individual with the utmost convenience. And they are also regulated by the SEC which offers additional assurance to the individual.

What do you look for in a country fund? First, you are hiring a highly professional manager who presumably knows the country well and can offer the best of its securities to investors; this person may be a native who has worked in the country's investment arena for many years. Secondly, in comparison to buying the individual securities of a country, that is, speculating on the fortunes of particular companies, there is the liquidity of the NYSE as well as someone to take care of the taxes and dividends, a task which can be a nightmare for the individual investor. So a country fund seems to fill the bill. They have a strong combination: diversification, professional management, liquidity, convenience, and flexibility.

Country funds made such a strong impression on investors in the 1980s that they are likely to be around for many years. But many have performance records that leave much to be desired or are too new to have established a record. Management fees and other expenses are higher for funds investing in non-U.S. securities, but the rewards can be great if your selection and timing are right. In fact, with country funds, timing is much more important than with other CEFs because of their volatility. These and other factors need to be considered before you invest.

In spite of what we have said, there is a strong case for investing in country funds. There are over 30 single-country funds at this writing and more are scheduled to come despite the slowdown in new issues. Funds are in the works for Germany (Germany Smaller Companies Fund), Finland (The Finland Fund), Mexico (The Mexico Capital Growth Fund), Poland, and New Zealand (First New Zealand Fund). Many of the funds offered recently are of the regional variety (which we cover later in the section on multi-country funds). There will be more and more of these to choose from, particularly those investing in Asia and Europe. Others, perhaps even a Hungary Fund or a China Fund will appear one day as stock exchanges in these regions develop. We understand that a Soviet Fund may soon be a reality. There is ample room for growth.

## COUNTRY FUND PROFILES

Space considerations will not allow us to profile each country fund. But, we have several illustrations which should indicate something about the nature of these funds. If you plan to invest, study the S&P *Stock Reports* profile and request the fund's recent shareholder reports.

**The Germany Fund (NYSE: GER)** With their origins dating back to the 16th century, the German securities markets are among Europe's largest. GER offered 7.5 million shares at $10 apiece in its 1986 IPO, making it the first U.S. fund to invest in Germany. A diversified fund, GER seeks long-term capital appreciation by investing primarily in equity securities of companies representing a broad spectrum of German industries. It tends to emphasize the bigger "blue chip" German companies. GER, which traded at a 58% premium at the end of 1989, was the tenth best performer on the NYSE that year. To increase invested assets, it had a second public offering of 4.5 million shares at $12.75 each in December 1989. Its assets were $173 million as of June 30, 1990.

The popularity of investing in Germany gave rise to three new CEFs underwritten in 1990: **New Germany Fund (NYSE: GF), Future Germany Fund (NYSE: FGF),** and **Emerging Germany Fund (NYSE: FRG).** All of these new funds are non-diversified. GF, the first one underwritten, raised $375 million, the largest country fund IPO in history. GF invests primarily in medium- and smaller-sized West German companies. FGF invests in West German companies that are going to do business in the East German bloc. FRG invests in medium- and smaller-sized West German companies likely to benefit from developments in East Germany and other parts of Eastern Europe. If listed securities markets develop in East Germany, these new funds may also start investing in East German-based companies.

Together the four funds have assets approaching $1 billion. Clone funds reduce premiums and create wider discounts. As of August 17, 1990 the original fund was trading at a slight discount and the new ones at discounts ranging from 21 to 24%. This is a case of too many shares chasing too few buyers. Those who want to invest in Germany now have several choices.

DB Capital Management International GmbH and Deutsche Bank Capital Corporation serve as adviser and manager, respectively, for GER, GF, and FGF. Both are subsidiaries of Deutsche Bank AG, the largest bank in West Germany. FRG's adviser, Asset Management Advisors of Dresdner Bank-Gesellschaft für Vermongensanlageberatung mbH, is a subsidiary of Dresdner Bank Aktiengesellschaft, second largest bank in West Germany.

**The Indonesia Fund (NYSE: IF)** A non-diversified fund, IF was underwritten in March 1990 when 4 million shares were sold at $15 each. Its primary objective is capital appreciation. The Republic of Indonesia is the fifth largest country in the world. It is regarded as the world's largest archipelago consisting of over 13 thousand islands off Southeast Asia. Java is the most densely populated of the islands. Indonesia's agriculture and mineral resources, large labor force, low wage rate, and pro-investment government policy have resulted in a strengthened economy.

The Jakarta Stock Exchange, the country's principal stock market, has a rather small number of listings characterized by high price volatility and relatively low liquidity. The exchange is expanding rapidly, however, thanks to deregulation measures designed to increase the role of the private sector in the Indonesian economy. As of February 6, 1990, 58 companies were listed on the Jakarta Stock Exchange. At that time their market capitalization was approximately U.S. $2.8 billion.

The fund does not normally expect to hedge against a decline in the value of the Indonesian rupiah. IF can invest up to 20 percent of its assets in unlisted Indonesian equities. Its adviser is BEA Associates, Inc., a U.S. investment counseling firm with some $10 billion in assets under management. James Capel (Far East) Ltd. of London serves as Indonesian economic adviser to the fund. **Jakarta Growth Fund (NYSE: JGF),** underwritten in April 1990 and managed by Nomura Capital Management, also invests in Indonesia. In addition to the two U.S.-based Indonesian country funds nine have been formed in other jurisdictions to invest there.[1] This obviously reflects investor optimism about the growth potential of Indonesia's stock market.

A word of caution. If you are interested in Indonesia try to buy IF or JGF at a discount. Relatively small, illiquid, exciting stock markets, like the Jakarta Stock Exchange, can become overpriced when investor demand outweighs supply. Don't overpay for growth!

**The Mexico Fund (NYSE: MXF)** The first single-country fund of the 1980s, MXF went public in June 1981 at $12 a share, raising over $100 million. With assets of $297 million at June 30, 1990, MXF is one of the larger country funds. MXF seeks long-term capital appreciation by investing in a broad cross-section of securities listed on the Bolsa Mexicana de Valores S.A. de C.V. (Mexican Stock

Exchange). It cannot, however, invest in all sectors of the economy.

The securities traded on the Bolsa tend to be less liquid and more volatile than those traded on U.S. exchanges. The fund has experienced extreme price volatility and wide discounts. It quickly fell from its $12 issue price to near $2 after a major peso devaluation in 1982. In November 1983 MXF sold about 10 million shares for under $3 apiece through a rights offering. Its price finally recovered, exceeding $14 in 1987, but then fell again to around $3 that year. In 1989 its price ranged between $5.25 and $12.75. It reached an all-time high of $17.13 in the summer of 1990. Value. investors who bought its shares at excessive discounts when it was trading in the $2 to $3 range and patiently held their shares were well rewarded. This is an example of good timing. MXF's adviser is Impulsora del Fondo Mexico, S.A. de C.V.

A second single-country fund investing in Mexico, **Mexico Equity & Income Fund (NYSE: MXE),** was offered in August 1990.

**Swiss Helvetia Fund (NYSE: SWZ)** SWZ is a $115 million fund founded in 1987. It is jointly owned by the Hottinger family of Paris and Zurich, one of Europe's oldest banking families, and Wilkinson & Hottinger, an investment advisory firm in New York. In the United States the fund is managed by Helvetia Capital Corp. SWZ has over half its holdings in registered shares which generally cannot be purchased by non-Swiss nationals. Registered shares offer the best value among the three classes of shares traded in the Swiss market and are the only class carrying voting rights. A non-diversified fund, SWZ has large holdings in a number of world class companies including a large position in Nestle AG (about 13% of net assets), the world's largest food company.

SWZ does not hedge against currency fluctuations. A strengthening of the U.S. dollar relative to the Swiss franc can hurt the NAV performance of U.S. investors unless Swiss corporate earnings gains offset the currency decline. Georges de Montebello, SWZ's executive vice president, feels that the Swiss franc is an excellent currency to hold as a long-term investment. "We are convinced that

when you buy Swiss assets you are buying worldwide purchasing power protection. We are going to protect your assets."[2] SWZ is the best way to own blue chip and special
situation Swiss companies which should benefit from the
1992 single market, as well as from the opening of Eastern
Europe, particularly in the sales of heavy machinery. The
fund, which is value-oriented, invests for the long term.

**The Turkish Investment Fund (NYSE: TKF)** The
$97 million nondiversified fund invests primarily in eq-
uity and equity-related securities of Turkish corporations.
As of April 30, 1990, 67% of TKF's assets were invested in
20 Turkish companies. The risks are high as the country's
securities markets are very small and illiquid and regulation is limited. Meaningful information is difficult to obtain on Turkish companies. High inflation has been a
problem in Turkey as well as a continuing devaluation of
the Turkish lira against the U.S. dollar. The Turkish stock
market plunged during the Middle East crisis. TKF is
managed by Morgan Stanley Asset Management Inc. and
has a Turkish adviser, TEB Ekonomi Arastirmalari A.S.
which collects a portion of the management fee. This fund
is an example of one investing in a Third World capitalist
economy. Others include those investing in Brazil, Indonesia, Mexico, the Philippines, and Thailand. These stock
markets can be highly volatile as illustrated by the recent
problems in the Philippines and their negative impact on
its stock market and the performance of The First Philippine Fund which plunged dramatically in 1990.


**COUNTRY FUND VALUATION**

As you know, some country funds can sell at huge premiums; others have traded at deep discounts. The swings
of investor sentiment, from extremes of optimism to pessimism and back again to optimism, can be swift and dramatic. Investors clearly have overreacted in the cases of
different country funds. In the late 1980s many of them
were the darlings of Wall Street—like exciting growth
stocks that trade at outrageous P/E ratios.

## Country Funds as Growth Stocks

One way to explain the overly inflated premiums seen on some country funds is to think of them as being comparable to the more glamorous growth stocks. If country fund investors view certain CEFs this way they would apply the principles of growth investing in valuing them. Growth investors will pay considerably higher P/Es than value investors would for stocks because their major objective is to find companies with high expected growth rates in earnings per share, not bargains on a price-earnings ratio basis. Country fund investors following this philosophy will pay higher price/NAV ratios for their funds because they are forecasting a much higher growth rate in the NAV than the average CEF could be expected to have. When the price/NAV ratio is above 100% the fund sells at a premium; when it is below 100% it sells at a discount. Some glamorous country funds have traded at price/NAV ratios of 200% or more, meaning their premiums were 100% or greater. For example, Spain Fund traded at a 130% premium at year-end 1989 reflecting a price/NAV ratio of 230%.

Value investors, on the other hand, focus primarily on the price/NAV ratio and less on the growth in NAV. They want to limit downside risk by paying a low price/NAV ratio for a fund. Value investors may also argue that the future is uncertain and it is impossible to predict the growth rate in NAV. The authors subscribe to this philosophy. In addition to the level of a fund's price/NAV ratio, investors should determine how the market (or markets) in which the CEF invests are being valued. This is explained in Figure 10–2.

## 1989 Country Fund Performance

Country funds were the darlings of Wall Street in 1989. Part of this was due to the excellent performances of the markets in which they invest. But an even bigger part in some cases was the fact that many were trading at significant discounts at the end of 1988. Many of the discounts had turned into enormous premiums by the end of 1989.

**Figure 10–2. International Stock Market Valuation**

An investor in single-country or regional funds should consider the valuation of the fund's stock market (or markets) in
terms of gauges such as the price/book value and price/earn-
ings ratios. Examine these valuation indicators along with the
fund's discount or premium level to gain a better feel for the
value you are getting. Valuation measures on a variety of different international indexes appear monthly in *Morgan Stanley
Capital International Perspective* (Morgan Stanley, 1251 Avenue of the Americas, New York, NY 10020; telephone, 212-
703-2965). Ask your broker about this publication. With this
data you can see how much value you are getting in terms of
four different valuation indicators for the specific country or
area. The ratios are: price to book value; price to cash earnings; price to earnings; and dividend yield. Lower price ratios
and higher yields normally reflect greater value.


Using Lipper data we can see the difference between the
performances of the funds in terms of NAV total return
and market price (Table 10–1). The multi-country funds
are included for comparison.

Observe the fat premiums on many of the single-
country funds. The reason for this in most cases was that
the market price increase far outdistanced the NAV total
return. Spain Fund is a good example. Its 1989 NAV return
of 31.79% was far below its 198.82% price change, resulting in a premium of 129.74%. The Germany Fund is a
similar case. Both rose from discounts at the end of 1988
to heady premiums. In the case of the Korea Fund the NAV
return was about the same as the price change because its
premium at the end of 1988 was also excessive.

These funds became the glamour stocks of the late
1980s for those who bought them right—they had ro-
mance that attracted the speculator—something will happen in the future to make you rich—now is the time to get
on the bandwagon. But, unfortunately, reality set in and
as in so many other cases, speculators lost money, sometimes large sums. The reasons are always the same. The
greater fool theory applies: someone has bid up the price
to the greater fool who will take it off the former's hands

**Table 10–1. 1989 NAV Total Return versus Market Price Performance* (12 Months to 12/31/89)**

| Single Country Funds | NAV Return (%) | Change in Price (%) | Premium or Discount (−) 12/31/89 (%) |
|---|---|---|---|
| The Brazil fund | 71.21% | 63.49% | −31.70% |
| First Australia Fund | 3.64 | 7.69 | −15.95 |
| First Iberian Fund† | 18.16 | 72.58 | 26.54 |
| Germany Fund | 51.21 | 156.67 | 58.31 |
| Swiss Helvetia Fund | 18.74 | 59.21 | 15.90 |
| India Growth Fund | 31.29 | 100.00 | 25.08 |
| The Italy Fund | 32.39 | 76.92 | 11.78 |
| Korea Fund | 30.20 | 30.95 | 85.31 |
| Malaysia Fund | 53.45 | 150.00 | 36.07 |
| Mexico Fund | 68.86 | 95.45 | −14.00 |
| Spain Fund | 31.79 | 198.82 | 129.74 |
| Taiwan Fund | 75.98 | 41.01 | 25.26 |
| Thai Fund | 108.87 | 174.47 | 71.63 |
| The United Kingdom Fund | 6.35 | 14.67 | −7.88 |
| **Global and International Funds** | | | |
| Asia Pacific Fund | 82.21% | 178.43% | 12.48% |
| Clemente Global Growth | 35.83 | 35.59 | −14.46 |
| Scudder New Asia Fund† | 48.59 | 78.87 | −3.85 |
| Templeton Emerging Markets | 46.19 | 87.30 | 10.07 |
| Worldwide Value Fund | 11.74 | 17.83 | −5.94 |

*NAV return reflects the change in NAV including reinvestment of all distributions. The percentage change in market price is not a measure of management performance.
†Fund is leveraged.
Source: *LIPPER Closed-End Equity Funds Analysis*, First Edition, 1990.

soon to unload it on the next person, perhaps an even bigger fool.

## 1990 Country Fund Fall Out

The dealings of Japanese brokerage firms appear to have been a major force underlying the 1989 speculative bubble in country funds. The firms had acquired substantial amounts of stock for their own accounts and greatly inflated prices by actively promoting country funds to their retail Japanese customers as long-term investments. As country fund prices rose, those firms that trade for their own accounts apparently sold the stock they had bought earlier, netting substantial profits.[3]

This kind of manipulation is illegal in the United States but the sad thing is that U.S. investors got taken to the cleaners, in spite of all the protections offered them. Some sophisticated investors and some stockbrokers who called *The Scott Letter* about this were aware of what was going on and tried to sell short, but for the most part couldn't because they were unable to borrow the stock. Even Tom Herzfeld, an expert at selling short for his closed-end fund clients, told us that he couldn't borrow many shares. When the Nikkei Index suddenly plunged more than 25% in the first quarter of 1990, many Japanese customers who had borrowed heavily had little cash and were forced to unload their country fund holdings to meet margin calls. The Nikkei Index is quite volatile and we may see these kinds of sudden sell-offs again in the future. The precipitous drop in country fund share prices, however, far exceeded any decline in the underlying country's stock market.[4]

## Discounts Prevail in August 1990

We counted a whopping 27 of the 31 single country funds at discounts as of August 17, 1990; 13 of those were at discounts greater than 15% and 9 were at discounts wider than 20%, the two deepest being 28 and 26% on The Turkish Investment Fund and Irish Investment Fund, respectively.[5] The four funds at premiums were at levels considerably below those prevailing at the end of 1989. The Korea Fund is the best example of one that has consistently sold at large premiums since it was formed in 1984 (it was at a 31% premium as of August 17 versus 85% at the end of 1989). The reasons for its persistent premium are twofold: the attractive, growing South Korean market and the fact that the Korea Fund has been the only way non-Koreans could invest in its stock market. Investors have always felt that CEFs investing in attractive markets that are either restricted or closed to foreign investors deserve a premium. We concur. Another example would be the Taiwan Fund (a 42% premium as of August 17). But if the restricted or closed market becomes more open the premium would decline. For example, in 1992 the Korean economy and stock market will start to open up to increased foreign investment. This could cut the fund's premium significantly.[6]

## Premium-Discount Fluctuations

The fact that country fund premiums can quickly turn to discounts and vice versa, especially during volatile periods as existed in 1988–90, is vividly illustrated in Table 10–2 which contains the 52-week high/low range in discount and premium levels of 28 single-country funds, two regional funds (Asia Pacific Fund and Scudder New Asia Fund) and Templeton Emerging Markets Fund. (If the fund has been in existence for less than 52 weeks the range reflects its shorter trading life).

Most of the ranges are quite dramatic. For example, Spain Fund ranges from a 145% premium to a 9% discount and Germany Fund from a 100% premium to a 15% discount. The First Philippine Fund plunged from a 61% premium to a 27% discount.

## Should You Pay a Premium?

As value investors, the authors have recommended buying at a discount. This same philosophy can be applied to country funds. But there are problems. The discounts often don't exist on the funds you'd like to own and you might not want the ones trading at excessive discounts. Jon Woronoff feels it is appropriate for investors to pay *reasonable* premiums for country funds which hold securities in promising foreign markets. Woronoff explains that funds with big discounts may deserve them since the foreign market could be excessively volatile, its securities overpriced, or the political risk high. Woronoff is more of a growth investor than a value investor. His viewpoints, as contained in *International Fund Monitor*, appear in Figure 10–3.

As you probably know, many of the most successful funds such as Templeton Emerging Markets Fund, Source

**Table 10–2. 52-Week Premium-Discount Range on
Single-Country Funds***

| Fund | Began | Prem. or Disc. (−) 52-Week Range | |
| | | High (%) | Low (%) |
|---|---|---|---|
| Asia Pacific Fund | 4/87 | 43 | −21 |
| Austria Fund | 9/89 | 85 | −20 |
| Brazil Fund | 3/88 | 27 | −55 |
| Chile Fund | 9/89 | 30 | − 7 |
| Emerging Germany Fund | 3/90 | 1 | −23 |
| First Australia Fund | 12/85 | 20 | −24 |
| First Iberian Fund | 4/88 | 87 | −19 |
| First Philippine Fund | 11/89 | 61 | −27 |
| France Growth Fund | 5/90 | 22 | −20 |
| Future Germany Fund | 2/90 | 8 | −24 |
| Germany Fund | 7/86 | 100 | −15 |
| Growth Fund of Spain | 2/90 | −3 | −24 |
| India Growth Fund | 8/88 | 47 | −13 |
| Indonesia Fund | 3/90 | 19 | −9 |
| Irish Investment Fund | 3/90 | 8 | −26 |
| Italy Fund | 2/86 | 38 | −21 |
| Jakarta Growth Fund | 4/90 | 26 | −3 |
| Japan OTC Equity Fund | 3/90 | 48 | −20 |
| Korea Fund | 8/84 | 120 | 16 |
| Malaysia Fund | 5/87 | 75 | −15 |
| Mexico Fund | 6/81 | 14 | −21 |
| New Germany Fund | 1/90 | 51 | −21 |
| Portugal Fund | 11/89 | 40 | −12 |
| Scudder New Asia Fund | 6/87 | −4 | −26 |
| Spain Fund | 6/88 | 145 | −9 |
| Swiss Helvetia Fund | 8/87 | 16 | −16 |
| Taiwan Fund | 12/86 | 98 | −23 |
| Templeton Emerging Mkts. | 3/87 | 14 | −12 |
| Thai Fund | 2/88 | 91 | −7 |
| Turkish Investment Fund | 12/89 | −10 | −32 |
| The United Kingdom Fund | 8/87 | −5 | −19 |

*The ranges were computed as of August 17, 1990.
Source: These data were provided courtesy Smith Barney Research.

**Figure 10–3. A Case for Paying a Premium**

. . . we would hardly recommend buying country funds just because they sell at a discount, let alone a big discount, since it may be deserved. To the contrary, we would tend to recommend funds which sell at a *reasonable* premium. For they usually reflect the fact that there is something particularly good about them. When you have places where the index nearly doubles in a year, like Korea and Taiwan earlier on, and Austria and Thailand more recently, it certainly seems worthwhile to pay a bit more to get vastly higher returns.

In practice, this advice has worked more often than not, and definitely more often than buying funds that sell at a discount. But it is still necessary to determine when a premium is reasonable and not exaggerated. That is easier said than done.

Unlike some advisers, we think it is justifiable for foreign funds, as opposed to domestic funds, to have at least a modest premium. After all, if you want to buy foreign stocks you would have to cover hefty commissions plus the cost of currency conversion and sundry items. It would run you at least 5%. So why shouldn't you pay 5% or so to get into a fund that does all that for you and which can be bought on the New York Stock Exchange in U.S. dollars? If the corresponding market is closed to foreign investors *except* through country funds, why shouldn't you pay even more to get in?

It would seem that more and more Americans agree with this logic because more and more country funds are trading at a premium. Indeed, if you want to buy country funds you almost have to accept that as a fact of life. Limiting yourself to funds which sell at a discount keeps you out of many, including the most successful.

Source: Jon Woronoff, *International Fund Monitor*, June 1990, p. 7.

Capital, and Bergstrom Capital, as well as many of the better bond funds, trade frequently at premiums. But, they never go to extremes like 60, 80, and 100% reached by some country funds. We still say that you should try to buy at discounts, or add to positions when discounts appear. We also feel it is the discounts which make CEFs attractive in the first place. But, Woronoff has a point. We want you to consider his viewpoint as well as ours.

**Funds at Large Discounts**

What about country funds that sell at large discounts? It
may be an untested market, such as Turkey, or one with
known problems such as Brazil or the Philippines. The
Mexico Fund sold at discounts near 50% when investors
were turned off by the country's problems. The United
Kingdom Fund has sold at large discounts because their
market was depressed for so long. As noted earlier, the
three new Germany funds were at discounts deeper than
20% because they all came to market at once in early
1990 and some investor disenchantment had set in with
so many similar funds. Additional possible reasons for
wide discounts would include a fund with an excessive expense ratio or one where the management capability is
suspect. These kinds of situations always attract bargain
hunters who are patient enough to wait for better times.

The $54 million **Irish Investment Fund (NYSE:
IRL)** which went public in late March 1990 and traded at
a 33% discount on October 12, 1990 is apparently an example of good value according to a *Forbes* article.[7] IRL invests most of its assets in stocks traded on the tiny Irish
Stock Exchange which has a total market capitalization
of $13.6 billion and nearly 120 listings. The Irish market
appears to represent good value at this writing with an average P/E of 9 times. IRL's annualized expense ratio of
1.8% based on its first several months of operation is not
excessive for a small country fund. The Bank of Ireland
based in Dublin is the primary adviser; Salomon Asset
Management Inc serves as co-adviser.

**THE MULTI-COUNTRY FUNDS**

The equity-oriented multi-country funds are identified in
Table 10–3. The number of CEFs in this group is still relatively small compared to their large number of open-end
cousins.

The global and international CEFs are a good way for
those new to foreign investing to get started. They are
more broadly diversified in a global sense and the fund
manager is making the decision about the relative weight-

**Table 10–3. Multi-Country Funds**

|                                      |         | Net Assets 7/31/90 |
| Fund                                 | Began   | (Millions) |
| ------------------------------------ | ------- | ---------- |
| Alliance New Europe Fund             | 3/90    | $263       |
| Asia Pacific Fund                    | 4/87    | 155        |
| Clemente Global Growth Fund          | 6/87    | 77         |
| The Europe Fund                      | 4/90    | 125        |
| The European Warrant Fund            | 7/90    | 66         |
| G.T. Greater Europe Fund             | 3/90    | 240        |
| The Latin America Investment Fund    | 7/90    | 56         |
| Pacific-European Growth Fund         | 4/90    | 40         |
| Scudder New Asia Fund                | 6/87    | 141        |
| Scudder New Europe Fund              | 2/90    | 204        |
| Templeton Emerging Markets Fund      | 3/87    | 200        |
| Worldwide Value Fund                 | 8/86    | 59         |

Source: Net assets were obtained from the individual funds.

ings given to the countries in the portfolio. At this writing several of the multi-country funds are trading at double digit discount levels. However, the regional funds (which we consider closer to country funds) and the internationally-oriented Templeton Emerging Markets Fund are highly specialized. You would want to limit your investment in any one of them based upon your risk tolerance. If you invest in a global fund, on the other hand, you may not be getting as much international exposure as you think if the fund invests half or more of its portfolio in the U.S.

Let's look at the individual funds and their objectives.


## FUND PROFILES

**Alliance New Europe Fund (NYSE: ANE)** A non-diversified fund, ANE seeks capital appreciation by focusing on equity securities of European companies. In March 1990 ANE issued 21 million shares at $12 a share. The fund invests in emerging growth companies but also in larger companies in growing economic sectors. ANE also looks for investment opportunities within the "east bloc" countries of Eastern Europe, and may invest up to 20% of its

assets in securities of issuers in these countries. Up to
25% may be invested in securities which are not readily
marketable. Because it experienced a significant discount
ANE may convert to an open-end fund in 1991.

**Asia Pacific Fund (NYSE: APB)** This regional fund
seeks long-term capital appreciation by investing mainly
in equities of companies doing business in emerging equity markets in the Asia Pacific region. These include
Hong Kong, Korea, Malaysia, the Philippines, Singapore,
Taiwan, and Thailand. APB does not invest in Japan. The
fund's adviser is Baring International Investment (Far
East) Limited.

**Clemente Global Growth Fund (NYSE: CLM)** CLM
seeks long-term capital appreciation through investment
in equities of small- and medium-sized companies ranging
in market cap between $50 million to $1 billion. The investment adviser is New York-based Clemente Capital,
Inc., headed by Lilia and Leopoldo Clemente, a highly regarded wife-and-husband global money management
team.[8] Clemente Capital also manages The First Philippine Fund.

A global fund, CLM concentrates on securities traded
both in the world's major stock markets and in many of
the smaller and emerging markets. The manager expects
normally to invest at least 85% of CLM's assets in securities traded outside the U.S. Over 30 countries are represented in the portfolio; about half of them are emerging
markets. Historically, CLM has had a large exposure to
Japanese securities. CLM is growth-stock oriented.

**The Europe Fund (NYSE: EF)** EF offered 7.25 million shares at $15 each in late April 1990, netting just un-
der $102 million. In June it exercised a so-called green
shoe to expand its capital to nearly $118 million. EF
seeks long-term capital appreciation through investment
primarily in European equity securities. Based in London,
it is managed by Mercury Asset Management, a division
of the S.G. Warburg Group. The adviser also manages The
United Kingdom Fund covered in Chapter 11 ("British and
Canadian Funds"). Annual distributions have been set at
7% of NAV. This is the first overseas fund to adopt a fixed
payout and this may reflect fears of hostile takeovers. In

the second quarter of 1995 EF's board will consider a tender offer at NAV, and, unless all shares are tendered, an open-ending proposal will be submitted to shareholders in early 1996.[9]

**The European Warrant Fund (NYSE: EWF)** A flexible fund, EWF invests mainly in several different types of equity warrants traded in European markets. Its objective is enhanced capital growth as European warrants provide a leveraged exposure to European equities. The European warrant market began to develop in the 1970s, but the big growth did not begin until the late 1980s. Germany has the largest warrant market. European warrants have maturities averaging about 3.5 years and some German warrants extend up to 10 years. EWF is the first fund of its kind to be publicly offered in the United States. States Julius Baer Securities Inc. serves as adviser. There are also two sub-advisers.

**G.T. Greater Europe Fund (NYSE: GTF)** A non-diversified fund, GTF seeks long-term capital appreciation. Its adviser, G.T. Capital Management in San Francisco, provides management services to ten G.T. Global Mutual Funds as well as other clients. GTF is its first closed-end fund offered to U.S. investors. The closed-end format was chosen for GTF as it will be investing a portion of its assets in less liquid securities. G.T. Capital is a part of the G.T. Group, an international investment advisory organization which manages assets of more than $10 billion most of which is invested overseas.

In March 1990 the fund offered 16 million shares at $15 per share. GTF seeks to identify those countries and industries where the economic and political changes affecting Western and Eastern Europe are likely to produce above-average growth. It expects to invest in a broad range of securities of European issuers in both established and emerging markets. The fund will also invest in certain special situations, such as joint ventures. GTF feels that these special situations could provide the initial means of investing in Eastern European countries. GTF will invest no more than a third of its assets in special situations and other illiquid securities.

According to a May 7, 1990 press release from G.T.

Group, GTF's first investment in Eastern Europe was a
private placement of equity securities of a Hungarian floor
and textile manufacturer, Graboplast. "This is an exceedingly westernized company with 40% of its products sold
to western companies," says GTF's London-based portfolio manager Nigel Ledeboer. The fund management is
reviewing many companies in Eastern Europe. "Privatization of companies is occurring at an accelerated rate in
Eastern Europe," says Ledeboer. "Poland and Czechoslo-
vakia are both planning to privatize approximately 10
companies, and Hungary plans to take private an estimated 200 companies." G.T. believes that by the end of
the decade Greater Europe will be one large economic
block of 700 million people.

**The Latin America Investment Fund (NYSE:
LAM)** A nondiversified regional fund, LAM focuses mainly
on listed equities of companies in Brazil, Chile, and Mexico. It may also invest up to 25% of its assets in unlisted
equities and up to 30% in external debt issued or guaranteed by Latin American governments or governmental entities ("sovereign debt"). BEA Associates, Inc. manages
most of LAM's investments and Salomon Brothers Asset
Management Inc. serves as adviser for investments in sovereign debt. The fund also has separate sub-advisers for
the countries in which it invests.

**Pacific-European Growth Fund (Amex: PEF)**
Another new regional fund, PEF defines its region more
broadly than the others. Its main investment territory
consists of the Pacific Basin and Europe with the initial
emphasis being on the former. According to its prospectus
it may eventually invest up to 25% of its assets in other
areas of the world, excluding U.S. companies. A relatively
small fund, PEF netted $36.5 million from its April 1990
offering.

Piper Capital Management Inc., a wholly-owned subsidiary of Piper Jaffray, is the adviser. Edinburgh Fund
Managers PLC, an international money manager based in
Scotland, is sub-adviser. That firm was founded in 1969
as a majority-owned subsidiary of American Trust PLC, a
Scottish closed-end fund founded in 1902. It's attractive
to use a U.K.-based sub-adviser for funds which invest in

the Pacific Basin. PEF's sub-adviser has had extensive experience in many of the former British colonies like Singapore and Hong Kong. The fees earned by both the adviser and sub-adviser are based on performance.

**Scudder New Asia Fund (NYSE: SAF)** A regional fund, SAF invests at least 50% of its assets in smaller Japanese companies. Recently, about half of its assets were invested in Japanese equities. It also has equity positions in companies in Hong Kong, India, Indonesia, Korea, Malaysia, the Philippines, Singapore, Thailand, and the United Kingdom. This fund is popular with institutional investors as they hold about 38% of its shares.

**Scudder New Europe Fund (NYSE: NEF)** This relatively new regional fund is non-diversified and invests in equity securities traded on smaller or emerging European securities markets. It issued 16 million shares at $12.50 each in February 1990. NEF invests in both Eastern and Western European companies. Its objective is long-term capital appreciation. Emphasis is placed on "specialized investments" like privately-held European companies, companies that have recently gone public, and government-owned or -controlled companies that are being privatized.

**Templeton Emerging Markets Fund (NYSE: EMF)** EMF is a diversified fund that invests in dozens of emerging markets around the globe which fit their investment criteria. It is the only international CEF profiled, as it invests in a large number of countries but not in the United States. In its prospectus the EMF defines an emerging country as one having a low or middle income economy, as determined by the World Bank. There are currently over 95 countries which meet the definition. EMF will consider investing in 42 of them as investment in many emerging countries is not feasible or may involve unacceptable political risk. Institutional investors hold about 27% of EMF's outstanding shares.

The fund manager, Dr. J. Mark Mobius, is located in Hong Kong because of the fund's extensive exposure to Asia, its large investments in the Crown Colony, and his interest in eventually investing in China. Mobius travels the world often to South America, Africa, the mid-East, and the other Asian countries in search of cheap stocks.

EMF employs the philosophy of John Templeton (explained in Chapter 4), chairman of the $17 billion Templeton International. Incidentally, the Templeton Emerging Markets Investment Trust, PLC, was launched in 1989 in the United Kingdom for local U.K. investors. It is also managed by Mobius.

The authors contacted Dr. Mobius to learn about his approach to investing in emerging markets in greater detail. He explained that at Templeton they use essentially the same techniques for all their global investments whether they be in developed or emerging markets. Excerpts from his response appear in Figure 10–4.

**Worldwide Value Fund (NYSE: VLU)** VLU is a global fund with the objective of long-term growth of capital. It invests primarily in equity securities throughout the developed world its adviser believes are undervalued—companies not closely followed or out-of-favor. Over half

**Figure 10–4. An Interview with Dr. Mobius**

**Fredman & Scott: Would you explain your approach to investing in emerging markets.**

**Mobius:** [Our analysis] . . . is based on a ground-up fundamental value-oriented approach. We are quite strict about selecting potential investments by seeking bargains regardless of the market trend or outlook. However, in applying our investment philosophy to emerging markets we make modifications. Since the universe of emerging markets is focused and more limited than a global portfolio we must be more flexible in the selection of criteria for evaluating companies. Criteria must differ among various countries and industries. For example, use of book value as a criterion may be flawed in some markets because of some idiosyncrasy of accounting methods used in that country, while in other markets it could be an excellent measure of value.

**F&S: Why do you favor a "bottom-up" approach?**

**Mobius:** We have found that the bottom-up value approach to investing is very appropriate in emerging markets because it forces the analyst to focus on essential company performance characteristics without filtering them through macropolitical and macroeconomic lenses. Emerging market countries tend to be perceived as subject to wide swings in political and economic activity. This tends to influence and perhaps distort the investor's perception of the individual company investment. We try not to allow those political and economic factors to influence our evaluation of the viability of an individual company investment, unless those factors have a direct bearing on the company's ability to operate and produce profits over the long term.

**F&S: Isn't it difficult to obtain meaningful information on emerging market companies?**

**Mobius:** Starting with this individual company focus places great demands on (1) the information-gathering and (2) the analytical skills of the investor. Emerging markets tend to have a shortage of adequately detailed company information gathered in a consistent way over a long historical time span. Templeton researchers sometimes ask for as much as ten years of audited company balance sheets and profit and loss statements when they analyze companies. However, the task of obtaining such information could be enormous in countries where regulations regarding company disclosure are inadequate (or inadequately enforced), and where public companies are often considered the private domain of the majority owner or his family and an information request from a minority stockholder is considered presumptuous. It is in such environments that good local contacts and sources of information are essential so that the required information can be obtained. It is thus of great importance for the investment organization to have a long history of local relationships.

**F&S: What are the difficulties investors face in analyzing data provided by emerging market companies?**

**Mobius:** As to the demands on the analytical skills of the investor in evaluating those emerging market companies, most daunting are the varying accounting standards used in each country and, more important, the varying taxation regimes that influence the way accounting standards are applied. It is essential, therefore, for the analyst to ensure that he understands what methods management and their accountants are using in an effort to minimize their tax liability. In addition, the high inflation and currency devaluation in many emerging market countries influence the accuracy of accounts since various (and differing) methods of inflation adjustments, decreed either by the accounting standards organizations or by the government, could render accounts all but meaningless for the value investor looking to the long-term growth prospects of a company.

its assets normally are invested in equities of non-U.S. issuers; only about 20% was invested domestically at this writing. The fund may hedge when its adviser believes the U.S. dollar will strengthen against one or another of the currencies in which VLU is invested.

VLU's adviser is London-based Lombard Odier International Portfolio Management Ltd., a subsidiary of Lombard, Odier & Cie, one of the oldest and largest private banks in Switzerland. The adviser also manages **The Second Market Investment Company** which invests in small French companies and **The Europe 1992 Fund,** a mutual fund organized under Luxembourg laws not available to U.S. investors.[10]

There are other global CEFs besides those identified in this chapter. Z-Seven (covered in Chapter 6) can now invest up to 80% of its assets abroad. Niagara Share (Chapter 5) has for many years invested between 20% and 35% of its assets overseas. Some domestic equity funds may invest 5% or 10% of net assets in foreign equities. For instance, Growth Stock Outlook Trust (Chapter 6) may now invest up to 15% in foreign securities. Charles Allmon would like to increase this percentage.

## THE QUESTION OF EXPENSES

Funds which invest in non-U.S. equities generally have significantly higher expenses than domestic equity funds. There are obviously greater expenses associated with overseas investing, including higher management fees, greater research costs, taxes, and so on. To get an idea of the differences in magnitude, examine the composite figures in Table 10–4.

**Table 10–4. 1989 Fiscal Year Median Expense Ratios***

| | |
|---|---|
| Global and international funds | 2.541% |
| Single country funds | 2.328 |
| Median—all funds | 1.414 |

*Total expenses as a percent of average net assets.
Source: *LIPPER Closed-End Equity Funds Analysis,* Second Edition 1990.

To determine the reasonableness of a particular fund's expense ratio you should consider the following:

1. The fund's expense ratio relative to other comparable funds—that is, those of about the same size and with similar investment objectives.

2. The size of the fund's expense ratio relative to its premium or discount level. Funds with higher expense ratios should sell at lower premiums or greater discounts than their peers, other things equal.

3. Any extraordinary items. Expense ratios can occasionally be affected by costs incurred in fighting off an unwanted raider. For example, Clemente Global Growth Fund's expense ratio was 3.05% in 1989 because it included extraordinary expenses associated with takeover litigation.

## CONCLUSIONS

Our position on single-country funds is summarized by two words: *USE CAUTION.* Country funds are the most volatile of all CEFs. This is clearly shown by their records in 1989 and 1990. We are conservative investors dedicated to a get rich slowly philosophy and, although we see a place for country funds in your portfolio, we do not want you to lose money on them.

For those new to international investing we recommend a well-diversified multi-country fund selling at an attractive discount. If you want to invest in regional funds you should diversify into both the Asian and European groups. Again, look for those discounts.

### Notes

[1]Michael T. Porter, "Indonesia: Exciting but Expensive," *Closed-End Country Funds Review* (New York: Smith Barney, Harris Upham & Co., Inc., May 1990), p. 5.
[2]*The Scott Letter: Closed-End Fund Report*, July-August, 1989, p. 4.

[3]Tatiana Pouschine with Nikhil Hutheesing, "How do you say 'manipulation' in Japanese?," *Forbes*, February 19, 1990, pp. 40–41.

[4]Nikhil Hutheesing, "What did in those country funds?," *Forbes*, May 28, 1990, p. 180.

[5]Based on data from *Barron's*, August 20, 1990, p. 114.

[6]Norman Tepper, *The Value Line Investment Survey*, March 30, 1990, p. 371.

[7]Michael Fritz, "A bargain," *Forbes*, September 3, 1990, pp. 148 and 150.

[8]Richard Phalon, "Family Portfolio," *Forbes*, September 7, 1987, pp. 148 and 150.

[9]*The Scott Letter: Closed-End Fund Report*, July-August, 1990, pp. 4–5.

[10]*Ibid.*, p. 5.

CHAPTER 11

# British
# and Canadian
# Funds

We want to give readers a taste of what the closed-end fund markets in Britain and Canada have to offer. After all, the CEFs we've written about trace their roots to the nineteenth century "investment trusts" of Britain. An overview of the London and Scottish funds should provide you with a richer background for understanding and analyzing the closed-end fund industry. We'll also give you an introduction to the much smaller Canadian closed-end fund market which provides a way to purchase good quality Canadian equities at substantial discounts.

Today, still known as investment trusts, the numerous British funds are well situated for investing in Europe, Asia, and North America where they have had exposure for more than a century. The discounts on British investment trusts apparently are of interest to certain sophisticated U.S. investors, as indicated in a recent *Forbes* article.[1]

251

## THE LONDON INVESTMENT TRUSTS

The earliest investment trust, which was private, was created by King William I of the Netherlands in Belgium in 1822. But the industry arising out of this didn't have much growth until the first public investment trust, **The Foreign and Colonial Investment Trust PLC,** was formed in London in 1868. Lord Westbury, a former Lord Chancellor, and four colleagues decided to form "a common law trust" to invest in overseas government bonds as British securities at the time were yielding only about 3% while those overseas offered over twice as much. The countries the trust invested in included Bolivia, Chile, Russia, and Egypt.

Originally named The Foreign and Colonial Government Trust, the company specialized in overseas government bonds. In 1891, Foreign and Colonial broadened its scope to include railway and industrial debentures and its present name was adopted. It pioneered the financing of the U.S. railroad industry. Funds investing solely in bonds have since fallen by the wayside in the United Kingdom as Foreign and Colonial and other British trusts have focused almost exclusively on equity investments since the 1920s. A number of British trusts which emphasize income have portfolios consisting of bonds as well as stocks, however. Investment trusts are technically no longer trusts but public companies with shareholders and boards of directors.

Foreign and Colonial has set the pattern for the British and American closed-end fund industry for over 122 years. A global fund, it pioneered the concept of international diversification in 1868. In 1961 it was one of the first U.K. investors to invest in Japanese equities. In 1987 it became the first British investment trust to be listed on the Tokyo Stock Exchange.[2] Its long-term performance record is impressive. Management attributes this success to an ability to identify good growth companies and undervalued stock markets. Based on the market outlook the fund may employ leverage or borrowing; it is increased or decreased (or eliminated) depending on market conditions. Finally, the management keeps a close eye on currencies and tries to anticipate major currency movements.

Today this investment trust has about 26,000 individual shareholders although 70% of its shares are held by 30 to 40 institutions. The manager, Foreign & Colonial Management Limited, has five other investment trusts: Enterprise Trust, Eurotrust, Germany Investment Trust, Pacific Investment Trust, and Smaller Companies.

Roger Adams, an investment trust specialist in London, provides a thorough overview of the London investment trust market in our Insights box. Adams explains that the London market is large, diverse, and undervalued. Many of the trusts are specialized and invest in other countries. Their capital structures are more intricate than those of U.S. closed-end funds and investment trust warrants are very popular there. In contrast to the largely retail U.S. fund market, the major investors in the U.K. trusts are institutional. Management fees on British trusts are very low and many leverage their capital structures moderately, a process they term "gearing."

---

**THE LONDON INVESTMENT TRUST MARKET**
**Roger Adams**
**Director U.K. Equities Division**
**S.G. Warburg Securities**

It was a distinguished American investor, Walter Eberstadt of Lazard Frères who, a few years ago, described the London investment trust market as "the largest pool of undervalued liquid assets anywhere in the world." Mr. Eberstadt was remarking not only about the sheer size of the London investment trust market, but also about the high discount at which U.K. investment trust shares traded in relation to their underlying asset values. Today, Mr. Eberstadt's remarks still hold true.

Representing about 3% of the total London market, some 230 investment trusts are quoted daily. Excluding trusts with fixed lives and split capital structures (known as dual purpose funds in the United States), total assets of U.K. investment trusts amount to around 35 billion U.S. dollars. The average geographical spread of these assets is about two-thirds in the United Kingdom, over a fifth in North America, and the rest divided equally between the Far East (including Japan) and Continental Europe. On average the shares of these funds trade at a discount of 15% to underlying asset values.

This large pool of "undervalued assets" includes only a few generalist funds. To a greater or lesser extent the majority of trusts have focused investment policies in such areas as income growth, international capital appreciation, smaller company specialization, and so on. In recent years there have been an increasing number of more specialized trusts. This has been caused by a determination on the part of fund managers to make their funds more appealing to both private and institutional investors.

Recently many specialist trusts, providing a particular service to investors, have appeared as new issues. For example, there are now six Japanese specialist funds, 11 Continental European funds, 13 Far Eastern regional funds, one Latin American regional fund, and European editions of the U.S., Korea and India funds. In addition there are other single-country funds specializing in Chile, France, Germany, Indonesia, Ireland, Malaysia, New Zealand, Singapore, Spain, Thailand, and Turkey. There are also about a dozen funds specializing solely in the United States, three of which have split capital structures. To give an example of the degree of specialization we can mention **The Leveraged Opportunities Trust** investing in U.S. stub equities, **The Mezzanine Capital and Income Trust** backing buy-out deals led by the Jordan Partners in New York, and the **London American Ventures Trust** supporting venture capital sponsored by Hambrecht and Quist in California. Within many specializations there are further specializations. For example, the **Baillie Gifford Shin Nippon Trust** invests only in smaller Japanese companies. **German**

**Smaller Companies Investment Trust** and **The Second Market Investment Company** do likewise in Germany and France, respectively.

The U.K. investment trust industry has a proud history going back more than a century. In 1868 the **Foreign and Colonial Investment Trust** was launched with the specific objective of enabling "the investor of modest means" to spread risk through a collective investment vehicle. Today Foreign & Colonial is still going and is one of the great success stories of the U.K. investment trust scene. By following a generalist investment policy it has, over the last 20 years, grown its net asset value by almost 1,000%. This compares to a U.K. inflation rate over the same period of just over 500%.

Many of the first U.K. investment trusts, launched a hundred years ago in Edinburgh and Dundee as well as in London, financed much of the growth of the U.S. economy at the end of the last century. Investing in such instruments as railway bonds and land mortgages, they survived the traumas of the 1920s and 1930s only to fall victim of exchange controls and an adverse taxation climate in the 1960s and 1970s. Even today the tax treatment of U.K. trusts means that, in contrast to the United States, there are no bond funds in the United Kingdom. Over the last 30 years many private investors have sold their investment trust holdings to institutional investors. The latter now control over 70% of the industry. Thus, the ownership of U.K. trusts differs markedly from that in the U.S. where most closed-end funds are owned by private individuals.

This ownership pattern partly explains the existence of a discount on most U.K. trusts. U.K. institutional investors are unwilling to offer a premium for the privilege of paying management fees to other people. Moreover, under U.K. tax laws investment trusts are not allowed to buy in their shares for cancellation by the use of their capital account. There is, therefore, no obvious defense against the discount problem. This factor has not been lost on various predatorial investors willing to exploit the obvious difference between share price and underlying asset value. The British Coal Board Pension Fund has recently completed a take-over bid for the **Globe Investment Trust,** the largest U.K. investment trust with assets around 2 billion U.S. dollars. In recent years limited partnerships have been formed with the specific aim of forcing investment trusts to unitize or "open-end." In 1988 the U.S. Grace-Pinto partnership successfully "open-ended" the specialized **Crescent Japan Fund.** At the same time the AJS Partnership, with surprising support from U.K. institutional investors, did much the same to the **Drayton Japan** trust.

Recently, the U.K. trust industry has been fighting back by tempting private investors with cheap savings schemes and imaginative capital structures. However, there is some way to go before the discount is narrowed and Walter Eberstadt's remarks no longer apply.

What are the major technical differences between U.K. investment trusts and U.S. closed-end funds? First, U.K. trusts are not registered with the U.S. Securities and Exchange Commission. As a result they are not promoted to U.S. investors. U.K. trusts are normally quoted in sterling on the London exchange. As with U.S. funds, U.K. trusts pay no capital gains tax. However, unlike their U.S. counterparts, they do not distribute realized gains. The result is that all gains are rolled-up tax free within the funds. However, up to 85% of their received revenue must be distributed to shareholders.

These arrangements actually pose a difficulty for U.S. investors who, under U.S. tax laws, are obliged to pay 'national capital gains tax' even if they have not actually realized their gain by selling their U.K. trust shares! However, for non-U.S. taxpayers, U.S. institutional investors and U.S. citizens with off-shore accounts, U.K. investment trusts can offer some exciting investment possibilities.

Apart from excellent long-term performance records U.K. funds have low management fees. For example, the management fee on the 1 billion dollar **Alliance Trust of Dundee** is only around 0.2% of assets per year. Launching costs for new funds are also lower in the United Kingdom where the method of syndicating new issues is not used. This means that underwriting expenses seldom exceed 2%. Finally, about a third of all U.K. trusts have warrant issues. Usually launched at the time of the issue of a new trust, with average lives of about five years, these warrants are extremely popular with private individuals who have made large profits during the bull markets of the 1980s. For example, the warrants of the **Edinburgh Investment Trust** have just expired with an intrinsic value of around 120 pence. When first issued five years ago Edinburgh Investment warrants could be bought in the market at around 20 pence each. Many newly created exotic specialist funds have warrant issues. Examples are **Abtrust New Thai, EMF Java, First Spanish Investment Trust,** and even the **Leveraged Opportunities Trust**—the ultimate warrants on warrants!

The U.K. investment trust industry is currently enjoying new popularity with international investors. It is not just the attraction of the discount anomaly but also the novelty of new share structures and various investment instruments that is tempting their interest. Apart from warrants, the U.K. investment trust industry can offer *stepped preference shares, zero-dividend preferred shares*, various types of capital and income shares, and various hybrid combinations of all types of shares. In fact the huge variety of investment choice makes the U.K. investment trust market one of the most fascinating investment areas anywhere in the world. It should not be overlooked by the serious international investor intent on finding value and building wealth.

Adams, who also researches and deals in U.S. closed-end funds, told *The Scott Letter* that he is critical of the high underwriting costs on new CEFs in the United States which take away assets from the investor. As Adams stated in the Insights box, these fees seldom exceed 2% on the U.K. funds. He also told *The Scott Letter* that "The U.K. directors are given warrants that can be exercised after seven years. So, if the fund does well, they will be able to exercise the warrants for a lot of money. If the funds do not do well, they get nothing for their time. It puts the manager on the same side as the shareholders."[3]

It is relatively easy for prospective trust investors to obtain information on the U.K. Trusts. There is a trade organization known as the Association of Investment Trust Companies which issues a monthly information service giving performance comparisons and rankings of the entire spectrum of British investment trusts. There is also a quarterly magazine, *Investment Trusts,* published by John Davis of the *Observer,* which covers every aspect of the industry.

At least five London-based investment managers have closed-end funds which trade on the NYSE. They are Mercury Asset Management (part of S.G. Warburg) with its United Kingdom Fund and The Europe Fund (Chapter 10); Kleinwort Benson which manages Kleinwort Benson Australian Income Fund (Chapter 14); Lombard Odier which manages Worldwide Value Fund (Chapter 10); and G.T. Management which runs G.T. Greater Europe Fund (Chapter 10). The most visible of these in the United Kingdom is the United Kingdom Fund. A profile of it, based upon a report published in *The Scott Letter,*[4] follows.

**The United Kingdom Fund (NYSE: UKM)** With assets of $46 million, London-based UKM began in August, 1987 and invests in equity securities of U.K. companies, seeking long-term appreciation. It may invest up to 35% of its assets in debt securities but has not done so to date. The equity market of the U.K. ranks third in total capitalization after the markets in Japan and the United States. The London Stock Exchange is the predominate U.K. equity market.

The fund's manager is Mercury Asset Management, a division of S.G. Warburg Securities of London, with offices in 15 countries. Mercury is the largest manager of pension funds in the United Kingdom, with some $40 billion under management. They are very keen on expanding their presence in the U.S. and spend much time in their New York office where UKM's executive offices and its chairman, Anthony Solomon, are located. Bear Stearns Funds Management Inc. serves as the administrator.

UKM has had a difficult time because of a bear market since 1987, high inflation, and the highest interest rates in Europe. Its portfolio contains a very aggressive list of securities mixed between small and large companies—about 70% blue chips and 30% smaller companies. UKM may hedge its assets when it believes the pound sterling may suffer a substantial decline against the U.S. dollar; however, it does not intend to enter into currency transactions on a regular basis.

There are no specific anti-takeover provisions, but management will submit an annual proposal to open-end if the average discount is over 10% during the first 12 weeks of each year. This criteria was met in 1990 (the discount averaged 10.68% during the 12 weeks ending March 31) and management submitted a proposal to shareholders at its annual meeting to open-end the fund, but it was defeated. Management hopes to continue as a closed-end fund because it considers UKM to be a "flagship fund" for its investment advisory business.


## THE SCOTTISH FUNDS

In Scotland there are 47 investment trusts and a number of unit trusts, the British name for mutual funds. Their oldest investment trusts are **The Scottish Investment Trust** (1887) in Edinburgh and **The Alliance Trust** (1888) in Dundee. The former was established to invest stockholders' funds in a portfolio of well-managed growth companies diversified on a worldwide basis. It had assets of about $1 billion at the end of 1989. The latter is now the largest self-administered (independent) investment trust in Scotland, with assets of about $1.2 billion.

Alex Hammond-Chambers, chairman of Ivory & Sime, PLC in Edinburgh, has had over a quarter of a century of experience in the business. Ivory & Sime, a global manager, was founded in Edinburgh in 1895 and is today one of the leading investment houses in Europe. To learn more about the Scottish investment trusts the authors wrote to Hammond-Chambers. He told us that the Scottish invest-

ment trust industry was created in the latter half of the
nineteenth century to provide international investment
opportunities for the considerable Scottish wealth that the
industrial revolution had spawned. Excerpts from his response appear in Figure 11–1 in interview format.

### Figure 11–1. Interview with Alex Hammond-Chambers

**Fredman & Scott: What are some salient features of the
Scottish investment trusts?**

**Hammond-Chambers:** [In the United Kingdom] . . . capital gains are not taxed, are not allowed to be distributed by
British law, and therefore have to be internally reinvested with
wonderful compounding results. This corporate structure also
allows for effective and (relatively) safe use of leverage, which
of course can and, over the years has, enhanced performance.
The I.R.S., it must be stated, assesses U.S. investors in British
investment trusts on the internally realized but undistributed
capital gains published in the annual reports.

**F&S: What is the size and general orientation of the Scot-
tish investment trust market?**

**Hammond-Chambers:** One quarter of all British investment trusts are Scottish, managed by 12 different money
management firms based in Scotland; their combined assets
amount to approximately $13.5 billion. The international tra-
dition of Scottish management is reflected in the international
mix of different trusts: of the 47 Scottish managed investment trusts, 20 have "global" or "continental" . . . objectives.
The other half (and by far the largest part by asset value) have
a traditional British bias to the portfolio, for income reasons.

**F&S: Could you describe some of newer internationally
oriented trusts?**

**Hammond-Chambers:** As new international investment
opportunities develop, so new Scottish investment trusts are
formed to take advantage of them. Investment remits can be
quite specialized: During the past five years, for instance, Ivory
& Sime's **Pacific Assets Trust** and Edinburgh Fund Manager's **Dragon Trust** have been launched to invest in fast-
growing South East Asian markets and Aberdeen Fund Managers has launched a Thai trust. A number of trusts have
been launched to take advantage of developments in Europe.
Murray Johnstone's **Smaller Markets Trust** invests in small
cap companies all over the world, while Baillie Gifford's **Shin
Nippon** concentrates on small cap investments in Japan.

## CANADIAN FUNDS

The Canadian closed-end fund market could be of some interest to U.S. investors. There are about 30 funds traded there although it can be difficult to get information on them—especially the more obscure ones. Net asset values for most of the funds are reported in the *Toronto Globe and Mail* weekly. The majority trade on the Toronto Stock Exchange, the largest, most active Canadian exchange. Among the funds traded there are Canadian General Investments, First Australia Prime Income Investment Co. Ltd. of Cook Island, Germany Fund of Canada, Goldcorp Investment Ltd. of Toronto, MVP Investments, Old Canada Investments, Third Canadian General Investments, and United Corporations. Canadian General Investments, Old Canada Investments, and Third Canadian General Investments originated in the 1920s.

First Australia Prime Income and Germany Fund of Canada resemble funds in the U.S. with similar names and objectives. Other funds include First Mercantile Currency Fund Inc. of Toronto which trades currency futures, and Growth Investment Corporation of Toronto, a dual fund. In Chapter 8 we profiled two of Canada's CEFs which are more popular with U.S. investors, BGR Precious Metals and Central Fund of Canada. The latter also trades in the United States on the American Stock Exchange.

Douglas Hitchlock of Midland Walwyn Capital is a Canadian financial advisor and broker specializing in closed-end funds. His address and phone number can be found in Appendix II. Hitchlock follows over two dozen funds. He estimates that the actively marketed Canadian closed-end funds have a market value in excess of $2 billion U.S. dollars. We understand that some deep discounts exist in the Canadian CEF market which could be appealing to value investors, but before investing you need to make a careful analysis considering factors like the fund's market liquidity, portfolio composition, and expense ratio. The Canadian funds are structured somewhat differently than those in the U.S., and prospective investors would want to be aware of these differences.

In this era of single-country funds, Hitchlock points out that there are some huge bargains in the Canadian market for those who want a high quality portfolio of Canadian equities. "If one were to look at a package of seasoned, high grade Canadian portfolios, the purchase of Canadian General Investments, Economic Investment Trust, Third Canadian General Investments, and United Corporations would represent an excellent way of buying institutionally-held Canadian securities at an average discount in excess of 40%. These four funds represent securities with a total market value of more than 730 million in U.S. dollars." A little arithmetic shows that at a 40% discount those securities sell for only $438 million.

## GETTING MORE INFORMATION

If you are interested in British or Canadian funds you should consider locating a knowledgeable broker who will be able to obtain shareholder reports and other information on these funds for you. Most brokerage firms have *The Thomas J. Herzfeld Encyclopedia of Closed-End Funds* which is published annually in the summer. The Herzfeld Encyclopedia contains the names and brief descriptions of about 170 British and 30 Canadian closed-end funds. For the Canadian funds addresses and phone numbers are also provided.

An extensive coverage of these funds is beyond the scope of this book. The average closed-end fund investor in the United States has plenty of choices on the New York Stock Exchange. In fact, the U.S. closed-end fund market with over $60 billion in assets is considerably larger in dollar terms than its British counterpart with assets of about U.S. $35 billion.

## CONCLUSIONS

This chapter should give you an idea of how the British investment trust industry, the model for our own, is organized. In regard to investing in the trusts by U.S. investors, it needs to be pointed out that they are not registered with the SEC and to invest small amounts of money in them can be expensive in terms of transaction costs. Thomas Herzfeld had been purchasing the London funds for his clients for some time, but told us that he is not doing so at the present time for three reasons. "The combination of an unfavorable change in the tax laws, the discounts narrowing, and the pound sterling becoming expensive has eliminated their former comparative advantage," Herzfeld said. He adds, however, that he has a flexible policy and would go back to the British market under the right conditions.

If interested readers have British connections, it is possible to purchase them with funds in the U.K. Another alternative for larger investors is the services of investment adviser George Foot of Newgate Management Associates in Northampton, Massachusetts who will take managed accounts of $250,000 or more (see Appendix II for his address and phone number). More and more British funds are seeking listing on the NYSE, which certainly opens up their markets, a trend which will hopefully continue.

## Notes

[1] Peter Fuhrman, "The British angle," *Forbes,* September 3, 1990, pp. 150 and 152.

[2] Facts on Foreign and Colonial were obtained from The Foreign and Colonial Investment Trust PLC, *Report and Accounts 1989,* p. 8.

[3] *The Scott Letter: Closed-End Fund Report,* July-August, 1990, p. 7.

[4] *Ibid.,* 1–2.

# PART III

# Fixed-Income Funds

## INTRODUCTION TO PART III
## ON FIXED-INCOME FUNDS
## A. MICHAEL LIPPER, CFA
## PRESIDENT, LIPPER ANALYTICAL
## SERVICES, INC.

Our comprehensive data on closed-end funds have been published on a monthly basis since the close of 1973. Over the first 12 years, through the close of 1985, the entire closed-end fund industry was a relatively small and stable segment of the entire fund industry—very small particularly compared with the mutual fund industry.

At the close of 1973 we initially tracked 66 closed-end funds, with a total net asset value of $5.5 billion. This subsequently increased to 76 funds and then tapered off at the close of 1985 to only 54 funds, with total net assets of $8.1 billion. Over this period, about one-third of the total value consisted of about 25 bond funds, mostly of fairly good quality, with the remainder in diversified and specialized equity, convertible, and dual purpose funds.

Over the next four years (1986–1989) and through the first half of 1990 an explosive and broadly diverse growth developed throughout the closed-end fund industry. The total number of funds increased from 54, with a value of $8.1 billion at the 1985 year-end, to 229 funds with a value of $60.9 billion as of June 30, 1990. The various reasons for this growth are well described in this book.

Prior to this new growth period, through the close of 1985, there had been few changes in the number or character of available closed-end funds and the variety of diversification available had been quite limited. For example, there had been no tax-exempt closed-end funds and very few international funds, both of which have became major categories in recent years.

However, the largest part of the 1986–1990 growth occurred in the bond fund segment, which increased from 26 funds with a value of $2.4 billion at the close of 1985, to 143 funds valued at $44.0 billion on June 30, 1990. As a percentage of the $60.9 billion total value of all closed-end funds, the bond funds increased from 29.9 to 72.3%, with 45 tax-exempt municipal bond funds accounting for 31.6% of the total on the latter date.

The scope of diversification available to closed-end bond fund investors as of June 30, 1990 is evident from the following percentage distribution of the total values of the principal types of funds:

Investment Grade Bond Funds                          4.0%
(at least 65% in top four quality grades)

General Bond Funds                                  13.7%
(no quality or maturity restrictions, but
largely of good quality)

High Yield Bond Funds                                4.2%
(largely lower grade issues)

Flexible Income Bond Funds                           8.2%
(relatively high income funds investing in
bonds, preferred stocks, convertible and/or
common stocks, and warrants)

Miscellaneous Bond Funds                            15.7%
(various, not otherwise classified)

U.S. Government Bond Funds                          15.2%
(at least 65% in securities and/or mortgages
issued or guaranteed by U.S. government or
its agencies)

World Income Funds                                   7.4%
(invest principally in worldwide debt instruments, but may also invest in common and
preferred stocks)

Municipal Bond Funds                                31.6%
(including general, high yield, insured and
specific state municipal debt issues)
                                        Total      100.0%

In each of the above categories there are at least ten different funds available, with no less than 45 municipal bond funds—a category not in existence four years earlier.

Unfortunately, during the explosive 1986–1990 growth period, investors in the many new issues of closed-end bond funds did not fare nearly as well as the underwriters or managers of the new funds. Reviewing the history of 138 closed-end bond funds—nearly the entire available universe—as of March 31, 1990 (of which 111 were issued during the years 1986–1990), we found that 119 funds were selling at prices below original offering prices, with only nine selling at premiums. The average discount below offering price for the entire group was −16.27%. No less than 36 funds (but not including any U.S. government or municipal funds) were selling at discounts of 25% or more, ranging up to a maximum of −64.38%.

Further, comparing March 31, 1990 market prices with net asset values on that date it was found that only 52 funds were selling at premiums and 81 at discounts, with an average discount of −1.07%. This suggests, as do the authors of this book, that after-market investors in closed-end bond funds may have fared much better than new issue investors since market prices have tended to settle down toward net asset values or less fairly soon after original issue.

We concur fully with the authors that the wide array of closed-end bond funds now available may offer attractive opportunities for alert and well-informed investors. We also concur that there are numerous complexities and pitfalls in this market so that investors would be well advised to do their homework with great care.

# CHAPTER 12

# *Bond Fund Basics*

As Michael Lipper documents in his Introduction, a great deal of money was invested in closed-end bond funds, or CEBFs, in the 1986–90 period. (We use the acronym CEBF for closed-end bond fund.) A handful of the newer ones have assets in excess of $1 billion. The oldest CEBFs came to market in the early 1970s. Most of these are investment grade bond funds; a few are convertible bond funds. In the 1980s many new CEBFs were offered which included new types of portfolios, such as government and municipal bonds. The MFS Municipal Income Trust, sponsored by Massachusetts Financial Services, went public in November 1987. This was the first municipal CEBF.

Bond funds represent an ideal means for most people to invest in bonds since the bond markets are geared to institutions that customarily deal in lots of several million dollars; in the bond market a round lot is usually $100,000. Individuals who typically transact in much smaller lots confront considerably higher transaction costs and less liquidity. Needless to say they find it difficult to diversify.

271

Bond funds are especially important to people seeking dependable monthly income and who view the potentially greater long-term growth in capital provided by the equity funds as less important given their situation. Individuals of any age, however, may want to have a certain amount of their assets invested in bonds for diversification purposes.

Bond funds can be quite volatile so you have to understand the various risk factors before investing. A recent example would be the massive declines sustained by the junk bond funds in 1989 (especially those that employed leverage). In general, the longer the maturity of the bonds and the lower their quality the more volatile the fund. If the fund is leveraged the volatility or risk is accentuated.

Besides just being larger, the newer CEBFs have gotten to be more complex and many have greater flexibility and more of a "tutti-frutti" flavor than the largely "plain vanilla" bond funds which came out in the early 1970s. A larger proportion of the newer ones may use options, futures, and other portfolio management techniques, like short selling, to enhance yield or attempt to reduce downside risk. Because of the large number of CEBFs, their diversity and, in a growing number of cases, their complexity, the selection process is difficult and confusing. But we feel strongly that a good case can be made for investing in closed- as opposed to open-end bond funds.

## CLOSED- VERSUS OPEN-END BOND FUNDS

CEBFs may offer the potential for better performance than open-end bond funds. Before we explain why a clear distinction between total return and yield must be made.

*Total return* is a complete performance measure incorporating changes in the value of the investment's principal or NAV along with the income generated. If principal or NAV declines during a period reflecting capital losses, total return would be adversely impacted even though the yield appeared attractive.

*Yield* relates an investment's income to its market

price or NAV and does not reflect increases and decreases in principal; as a simpler performance measure it tells only part of the story.

Both yield and total return are expressed as percentages.

Jonathan Clements explained in a *Forbes* article that CEBF managers have more incentive to manage their portfolios for total return as opposed to maximizing yield, which is very shortsighted. Some open-end funds may try to maintain the highest possible yields to attract more shareholder money and build-up assets and management fees. To increase the assets of a closed-end fund, on the other hand, the manager must gradually increase portfolio value by earning a higher total return.[1] We are not in complete agreement with this reasoning, however, since closed-end funds do have other ways to increase assets. These include reinvestment of income (that is, retained earnings); rights offerings and additional public offerings; establishing clone funds as a number of the bond funds (for example, Nuveen) have done; and acquisitions and/or mergers.

The 1838 Bond-Debenture Trading Fund has been an outstanding performer over the years. It is a good example of a CEBF which seeks total return. Robert Vitale, its manager, prudently reduced the fund's dividend to $1.86 in 1987 after consistently paying $2.00 per year for many years. Vitale would not want to dip into principal to doctor up the yield.[2] CEBFs, of course, may also focus on yield at the expense of total return. We'll show you how to spot funds which do this. A fund which reaches for the highest possible yield might be doing shareholders a disservice, since the higher yield could come at the expense of a lower total return. For instance, a portfolio packed full of risky, high-yielding bonds may experience a substantial price decline, producing a disastrous total return.

An advantage enjoyed by the CEBF, which should lead to better performance, is that the manager need not keep an extra buffer of cash on hand to meet redemptions. More of the portfolio could, therefore, be invested in higher yielding bonds.[3] The authors cannot, however, offer any conclusive proof that CEBFs consistently exhibit superior performance to open-end bond funds. We leave this for a thorough academic study.

Of course, there are other advantages of CEBFs in addition to their possible performance edge. As with the equity funds, you can buy shares at a discount, although the average discount on bond funds is less than that for equity funds. Any discount offers potential value though. Furthermore, there is some indication that windows of opportunity may be forthcoming to buy CEBFs at attractive discounts because of increased supply, resulting from so many offerings during the latter part of the 1980s. Finally, remember that you have a trading advantage with any closed-end fund, as you have control over when you place your limit orders to buy and sell shares. Thus, you can nail down more favorable prices.

## BOND BASICS

The better your understanding of bonds and how the bond markets work the better you will be able to analyze the funds and fit them into your portfolio. A *bond* is a promissory note issued by a corporation or public body. Bonds typically pay semiannual interest and return their par or principal value at maturity. *Zero coupon bonds* do not pay periodic interest. Instead, they make one lump sum payment at maturity. The CEBFs pay dividends at least quarterly and many do so monthly.

### Bond Types

Different CEBFs invest in different types of bonds in accordance with their prospectuses. Their portfolios reflect the characteristics of sectors represented. The sectors are as follows:

*Straight Corporate Bonds.* A great deal of diversity exists here. Qualities range from triple-A for the highest grade obligations down to Standard & Poor's single-D classification for bonds in default. Investment grade corporates are rated within the top four grades (triple-B or higher) by the major rating agencies (Moody's and S&P's

are the two largest and best known). High yield or junk bonds are rated double-B or lower.

**U.S. Treasury Securities.** This sector consists of Treasury bonds (original maturities of 10 years or longer), notes (maturities of one to 10 years), and bills (maturities of one year or less). Treasuries have no credit risk.

**Foreign Bonds.** Bonds issued by foreign governments can offer attractive yields at times and could lead to currency gains (or losses) as the value of the dollar changes relative to a particular country's currency.

**Mortgage-Backed Securities.** Mortgage-backed *pass-through securities* or *participation certificates* are primarily issued by three federal agencies: Ginnie Mae (Government National Mortgage Association, the largest and oldest issuer), Freddie Mac (Federal Home Loan Mortgage Corporation), and Fannie Mae (Federal National Mortgage Association). A pass-through security is like a cross between a bond and a single family mortgage. Ginnie Maes are based on a pool of federally insured FHA and VA mortgages. Monthly payments of interest and principal, including prepayments of mortgages, are passed through a mortgage banker to the investor.

**Municipal Bonds.** The appeal of municipal bonds is that their interest is exempt from federal taxes and may be exempt from state taxes as well. Single-state muni CEBFs have been offered in recent years which hold California or New York state bonds in order to offer investors in those states tax exemption at the state (and possibly city) level as well as the federal level.

**Convertibles.** Convertible bonds and preferred stock can be exchanged for shares of the underlying common stock of the issuer at the holder's option. Convertibles offer the downside safety of a bond and the upside potential of common stock.

## Bond Risks

Bonds carry a variety of different types of risks which can affect investors. Even though bond funds generally diversify away company-specific risk factors, the bond risks still affect the fund itself as well as the individual bonds. Just how a particular fund would be affected would depend on the composition of its portfolio.

The basic risks are as follows.

**Interest Rate Risk.**  Bond prices fall when interest rates rise and vice versa. The bonds with the longest term to maturity and the lowest coupons are the hardest hit by an increase in rates, but would appreciate most in price when rates fall. A bond's *duration,* rather than time to maturity, would be the most precise gauge of interest rate risk since it reflects the size of the coupon payment in addition to time to maturity. The longer the duration of a bond (or bond portfolio), the more extreme its price fluctuations in response to a given change in rates. Duration is explained in Figure 12–1.

**Reinvestment Rate Risk.**  This risk is a problem during periods of *falling interest rates.* It impacts coupon

### Figure 12–1. What Is Duration?

Sophisticated bond fund investors want to compare durations of different funds in order to assess relative riskiness. Simply put, a bond's duration is a weighted average time to maturity where each payment date is weighted by its associated payment. The duration of a coupon bond would be a number smaller than its time to maturity; for a zero coupon bond duration equals time to maturity. Thus, zeros are more volatile than coupon issues for a given maturity. For instance, the duration of a 20 year zero would simply be 20. The duration of a 10% coupon bond trading at par and maturing in 30 years would be 10.37. Roughly speaking, the former would be nearly twice as risky as the latter.

Suppose a CEBF has an average portfolio duration of 5. Its portfolio would fall (rise) about 5% for a 1 percentage point increase (decrease) in rates. If its duration was 10 its portfolio would fall (rise) 10% for a 1 percentage point increase (decrease) in rates.

Some CEBF managers, like Wayne Lyski, senior vice president at Alliance Capital and manager of the five ACM government bond funds, may use zeros to adjust the duration of their portfolios in response to anticipated shifts in interest rates. For example, if they expect rates to decline they would lengthen the portfolio's duration by adding a larger proportion of long-term zeros to the mix.

issues during such times; the higher the coupon the greater the impact. The problem is that the coupons would have to be reinvested at successively lower rates reducing the investor's realized return on the bond. A more significant problem is that the high coupon bonds could be called by the issuer in order to replace them with a lower coupon issue. The holder of the bond would then be forced to reinvest the proceeds of the call at a lower interest rate. Funds which hold long-term Treasuries have call protection since Treasury bonds are generally not callable until during the last five years of their life. Reinvestment risk would affect funds which hold a lot of shorter term debt since at maturity the principal would have to be reinvested in debt with lower interest rates during a period of falling rates.

**Credit Risk.**   Credit (or default) risk is customarily judged by the bond rating. The rating is an assessment of the likelihood that the issuer will be able to make promised payments of interest and principal on time and in full. The weaker the issuer's financial condition the greater this risk. To determine the degree to which the bonds held by a particular fund would be affected, you would want to know the proportionate breakdown of its portfolio in terms of bond ratings. The percentage breakdown is more important than the average rating since a fund with an average rating of triple-B could have a significant amount of low grade bonds in its portfolio. Credit risk would pose the greatest problem with the high yield CEBFs.

**Event Risk.**   As its name implies this risk relates to an unexpected occurrence that would have an adverse impact on a company, causing its bond prices to drop sharply. Event risk would commonly be something like a leveraged buy-out, which unfavorably impacts a high quality company's bonds because it greatly increases its debt burden. The RJR Nabisco LBO is a case in point.

A CEBF that has a high concentration in industrial companies would have greater exposure to that part of the market that is beleaguered by event risk. A higher concentration in utilities, financial companies, and governments lessens event risk exposure. Of course, the diversification offered by a diversified investment company would lessen the impact of event risk as well as credit risk.

***Purchasing Power Risk.*** This risk results from an unanticipated increase in the rate of inflation that erodes the purchasing power of the dollar. Fixed income investors would experience an erosion of their purchasing power during inflationary periods. This is the reason the authors emphasized the importance of maintaining a sufficient proportion of a long-term portfolio in stock funds.

***Liquidity Risk.*** In general, the larger the bond issue and the wider the distribution of ownership the better the marketability and liquidity. Private placements tend to have the lowest liquidity, and CEBFs that hold a large amount of privately placed debt tend to sell at wider discounts.

***Currency Risk.*** This risk impacts bonds denominated in a foreign currency, such as the Japanese yen. This would be a problem for a U.S. investor if the yen decreased in value relative to the dollar during the period of investment in yen-denominated bonds. The total return in U.S. dollars would be reduced as a consequence.

## BOND FUND BASICS

Basic considerations confronting the CEBF investor include the following.

***The Portfolio Composition.*** The most elementary difference between CEBFs would be found in the make-up of their portfolios. Some, called multi-sector funds, may invest in several different bond market sectors, typically three. Going to the extreme, Oppenheimer Multi-Sector Trust can invest in seven. Other CEBFs limit their investments to the tax-exempt bonds of a single state. You obviously want the fund with the portfolio which best suits your objectives. The current portfolio composition of a fund can be found by consulting S&P's *Stock Reports* or the fund's most recent shareholder report.

***The Quality of the Bonds Held.*** Some funds concentrate on junk bonds. Others hold only investment grade corporates or governments. Risk and return usually go hand in hand. When you invest in CEBFs holding corporate or municipal securities, you must have information on the breakdown of the portfolio in terms of bond ratings.

***The Average Maturity (or Duration) of the Bond Portfolio.*** Those funds which have the longest average maturities (or durations) would generally offer the highest long-run return, other things equal, but would be expected to be riskier in the sense that their NAVs would be more volatile since the bonds would be subject to greater interest rate risk.

***The Portfolio Turnover.*** How actively is the bond portfolio managed? Some funds have a policy of switching back and forth between sectors based upon changing market conditions. Others tend to remain fully invested in a particular sector and, consequently, experience relatively low turnover. Keep a fund's basic philosophy in mind when studying its turnover and compare its trading activity to others with a similar strategy. Also, look at turnover for several years since the numbers can vary widely from year to year. For instance, a fund that ordinarily does not actively trade bonds may decide to shift a large portion of its portfolio into higher quality paper because the management anticipates a difficult economic environment. Or a new portfolio manager may step in and restructure the holdings to suit his or her philosophy.

***The Use of Leverage or Borrowing on Assets.*** Leverage amplifies gains and losses. A vivid illustration of its negative impact can be seen in the 1989 performances of the leveraged junk bond funds. Particularly hard hit were The New America High Income Fund and Prospect Street High Income Portfolio. According to *LIPPER Closed-End Bond Funds Analysis,* New America and Prospect Street tumbled 40 and 41.25 percent in price, respectively, over the year ended December 31, 1989. Their NAV total returns, although not as bad, were still negative in the double digits.

***Hedging with Options and Futures.*** This can be good if the hedge is placed and lifted at precisely the right time. But that is easier said than done, and too much hedging may turn out to be more of a drag on long-run performance.

***Option Writing.*** U.S. Government bond and multisector CEBFs may write call options to generate additional income. It works well during periods of stable interest rates. But it could adversely affect total return during a period of falling rates as higher coupon bonds could be called away, forcing reinvestment in lower yielding debt. For a call writing program to work effectively *a correct forecast of interest rates is crucial.* But who can consistently make accurate interest rate forecasts?

**Security Lending.**   Some funds may, from time to time, loan some of their bonds to brokers or other financial institutions, in order to earn additional income. The borrowing firm often has a short position in the securities and needs to use them for a few days so they can be delivered to the owner of the bonds. These would typically be actively-traded, liquid government securities and agency paper loaned for short periods. Lending may present a slight risk in that the borrower may fail to return the securities on time.


## ANALYZING A CEBF

The basic information you need to know to analyze a fund was covered in Chapter 3 and most of the techniques explained there would apply to bond funds as well as stock funds. In addition to past performance, you should analyze such things as past expense ratios, turnover rates, and discount/premium levels. However, CEBFs have certain unique characteristics which mean that investors must undertake some additional analysis. In fact, some of the newer CEBFs are quite complex and require careful scrutiny.

First of all you should examine the portfolio. If you are studying a multi-sector or flexible portfolio fund you want to see which sectors are presently being given the greatest weight. Dramatic shifts in emphasis can occur.

You should also evaluate the quality of the portfolio. What is the average rating of the portfolio? Study portfolio changes over a period of a year or two using past shareholder reports. Has the fund manager tended to lower the quality of the holdings in order to maintain yields? The average maturity (or duration) of the portfolio is also important. Longer maturities mean generally higher yields but greater volatility of NAV. Has the fund manager lengthened average maturity in order to increase yield? On the other hand the manager may have lengthened maturity in anticipation of a decline in interest rates. But if interest rates rise instead of fall losses invariably result.

## TWO SPECIAL RATIOS

Two ratios are particularly helpful in analyzing a CEBF. They are:

1. Income dividends as a percent of *net* investment income.
2. Expenses as a percent of *gross* investment income.

Let's look at each one in turn.

### Income Dividends versus Income

You should always check to see whether your CEBF is paying more in dividends from investment income than it is earning. This can be determined by calculating the ratio of per share dividends paid from investment income to investment income per share. Investment companies are required to distribute nearly all investment income to avoid taxation at the corporate or trust level. *However, a fund may decide to pay out more than it earns to try and please shareholders and keep share price from declining.* When a bond fund's income distributions significantly exceed net earnings, it is essentially "cannibalizing" assets in order to maintain shareholder distributions. This practice, if followed consistently, is undesirable as it depletes the fund's asset base and hence its earning power.[4]

The past data necessary to determine whether or not a fund is cannibalizing assets appear in Table 12–1. Here we have two CEBFs, American Capital Bond Fund and Bunker Hill Income Securities. The information needed to calculate the ratio can be found in the selected per share data and ratios exhibit in the fund's annual or

**Table 12–1. Investment Income Paid Out in Income Dividends**

| Year | American Capital Bond Fund | | Bunker Hill Income Securities | |
|---|---|---|---|---|
| | Income Dividends | Net Invest. Income | Income Dividends | Net Invest. Income |
| 1989 | $2.20 | $1.90 | $1.87 | $1.98 |
| 1988 | 2.20 | 1.95 | 2.01 | 1.88 |
| 1987 | 2.20 | 1.94 | 2.16 | 2.17 |
| 1986 | 2.20 | 2.15 | 2.16 | 2.11 |
| 1985 | 2.20 | 2.23 | 2.16 | 2.12 |
| TOTALS | $11.00 | $10.17 | $10.36 | $10.26 |

Source: Shareholder reports of the individual funds.

semi-annual report or from data in S&P's *Stock Reports.* To calculate the ratio, divide the per share total income dividends distributed over a five year period by the total net income per share (investment income less expenses) over the same period. The lower the ratio the better.[5]

The ratio of income dividends to net investment income for American Capital is 1.08 ($11.00/$10.17) and for Bunker Hill it is 1.01 ($10.36/$10.26). The lower this value the better. Thus, at this writing, American Capital faced the prospect of having to reduce its $2.20 dividend, as noted by Norman Tepper in his May 1990 *Value Line* profile of that fund. Tepper also noted that American's discount had widened making it one of the largest for a bond fund.

### Expense Analysis

The significance of the expense ratio has already been discussed. However, one can carry expense analysis a step further for a CEBF by calculating the ratio of expenses to gross (or total) investment income. This discloses what percentage of income is being consumed by expenses. S&P's *Stock Reports* supply the ratio for a number of years. Again, it is desirable to look at a five-year average value for this ratio if the fund has been in existence that long. It is possible to calculate the ratio from numbers given in the schedule of selected per share data and ratios in the fund's annual or semi-annual report. Based upon a group of funds that he was working with, Thomas Herzfeld recommended that this ratio should be 10% or less unless the fund is trading at a discount of 10% or more. If interest expense is included in the expenses portion of the ratio, Herzfeld recommends taking it out and calculating the ratio, ignoring interest. Interest should be viewed as a trading expense rather than an operating expense, wrote Herzfeld.[6]

If the ratio for a particular fund is high you would want to know why. More often than not it will be because there is interest expense associated with the use of leverage. As has been said before, there is a tendency for funds with higher expenses to sell at smaller premiums or wider discounts than similar funds with lower expenses. Thus, you should also look at the discount when evaluating expenses.

## SET YOUR SIGHTS ON TOTAL RETURN, NOT YIELD

The best kind of CEBFs for the long-term investor, seeking preservation of capital as well as income, are those that manage their portfolios for total return. The high total return funds may have relatively low dividend yields (from the fund's interest income), but high yields are illusive and can serve as a red flag, indicating that inferior total returns may be forthcoming.

There are at least three ways in which a bond fund could increase its yield at the expense of total return:

1. By moving the portfolio into higher yielding, lower quality bonds. This produces a higher yield at the moment, but can lead to damaging price declines due to the higher volatility of lower quality bonds. For instance, suppose a fund with a 9% dividend yield decides to boost that yield to 12% by shifting into lower rated bonds. But then the value of the portfolio may subsequently decline 8%, resulting in a measly 4% total return for the year.

2. By dipping into principal to maintain a fixed dividend payment. This is irresponsible when it would be better to reduce the dividend to preserve the principal. Remember that Vitale, who manages 1838 Bond-Debenture Trading Fund, reduced the dividend in order to preserve principal and maintain a higher total return in the long run.

3. By writing options to generate additional income to bolster the yield. Funds that write options may be forced to sacrifice considerable upside appreciation potential in exchange for their higher distributions. When you examine the yield of a fund that writes options, make sure you look at a conservative figure that does not include the option premiums. The advertised figure has the option premiums in it.[7]

## ALWAYS RELATE TURNOVER
## TO TOTAL RETURN

When analyzing portfolio turnover be sure to look at the numbers over several years taking the fund's objectives into consideration. Relate these numbers to total return to see if any above-average turnover rates made a positive contribution to performance.

Bond funds commonly use short-term trading in anticipation of changes in interest rate levels and to take advantage of attractive yield disparities between securities of comparable quality. A yield disparity could exist when, for example, triple-A corporate debt is yielding considerably more than Treasury bonds based on their historic yield differential. Yield disparities generally occur in response to changes in demand or supply.

Turnover can thus vacillate from year to year depending upon market trading opportunities. It can also vary with market liquidity. In periods of market illiquidity, such as existed after the October 1987 crash, it becomes more difficult to trade outstanding bond issues and the supply of new issues shrinks dramatically. Thus, turnover would be expected to be lower.

Of course, a fund which is poorly managed could be adversely affected from short-term trading. The bottom line is: Don't make a decision to accept or reject a fund on turnover by itself. Try to determine how turnover has affected performance.


## CONCLUSIONS

Bond funds can be complicated and special expertise is needed to understand them. This chapter has provided you with an introduction to the CEBFs and what to look for when analyzing them. The long-term performance of the CEBFs as a group is below that of the equity funds. However, bond funds should produce more stable returns than equity funds (although some which assume greater risks may not). This is important to many people. For instance, suppose a parent wanted to set aside a lump sum for a minor who will be attending college in three years. An investment grade bond fund *with a short duration* would be a safer choice since the stock market could be down considerably at the end of a given three-year period.

We want to stress that investors who buy individual bonds have higher transaction costs. Due to changing market conditions it doesn't make sense to buy a 30-year bond and hold onto it for 30 years. A bond fund portfolio manager is better equipped to react to changing market conditions and, if he's good, could create a higher long-run total return.

The authors feel that, as a group, CEBFs are superior to open-end bond funds. They offer you a chance to buy at a discount even though that discount typically is less than you would find on equity funds. There are also reasons why they might be somewhat better long-run performers than their open-ended cousins, although we are unable to substantiate this with a risk-adjusted performance study.

## Notes

[1]Jonathan Clements, "Yielding to total return," *Forbes*, December 11, 1989, pp. 312 and 314.

[2]Jonathan Clements, "Yield versus total return," *Forbes*, September 4, 1989, pp. 162–63.

[3]Clements, "Yielding to total return," p. 314.

[4]Norman Tepper, "Some Things To Be Aware Of Before Investing In Closed-End Funds," *The Value Line Investment Survey*, December 15, 1989, pp. 2090 and 2139.

[5]Another approach to test whether a fund is paying out more than it earns is to annualize its most recent monthly or quarterly dividend (that is, multiply it by 12 or 4, respectively) and divide the result by the fund's annualized net income for the most recent quarter. This approach can help you pinpoint a fund starting to pay out of principal. See Leslie Eaton, "Mutual Benefits," *Barron's*, July 2, 1990, p. 17.

[6]Thomas J. Herzfeld, *The Investor's Guide to Closed-End Funds* (New York: McGraw-Hill Book Company, 1980), p. 51.

[7]William Baldwin, "Cannibal bond funds," *Forbes*, September 4, 1989, pp. 166 and 171.

# CHAPTER 13

# *Older Bond Funds*

About two dozen CEBFs were formed in the early 1970s. This was a period when interest rates began to look attractive relative to historic levels, even though they were destined to go higher later in the decade. Many of these funds were started by banks and insurance companies interested in utilizing their capability to manage bonds in a way they hadn't done before and earning management fees on an ongoing basis. It was another way to gather assets and a way for these institutions to enter the investment company business. Another factor prompting the offerings was the investment banking industry itself which was in the doldrums and looking for something to provide additional income.

The majority of the older CEBFs hold primarily higher quality debt. We categorize them mainly as *investment grade bond funds.* The funds in this category invest primarily in corporate debt rated triple-B or higher and, to

a lesser extent, in U.S. government securities. Their portfolios may also contain modest amounts of investment
quality foreign debt.

These funds are relatively straightforward. They are
our favorite group for the average bond fund investor. The
first CEBF offering was American Capital Bond Fund (formerly American General Bond Fund) which began in October, 1970. On January 29, 1971 it became the first
CEBF in history to be listed on the New York Stock Exchange.


## PAST PERFORMANCE

Since these older funds have long track records we can
examine their past performance. Again, we'll turn to Lipper data. Table 13–1 displays compound annual total returns of 25 older CEBFs over recent 5- and 10-year periods. Total net assets are also reported as an indicator of
fund size.

Total assets range from a high of $209.1 million (In-
terCapital) to $22.7 million (Revere Fund). Altogether
these older bond funds have assets of $2.3 billion, which
is only about 5% of the $44.0 billion in assets of all CEBFs
at June 30, 1990. The older bond funds are generally
smaller than many of the newer ones, some of which have
assets of $1 billion or more.

The 5-year performance ranges from 12.83% (Mass-
Mutual Corporate Investors) down to 0.06% (Revere Fund)
with a median of 10.14% for the group. The 10-year numbers range from 14.42% (MassMutual) to 5.01% (Revere
Fund); the median for the 10 years is 11.44%. MassMutual
invests in private placements of small to medium-sized
companies. In contrast, the performance for the Revere
Fund, which also invests in private placements, was considerably below that for the second worst performing fund
for each of the periods. Its June 30, 1989 quarterly report
indicated that the coincidence of two holdings filing for
bankruptcy protection and major fraud in two others substantially reduced NAV and income. Of course, past per-

formance is not necessarily a good indicator of future performance.

## OLDER INVESTMENT GRADE
## FUND PROFILES

Let's examine seven of the older investment grade bond funds more closely. Averages of past expense ratios and turnover rates for these funds appear in Table 13–2.

**Current Income Shares (NYSE: CUR)** CUR has maintained an investment grade portfolio over the years with about 90% of its bonds in the top four rating categories. Union Bank serves as adviser. The fund could use leverage but never has. Options and futures cannot be used. It does not invest in private placements.

The bottom line is that this fund is very plain vanilla compared to the newer ones. "We don't regard this as a fancy, tutti-frutti vehicle where we're trying to make fancy bets one way or another, all of which entail a good deal of risk in our opinion," says Richard Grayson, the fund's president. CUR remains fully invested in marketable, longer-term bonds and does not try to time the market by switching between long- and short-term debt. The average maturity of its portfolio tends to be in the 16- to 17-year range.

The broadly diversified portfolio of about 40 issues consists mainly of high quality corporate and utility bonds. At this writing about 10 percent was in Treasury bonds. Over the years the fund has maintained about 10 percent in high quality Canadian bonds which are denominated in U.S. dollars and thus do not have a currency risk. These bonds are guaranteed by Canadian provinces and offer a long call deferment period. (The call deferment period refers to the period during which the bond could not be called in by the issuer).

Stephen Dunn, the portfolio manager, strives to maintain an attractive quarterly dividend. Within the group of bonds that meet Dunn's criteria for safety and income he selects those which offer the longest call deferment pe-

**Table 13–1. Five- and Ten-Year Performance of Older CEBFs**

| | Net Assets 6/30/90 (Millions) | NAV Performance* | |
| --- | --- | --- | --- |
| | | 5-Year | 10-Year |
| American Capital Bond Fund (L) | $ 205.1 | 9.22% | 11.17% |
| AMEV Securities | 106.3 | 9.07 | 10.24 |
| Bunker Hill Income Securities | 41.8 | 9.82 | 10.29 |
| Circle Income Shares | 32.3 | 9.70 | 10.99 |
| CNA Income Shares (L) | 75.8 | 9.66 | 11.43 |
| Current Income Shares | 44.1 | 12.03 | 12.61 |
| 1838 Bond-Debenture Trading Fund | 52.9 | 11.02 | 12.61 |
| Excelsior Income Shares | 39.0 | 8.69 | 9.97 |
| Fort Dearborn Income Secs. | 103.5 | 11.76 | 12.22 |
| Hatteras Income Securities | 48.3 | 10.00 | 11.68 |
| INA Investment Securities | 84.0 | 10.14 | 10.81 |
| Independence Square Income Securities | 30.0 | 9.92 | 11.09 |
| InterCapital Income Secs. | 209.1 | 10.60 | 11.96 |

| | | | |
|---|---|---|---|
| John Hancock Income Secs. | 147.2 | 10.56 | 11.89 |
| John Hancock Investors | 143.7 | 10.41 | 12.13 |
| Lincoln National Income Fund | 68.2 | 11.75 | 13.78 |
| MassMutual Corporate Inv. (L) | 124.0 | 12.83 | 14.42 |
| Montgomery Street Income Secs. | 145.8 | 9.28 | 10.93 |
| Mutual of Omaha Interest Shs. | 94.8 | 11.09 | 11.44 |
| Pacific American Income Shs. (L) | 105.5 | 10.66 | 12.07 |
| Revere Fund Inc. | 22.7 | 0.06 | 5.10 |
| State Mutual Securities Trust | 88.6 | 9.86 | 11.09 |
| Transamerica Income Shares | 118.9 | 12.53 | 13.05 |
| USLIFE Income Fund | 46.7 | 7.24 | 10.92 |
| Vestaur Securities | 87.7 | 12.49 | 13.03 |
| Total and medians | $2,266.0 | 10.14% | 11.44% |

L denotes leveraged fund.
*Returns reflect the compound average annual change in NAV, including reinvestment of all distributions. Both performance periods end 6/30/90.
Source: Adapted from *LIPPER Closed-End Bond Funds Analysis*, Third Edition, 1990.

**Table 13–2. Selected Data on Seven Older Investment Grade Bond Funds**

|  | Began | Expense Ratio | Portfolio Turnover |
|---|---|---|---|
| Current Income Shares | 3/73 | 0.90% | 138.46% |
| 1838 Bond-Debenture Trading Fund | 10/71 | 1.13 | 123.62 |
| Excelsior Income Shares | 5/73 | 0.99 | 286.72 |
| John Hancock Income Securities Trust | 2/73 | 0.69 | 40.88 |
| John Hancock Investors Trust | 1/71 | 0.69 | 36.83 |
| Pacific American Income Shares | 3/73 | 0.91* | 59.89 |
| Transamerica Income Shares | 7/72 | 0.68 | 113.60 |

*Exclusive of expenses relating to convertible notes.
Source: Data provided by individual funds. Expense ratios and turnovers represent averages of 5 years through fiscal year 1989.

riod. He avoids high coupon, callable bonds that might be called away in a year or two. At the minimum he likes to have a five-year call deferment period. This call protection helps Dunn lock in the rates he wants for longer periods.

Short-term trading of debt is done in anticipation of market developments and to take advantage of yield disparities. Short-term trading is typically done with higher quality, non-convertible debt which generally trades in markets with greater depth and liquidity than lower quality debt. Over the past five years CUR's portfolio turnover has averaged about 138%. Dunn said that he took advantage of many attractive swap opportunities that were widespread during the 1984–87 period. "It was a time of tremendous disparities in the whole yield universe." Swaps are done to improve yield without incurring additional risk, to obtain a longer call deferment period, or in anticipation of a rating change in a particular issue.

About 93% or 94% of CUR's 5,000 shareholders take their quarterly dividends in cash. Quarterly dividends lead to slightly lower administrative costs than monthly dividends. Over half of the older funds pay dividends quarterly. CUR's long-term performance record is above-average and its expense ratio is low for a relatively small fund with assets of $44 million. Its discount has averaged about 7% over the past 12 years.

**1838 Bond-Debenture Trading Fund (NYSE: BDF)** Formerly Drexel Bond-Debenture Trading Fund, BDF's long-term performance record is excellent as noted in Chapter 12. Its objective is a high total return from interest income and short-term trading activity. Lipper Analytical Services rated BDF Number 2 performer among all closed-end taxable bond funds for the 12 years ended December 31, 1989. BDF also received certificates for outstanding performance in past years. Michael Lipper commended 1838's management for performing well in both inflationary and deflationary periods.

BDF seeks to take advantage of abnormal yield spreads between different sectors of the high grade securities market, adding value through active management. For instance, in 1989 the fund acquired a large amount of Ginnie Maes when their yield spread over Treasuries widened. It then sold about half the holdings during the final quarter of 1989 when the spread narrowed.[1] The fund's portfolio turnover averaged about 124% over the past five years.

1838 pays quarterly dividends. In 1989 it lowered the dividend slightly. In commenting on this in the 1989 annual report, Robert Vitale, the fund's president stated:

> Most of the other closed-end bond funds with which we compare ourselves have taken similar dividend-reducing action over the last several years, as older, higher coupon bonds are retired by call or maturity. Also, we believe it is in the best long-term interest of the stockholders to give up a little income, when necessary, to endeavor to maintain or improve quality and/or the call protection and appreciation potential of the portfolio.

The authors are in total agreement with Vitale's reasoning and feel that investors should always understand the logic and implications of a dividend reduction before becoming disturbed. *The fund that does not reduce its dividend under circumstances such as these may be doing long-term investors a disservice.*

The adviser is 1838 Investment Advisors, L.P. in Philadelphia which manages more than $2 billion of other fixed income assets. Long-term, its discount has averaged about 2%.

**Excelsior Income Shares (NYSE: EIS)** EIS raised about $51 million when it went public in 1973 but its net assets are now about $39 million. Its assets today are lower than they were on the offering as is true of a number of the older CEBFs. What happened to the assets? These older funds bought long-term bonds at a time when interest rates were low relative to where they were destined to go. When rates rose later in the decade and in the early 1980s, many of the funds experienced major contractions in their NAVs. Since closed-end funds must distribute virtually all income and gains it would be difficult to restore the corpus of the fund.

Although a diversified investment company, Excelsior has a relatively small number of holdings in its portfolio. At this writing nearly 80% of its assets are in U.S. government and federal agency obligations. Most of the balance is in high quality corporates. The average maturity is about 10 years. EIS could invest in Treasuries, agencies, mortgage-backed securities, and corporates in whatever proportions management deems advisable. But, strictly speaking, Excelsior would not be classified as a multi-sector fund since its policy has consistently been to hold only high grade securities. The true multi-sector funds are able to invest in below investment grade debt as well as in high grade securities.

Its portfolio turnover ratios have been unusually high in certain years, 469 and 428% in 1988 and 1987, respectively. According to Edwin Heard, Excelsior's president, this reflected a decision made in early 1987 by the fund's board of directors and its adviser to try and manage the portfolio for total return rather than just income. "The activity is generated by possible changes in interest rates and shifts in relative values among the high grade sectors," said Heard. He expects that the fund's annual turnover would normally range between 100 and 200%.

Excelsior's discount has been relatively wide for a CEBF at times. It has averaged about 8% over the past 12 years. As evident in Table 13–1, EIS has been a below

average long-term performer in terms of total return. The
fund pays quarterly dividends and has about 5,000 shareholders. United States Trust Company of New York is the
adviser.

**John Hancock Income Securities Trust (NYSE:
JHS)** and **John Hancock Investors Trust (NYSE: JHI)**
are managed by John Hancock Advisers, Inc., a subsidiary of John Hancock Mutual Life Insurance Co. Both
funds are managed by Barry Evans with the assistance
of James Ho. Evans and Ho also manage the company's
largest fund, the **John Hancock Bond Trust**, an open-
end fund with assets of $1.1 billion.

JHS and JHI both invest primarily in high quality
corporate debt and are managed very similarly today even
though they began with somewhat different objectives as
reflected in their prospectuses. Neither fund uses options,
futures or leverage—although leverage could be used.
Both have a very high single-A composite rating. The
funds are similar in size and have very low expense ratios.
At this writing the stated average maturities of JHS and
JHI were 16.9 and 17.8 years, respectively. Dividends are
paid quarterly.

Investors Trust, the oldest of the two, primarily seeks
income, with capital appreciation as a secondary objective. Its portfolio could potentially be of somewhat lower
quality than JHS's according to its prospectus. It could
invest up to half its assets in directly placed debt, which
is illiquid. In the summer of 1990 only 3% of its portfolio
was in private placements because Evans didn't see prudent investments in the private placement market.

Income Securities Trust's objective is to generate income through a portfolio of high grade, marketable debt
securities. It may invest up to 20% of its assets in income-
producing preferred and common stock. It generally has
not used this option and holds no stock at the present
time.

The discounts for JHS and JHI have averaged 8% and
7%, respectively, over the past 12 years.

Evans and Ho explain why active management is necessary for closed-end as well as open-end bond fund portfolios in the Closed-End Insights box.

## ACTIVE MANAGEMENT IN CLOSED-END BOND FUNDS
### Barry H. Evans and James K. Ho
### Senior Portfolio Officer and Senior Vice President, respectively
### John Hancock Advisers, Inc.

In the management of open-end bond funds we have always emphasized active bond management in the pursuit of maximizing shareholder value. This premise should equally apply to the management of closed-end bond funds. Unlike equities, where a portfolio of quality stocks would have provided a respectable return over the past five years through a buy and hold strategy, a similar portfolio of bonds would have required more active management to adjust the coupon, call structure, duration and sector exposure of the portfolio to changing interest rate and credit conditions. The need to pay close attention to these attributes has been brought about by the increased volatility in the bond market, the rapid changes in the credit quality characteristics of many issuers, and the continual change in the supply/demand equation for debt securities.

There may be a tendency for managers of closed-end bond funds to manage their portfolios less actively since the assets are securely under management and, absent changes in the market, should remain about constant. In an open-end fund, poor performance may cause investors to redeem their shares, reducing the assets under management. Poor performance in a closed-end fund should not affect the manager's ability to retain those assets, but should merely cause investors to sell their shares to another investor. Low turnover may be symptomatic of an investment manager's failing to satisfy the performance priority one may find in an open-end product. Evaluating the nature of the fund's turnover for the past several years should provide many clues to effective active management.

Consider a portfolio of bonds purchased during the early to mid-1980s by a closed-end corporate bond fund which was issued during that period. Most holdings would have consisted of high coupon (11% and up) securities, many with optional call features. With the sharp decline in interest rates since that time, many of the securities would have either failed to appreciate beyond their call price or would have been called, forcing reinvestment at significantly lower interest rates. A program of actively swapping callable or refundable securities for non-callables during periods of low interest rate volatility (when the call option on a bond is worth less) would have resulted in better long run income potential and price performance.

Active management was also necessary during the last several years when American corporations were releveraging their balance sheets as a result of management-led buyouts and other forms of recapitalization. During the last three years many bond portfolios heavily concentrated in high grade industrial debt securities faced significant principal losses as many of these credits fell below investment grade. A fund required active credit management during this period to limit the exposure to event-prone companies.

These two examples highlight the need to actively restructure bond portfolios to reflect changing market conditions. Furthermore, transactions in most bond market sectors are negotiated and do not take place on any organized exchange. Often, value can be added through astute trading of securities, capitalizing on gluts in new issue and secondary market supply as well as knee-jerk reactions to economic and credit quality trends.

Active bond management will naturally lead to higher portfolio turnover. However, given that over the last decade the debt markets have become much more dynamic, higher turnover is easily justifiable, so long as the return to the shareholder remains competitive.

**Pacific American Income Shares (NYSE: PAI)** PAI seeks high income through a diversified portfolio of debt securities. Capital appreciation is a secondary objective. Its policy is to invest at least 75% of assets in investment grade debt, government securities, and short-term debt. Up to 25% can be invested in other debt securities, convertibles, and preferred stock. No more than 25% can be in restricted securities; recently this figure amounted to about 4%.

The fund has recently increased the quality of its holdings, reduced its exposure to the industrial segment of the market, and increased its position in utilities. Exposure to event risk is lessened with the reduced exposure to industrial companies. At this writing the average maturity of its portfolio is 14.5 years and its composite rating is close to double-A. With assets of over $100 million, PAI loans some of its securities to broker-dealers to generate additional interest income. At the end of 1989 about $11 million in securities were on loan.

PAI's capital structure is leveraged modestly with $5 million of convertible extendible notes issued in 1983. Of the original $18.5 million issuance, $13.5 million of the notes have already been converted into common stock of the fund. The notes were issued to increase assets which, in turn, would lead to greater income.

Western Asset Management Co., a wholly owned subsidiary of Legg Mason, Inc., serves as adviser. PAI's discount has averaged 10 percent over the past 12 years.

**Transamerica Income Shares (NYSE: TAI)** High income as consistent with prudent investment is the fund's primary objective: capital appreciation is a secondary objective. TAI does not use options, futures, or leverage, and presently over 80% of its portfolio is in debt rated triple-B or better. It has generally maintained a longer average maturity portfolio, which was 23 years at this writing.

TAI was ranked Number 2 performing CEBF for the 10 years ended December 31, 1989 by Lipper Analytical Services. Looking at a slightly different period (Table 13–1), TAI's compound annual total return for the 10 years ending June 30, 1990 was 13.05% compared to the 11.44% median for the group of older bond funds.

TAI's turnover has averaged about 114% over the past 5 years. But, the rates do vary widely from year to year—from 15% to over 150%. The short-term trading has enhanced total return as evident from TAI's performance.

The adviser is Transamerica Investment Services, Inc., a division of Transamerica Corp. The fund pays monthly dividends. Its expense ratio is very low.

## DIRECT PLACEMENT FUNDS

The portfolios of three older funds have held major positions in private or direct placement securities over the years. These include **MassMutual Corporate Investors (NYSE: MCI), Lincoln National Income Fund (NYSE: LND),** and **The Revere Fund (NASDAQ: PREV).** Since these funds invest in a different type of security than the investment grade funds their performance numbers in Table 13–1 are not really comparable with those of the latter. The direct placement funds comprise a very small fraction of the total bond fund universe. This will probably be true to an even greater extent in the future because of the limited availability of small company private placements that would be of interest to these funds.

Direct placement funds acquire securities directly from the issuer or in privately negotiated transactions with a seller. These securities commonly have equity participation features such as conversion privileges or warrants to purchase common stock. Direct placement investments are restricted securities and generally can be sold only in a directly negotiated transaction. They must be registered with the SEC before they can be sold in the open market. Thus, they have no quoted market value. Their estimated fair values as reported by the fund represent a valuation approved by its board of directors or trustees. Direct placement debt securities are generally long-term investments and may be held to maturity. Direct placement investing requires especially careful analysis, the close monitoring of portfolio companies, and the ability to assist in the restructuring of deteriorating situations.

All else equal, funds that invest in direct placements tend to trade at wider discounts than those that hold predominantly publicly-traded securities because direct placements have no market and are therefore illiquid. For instance, LND's year-end discounts averaged 15% since 1978. Recently, LND's discount has been running at 10% and under, which could be attributed to the fact that the proportion of its portfolio invested in private placements has declined over the years.

Let's briefly examine these funds.

LND changed its name in 1989 from Lincoln National Direct Placement Fund to Lincoln National Income Fund, reflecting the modification of its investment policy which now is to focus on publicly-traded as well as privately placed issues. When LND was established in 1972 it focused primarily on the private placement sector. It is now the least direct-placement oriented of the three funds examined here, with about 20% of its portfolio in direct placements at this writing. The kind of small private placements of interest to LND have not been available to the extent they were in the past. LND's expense ratio averaged 0.96% and its turnover 41.13% over the past five years. Lincoln National Investment Management Company is the adviser.

MCI is a non-diversified investment company which began in 1971. About 90% of its portfolio is in restricted securities. Approximately 41% of the portfolio consists of equity or equity-related securities. Its primary investment objective is current income with the opportunity for capital gains. Its investments provide a fixed yield and capital gains potential through warrants, conversion rights, or other equity features. Capital gains may be realized on holdings of restricted securities through different methods, including directly negotiated sales, exercise of put options, and initial public offerings of stock. MCI's expense ratio averaged 2.11% and its turnover 36.37% over the past five years.

Massachusetts Mutual Life Insurance Company serves as investment adviser to MCI and also to **Mass-Mutual Participation Investors (NYSE: MPV),** which was started in October 1988. With net assets of about $83 million, MPV's objectives are similar to those of its sister fund MCI. A higher proportion of MPV's portfolio is in public securities, however.

PREV is a small, non-diversified investment company. As noted earlier, it has had some problem issues in its portfolio. The vast majority of its assets are invested in directly-placed securities. PREV's focus is primarily on the second stage of venture capital financing; it does not provide seed, startup, or first stage financing. It generally invests in companies with annual sales between $5 million and $100 million. PREV's expense ratio averaged 1.36% over the past 5 years. Data on its turnover were unavailable. In August, 1989 shareholders approved transfer of the advisory agreement to Sunwestern Advisors, L.P.

In conclusion, funds specializing in direct placements require special expertise and greater risk tolerance on the investor's part because of the potential existence of non-performing issues. They are a much different product than the investment grade bond funds and their potentially higher returns come at the expense of greater risk. All else equal, the greater the proportion of the fund's portfolio in direct placements the higher its risk. Although LDN's discount to NAV can be tracked weekly in the closed-end funds box the others cannot since their holdings are primarily direct placements which are difficult to value precisely. Contact the funds themselves for further information.

## CONCLUSION

For those who are looking for a simpler, more straightforward type of bond fund with a long track record, the older plain vanilla investment grade CEBFs are the place to start. Many of them appear to have performed well in the past and have had relatively low expense ratios. We reached the same favorable conclusions about the older stock funds.

## Note

[1] Norman Tepper, *The Value Line Investment Survey,* April 27, 1990, p. 980.

CHAPTER 14

# *Bond Fund Types and Their Characteristics*

Perhaps the greatest lesson investors have learned in the 1980s, particularly in the last three years of that decade, has been to pay more attention to *total return* from whatever investment they make. The explosive growth of the CEBF industry underscores this. After seeing what program trading did to the U.S. stock market in late 1987, and its repercussions in every other stock exchange around the globe, nervous investors began to search for yield in the form of a monthly check from a bond fund.

Bond fund sponsors quickly became aware of this phenomenon and have "captured assets" achieving record growth. Large mutual fund complexes began to offer CEBFs. Included were Alliance Capital Management, Massachusetts Financial Services (MFS), Nuveen Advisory Corp., and Putnam Management Company. History buffs will be interested to know that MFS started **Massachusetts Investors Trust** in 1924, the first open-end fund offered to U.S. investors which today has about $1.4 billion in assets. Nuveen introduced the first municipal bond unit investment trust (UIT) in 1961 and has issued more than $28 billion in tax-exempt UITs since then. (In contrast to open- and closed-end funds which have managed portfolios, UITs hold unmanaged portfolios, generally consisting of fixed income securities.)

The newer CEBFs can be highly complex and require careful analysis on your part. A large number of them hold a varied assortment of debt security types and may use options and futures with the goal of achieving better performance. *The Scott Letter* tracks 140 bond funds.

## BOND FUND CATEGORIES

CEBFs can be separated into at least ten distinct categories. Many of these were popularized in the 1980s. Thinking of bond funds in terms of categories can help you select the one which best meets your objectives. In certain cases it may be difficult to decide which category a particular bond fund should be placed in. In fact, a few of them may seem to bear a closer resemblance to equity funds. But the groups represent a useful starting point. The portfolio of each fund in a particular category should be examined carefully since there can be wide differences among funds within a given classification.

The basic categories of CEBFs are named in Figure 14–1. Funds in all categories are taxable with the excep-

**Figure 14–1. CEBF Categories**
1. Investment grade bond funds.
2. Direct placement funds.
3. High-yield corporate bond funds.
4. U.S. government bond funds.
5. Mortgage-backed securities funds.
6. Global and international bond funds.
7. Multi-sector bond funds.
8. Flexible portfolio funds.
9. Municipal bond funds.
10. Loan participation funds.
11. Convertible funds.

tion of the municipal bond funds which are largely tax-exempt.

Investment grade bond funds and direct placement funds were dealt with in Chapter 13. The other categories are examined here with the exception of convertible bond funds which are covered in Chapter 15. One or more representative funds from each group are profiled. Other funds belonging to each of these categories are identified in our directory in Appendix II.

## HIGH-YIELD CORPORATE FUNDS

These funds (also known as junk bond funds) invest the vast majority of their assets in domestic issues of corporate debt which carry ratings below investment grade (that is, below triple-B). Although they may offer high returns, their portfolios have a high level of credit risk. On top of that, some of them use leverage which adds greater volatility for the investor.

The performance of this group during 1989 serves as a good illustration of their downside risk potential (Table 14–1). It was a very difficult year for the junk bond sector and many high-yield issues declined sharply amid well-publicized negative developments. The collapse of several major high-yield issuers, regulatory changes that forced thrifts to liquidate their high-yield holdings, and substantial net redemptions in many high-yield open-end funds all contributed to the turmoil.

The data in Table 14–1 reflect both the NAV performance, adjusted for reinvestment of all distributions, and the change in market price. Investor experience is not as bad when the reinvestment of distributions is considered. But these data do underscore the substantial risk facing the high-yield bond investor. High-yield funds are appropriate for speculative individuals who understand the nature of the risks and are able to live with the potential volatility. The risk tolerance would be similar to that needed for equity investment.

Of course, the funds, with their diversification and professional management, offer far greater safety than the

**Table 14–1. 1989 Performance of High-Yield Bond Funds**

| | Performance[1] | |
| --- | --- | --- |
| | Net Asset Value | Market Price |
| CIGNA High Income Shares | −6.24% | −17.33% |
| CIM High Yield Securities | −9.89 | −26.32 |
| Colonial Intermediate High Inc. (L) | −2.97 | −21.62 |
| High Income Advantage Trust | −15.00 | −25.68 |
| High Income Advantage Trust II | −9.32 | −23.29 |
| The High Yield Income Fund | −1.63 | −16.90 |
| The High Yield Plus Fund | −2.39 | −13.04 |
| Kemper High Income Trust | −9.96 | −24.18 |
| The New America High Income Fund (L) | −12.21 | −40.00 |
| Prospect Street High Income Port. (L) | −18.89 | −41.25 |
| USF&G Pacholder Fund, Inc. | +2.22 | −10.79 |
| Zenix Income Fund Inc. (L) | −10.37 | −24.66 |
| AVERAGE | −8.05% | −23.76% |

[1] Net asset value performance reflects the change in NAV adjusted for reinvestment of all distributions. Market price performance reflects the change in market price only. The one year performance period ends 12/31/89.
L denotes the fund is leveraged.
Source: Adapted from *LIPPER Closed-End Bond Funds Analysis.*

individual would have with direct investments in one or a few high-yield bonds. It takes an experienced bond analyst to "cherry pick" the best of the junk issues. The closed-end format has a special advantage for a high-yield portfolio as fund managers are not forced into selling illiquid holdings to deal with redemptions.

Investor sentiment towards high-yield bonds can be monitored with yardsticks like the **Treasury-Junk Yield Spread** appearing weekly in *Barron's*. The higher the spread (the amount by which the yield on an index of junk bonds exceeds the yield on Treasuries) the lower investor confidence is in junk bonds. This spread widened to over 700 basis points at times during the fourth quarter of 1989 and the first half of 1990. In the third quarter of 1990 the spread reached over 800 basis points. This is considered extremely wide based on past history. The contrarian would become more interested in junk bond CEBFs when the spread is wide. Presumably this would be a time when discounts on the high-yield funds are relatively wide. In mid-October 1990 we noticed that the discounts on some of the junk bond funds were huge. For example, The New America High Income Fund and Prospect Street High Income Portfolio both had discounts of over 40 percent!

Our illustrative fund for this category is **USF&G Pacholder Fund, Inc. (Amex: PHF).** PHF issued 1.8 million shares in 1988 at $20 each. Recently its net assets amounted to $31.1 million making it one of the smaller CEBFs. The fund seeks high total return through current income and capital appreciation by investing chiefly in very high-yielding domestic low-rated or unrated debt. The issues it selects generally trade at deep discounts to par which the management feels are due to market inefficiencies. Some of the companies may be involved in restructurings or Chapter 11 bankruptcy proceedings. The bonds may not even be paying interest. But it is thought that credit quality will improve or a reorganization or liquidation would increase their value. The fund's management wants to be an active participant in any reorganizations in an attempt to maximize its returns. PHF fared relatively well in 1989 (Table 14–1) since it maintained a very large cash position. At year-end, over half its assets were in high-rated commercial paper.

Pacholder & Co., the adviser, is jointly owned by Pacholder Associates and USF&G Marketing Services Co. Pacholder Associates, which has $2.3 billion under management, specializes in high-yield debt. Dr. Asher Pacholder, its chairman, has had over 20 years experience in the investment industry. PHF has an above-average expense ratio because of the nature of the securities in which it invests and the research it must undertake. The management fee is tied to performance. PHF's discount was nearly 21% on October 12, 1990.

## U.S. GOVERNMENT FUNDS

These funds invest at least 65% of their assets in U.S. Treasuries or agencies. Generally, up to 35% may be invested in foreign government debt or perhaps corporate bonds. A number of them write options to generate additional income. Many of these funds have portfolios with average maturities of five to ten years. They are categorized as intermediate term government funds. Some others may have longer maturities and, therefore, greater interest rate risk.

Wayne Lyski at Alliance manages five U.S. government bond CEBFs.[1] **ACM Government Income Fund (NYSE: ACG)** and **ACM Government Securities Fund (NYSE: GSF)** are virtually identical. U.S. Treasury securities and government agencies comprise at least 65% of their portfolios. The balance can be invested in foreign government debt or investment grade domestic corporate debt.

**ACM Government Spectrum Fund (NYSE: SI)** follows somewhat stricter guidelines. For instance, it cannot invest in corporate debt or in mortgage-backed securities like collateralized mortgage obligations (CMOs) which are not backed by the U.S. government. It tends to hold a higher percentage in domestic governments.

**ACM Government Opportunity Fund (NYSE: AOF)** and **ACM Managed Income Fund (NYSE: AMF)** generally invest about 65% in U.S. government securities and agencies. AOF may invest up to 20% in equities whereas AMF may hold up to 50% in domestic junk bonds. Both have invested well below those limits.

All five of the ACM funds are managed as intermediate term funds. At this writing their durations ranged from 3.8 to 4.5 years. Duration is the best single indicator of interest rate risk says Lyski. He will adjust it based on his interest rate outlook—lengthening duration when interest rates are expected to decline and shortening it if rates are expected to increase. The most important duration adjuster in these funds is the degree to which zero coupon bonds are used, explains Lyski. The more bullish he is on bond prices the higher the weighting for zeros which would give a longer duration.

## MORTGAGE-BACKED SECURITIES FUNDS

Mortgage securities offer investors very high credit quality and attractive yields relative to U.S. Treasury securities. For instance, Ginnie Maes yield between 100 to 160 basis points more than U.S. Treasuries. But, they are highly complex in comparison to the ordinary corporate or Treasury bond. Monthly cash flows consist of interest and amortization of principal, unlike the standard coupon bond which pays semiannual interest and principal at maturity. Prepayments of mortgages by homeowners accelerate the maturity date in an unpredictable way and complicate the usual calculations of duration and yield which are meaningfully applied to ordinary bonds. Professional management by an astute adviser is especially important with these securities.

The mortgage funds invest at least 65% of their assets in various types of mortgage-backed securities and mortgage derivatives. They are somewhat similar to the U.S. government funds since most of the mortgage-backed securities have the direct or implicit backing of the government. The objective is high current income generally paid to investors monthly.

An example of CEBFs investing in mortgage-backed securities would be the Blackstone family consisting of **Blackstone Income Trust (NYSE: BKT), Blackstone Target Term Trust (NYSE: BTT),** and **Blackstone Advantage Term Trust (NYSE: BAT).** BKT, the oldest of the three, was offered in July, 1988. Its primary objective is to generate high monthly income through a high quality mortgage asset portfolio. BTT, on the other hand, is a *finite-life* CEBF with the dual objective of generating high monthly income and returning $10.00 per share to investors in December, 2000. BAT, also finite-life, matures in the year 2005. All three funds are leveraged and may engage in a variety of hedging transactions. The adviser is Blackstone Financial Management, L.P. in New York.

Robert Kapito of Blackstone provides an overview of the mortgage-backed securities market and explains the unique structure of BTT in our Closed-End Insights box.

**Hyperion Total Return Fund (NYSE: HTR)** HTR went public in July 1989 and has net assets of about $269 million. It invests at least 70% of its portfolio in triple-A and double-A rated mortgage-backed securities and mortgage derivatives. Up to 30% is invested in high-yield corporate bonds rated double-B or single-B. Thus, HTR has a relatively unique personality. Because it limits its high-

## BRINGING SOPHISTICATED ASSET MANAGEMENT TO THE INDIVIDUAL
### Robert S. Kapito
### Principal
### Senior Portfolio Manager
### Blackstone Financial Management

The U.S. mortgage securities market has developed into a very large and liquid market over the last ten years. Currently, over $800 billion of the $2.7 trillion mortgages outstanding have been securitized by three government entities (the Government National Mortgage Association, the Federal National Mortgage Association, and the Federal Home Loan Mortgage Corporation). Due to their government sponsorship, these mortgage securities are extremely high in credit quality.

While the mortgage market provides excellent liquidity and credit quality, the securities themselves have very complex investment characteristics. The cash flows of mortgage securities depend on the level of home owner prepayments since interest, amortization, and prepayments of the underlying mortgage loans are passed through to the mortgage security holders. The interest rate risk and prepayment risk of mortgage securities is magnified in derivative mortgage securities such as collateralized mortgage obligations (CMOs), real estate mortgage investment conduits (REMICs), and mortgage strips. Blackstone utilizes proprietary analytics and portfolio strategies that typically are only available to sophisticated institutional investors, and has developed a structured product to fit the individual investor's needs.

The Blackstone Target Term Trust (BTT) is an example of bringing institutional expertise to the individual investor. In the recent environment of volatile interest rates and increased credit concerns, the typical investor clamored for high quality, high monthly income, liquidity, and return of their initial investment. Blackstone responded by offering BTT, the first closed-end fund rated AAA by Standard and Poor's and the first closed-end fund to state as an objective the return of the investor's initial investment. In order to achieve this objective, the Trust invested approximately 30% of its assets in zero coupon bonds whose value would equal the initial investment per share as of the final distribution date. The balance of assets were invested in a diversified portfolio of mortgage-backed securities to provide high monthly income. The finite life of the Trust gives the investor the best features of both a managed bond and the liquidity of an NYSE stock. The Trust is $955 million and has provided a high monthly income, a stable net asset value, and stock price.

yield exposure in terms of rating and amount it would have considerably less risk than funds that invest more heavily in this sector. Hyperion Capital Management, Inc., the adviser, is headed by Lewis Ranieri, a pioneer in the development of the secondary mortgage market. The high-yield portion of the portfolio is managed by Pacholder Associates, the sub-adviser.

## GLOBAL AND INTERNATIONAL FUNDS

The global and international bond funds are a logical development since about half of the world's debt is non-U.S. These funds have a wide range of flexibility as to where they can invest geographically. As well as holding domestic bonds they can invest in foreign bonds, mainly foreign government bonds. There would be some currency risk inherent in the portfolios of these funds which could increase the volatility of returns.

Two illustrative funds for this category are **Templeton Global Income Fund (NYSE: GIM)** and **Templeton Global Governments Income Trust (NYSE: TGG)**. Both funds are non-diversified and invest in domestic as well as foreign debt. GIM has net assets of $968 million whereas TGG's are $186 million. As well as having positions in U.S. debt, the two funds have substantial holdings in Australia, Canada, and New Zealand. TGG must invest at least 65% in government securities; the balance may be invested in U.S. and foreign corporate debt and preferred stock. GIM has greater latitude in terms of the kinds of debt it can invest in. Both funds can buy puts and write calls.

In contrast to the more diversified global funds are two which invest mainly in Australian debt, **First Australia Prime Income Fund (Amex: FAX)** and **Kleinwort Benson Australian Income Fund (NYSE: KBA)**. Both seek high current income. These funds are riskier than the more broadly diversified global funds and carry an exchange rate risk due to U.S. versus Australian dollar exchange rate fluctuations. FAX, which is much larger than KBA, is leveraged with auction rate preferred stock.

## MULTI-SECTOR FUNDS

The typical multi-sector fund invests in three bond market sectors: U.S. government bonds, corporate bonds (generally high-yield), and foreign government bonds. The primary objective is high current income; capital appreciation is secondary. By diversifying into several sectors the overall volatility of the portfolio should be smoothed out. These funds may use income enhancement strategies like call writing to increase distributions. The multi-sector funds use junk bonds to increase their yield but they don't have exposure to this sector to the extent that a pure junk bond fund would. They may also trim back their junk bond holdings when they feel that circumstances warrant.

Putnam has four multi-sector CEBFs which invest in the three traditional sectors. A large investment company complex, Putnam has total assets under management of over $42 billion represented by about 2 million shareholder accounts. Taken together its nine closed-end funds have assets amounting to nearly $4 billion. Gary Coburn of Putnam explains the merit of the multi-sector concept in our Closed-End Insights box.

## PUTNAM'S OPTIMAL PORTFOLIO: THE "CYCLE OF STABILITY" STRATEGY
### Gary N. Coburn
### Senior Managing Director and Chief of U.S. Fixed Income Investments
### The Putnam Companies

What kind of investment best meets investors' increasing need for income while suiting their lower tolerance of volatility? To answer this question, Putnam's fixed income group studied monthly returns, standard deviations, and correlation coefficients for a variety of fixed income instruments over ten years. Reviewing cash, mortgage-backed securities, corporate bonds, international bonds and U.S. government and agency securities, we found the best combination of high current return and relatively low volatility occurring with one particular blend of investments: equal weightings of U.S. government securities, high-yield corporate bonds, and international fixed-income securities. This combination became the key to our "Cycle of Stability" strategy.

Each "Cycle" investment has its own advantages. U.S. government securities, for example, offer attractive income and an unsurpassed credit record. High-yield corporates have substantial yield advantages over Treasuries, with an average spread of about 350 basis points. And international fixed-income investing is an opportunity to take advantage of interest rate and currency trends around the globe.

There are trade-offs in each case, though, and that's where the "Cycle" strategy comes in. Economic events, such as the U.S. dollar's value, the rate of economic activity, and interest rate trends, influence performance, with some factors affecting each sector to a greater extent. For example, U.S. government securities are most sensitive to interest rates, while high-yield corporates respond to changes in economic activity. Consequently, these sectors move somewhat independently, on occasion traveling in opposite directions simultaneously. Given this relationship, each sector's strengths have the potential to cushion the others' vulnerabilities, the reason a combination of all three brings you pretty close to that "optimal portfolio."

Two recent one-year periods show how the strategy would have operated:

In 1987, U.S. government securities declined due to an upturn in interest rates. High-yield bonds were relatively unaffected, since the economic growth rate was continuing. Meanwhile, declines in the U.S. dollar's value meant higher prices for international bonds.

In 1984, early interest rate increases followed by a decline meant a strong environment for U.S. government securities. Economic activity moved in reverse, beginning with a bang, then slowing substantially, contributing to a middle-of-the-road year for the high-yield sector. With a strong U.S. dollar throughout the year, international bonds significantly underperformed the other sectors.

In each case, a downtrend in one sector was balanced by more favorable results in others. Of course, this can't be the case every year, but generally, an investment equally diversified across these sectors can be expected to produce attractive returns over the long term, plus greater relative stability than an investment in any *one* sector.

The principle is even more apparent over longer periods, as the accompanying chart shows. It shows performance results (graphed as percentages) for three different unmanaged indexes, each representing a "Cycle" sector, and a hypothetical portfolio equally weighted in each index. While the "Cycle" can't be expected to operate effectively if all three sectors decline simultaneously, this long-term picture puts the recent downtrend in its proper perspective, a relatively rare event. No one strategy is infallible, but we continue to believe that this approach is an excellent recommendation for investors who want attractive returns plus greater relative stability.

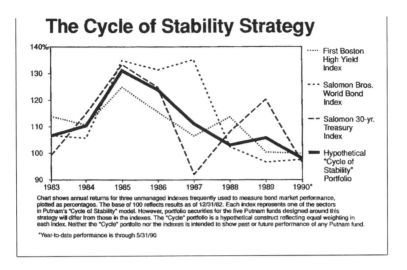

## The Cycle of Stability Strategy

First Boston High Yield Index

Salomon Bros. World Bond Index

Salomon 30-yr. Treasury Index

Hypothetical "Cycle of Stability" Portfolio

Chart shows annual returns for three unmanaged indexes frequently used to measure bond market performance, plotted as percentages. The base of 100 reflects results as of 12/31/82. Each index represents one of the sectors in Putnam's "Cycle of Stability" model. However, portfolio securities for the five Putnam funds designed around this strategy will differ from those in the indexes. The "Cycle" portfolio is a hypothetical construct reflecting equal weighting in each index. Neither the "Cycle" portfolio nor the indexes is intended to show past or future performance of any Putnam fund.

*Year-to-date performance is through 5/31/90

**Oppenheimer Multi-Sector Income Trust (NYSE: OMS)** OMS is rather unique among multi-sector funds as it can invest in seven different fixed income sectors. Its objective is high current income consistent with preservation of capital with a secondary objective of capital appreciation. OMS has carried the multi-sector concept further than others in order to gain greater flexibility.

The eligible sectors include U.S. Treasury securities, corporate bonds, mortgage-backed securities, international securities, convertible bonds, municipal bonds, and money market instruments. OMS can have up to 95% of its portfolio in U.S. governments, up to 50% each in U.S. corporates and money markets, and up to 25% each in the other four sectors. It must be invested in at least three sectors at any one time.

We met with Paul Suckow, executive vice president at Oppenheimer to discuss the fund. "Basically, we felt that there are certain sectors that perform best in certain economic and interest rate environments," Suckow told us. "You shouldn't preclude some of the sectors in a true multi-sector fund. We look at it as sort of the 'eclectic bond fund.' Whatever seems to be the sector that's going to work we'll invest in. It's not an all-or-nothing bet. It's based on the probabilities that this sector is going to do better than that one so we overweight this sector and underweight that one."

The fund may invest in taxable as well as tax-exempt munis. We thought it was kind of unique that OMS could invest in the municipal sector and asked Suckow about it. "It's not in there to create tax-exempt income, it's in there because the municipal sector sometimes performs extremely well," he replied. OMS investors would have to pay tax on the portion of the fund's income derived from the tax-exempt munis since it would not have a large enough proportion of its portfolio in munis to generate tax-free income for shareholders. The munis would be held more for total return than strictly for income, says Suckow.

Several of the closed-end funds managed by MFS have a multi-sector orientation with emphasis on the three traditional sectors. Their newest offering, MFS Special Value Trust, is closer to a flexible portfolio fund. It will be covered in the next section.


## FLEXIBLE PORTFOLIO FUNDS

These funds (also known as "asset-allocation funds" and "total return funds") would typically have lower yields than the average bond fund because they seek greater capital appreciation. Using "top-down" analysis, fund managers can vary portfolio composition between bonds, stocks, derivative securities, and money market instruments depending upon their outlook. For instance, a flexible fund might move from a 75% position in Treasury bonds to a 75% position in stocks.

When analyzing a flexible fund the reputation and track record of the investment manager is especially important since the manager has considerable freedom to rearrange the portfolio. Also check the portfolio turnover to see how much switching is being done. Excessive turnovers translate into relatively high transaction cost so the high turnover is good only if impressive results are being achieved. Four illustrations will give you the idea of how some of these funds are managed and the wide differences that can exist among them.

**America's All Season Fund (NASDAQ National Market System: FUND)** FUND is non-diversified and seeks long-term capital appreciation without undue risk. Any income earned will be incidental. It could be heavily invested in equities as it was during the summer of 1990. In fact, it may best be categorized as a global equity fund. We decided to include it here because it is flexible and could invest heavily in debt.

FUND was offered in April, 1988 at $6 a share and had net assets of about $52 million at this writing. Diego Veitia, the manager, uses top-down analysis and can make fixed income and equity investments "anywhere in the world." Veitia uses a variety of different strategies which include short selling and writing options on securities FUND holds. It could use leverage and could hold foreign currencies and gold and silver if circumstances warrant. FUND could be up to 133% invested. Veitia is chairman of International Assets Advisory Corp. in Winter Park, Florida. Global Advisors, an affiliate of International Assets, is the fund's adviser. It manages total assets of about $100 million.

FUND's shares have traded at discounts as high as 30%. Perhaps investors feel the management isn't sufficiently focused. Veitia maintains that the focus is clear as he told *The Scott Letter* (November, 1990):

> We are very focused on preservation of capital. While world markets are down about 27% this year [the first 9 months of 1990], we have preserved almost 100% of our shareholders' capital in 1990. [FUND shifted from almost 80% in stocks to 95% in cash over the period from mid-July to the end of August, 1990]. Performance is the bottom line. This year we are in the top 1% of all capital appreciation funds.
>
> You also have to have a discipline. My philosophy is that I look at the fund as a family of funds. Unlike a balanced fund which has to have certain assets in certain categories, I have no minimal requirement for any sector. We use a strategy of timing the use of

assets which most individual investors usually cannot do.[2]

As a relatively low priced NASDAQ-traded stock FUND has had a fairly wide bid-asked spread (as a percent of its bid price) which means investors purchasing its shares at the offering price or selling at the bid face higher transaction costs.

**Comstock Partners Strategy Fund (NYSE: CPF)** With net assets of about $1.2 billion, CPF is one of the largest CEBFs. It began in May, 1988 with a $1.2 billion offering. CPF's objective is to maximize total return over a long time horizon by investing primarily in fixed income securities. Comstock Partners, Inc. is the adviser. Stanley Salvigsen, Charles Minter, and Michael Aronstein are the firm's principals. The adviser, which also manages discretionary accounts, publishes the *Comstock Investment Strategy Review* and the *Comstock Investment Strategy Commentary.*

CPF will invest 75% or more of its net assets in debt securities rated single-A or higher. The remaining 25% can be invested in debt rated as low as single-C. Being non-diversified, CPF could invest more than 5% of its assets in the obligations of a single issuer.

During 1989 the fund divested all its corporate and foreign debt and equity holdings and invested the balance in U.S. Treasury securities including some zero coupon Treasuries. The adviser wanted the highest quality, most liquid, and long duration securities because further declines in interest rates were expected. Its outlook changed and beginning in January 1990 CPF divested the Treasury zeros and invested the balance in Treasury bills. The long-term Treasury positions were hedged with put options and futures contracts in order to insulate the portfolio from a possible rise in interest rates. This made CPF a bystander in the debt marketplace positioned to take advantage of whatever opportunity arises. CPF's portfolio turnover was about 40% for its 1990 fiscal year. We noticed that CPF was trading at a small discount in October, 1990.

CPF will make a tender offer during the second quarter of 1991 to purchase its shares at the NAV determined on the day the offer terminates. If the board decides not to purchase any shares under the tender offer a subsequent one will be made. If all shares tendered are not purchased by the fund shareholders will be given the opportunity to vote to open-end the fund.

**MFS Special Value Trust (NYSE: MFV)** is the eighth CEBF offered by MFS and is the first one which contains equities in the portfolio. MFV came out in November, 1989 and raised under $100 million. The fund is a little hard to categorize. A non-diversified fund, MFV invests in U.S. government securities, junk bonds, and stocks. At least half its portfolio is invested in government securities. It is total-return oriented as it seeks out-of-favor, undervalued securities. Some of its holdings are of above-average risk and may be involved in reorganizations or capital restructurings. It also has a current income component, and seeks to pay out a monthly distribution at an 11% annual rate, which comes primarily from investing in Treasuries and writing options against them. A high distribution rate like this means that a portion of the return may be paid from the trust's assets and thus represent a return of capital. MFV's high distribution makes it a hybrid between a multi-sector fund and a flexible fund.

One of the large mutual fund complexes, MFS, a wholly-owned subsidiary of Sun Life Assurance of Canada (U.S.), manages $25 billion in net assets for more than one million investor accounts. MFS has $4.8 billion of assets in its eight closed-end funds.

**The Zweig Total Return Fund (NYSE: ZTR)** ZTR will normally invest between 50% and 65% of its assets in high quality debt securities including U.S. government and agency securities and domestic corporate debt rated double-A or triple-A. Between 25% and 35% would normally be invested in equities, but up to 75% could be invested in equities. ZTR is fairly large with assets of about $590 million at this writing. The fund employs the market timing techniques developed by Dr. Martin Zweig, as ex-

plained in Chapter 6. ZTR's portfolio turnover has averaged about 150%. The fund distributes a total of 10% of
NAV annually; distributions are made monthly.


## MUNICIPAL BOND FUNDS

Municipal bonds are attractive to many investors since
they are one of the few remaining vehicles which can shelter income from taxes. The income from most municipal
bonds is exempt from federal taxes and from state taxes
as well if the bonds are issued within your state. Several
states have no income tax and a few others exempt income from out-of-state as well as in-state municipal
bonds. Capital gains realized on the sale of a municipal
bond would be subject to tax though.

The basic advantage of a tax-exempt bond depends
upon the relative values of three variables:

1.   The yield on tax-exempt bonds.
2.   The yield on fully-taxable bonds of equivalent
     risk.
3.   The investor's tax bracket.

In late July 1990 high grade corporate bonds were
yielding about 9.2% to maturity as reflected by *Barron's*
**Best Grade Bonds** index, and the **Bond Buyer 20 Bond
Index** showed a yield of nearly 7.2% on general obligation
municipals.[3] Using a simple equation we can determine
the break-even marginal tax rate (T) at which we would
be indifferent between the taxable and tax-exempt bonds:

(1 − T) × Taxable Bond Yield = Tax-Exempt Bond
Yield
(1 − T) × 9.2% = 7.2%
(1 − T) = 7.2%/9.2%
T = 0.22

In this illustration investors in tax brackets above
22% would prefer tax-exempt bonds whereas those in tax

brackets below 22% would prefer the fully taxable bonds. Thus, 22% represents the break-even marginal tax rate.

The municipal bond fund group amounts to the largest sector in the CEBF universe. Most invest in munis issued by a variety of states, some restrict their investments to either California or New York state obligations. The funds also differ in quality and there is a group of high-yield muni funds which hold lower quality obligations. Figure 14–2 contains a breakdown of municipal bond fund types as determined by Lipper Analytical Services, whose definitions are widely accepted and used throughout the industry.

## The Nuveen Funds

John Nuveen & Co. is the oldest and largest investment banker specializing in the underwriting and distribution of tax-exempt securities and the largest sponsor of tax-free funds. Founded in 1898 by wholesale grocer John Nuveen, it has $38 billion under management and 700,000 shareholders. Its first open-end municipal bond fund came out in 1976, the year in which it became legally possible to pass along tax-free income to investment company shareholders. The first of the Nuveen CEBFs was **Nuveen Municipal Value Fund (NYSE: NUV)** offered in

**Figure 14–2. Municipal Bond Fund Types**
**GENERAL MUNICIPAL BOND FUNDS**
Invest at least 65% of assets in municipal debt issues rated in the top four grades.
**HIGH YIELD MUNICIPAL BOND FUNDS**
May invest 50% or more of assets in lower rated municipal debt issues.
**INSURED MUNICIPAL BOND FUNDS**
Invest at least 65% of assets in municipal debt issues that are insured as to timely payment.
**SPECIFIC STATE MUNICIPAL BOND FUNDS**
Limit investment of assets to municipal debt issues that are exempt from taxation of a specific state (double tax exempt) or city (triple tax exempt).
Source: *LIPPER Closed-End Bond Funds Analysis.*

June 1987. Net proceeds of that offering were $1.6 billion. NUV is unleveraged and invests at least 80% of its assets in munis rated triple-B or higher. NUV's portfolio is managed by Thomas Spaulding, vice president and manager of Nuveen Advisory Corp., a subsidiary of John Nuveen & Co. Incorporated.

Nuveen now manages 15 CEBFs with total assets of about $7 billion. Four of these invest in California munis and four in New York state munis. Of the 15 funds 11 are leveraged with preferred stock representing about 34% of the fund's assets. The primary distinctions among the 15 Nuveen funds are state or national and leveraged or unleveraged. Otherwise they do not differ that much from one another. As of this writing Nuveen's most recent offering was **Nuveen Investment Quality Municipal Fund (NYSE: NQM).** The offering was for 30 thousand shares at $15 in June 1990. NQM, which invests exclusively in investment grade securities, uses value investing as it seeks municipal bonds with high safety that are undervalued. In selecting munis the management looks for 7 to 8 years of call protection to protect the dividend stream. NQM's capital structure is leveraged with preferred stock.

The Nuveen funds tend to trade at modest premiums. "Historically, our 15 closed-end funds generally have traded at or above their net asset values," says Timothy Schwertfeger, executive vice president, John Nuveen & Co. Incorporated. "We believe this strong performance is primarily due to the ability of our funds to deliver superior taxable equivalent total returns, and also to our widely recognized brand name and our diverse shareholder base."

Other sponsors of closed-end municipal bond funds include Allstate, Colonial, Dreyfus, Putnam, and VanKampen Merritt.

## Choosing a Muni Fund

Selection of a municipal bond fund is tricky and a number of factors must be kept in mind.

1. Examine the quality of the fund's holdings by looking at the breakdown in terms of agency ratings.

2.  Determine whether or not the fund uses leverage. If it does you should understand the nature of the leverage and the potential risk it entails as well as its advantage. Simply put, leverage can increase returns under favorable interest rate conditions but it also increases risk and can lead to greater fluctuations in share price, NAV, and yield. This is explained by Jeff Hopson of A.G. Edwards in his *Closed-End Fund Update.* A portion of his discussion appears in Figure 14–3.

### Figure 14–3. How Leverage Works

In the municipal sector, the most common leverage technique has been the issuance of auction rate preferred stock. The most common capital structures have the preferred stock equal to 30% to 40% of the total capital of the fund.

Preferred stock is generally issued with a variable rate, while the proceeds of the issue are invested in long-term bonds. To the extent that the short-term rate is lower than the return initially generated by the proceeds, the fund earns a spread and the holder of the common shares can receive above-average dividend distributions. From that point forward, the returns to the common holders will be a function of the trend of short-term interest rates. If short-term rates fall/rise, the earned rate to the common will increase/decrease. As long-term rates fall/rise, the market value of the portfolio and the NAV will increase/decrease by a leveraged amount.

The worst-case scenario for these funds is one in which both long-term and short-term interest rates rise dramatically. In this case, the short-term rate on the preferred would rise and reduce the earned income (and eventually the dividend) of the fund. With long-term interest rates rising as well, the net asset value of the common shares would fall by a leveraged amount. The fund does have some flexibility to react to such a change in interest rates. The fund has the ability to call in the preferred at any time at par. However, the fund would have to liquidate portfolio securities to meet this call, and common holders could suffer capital losses if the value of the portfolio securities had dropped in reaction to higher interest rates. The fund could also shift a portion of its portfolio securities to short-term instruments, reducing its negative exposure to a rise in rates.

Source: J. Jeffrey Hopson, *Closed-End Fund Update* (St. Louis, MO: A.G. Edwards & Sons, Inc., January 23, 1990), p. 5.

3. If you live in California or New York state the single state fund would generally be your first choice. A broker or financial planner could assist you in determining the after-tax yield advantage of the single state fund. These funds have lower yields than multi-state funds and their limited geographic diversification exposes investors to greater risk.

4. Determine the average maturity or duration of the fund's portfolio. The longer the maturity the more volatility the fund could experience.

5. Do municipal bonds offer attractive returns relative to equivalent risk taxable bonds? Examine the current relationship between yields on municipal bonds and corporate bonds relative to their historic relationship. The **Bond Buyer 20 Bond Index** and the **Bond Buyer Municipal Bond Index** reported weekly in *Barron's* are helpful in this regard.

6. The higher your combined federal and state tax bracket the more attractive municipal bonds become. If you are subject to the alternative minimum tax (AMT), a municipal bond fund may not be attractive, however, since most have the ability to invest in those municipal bonds the income from which may be taxable at the AMT rate. *But, very few people are subject to the AMT.*

## LOAN PARTICIPATION FUNDS

You may have noticed the relatively small "Loan Participation Funds" category that appears weekly in the closed-end funds box in *Barron's*. You might have been puzzled by the fact that only an NAV is reported, not a price and a related discount or premium, and they are not traded on any exchange.

What are these funds? While legally they are closed-end funds, we do not consider them CEFs from a practical point of view since they are not publicly traded. These funds hold portfolios of bank loans. Loan participations are nothing new—they've been in use for more than 20 years. Banks sell off portions of their loans to institutional investors, including these funds, for a fee. Typically, each loan interest is at least $5 million. This provides the banks with capital to make more loans.

Loan participation funds pay dividends which vary with the prime rate. Investors can buy shares daily through a broker. But you cannot sell shares daily; shares are purchased by the fund periodically, like once a quarter at NAV. **Pilgrim Prime Rate Trust,** originally offered in May 1988, was the first loan participation fund. It has assets of about $1.1 billion. Since we do not consider loan participation funds to be true closed-end funds we will not cover them further and do not include them in our directory.

## CEBF SELECTION GUIDELINES

1. It is useful to think of CEBFs in terms of categories but fund variations within a given category can be extreme in terms of portfolio composition, management philosophy, and so on. And funds can change their philosophies over the years. The categories are only a starting point.

2. Before investing it is essential to know what guidelines the fund operates under. Try to obtain a prospectus, but, if you can't, at least you should understand the general parameters. Then look at the portfolio composition. The breakdown of the portfolio in terms of quality rating is also critical. Finally, determine the average maturity, or better yet, the average portfolio duration.

3. As we've said before, beware of funds with above-average yields. They may be taking on excessive risk or cannibalizing assets, using high current income to appease shareholders. A dividend cut may be a wise move on the part of the manager.

4. While the discount is highly important you can't always accept it at face value. A high yield and a big discount could be illusive. The CEBF may be writing call options to jack up the yield. The danger is that funds heavily involved in writing options lose out if interest rates decline, since their optioned bonds get called away. Total re-

turn suffers and the fund faces reinvestment risk since the money would generally have to be reinvested in lower yielding issues.[4]

5.  CEBFs with relatively high portfolio turnovers can be attractive if the portfolio manager is adding value through active management. But a high turnover accompanied by consistently poor performance is a negative. A very low turnover accompanied by poor performance is also a negative since management may not be fulfilling its responsibilities.

6.  Finally, if you don't understand a particular CEBF don't invest in it. Investors in complex funds must be sophisticated and be able to tell whether they are getting value or gimmicks.

## CONCLUSION

This chapter provides an overview of the CEBF universe. Readers should recognize that many of the newer bond funds are quite complex and must be analyzed thoroughly before investing. The first step to becoming a knowledgeable bond fund investor is to familiarize yourself with the different bond fund categories and their general characteristics including their risk factors. Individual funds have been profiled for illustrative purposes only, not because we want to recommend for or against purchasing their shares. If you are interested in a particular category you need to go further and examine the other funds in that category. The next chapter covers convertible funds which are sort of a hybrid between a bond fund and an equity fund.

### Notes

[1]Randall D. Forsyth, "All in the Family," *Barron's*, May 21, 1990, p. 41.

[2]*The Scott Letter: Closed-End Fund Report*, November, 1990, pp. 3 and 6.

[3]*Barron's*, July 30, 1990, p. 139.

[4]Leslie Eaton, "Mutual Benefits," *Barron's*, July 2, 1990, p. 17.

CHAPTER 15

# *Convertible Funds*

Convertible funds (or convertible bond funds) have characteristics of both bond and stock funds. If you are seeking an investment that is a bit more conservative than the typical equity fund, but may offer most of the upside potential of stock, you should consider the closed-end convertible funds. A convertible fund is similar in nature to a balanced fund which invests in both bonds and common stock. Convertible fund portfolios typically include convertible preferred stock as well as convertible bonds. Discounts on some of the convertible funds are greater than those on the average "straight" (or nonconvertible) bond fund. Thus, you may be able to find value here.

## THE BASICS OF CONVERTIBLES

No one should invest in a convertible fund without a basic understanding of how convertibles themselves work.[1] Convertibles (or CVs) have been called the "ideal security" as they offer investors potentially the best of both the stock world and the bond world in a single investment. Convertible bonds and convertible preferred stock are quite similar in most respects, so let's focus on bonds for simplicity. CVs can be converted into shares of the underlying common stock at the holder's option. A convertible bond is similar to a straight bond, as it pays a fixed coupon semi-annually and has a fixed maturity date. Convertible bonds have a kind of dual personality since they may act like bonds at certain times and like stock at other times.

CVs are complex and difficult to analyze and diversification is important. As bonds, your transaction costs would be high if you want to buy them in small lots since you would be faced with retail rather than wholesale prices. Furthermore, convertibles may carry lower credit ratings since smaller companies and/or those with weaker balance sheets often use them to raise money on more favorable terms. Convertibles on average, however, are of higher quality today than they were 20 years ago.

The conversion feature acts as a "sweetener" since investors have the safety of the bond plus the opportunity to participate in the growth of the company if it becomes successful. This enables the issuer to offer the bonds with a lower coupon than would be required on a nonconvertible issue, thus making borrowing feasible where otherwise it might be prohibitively costly. The income stream on a convertible would typically be 20% to 25% below that of a similar bond without the conversion feature. The investor is giving up some income in return for upside potential if the stock performs well in the future.

In comparison to the underlying common stock, CVs generally offer a higher yield, advance less in rising markets, and decline less in falling markets. CVs decline less because they have a price "floor" provided by the bond side of their personalities.

## The Bond Value

The *bond value* (also known as investment value) of a convertible is its value stripped of the conversion feature. It is based upon the CV's agency rating, coupon rate, maturity, and the general level of interest rates. The bond value can be calculated by discounting the CV's interest payments and face or maturity value at a rate corresponding to the yield to maturity on an equivalent nonconvertible bond.

**Example:**   The 10% coupon, $1,000 face value, single-B rated convertible debentures of the Emerging Growth Co. mature in 20 years. Nonconvertible single-B bonds which mature in 20 years now yield 12%. The bond value works out to be about $850.


*The convertible should never sell below its bond value regardless of what happens to the price of the stock.* The CV is clearly safer than the common stock of the issuer. As in the case of any corporate bond, a CV's bond value can change due to a change in interest rates and/or a change in the company's creditworthiness. The CV will usually sell at some premium above its bond value since it offers the potential of appreciation if and when the stock does well.

## The Conversion Value

The *conversion value* (also known as *parity*) represents the value received if one bond is exchanged for common stock at the present market price. Parity equals the conversion ratio (the number of shares of common stock obtained per converted bond) times the market price per share of the stock.

**Example:**   Assume that the Emerging Growth Co. bond had a conversion ratio of 100 (that is, each $1,000 face value bond is convertible into 100 shares of Emerging Growth Corporation common).

If the stock is trading at $11, the CV's conversion value would be $1,100 ($11 × 100).

If the stock rises to $12, parity would increase to $1,200, and so on.

## The Two Premiums

The convertible bond will usually sell at some premium above the *greater of* its conversion value or bond value. The CV would simultaneously be trading at an even higher premium above the lesser of those two values. If the bond value is $850 and the conversion value is $1,200 the CV would sell at a premium above the $1,200. If the premium was 20% it would be selling for $1,440. The CV trades at a premium over conversion value because it offers an income advantage over an investment in the company's stock. Note also that the $1,440 market price would represent a 69% premium over the $850 bond value. All else equal, appreciation-oriented convertible investors like low conversion premiums (20% or less is considered low) since the lower the premium the more appreciation you would realize with the convertible when the stock advances.

## A Closer Look at the Premiums

The relationship between the market price of a convertible and its bond value and conversion value can be seen in Figure 15–1. The amount by which the market price curve exceeds the bond value or conversion value represents the premium over that value. Three areas on the diagram are identified to illustrate the nature of the two premiums.

## Forcing Conversion

Convertible bonds are callable, and the issuer would call the bond to "force" conversion when the conversion value exceeds the call price by a sufficient amount. The reason the issuer would force conversion would be to get the bonds off its balance sheet, since the original reason for issuing the CV was to sell stock at prices above the current level. The issuer would not want the bonds to remain outstanding any longer than necessary. By forcing conversion the fixed interest payments are eliminated. Convertible investors would generally not want to hold the stock.

**Example:** The Emerging Growth Co. bonds are callable at 110, or a price of $1,100 per $1,000 bond. If the stock is trading at $12 and the conversion value is $1,200, investors would not want to tender their bonds for $1,100 when they could sell them for at least $1,200 on the open market or convert into stock with a current

**Figure 15–1. Convertible Bond Price Versus Common Stock Price**

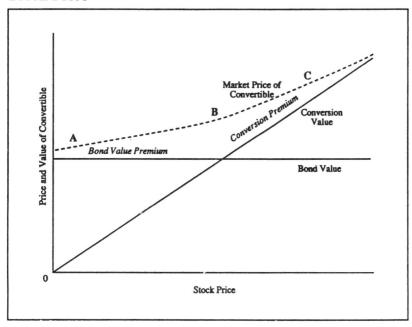

**AREA A:** In this area the convertible trades at a modest premium above its bond value and at a large premium over conversion value. At A the CV would be similar to a straight bond investment. Its yield would be greatest here. The stock price would have to increase considerably for the convertible to rise in price unless interest rates decline.

**AREA B:** The premiums over conversion value and bond value are now similar in size; around this area the convertible would have both stock and bond attributes. Since the CV is attractive to investors here its conversion premium is moderately high.

**AREA C:** Now the conversion premium is very small and the premium over bond value very large. The convertible acts like a stock and has a lower yield than it did at lower stock prices. The downside price risk is greatest here. You'll also notice that the premium over conversion value practically disappears at high conversion values. This is because the issuer is likely to force conversion.

value of $1,200. Thus, the issuer has forced conversion by calling in the bonds at 110.

Of course, if the stock languishes, conversion may never take place and the issuer would be stuck with an "overhanging" convertible.

## THREE CONVERTIBLE STRATEGIES

There are basically three alternative strategies that a convertible fund manager could use. They correspond to the three areas on the convertible price curve shown in Figure 15–1. Essentially, convertible funds could be structured as bond portfolios with the emphasis on yield, stock portfolios with emphasis on appreciation, or balanced portfolios with approximately equal weight given to yield and appreciation. This is explained in the Closed-End Insights box by Thomas Dinsmore, president of Davis/Dinsmore Management Company, the adviser to two closed-end convertible funds.

---

### CONVERTIBLE PORTFOLIO STRATEGIES
### Thomas H. Dinsmore, CFA
### President
### Davis/Dinsmore Management Company

Convertible securities are more complex than common stocks or bonds. The market values of convertibles are affected by both stock prices and interest rate levels. This makes it possible to structure portfolios of convertibles to participate in upward moves in either market while providing a hedge against downward moves.

There are three fundamental approaches to a buy and hold convertible investment strategy. They are the bond equivalent, equity equivalent, and mixed strategies.


## BOND EQUIVALENT STRATEGY

The investor using this approach would seek out convertibles that have fallen to levels where their yields are roughly the same as non-convertible bonds, or preferred stock, issued by the same company. These issues would most likely have large premiums to conversion value (usually greater than 50%). Provided the issuers are sound, a portfolio of these issues should do as well as a similar fixed income portfolio, while providing the potential for outperforming it if one or two of the underlying common stocks revive. Just such a revival occurred with MCI. In 1985 the MCI 7.75% convertible debenture fell into the 60s and had conversion premiums over 100%. By 1989 these bonds were trading near 110 with very little premium just before they were called.

Investors using this strategy should be satisfied with the credit quality of the issuer and with the potential of the common to revive. Further, this is a long-term strategy.


## EQUITY EQUIVALENT STRATEGY

There are some convertibles that are more attractive than the common stock. These issues have low or negligible premiums (0% to 5%) to conversion value while still providing a yield advantage to the common stock. If there are no serious disadvantages such as an imminent call that would force conversion, a portfolio of such issues would outperform a similar portfolio of common stocks.

This is usually not a long-term strategy as convertibles selling near conversion value are often called. The investor should have done a thorough equity analysis of the underlying common stock. It is a useful supplement to an equity portfolio.

**MIXED OR BALANCED CONVERTIBLE STRATEGY**

A portfolio of issues with moderate premiums to conversion value (usually 15% to 30%) and significant yield advantages over the underlying common stock (perhaps 300 to 600 basis points, or 3 to 6 percentage points, over the common dividend yield) is a mixed or balanced strategy. Such a portfolio can provide performance that has much of the profit potential with less volatility and greater current income than the equivalent equity portfolio.

This strategy is usually long-term in nature and requires monitoring. The investor should like the underlying common stock.

Now we're ready to look at the convertible funds themselves.

## THE CONVERTIBLE FUNDS

There are nine closed-end convertible funds, one of which is a dual purpose fund, Convertible Holdings. They are identified in Table 15–1. The convertible funds range in size from assets of $47.9 million for Castle Convertible Fund to $265 million for Convertible Holdings. These funds normally invest at least 65% of their assets in convertibles.

Three of the convertible funds were started in the early 1970s and thus offer us the opportunity to examine their longer-term performance. The performances of these funds for 5- and 10-year periods based on Lipper data appear in Table 15–2. Relevant benchmarks are also included. American Capital was the best performer among the convertible funds for each of the periods and outperformed the performance benchmarks for the 10-year period. Due to their hybrid nature, one would expect convertible funds to perform somewhere in between the average performance of a group of bond funds and a group of equity funds. The actual return earned by the fund

**Table 15–1. Selected Data on Closed-End Convertible Bond Funds**

| Fund | Began | Net Assets 6/30/90 (Millions) | Expense 1989 | Ratio 1988 |
|---|---|---|---|---|
| AIM Strategic Income Fund | 3/89 | $ 61.5 | 1.40%* | n.a. |
| American Capital Convertible Securities | 6/72 | 72.2 | 0.84 | 0.82% |
| Bancroft Convertible Fund | 4/71 | 53.9 | 1.50† | 2.40† |
| Castle Convertible Fund | 11/71 | 47.9 | 1.26 | 1.20 |
| Convertible Holdings | 7/85 | 265.0 | 0.80 | 0.79 |
| Ellsworth Convertible Growth & Income Fund | 6/86 | 51.4 | 1.40 | 1.40 |
| Lincoln National Convertible Securities | 6/86 | 95.9 | 0.94 | 0.96 |
| Putnam High Income Convertible and Bond Fund | 7/87 | 93.0 | 1.15 | 1.18 |
| TCW Convertible Securities Fund | 2/87 | 167.2 | 0.95 | 0.94 |

n.a.: Not available.
*Annualized and after partial waiver of fees.
†Includes extraordinary expenses for tender offer and litigation.
Source: Net assets from Lipper Analytical Services, Inc. Expense ratios provided by individual funds.

**Table 15–2. Five- and Ten-Year Performance of Older Convertible Funds**

|                                          | NAV Performance* | |
| ---------------------------------------- | --- | --- |
|                                          | 5-Year | 10-Year |
| **Convertible Funds**                    |     |     |
| American Capital Convertible Securities  | 11.04% | 15.76% |
| Bancroft Convertible Fund†               | 8.11 | 10.96 |
| Castle Convertible Fund†                 | 4.42 | 12.55 |
| **Performance Benchmarks**               |     |     |
| Closed-end bond funds                    | 10.09% | 11.57% |
| Closed-end diversified equity funds      | 14.83 | 15.47 |

*Returns reflect compound average annual changes in NAV including reinvestment of all distributions. Performance periods end 6/30/90. Benchmarks represent averages for categories.
†Not adjusted for rights offering.
Source: Adapted from data provided by Lipper Analytical Services, Inc.

would depend on whether it is being managed more like an equity fund or closer to a bond fund.

## CONVERTIBLE FUND PROFILES

Since there are only nine members of the closed-end convertible universe we will provide a profile of each.

**AIM Strategic Income Fund (Amex: AST)** The newest member of the group, AST's rather unique strategy involving the use of convertible securities combined with short sales sets it apart from the traditional convertible funds. Its objective is to earn above-average income and to have a low volatility in its NAV. Basically, AST invests in convertible securities while selling short the underlying common stock. The short selling is done to hedge against market risk and to enhance income with interest earned on its short sale credit balances. The fund's primary objective is to distribute monthly dividends equal to 130% to 140% of the 90-day U.S. T-bill rate.

AST's adviser is A I M Advisors, Inc., a subsidiary of A I M Management Group, Inc., which manages investment companies with assets totaling about $14 billion. AST is its only closed-end fund.

**American Capital Convertible Securities (NYSE: ACS)** Formerly American General Convertible Securities, ACS is managed by American Capital Asset Management, Inc., a subsidiary of Primerica Corp. The fund's portfolio is broadly diversified across industries and normally at least 80% invested in convertibles. Nearly 16% of ACS's portfolio was invested in common stocks at this writing. An outstanding performer over the years, the fund has maintained a low expense ratio.

"It's an investment grade fund with an average portfolio rating of around triple-B," says James Behrmann, the fund's portfolio manager and a vice president at American Capital. "We're attempting to provide income, capital appreciation, and capital preservation. We use a bottom-up approach focusing first on the fundamentals of the underlying company. We tend to follow more of an equity oriented philosophy towards convertibles, although we have one of the higher yielding convertible funds. We don't try to time the market and remain fully invested." Behrmann also manages the $377 million, open-end American Capital Harbor Fund using the same philosophy.

**Bancroft Convertible Fund (Amex: BCV)** and its sister fund **Ellsworth Convertible Fund (Amex: ECF)** are both managed by Davis-Dinsmore Management Company. Ronald and Thomas Dinsmore, a father-and-son team, manage the funds. BCV, the first "pure" convertible fund, began in April 1971 when it raised $50 million. Over the years BCV has followed the policy of investing at least 80% of its assets in convertible securities. Its strategy is simply to buy and hold convertible bonds and convertible preferred stock for long-term capital appreciation and income.

Bancroft has a long, successful history of fighting off raiders. Since the first takeover attempt in the mid-1970s, Bancroft fought off three additional raiders. After a 1982 takeover attempt Bancroft, and later Ellsworth, installed the standard anti-takeover provisions in their charters. These include staggered boards and super majority voting provisions.

But in 1987 a South African group, ZICO Investment

Holdings, tendered for a simple majority of BCV's shares at a *premium* over its market price, which is unusual and caught management by surprise.[2] ZICO, which had successfully pyramided closed-end funds in Europe, was attempting to get started in the U.S. and thought Bancroft would be a good starting point. Although legal in Europe, the pyramiding of closed-end funds is illegal here. BCV thus defeated ZICO and tendered to buy back their stock from ZICO as well as from other stockholders who wished to sell. Then a shareholder rights offering was undertaken in November, 1988 to restore Bancroft's assets from their $38 million level, subsequent to the repurchase of the shares from ZICO, to their former $50 million.

What attracted these suitors to Bancroft over the years? "We're one of the few closed-end funds of any significant size that doesn't have a large organization behind it," Tom Dinsmore told us. "So you're not dealing with a management company that has enormous assets to fight a battle. We're just a couple of guys that had been running it for a long time." Dinsmore added that Bancroft's good long-term performance record had also attracted ZICO. "It was a record that they could go back to Europe and sell." In the more typical case, raiders will go after a fund with a *poor* performance record.

Ellsworth, launched in June 1986, is generally similar to Bancroft, but has less of a plain vanilla orientation. It will normally invest at least 65% in CVs. The management has a bias towards holding investment grade securities in both funds. Both funds follow the mixed or balanced convertible strategy as outlined by Dinsmore in the Closed-End Insights box. ECF can use options to enhance yield and protect its portfolio. It can also use an "economic hedge" which entails buying the convertible and selling the common short against it. Further, it can purchase restricted securities to a limited degree and invest a modest amount in foreign securities.

Some of these additional strategies have been used sparingly, if at all, according to Tom Dinsmore. He emphasized that Ellsworth will use a strategy only when conditions are clearly favorable. For instance, before the crash of 1987 the fund wrote a lot of calls on its convertibles because conversion premiums were low and call premiums were high. It was very profitable at that time. Then for an 18-month period the fund wrote no calls because it appeared conditions were unfavorable.

**Castle Convertible Fund (Amex: CVF)** CVF normally invests about 80% of its assets in CVs. Fred Alger Management, Inc. has served as adviser since 1974. The adviser and its affiliates own about 14% of the fund's shares. According to David Alger, CVF is oriented towards buying convertibles at modest premiums over their bond values so as to realize a high yield. The fund is thus being run more as a fixed income portfolio than as a stock portfolio. Alger explained that he does his own credit analysis rather than using agency ratings; he will often buy non-rated, high-yielding convertibles of firms he feels are sound credit risks.

**Convertible Holdings (NYSE: CNV, CNV PR)** A specialized dual fund with capital and income shares, CNV was introduced in Chapter 7. With $265 million in assets, CNV is the largest closed-end convertible fund. At least 70% of its assets would normally be invested in convertibles. At the end of 1989, 74% of the portfolio was in convertibles, 10% in common stock, and 14% in short-term investments. Merrill Lynch Asset Management is the adviser. If you plan to invest in CNV be sure you are thoroughly familiar with the unique characteristics of dual funds covered in Chapter 7. CNV's capital shares were trading at a 47% discount in late October, 1990. The income shares will be redeemed in 1997. The capital shares will then own all remaining assets and the fund will either liquidate or continue as an open-end fund.

**Lincoln National Convertible Securities (NYSE: LNV)** LNV's primary objective is to provide a high total return through capital appreciation and income. Net realized long-term capital gains are retained to increase the fund's asset base. LNV may borrow or use leverage in an amount not exceeding one-third of its net assets. The fund concentrates in higher quality securities but may invest in some direct placement convertibles. The adviser is Lincoln National Investment Management Company. Since 1988 Lynch & Mayer, a wholly owned subsidiary of Lincoln National, has served as sub-adviser. The sub-adviser may perform some or nearly all of the advisory services. A leading growth stock manager, Lynch & Mayer seeks companies demonstrating "significant fundamental change." Because Lynch & Mayer are growth investors, some of the dynamic companies undergoing fundamental change they select may appear too expensive to value investors. Lynch & Mayer focuses on the attractiveness of the underlying equity in selecting convertibles. Top-down analysis and investment timing do not play a significant role.

**Putnam High Income Convertible and Bond Fund (NYSE: PCF)** As its name implies, PCF invests in high-yielding convertibles and high-yielding nonconvertible bonds that carry lower ratings or are unrated. The objective is high current income with the potential for capital appreciation. Capital appreciation would be limited with high-yield convertibles as they trade at a high premium to conversion value, as has been explained earlier. But the conversion feature may add to total return in the long term.

A recent portfolio breakdown indicated that 66% of its bonds were rated double-B and below. The minimum rating the fund will invest in is triple-C. Unrated bonds must be judged by the management to have the equivalent of a triple-C rating or better. PCF has above-average credit risk due to the concentration of its portfolio in high-yield securities. The fund may write covered call options. PCF distributes dividends from investment income monthly.

**TCW Convertible Securities Fund (NYSE: CVT)** With assets of $167.2 million and over 100 convertibles in its portfolio, CVT is the second largest convertible fund. CVT had its initial public offering of 20 million common shares at $10 each in February, 1987. The fund seeks total investment return, comprised of current income and capital appreciation. Dividends are paid monthly. Its policy is to be fully invested in CVs at all times. The average rating ranges between double-B and triple-B.

TCW Funds Management, Inc., a wholly-owned subsidiary of TCW Management Company, Los Angeles, is

CVT's adviser. As of December 31, 1989, Trust Company of the West and other subsidiary companies of TCW Management Company had approximately $17.0 billion of assets under management, of which more than $2.0 billion were represented by investments in convertible securities. This makes them the largest manager of convertible securities portfolios in the U.S.

CVT's portfolio managers, Howard Marks and Glenn Weirick, are both long and seasoned veterans in the convertible business.[3] Each manages over $1 billion of convertible securities for TCW. Responsibility for the CVT portfolio lies equally between Marks and Weirick. They have two entirely different styles that they feel fit together to the advantage of the shareholders. Marks follows a bottom-up approach, focusing on the individual company and security, whereas Weirick uses a top-down approach, focusing on the economy and different industries. Marks uses options to a limited extent, Weirick does not; neither manager uses leverage.

Marks discusses his philosophy of investing in convertibles in the Closed-End Insights box.

---

### WHAT IS THE RIGHT TIME FOR CONVERTIBLES?
#### Howard S. Marks, CFA
#### Vice President
#### TCW Convertible Securities Fund, Inc.

This question has come up many times over the twelve years I've been managing portfolios of convertible securities, and my tongue-in-cheek answer always starts off the same: "There's no right time for convertibles. If the stock market goes up, you want to be in stocks. If it goes down, you want to be in cash. So convertibles are never the right tool. . . ."

"Unless," the answer continues, "you don't know what the future holds." If that's the case, you want convertibles, because they will deliver participation if the market rises and protection from the full impact if it falls. And, throughout, their yield will exceed that of stocks.

Simply put, convertibles combine bond characteristics with responsiveness to stock market trends and are hedged vehicles. As such there is no scenario for which they are the best vehicle. But there are numerous scenarios in which they will be generally helpful, and they're unlikely under any circumstances to be the worst performers.

When are hedged vehicles desirable? When the outlook for the future is uncertain. And in my opinion, the outlook is always uncertain. So when are convertibles the ideal vehicle? All the time!

## CONCLUSIONS

Convertible funds merit your consideration. Because our personal bias is towards equity investment, the authors find them more interesting than the straight bond funds. They offer a large share of the appreciation you would get with an equity fund while providing some downside protection. You may also be able to buy them at wider discounts than you could find on the typical bond fund. The majority were trading at double-digit discount levels at this writing.

But they can be risky since the convertible market can be hit hard under adverse economic conditions. The worst scenario would be a time of skyrocketing interest rates and plunging stock prices. The funds that have more of their portfolios invested in below investment grade (that is, high yield or junk) convertibles obviously carry greater risk. They performed much worse than the convertible funds with better quality portfolios during the 1990 bear market. As they are specialized, convertible funds do not represent a complete investment program but should provide a nice addition to the other holdings of the CEF investor.

## Notes

[1]Readers interested in a more extensive and detailed treatment of convertibles are referred to Thomas H. Dinsmore, "Convertible Securities," in *Encyclopedia of Investments*, Second Edition, Jack P. Friedman, Editor-in-Chief (Boston: Warren, Gorham & Lamont, 1990), pp. 151–167.

[2]Richard Phalon, "$11 for a $10 bill?," *Forbes*, January 26, 1987, p. 99.

[3]Albert J. Fredman, "TCW Convertible Securities Fund," *The Scott Letter: Closed-End Fund Report*, June 1990, pp. 1–3.

# PART IV

# Putting It All Together

# CHAPTER 16

# *Dealing with Your Broker*

Closed-end bond and equity funds are traded through brokerage firms just like the shares of other publicly traded corporations. The majority trade on the New York Stock Exchange, a smaller number on the American, and about ten trade over-the-counter—mainly in NASDAQ. Experienced CEF investors have found that funds trade differently than other listed stocks do. Their prices react to changes in weekly discounts and premiums but not to quarterly earnings.

In this chapter we discuss strategies for buying and selling closed-end funds, how to save on transaction costs, and whether to use market or limit orders. We'll also make recommendations as to what type of brokerage firm to use in executing your trades. By following our recommendations, you should have a higher return on your investment.

You should first seek out a broker with expertise in closed-end funds. Most of the large firms have one or more; it may even be advisable to deal with a broker in a location other than where you live or work because it may pay to have the advantage of that person's expertise. If your portfolio is large enough, or if you find your time is limited, you may even want to consider the services of an investment adviser. The adviser is compensated by a fee based on a percentage of the assets rather than by a commission. A few use an incentive fee tied to performance.

Some people think there is a conflict of interest in using a broker, but brokers who do well for clients build their books by referral. The directory in Appendix II lists some brokers and investment advisers who specialize in CEFs traded in the U.S. as well as overseas. This is not intended to be a complete list; it identifies those individuals with whom the authors are acquainted. The choice depends on how involved you want to become in managing your own investments. As was indicated in Chapter 3, a number of brokerage firms see the importance of follow-up research and have added analysts to cover closed-end funds. This research can be especially helpful for larger retail investors and institutions. Brokerage firms such A.G. Edwards; Kidder, Peabody; PaineWebber; Prudential-Bache; Shearson Lehman; and Smith Barney do a good job following closed-end funds. These full service firms will offer commission discounts to larger, more active clients. Don't be afraid to ask for this break.

## TRADING BASICS

All else equal, you're better off from a liquidity standpoint with NYSE-traded funds. Of course, the primary consideration is whether you really want the particular fund— where it happens to be traded is certainly secondary.

### Liquidity

Liquidity refers to the ease with which a stock can be traded without disturbing the price. The more shares you can buy or sell at the current quote the higher the liquidity. Funds traded on the NYSE are usually more liquid than those on the Amex which, in turn, may be more liquid than those traded over-the-counter. The most illiquid

CEF we've encountered is the tiny Spectra Fund (Chapter 5) which trades exclusively in the "pink sheets." The pink sheets contain over-the-counter stocks, including those not in the NASDAQ system, and are usually available only in brokerage offices. A moderately big order to buy or sell an illiquid stock could push its price up or down quickly, resulting in a poor execution. This is a good reason to buy actively traded, listed funds if possible. Underwriters know this and are seeking the NYSE for every new issue they bring to market.

It is always important to consider the liquidity of a fund when examining its discount as the two are related. A discount of 25% percent or more on a highly illiquid fund might not offer you much value if you want to take a significant position because it would be difficult to buy without driving the price up dramatically, narrowing the discount significantly. Thus, the fund may not be as much of a bargain as you first thought. A way around this difficulty is to enter a series of smaller limit orders, spaced over time, so as to lessen the pressure on price. Even though the brokerage commissions will be higher (if trades are executed on different days) the purchase prices should average out lower, giving you a lower total cost for your investment. This is another reason to work with a broker experienced in closed-end fund investing, as he's aware that it's a different ball game than buying other listed stocks.

## Average Daily Volume

Always determine the *average daily trading volume* for funds you plan to buy or sell. For any market, the higher the daily trading volume the more liquid the fund. To compute average daily volume consult the most recent issue of Standard & Poor's *Security Owner's Stock Guide* for the fund's recent monthly sales (share volume). Translate this figure into an average daily volume. Compare the size of your order with the average daily volume. Is the order going to be so large that it will move the bid or asked? If so, consider breaking it into a number of smaller orders that can be spaced out over a period of a week or so.

**Example:**   NYSE-traded Salomon Brothers Fund (SBF) had total sales in May, 1990 of 1,041,400 shares, according to S&P's June 1990 *Stock Guide.* Dividing this by 20 (the average number of trading days in a month) SBF's average daily volume amounts to 52,070 shares. This high volume indicates plenty of liquidity. If you wanted to buy 10,000 shares of SBF in a single day there shouldn't be any problem.

**Example:**   Engex (EGX), which trades on the Amex, had total sales in May 1990 of 15,200 shares, which translates into a daily volume of 760 shares. If you placed an order to buy or sell 4,000 shares of EGX you would probably move the price. The best course of action in lightly traded funds would be to break a large order down into a number of smaller ones and go to the market every other day or so to execute these smaller orders. With EGX, one could place orders of several hundred shares a day. Getting better prices will more than offset the higher brokerage commissions.

## The Bid-Asked Spread

The quote on every stock consists of two prices: the *bid* and the *asked.* The bid is the highest price someone is willing to pay to buy the stock, and the ask is the lowest price someone is willing to take to part with it. The bid is always below the asked.

More liquid funds which trade higher daily volumes tend to have tighter (or narrower) bid-asked spreads. Actively traded NYSE funds typically have a 1/8th point spread. At the opposite extreme, a thinly traded OTC fund could have a quote like 5 bid, 5 1/2 asked, a 1/2-point spread. Examples of thinly traded CEFs include Dover Regional Financial Shares (Chapter 8), Fund Alabama (NASDAQ: FALI), and Spectra Fund (Chapter 5). FALI is a $6.4 million specialized equity CEF which invests mainly in Alabama-based companies.

You must recognize that the spread is part of the total transaction cost along with the brokerage commission. In fact, the spread is even more important because it has a greater monetary impact. This is especially true for over-the-counter funds. For instance, take the fund bid for at 5 and offered at 5 1/2. If you bought 1,000 shares at 5 1/2 it would cost you $5,500 ignoring commissions. But, if you immediately decide to sell it you would get 5, or $5,000. The spread has cost you $500 on 1,000 shares. The spread should be important to one who trades funds based upon short-term changes in discount and premium levels. For long-term investors it would have less significance.

## The "Size" in the Quote

The *size* is another piece of useful information for exchange traded stocks. It comes directly from the specialist's book. The size shows you the number of shares being bid for and the number offered in the current quote. Size changes throughout the day and can be obtained from your broker. Size should be considered when placing an order, especially a large one. Size quotes are not available for OTC-traded stocks, another advantage for a fund to be listed.

**Example:** Suppose Fund A is quoted at 8 to 8-1/8, 30 × 100. This means that 3,000 shares are being bid for at 8 and 10,000 are offered at 8-1/8. Thus, if you wanted to buy 10,000 shares at 8-1/8 your order could get executed in full since 10,000 are being offered at that price. This is true despite the fact that Fund A might trade an average volume of just 2,000 shares a day.

## ENTERING ORDERS—TIMING IS IMPORTANT

A significant advantage of closed-end funds over their open-end cousins is that they trade on an exchange and this enables investors to have some control over the price at which they buy or sell. They also have access to important trading information which they wouldn't have with an open-end fund. Knowing how and when to place buy and sell orders is highly important. *Buy when markets are weak and, when you sell, sell into strength. This is the essence of good timing.*

## The Market Order

The *market order* is the most common, simplest type of order. It is to be executed as soon as possible at the best obtainable price. Those investors who place market orders generally buy at the asked and sell at the bid, unless their order is fairly large relative to the stock's average daily volume and causes the price to move up or down. They would then be paying more than the original asked, or selling for less than the original bid, which often happens. In fact, the bid or asked is technically supposed to be good for just 100 shares although in practice one is usually able to trade more than 100 shares without disturbing the quote.

## The Limit Order

Our advice is that you should use *limit orders*, which are to be executed at a specific "limit" price or better.

**Examples:**  Buy 300 shares of XYZ Fund at 15. This order specifies that you would never pay more than 15 for XYZ Fund although you might get it at less than 15 if the market moves down. Another example would be to sell 300 shares of XYZ Fund at 15. In this case you would not receive less than 15 although you could do better if the market moves up. A limit order would be partially executed if it cannot be filled in full. For instance, you may be able to sell only 200 shares of XYZ Fund at 15 on a particular day.

If you use these orders and have a little patience you'll often be able to sell at the asked and buy at the bid— or, at least, trade at a price between the bid and asked. A limit order could be entered as a *day order* which would expire at the end of that day if it is not executed. Or it could be entered as an *open* or *good-till-canceled (GTC)* order where it would remain outstanding until either executed or canceled by the customer.

The stock exchange has been called a "double auction" market, because there is bidding going on among both buyers and sellers. When the specialist's spread is 1/4 point or more, trading can take place between the bid and asked.

**Example:**   Suppose XYZ Fund is quoted at 14-7/8 to
15-1/8. You want to sell 600 shares of XYZ. By simply
entering a market order you would probably sell it at 14-
7/8; maybe part of the order would end up being executed at a price below that if the fund is relatively illiquid. A better strategy would be to enter a limit order.
Say you enter a limit order to sell 600 shares at 15—
midway between the bid and asked. Perhaps another investor wants to buy 600 shares of XYZ at 15. Your
orders could be matched and paired off at the specialist's post. This is an important advantage of the exchange system: customer order meets customer order
and trades take place between the bid and asked, bene-
fiting both buyer and seller.

Carrying the example further, your trade could be
even more profitable if you were able to sell your shares
at 15-1/8, the asked price. If you are not in a rush to sell
you could enter a GTC order to sell 600 shares at 15-1/8.
The GTC order would allow you to keep your place in
line in the specialist's book and when your turn comes
you may be able to sell your shares for 15-1/8 if it trades
at that price again.

With the small number of CEFs that trade on
NASDAQ it is more difficult to trade between the bid and
asked or buy at the bid and sell at the asked. This is because customer orders are not matched and paired off as
they are on exchange-traded stocks. Orders to buy below
the asked or sell above the bid usually don't get executed
unless the quote moves. Since prices do fluctuate up and
down from day to day, it still makes sense to try to buy
for less than the asked or sell for more than the bid on a
NASDAQ stock. The investor should exercise patience in
waiting for his price. It's always best to use limit orders in
any market—even if you're going to buy at the asked or
sell at the bid—as you might have to do with a fund traded
in NASDAQ. This will ensure that the order will not get
executed at a price beyond your limit.

Finally, you should be aware that it can be tough to
buy the more volatile country funds at a limit price. Since
you may miss out on a buying opportunity by placing a
limit order on a country fund there might be some justifi-

cation for using a market order. You need to decide this for yourself. As you know, we are value-conscious, long term investors not traders.

## Stop Orders

*Stop orders* (or stop loss orders) could be placed on the sell side with highly volatile funds, like country funds, to help protect your profits or limit losses. A stop order is nothing more than a "delayed market order." It is placed at a price below the current market price but when the stop price is hit the order is activated, turning into a market order for execution as soon as possible at the best obtainable price.

**Example:**  You own 2,000 shares of XYZ Country Fund. You paid 10 per share for the stock and now it is trading at 18 but you don't want to sell it just yet since you feel it still has potential to advance. You would want to sell if the price starts to deteriorate, however. Since you plan to go on a three week vacation abroad and want to protect your profits, you enter a stop-loss order to sell at 15. If the price falls to 15 the stop order would turn into a market order. If the market is falling fast, however, the order may end up being executed at a price significantly less than 15. For added protection you could place a *stop-limit order,* which is a hybrid of a stop-loss order and a limit order. For example, you might set the stop price at 15 and the limit at 14-1/2. The problem is that if the market is falling very fast your limit price could quickly be left behind and the order would go un-executed. Thus, you assume a risk with a stop-limit order.

The authors don't like stop orders and prefer not to use them. But there may be a few cases where they would be appropriate. We've explained them here to make you aware of the pitfalls you face in using them.

## Do Not Reduce ("DNR") Orders

Closed-end fund investors generally get quarterly dividends, and many bond fund investors receive monthly dividends. Thus, you need to consider the effect of an upcoming dividend payment on the limit price you established. With the ordinary limit order the limit price will be reduced automatically by the amount of the dividend on the date the fund goes *ex-dividend.* On the ex-dividend date the price of a stock ordinarily falls by the amount of the dividend to be paid because the buyer would not be entitled to the payment.

**Example:** Suppose you placed a GTC limit order to buy 300 shares of Fund A at 8. But the order is not executed right away and the fund goes ex-dividend for its 25 cent quarterly dividend. The price on the limit order would automatically be reduced to 7-3/4. The *do not reduce* order is a limit order with a special instruction telling the broker not to reduce the limit price when the stock goes ex-dividend. If you had placed a DNR order the limit price would remain at 8 in our example after the fund goes ex-dividend. You would lose the dividend, however, if you buy the stock after it has gone ex-dividend. The choice is yours.

### All-or-None ("AON") Orders

The all-or-none order is to be executed in its entirety or not at all, usually at a limit price. It is used to save commissions. An ordinary limit order (without the AON qualification) might end up being executed piecemeal over several days with commissions being computed on the individual trades and thus totaling more than if the order had been executed on one day in its entirety. The AON order has its disadvantages because it may cause you to miss out on a trade since the order would not have high priority in the specialist's book. If you are placing a small order in a stock which trades in heavy volume you probably wouldn't need to use an AON order.

**Example:** "Buy 1,000 Fund A at 8 GTC, AON." This GTC order specifies a limit price of 8 but it would not be executed unless you can get the full 1,000 shares. Patience is required.

### Discretionary Orders

Some brokerage firms will take what are known as *discretionary accounts* which give the broker the power to trade the customer's account without the latter's knowledge or

consent on each trade. The customer must sign power of
attorney agreements for this, and the firm's manager has
to approve each trade. Discretionary accounts are discouraged by most firms. The authors fully agree with this as
they give the broker too much power over the customer's
account. We bring this up only in relation to what is
known as *limited discretion* in buying a particular stock,
such as a CEF. It may be 1/8 or 1/4 of a point discretion
on a specific order given to the broker to prevent missing
the purchase entirely. You should be able to buy most
funds at the bid and sell at the ask (when a strict limit
appears to make sense), but there are times when you
may have to be more flexible. These guidelines we hope
are helpful, but are not intended to be specific advice to
our readers.

## WATCH OUT FOR THE NAV SYNDROME ON MONDAYS

The authors won't go so far as to say "don't buy on Mondays." But, at least, use caution if you do want to buy on
a Monday. This is because eager investors will be eying
the discounts in the weekly closed-end funds box on week-
ends and early Monday morning. They will place market
orders to buy funds with discounts that look particularly
attractive. This may push prices higher temporarily. Our
experience tells us that you are better off to buy later in
the week. But it would be all right to buy later in the day
on Monday if it turns out to be a big sell-off, as Mondays
often do. This coincides with our general rule, which is to
buy on weakness and sell on strength.

## CASH VERSUS MARGIN

There are two basic types of accounts you can open with
a broker: a *cash account* and a *margin account*. With the
cash account you must pay for your purchases in full.
With a margin account you may borrow a portion of the
cost of the securities through your broker. Virtually all
CEFs are marginable; however, most brokers won't mar-

gin a stock selling for less than $5 a share. Buying on margin introduces leverage and therefore increases your risk and potential return. The amount of cash or eligible securities you put up as collateral is called the *margin*. The leverage is favorable if your total return exceeds the interest cost of the borrowed money. Otherwise, you would be better off without the leverage. This is illustrated in Figure 16–1.

## Figure 16–1. How Leverage Works

Assume you purchase 2,000 shares of Fund A at $10 per share. The total cost is $20,000. If you buy on margin you could borrow up to 50% of the cost from your broker under prevailing initial margin requirements. Thus, you could use $10,000 of your own cash or eligible securities and borrow $10,000. The fund's distributions would offset your interest cost.

Using a one-year time horizon, we assume Fund A's price (1) increases 25% from $10 to $12.50 and (2) decreases 25% from $10 to $7.50. The interest cost is 10% and Fund A makes a distribution equal to 6% of the $20,000 cost of the shares. In the first case the leverage is favorable and you earn a 52% total return. In the second case, however, your return is a *minus* 48%. The computations follow:

|  | Favorable Leverage | Unfavorable Leverage |
|---|---|---|
| Stock price at end of period | $12.50 | $ 7.50 |
| Change in price | +25% | −25% |
| Value of stock at end of period | $25,000 | $15,000 |
| *Less* cost of stock | −20,000 | −20,000 |
| *Less* interest on loan (10% × $10,000) | − 1,000 | − 1,000 |
| *Plus* fund distributions (6% × $20,000) | + 1,200 | + 1,200 |
| Profit (or loss) | + 5,200 | − 4,800 |
| Total return on $10,000 investment | +52% | −48% |

For margin buying to be successful, a good prediction of near-term price movements is essential, since the interest you pay on your borrowed money can hurt your performance if the fund doesn't move up sufficiently within a reasonable period of time. Buying CEFs on margin can be highly risky if the fund's price falls sharply. You would receive a *margin call* from the broker to place more cash or eligible securities into your account to meet the *maintenance margin requirement.* If you are unable to come up with more collateral, some or all of your securities would have to be sold to satisfy your obligation. For larger, more sophisticated investors a margin account may make sense for timing purposes; for example, to take maximum advantage of deep discounts in bear markets or during tax selling season. IF YOU WANT TO BUY A FUND ON MARGIN MAKE SURE YOU ARE THOROUGHLY FAMILIAR WITH YOUR BROKER'S POLICY ON MARGIN CALLS. DON'T BUY YOUR FUNDS ON MARGIN UNLESS YOU ARE PREPARED TO ACCEPT THE ADDITIONAL RISK.

## STOCK CERTIFICATE CONSIDERATIONS

In establishing a brokerage account, you have to make a decision as to whether you want your shares held in "street name" (the name of the brokerage firm), with you as the beneficial owner, or whether you want to take delivery of the certificates. With open-end funds investors virtually always elect to have the fund custodian hold their certificates. Certificates can be bothersome if one takes delivery of them, and there is always the chance that they could be lost, stolen, misplaced, or destroyed. If you do take delivery of the certificates they should be kept in a safe place such as a safe deposit box. The problems are not inconsequential if you lose your certificates since there would be red tape in obtaining a replacement, as well as fees associated with a lost instrument bond, and delays.[1]

Ordinarily, it would be better to hold certificates in street name. But in some cases it may be easier to participate in a fund's dividend reinvestment plan if you take delivery of the certificates. Brokerage firms that don't have a lot of clients in closed-end funds may not do a good job of handling dividend reinvestments so you need to be careful.

## A BROKER'S ADVICE

Steve Samuels offers useful advice in the Closed-End Insights box which will help you bring together some of our most important points.

---

### CONTROLLING TRANSACTION COSTS
### Steven Samuels
### Samuels Asset Management

WATCH THOSE PENNIES! Three small words that can mean either success or failure when investing in closed-end funds. Why? Simple. The price of closed-end funds. Closed-end funds typically come public at or around $10 per share. This is done so that investors can purchase a sizable number of shares with a relatively small capital outlay. Since the majority of closed-end funds will trade at these relatively low prices, a seemingly small price difference can mean dramatically different results.

As a broker I have seen investors make two major mistakes.

1. *Not placing limit orders.*

Investors should never, never buy or sell at the market. The difference between the bid and ask prices can substantially alter your investment results.

For example, closed-end fund XYZ is trading at 7 bid 7 1/4 asked. By paying 7 1/4 instead of 7, you have increased your cost over 3%. In other words, your investment must do 3% better just to be even. Not very good odds at all!

2. *Not getting a large commission discount.*

If you are not getting a commission discount you are either dealing with the wrong firm, or you just don't have enough dollars to invest to make sense.

For example, closed-end XYZ is trading at 7 bid 7 1/4 asked. Even if you were able to buy at the bid of 7, look what happens if you pay regular commissions. If you were to buy 1,000 shares at 7, the commission at a typical brokerage firm will be around $200. This trade will cost almost 3%. We typically pay between 8 and 10 cents per share, keeping transaction expenses at roughly 1% of the dollar value invested. Again, as with buying at the asked, large commissions make it tough to make a profit.

Making both mistakes would obviously lead to very poor results. Another way to illustrate how important it is to watch your costs is to compare the costs presented above and the returns of the best money managers of all time. The very best, like Lynch, Templeton, and Neff, outperform the market by 2% to 3% per year (with very low commissions and costs). The chances of you outperforming the market giving "away" up to 6% doesn't seem like too good a bet.

A couple of other tips. Check to see how many shares on average a fund trades per day. Usually those listed on the New York Stock Exchange are more liquid than those on the American and Over-the-Counter Exchanges. The less liquid, the more important it is to place limit orders. Also we almost always use good-till-canceled orders. This is done because sometimes it can take from a few days to a few weeks either to buy or to sell a full position. Good-till-canceled orders will make it much easier.

Lastly, one very important point. If you haven't done so before, memorize the following statement: NEVER BUY ON THE INITIAL OFFERING. While you might be told by a broker that there is no commission, this is not really true. A fund that initially comes out at $10 will be worth $9.30 the very next day after fees and expenses. A premium of over 7%. Not a very good deal.

In summary, it is crucial to watch your costs. As

> illustrated it can make a major impact on your results.
> Following the above guidelines will hopefully help you
> keep more dollars which, come to think of it, is the
> whole idea anyway.

The authors agree with Samuels's advice, but wish to advise readers that to get big discounts from most brokers you have to be trading at least 1,000 shares.

## CONCLUSION

The authors want to encourage readers to take more responsibility for their investments. To do this one needs to be familiar with the different types of orders and proven strategies for buying and selling stocks. This includes the details of knowing how to obtain the best possible prices when you are buying or selling shares through a knowledgeable broker. Using good-till-canceled limit orders gives you the time to get a feel (and often a better price) for the particular stock you are buying. We have been able to fill limit orders on closed-end funds as much as 90 percent of the time. Those few you miss will be made up with better prices obtained on those you do fill. Limit orders for CEFs, with the exception of the more volatile country funds, are usually no problem. Buy country funds when they have had a large price decline or wait until they are at bargain prices, such as in late 1990. John Templeton says never to buy a stock unless it is at a bargain price; we concur—never pay too much or your performance will suffer.

The OTC market is different from the listed markets; you probably will not be able to buy as close to the bid on a limit order as with stock exchange-traded securities. In the final analysis it depends on how badly you want the fund and how patient you are. There will always be buying opportunities for the patient investor. We hope we have made a clear case that closed-end funds are one of the better ways to find value and to build a portfolio. Once you see it happen, you'll agree.

## Note

[1]Albert J. Fredman and Donald F. Donahue, "The Securities Depository," *AAII Journal*, August 1988, p. 8.

CHAPTER 17

# Building Your Portfolio

Closed-end funds are excellent portfolio building blocks. With a wide range of fund types available today investors can fine-tune a portfolio of CEFs to closely match their needs and preferences. Having read this far most readers would probably agree that one could have a well-balanced portfolio consisting exclusively of CEFs. Still, many investors may wish to hold mutual funds, as well as individual stocks or bonds, along with their CEFs. There is nothing wrong with this. It is a personal choice. But as long as you find good value in CEFs we urge you to give them high priority in building your portfolio.

This chapter will provide some general ideas for managing investments. We'll cover basic concepts like the risk-return tradeoff and the benefits to be gained from diversifying among different types of CEFs. We won't give hard and fast guidelines for investing your money, however, since each individual's needs and objectives are unique. There is no simple answer to the questions of how many and what types of funds an investor should hold.

363

**LET'S REVIEW OUR PHILOSOPHY**

1. Most importantly, *we are investors, not specula-tors.* We look for investments that allow us to protect our capital (within reason) as it grows over the years. Speculations which can lead to unmanageable losses are the wealthbuilder's major enemy. Our view is that individuals will do best following a get rich slowly, buy and hold investment strategy.

2. *Always seek value.* You've seen how the power of compound interest can help to build a substantial sum of money over the years. A seemingly modest increase in the rate of growth of one's capital can lead to a huge difference in the results over many years. For example, if you set aside $1,000 at the end of each of the next 30 years, it would grow to $164,490 at 10% compounded annually (ignoring taxes). Increasing the growth rate to 12% you would have $241,330. CEFs are excellent vehicles for this purpose as you can sometimes buy at attractive discounts thereby enhancing your long-term performance. *The wise CEF investor maintains cash reserves in a money market fund in order to take advantage of unexpected market weakness and unusually attractive discount levels.*

3. *Don't move in and out of funds and don't try to shift your portfolio holdings on the basis of every antici-pated market move.* If you use dollar cost averaging you don't have to time the market. You can select one or more funds and invest a fixed amount of money in them at regular intervals. The mutual fund industry makes the most of this strategy.

4. *You should always reinvest your dividend and capital gains distributions if you possibly can.* Reinvesting is an excellent way to maximize your total returns and thereby build capital through the power of compound interest. This is true for investors in bond as well as equity funds, if they can forgo the income. According to a Shearson Lehman Hutton report, reinvesting is especially beneficial in the more aggressive, volatile CEBFs, such as those investing in junk bonds, as it can help cushion principal erosion in a declining market.[1] There is a special advantage with any CEF when the shares are trading at a

discount since reinvestment is generally made at the market price which is below NAV.

A reinvestment program is beneficial in a declining market since more shares will be acquired at lower prices with the reinvested distribution (assuming that the distribution is not cut significantly). This will allow the shareholder to dollar cost average. Further, if more shareholders reinvest it can have a beneficial effect on the fund since the management will be buying shares in the open market to be allotted to reinvesting shareholders. The buying of shares will help support the fund's share price.[2]

5. *It is generally unwise to pay premiums for CEFs—including the "hottest" country funds.* Those who pay a premium are not getting any value and expose themselves to greater risk, since the premium could easily turn to a discount. It's analogous to the idea of avoiding stocks selling at excessive P/E ratios. In fact, if you have bought earlier at a discount you may wish to consider selling when the premium to NAV on any CEF reaches 10% or more.

6. *Don't overdiversify among CEFs.* We recommend holding no more than six or eight funds. Too many will complicate record keeping and may hurt your overall performance since you may be investing in funds that don't offer value, simply to "fill out" the portfolio. Focus on a select group of funds that have good long-term performance, low expenses, and offer good value.

7. Finally, *watch those pennies* as Steve Samuels explained in the Insights box in Chapter 16. By knowing how to place limit orders so as to minimize transaction costs, you will realize better long-run performance. Savings of a fraction of a point on each trade add up over the years.

## DEVELOPING YOUR INVESTMENT PLAN

There are five basic variables that you need to examine in formulating an investment plan.

1. *Your age.* Your point in your life cycle (early career, mid career, late career, or retirement) is one of the

most important considerations in developing an investment plan. Younger investors can assume greater risk and should seek investments that will lead to favorable long-term growth of capital. They would want to give the heaviest emphasis to equity funds in order to build a substantial net worth over the years. Older investors who are at or near retirement would place high priority on income and preservation of capital. They would want to invest less in equities. Besides your age, the proportion of your portfolio you should allocate to equities would depend upon (a) your risk tolerance, (b) your income and job security, and (c) your liquidity needs.

2. *Your risk tolerance.* Are you more interested in eating well or sleeping well? Some people just don't feel comfortable with much risk. You shouldn't invest in a way that makes you feel uncomfortable. If you are highly risk adverse you obviously shouldn't have a major position in a volatile country or sector fund. Those with a low risk tolerance would want to hold a greater portion of their portfolios in conservative fixed income funds and money market mutual funds.

3. *Your income and earnings potential.* For many people the most important asset they have is their job. The loss of a good job represents a major financial setback since the earnings stream could be interrupted or reduced. If you have a secure job with high earning potential you should be able to place a larger proportion of your assets in equities—including some of the more volatile CEFs.

4. *Your liquidity requirements.* Some people need more liquidity than others to protect themselves against unforeseen circumstances. A person with a relatively low degree of employment security would need greater liquidity. Some people have an earnings stream that varies in an unpredictable manner. If liquidity is important, select more stable funds, like investment grade CEBFs, that will allow you to preserve capital and avoid substantial declines in portfolio value. Naturally, everyone should have some liquid holdings to protect against an unexpected misfortune and to take advantage of an exceptionally good investment opportunity in a weak market.

5. *Your tax bracket.* If you are seeking a tax shelter the closed-end muni funds would have a place in your portfolio. Of course, you may also be able hold some of your CEFs in a tax-sheltered retirement plan, like an IRA or Keogh.

## THE RISK-RETURN TRADE-OFF

Risk is a part of everyone's life. You simply can't avoid it. But you can control it within certain limits. One of the most important principles in the field of finance is *the risk-return tradeoff* which has its origins in Modern Portfolio Theory. In order to have the opportunity of earning higher returns you've got to take on more risk. But, this doesn't mean betting the ranch on the one stock or one asset that appears to promise the highest return. We're talking about investing in *more volatile, diversified portfolios* in order to increase the odds of earning higher returns *over the long term.*

Our focus is exclusively on diversified portfolios, like CEFs, which contain little or no company-specific risk. We've already explained that it's foolish to invest heavily in a single stock since it may fall to a low price and never recover. But individual CEFs, which are diversified, inevitably recover after a decline.

The risk-return trade-off is illustrated by the upward-sloping line in Figure 17–1. Return is measured on the vertical axis and risk on the horizontal. Different types of CEFs plot at various points along the risk-return line. Risk could be measured by the period-to-period fluctuations of the fund's returns or by its beta coefficient. At the far left on the risk-return line there is virtually no risk. This point would correspond to investing all one's money in U.S. Treasury bills or an insured money market account. If you always keep all your money in such risk-free assets, however, your long-run after-tax returns may be insufficient to protect you against inflationary forces.

Let's move up along the risk-return trade-off line and see what we find. You might settle for a somewhat higher return than you could get on T-bills by investing in a con-

**Figure 17–1. The Risk-Return Trade-Off**

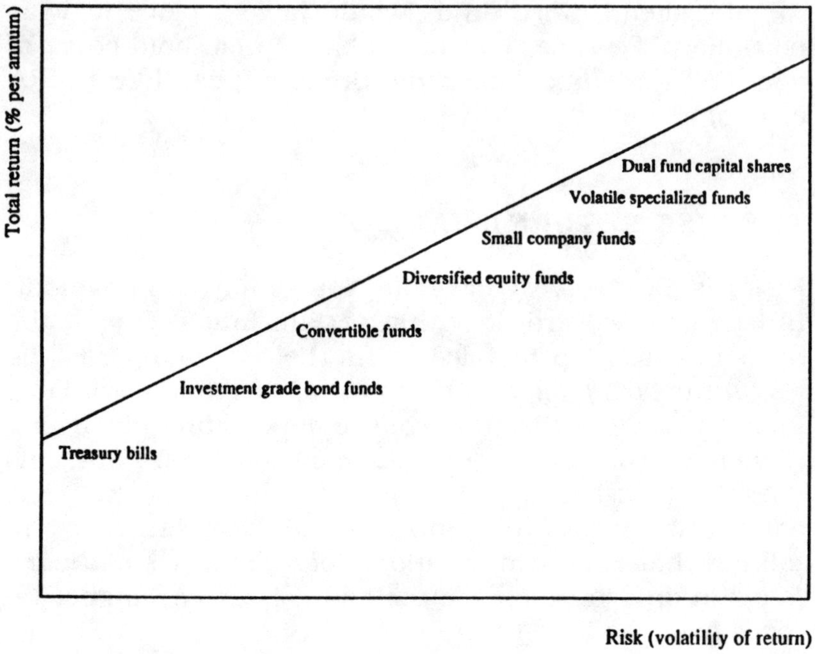

Risk (volatility of return)

servative, high quality, low duration bond fund. Moving along further you would find the balanced funds, which hold both debt and equity, or the convertible funds, which behave like balanced funds. Going still further you would have the diversified equity funds like Adams Express and Tri-Continental. The small company CEFs would be a bit riskier than those that invest in bigger equities, so they would lie further up on the line. Continuing up you would find some of the specialized funds like those that invest in the gold sector, the single country funds, and the capital shares of dual funds.

## RISK—A CASE STUDY

We can show more clearly what is meant by a riskier fund with a table of past annual returns from ASA Limited, which invests mainly in South African gold shares, in relation to those of Adams Express Company, a diversified domestic equity fund (Table 17–1). These data show how volatile the performance of some sector funds can be. For instance, ASA experienced a big slide in 1988 with a −31.69% return but then was up 48.88% in 1989. In comparing ASA's returns with those of Adams Express you observe dramatic differences in year-to-year volatility. ASA had substantial negative returns in four years ranging from −9.06% in 1983 to −31.69% in 1988. Adams Express had negative returns in only two years—the most negative value was −1.23% in 1987.

*There is nothing wrong with a volatile fund provided the investor is prepared to accept the greater risk.* In fact, as the risk-return trade-off line in Figure 17–1 illustrates, more volatile funds could be expected to produce higher long-run returns. Of course, some sector funds are more volatile than others. The volatility depends mainly on the particular sector or country the fund invests in. The capital shares of dual funds can also experience considerable volatility because of their leverage. Thus, sector equity funds, single country funds, and dual fund capital shares

**Table 17–1. Annual Returns of ASA Limited Versus Adams Express Company**

|         | Total Returns* | |
| --- | --- | --- |
| Year | ASA | Adams Express |
| 1989 | 48.88% | 27.32% |
| 1988 | −31.69 | 13.27 |
| 1987 | 16.34 | −1.23 |
| 1986 | 81.69 | 17.82 |
| 1985 | −1.72 | 27.46 |
| 1984 | −23.47 | 4.54 |
| 1983 | −9.06 | 17.32 |
| 1982 | 39.18 | 17.50 |
| 1981 | −24.56 | −0.95 |
| 1980 | 73.76 | 34.09 |
| 1979 | 114.81 | 21.94 |

*Data reflect change in NAV, including reinvestment of all distributions.
Source: Adapted from data provided by Lipper Analytical Services, Inc.

tend to be more volatile than diversified equity funds like Adams Express. For this reason, more conservative investors would not want to make them too big a part of their portfolios.

But if you have a high tolerance for risk, a long period of time over which you can hold the fund, a good secure job, and low liquidity needs, you may wish to invest more heavily in the volatile funds. If you do it would be a good idea to use dollar cost averaging since it works especially well with more volatile securities.

Further, more volatile funds *held in combination with other funds* can be excellent portfolio "building blocks." They can lead to higher long-run returns with little or no increase in overall portfolio volatility. We explain why in the next section.


## DIVERSIFYING AMONG FUND TYPES

We're convinced that the key to achieving good results with your portfolio is to diversify among fund types or categories. As rational investors we would agree that return is desirable and risk is undesirable. Nobel laureate Harry Markowitz, the father of Modern Portfolio Theory, laid the foundation for portfolio analysis in a 1952 article in *The Journal of Finance*.[3] We should, Markowitz explained, always hold a portfolio that will produce the most return for any given level of risk or result in the least amount of risk for any given return. For our purposes we will consider a portfolio to be a group of CEFs plus a money market mutual fund held to meet liquidity needs.

While a particular fund may appear risky by itself, it could make a favorable addition to one's overall portfolio, allowing you to experience higher long-run returns, while maintaining risk at an acceptable level or even reducing it. You would benefit by holding several volatile funds, which have portfolios representing different sectors or countries, along with your more conservative "core" holdings like an older domestic equity fund and an investment grade CEBF. Thus, there are special diversification benefits from holding funds like ASA, since their returns may have a low correlation with those on your diversified funds or other specialized funds. This is the same as the fundamental principle underlying international diversification outlined in Chapter 9. For example, during a particular year a fund investing in the gold sector could have a *negative* 20% return, whereas one investing in the German stock market could have a *positive* 30% return. This can reduce the risk of your overall portfolio. In Table 17–1 you see that ASA had a + 16.34% return in 1987 when Adams Express had a − 1.23% return. ASA also had significantly higher returns than Adams in five other years.

A fund usually does diversify within its own investment category. But, as Professors Jeff Madura and John Cheney explain, a given fund's diversification capabilities are limited to the category of securities in which it invests.[4] The professors examined the benefits to be gained from diversifying among different categories of open-end funds, although their findings should apply to closed-ends as well. They studied return interrelationships among international stock funds, small company stock funds, growth stock funds, corporate bond funds, Treasury bond funds, and money market funds. The bottom line is that investors could benefit from diversifying among funds that invest in different categories of securities, since they could reduce risk without sacrificing much, if any, return. For example, Madura and Cheney state: "A combination of international stock, small-company stock, and growth stock mutual funds achieved a portfolio return that is only 1% less than that of the international funds alone [which had the highest average annual return among the three categories], but with 18% less risk."[5]

In sum, if you hold several funds your portfolio risk would be based on the overall riskiness of the group, which would depend not only on the riskiness of each individual fund but on *how the NAVs of the funds fluctuate relative to one another*. If you hold funds whose NAVs move somewhat *independently* of each other your portfolio risk would be reduced. On the other hand you would not have good diversification if you invest in different funds specializing in the same sector, such as gold.

## TIME DIVERSIFICATION MAKES EQUITY INVESTING LESS RISKY

Burton Malkiel, in his book *A Random Walk Down Wall Street*, explains that one of the most important determinants of the proportionate allocation an individual would want to make to common stocks would be the amount of time that person has to work with.[6] A 25-year-old, for example, may want to allocate 70%, or more, of a portfolio to equities. An older, retired individual may choose to hold little of his portfolio in equities.

We've explained the importance of time diversification in Chapter 4. It's an important concept and worth reviewing. The longer your time horizon, the more likely you are to earn the long-run total return on equities that has averaged about 10% annually since 1926. Younger investors can benefit greatly from time diversification since their investment results will be averaged over different economic and stock market environments. Inferior returns during bad periods should be more than offset by superior results during the more numerous good market environments. If you are investing a relatively large amount that you are going to need at the end of a few years, you would not want equities, however, since the market averages could be down considerably at the time you want to sell.

## USE DOLLAR COST AVERAGING

Dollar cost averaging is one of the authors' favorite strategies since it is based on a strict savings plan, and fixed dollar investments buy more shares when prices are depressed, which is often when discounts are at their widest. We've explained and illustrated dollar cost averaging in Chapter 8. We suggest you review the illustration in Table 8–2 if you are not certain about the mechanics.

In all fairness, it should be pointed out that dollar cost averaging works best with no-load mutual funds for those who want to invest *small sums of money* at *frequent intervals*, like $500 a month, since there would be no transaction cost on the purchase of fund shares. The transaction costs on the CEF would be higher as a percentage of small dollar investments if the shares are purchased through a brokerage firm. A better way to use this strategy with a CEF would be to invest larger sums less frequently—say, $3,000 every six months rather than $500 every month so as to hold transaction costs to a reasonable level. On the other hand, if the CEF has a *cash purchase plan*, as Tri-Continental and some others do, one could send in small cash payments once or twice a month, or even weekly, and dollar cost average at low transaction costs. For larger investments, however, we recommend dealing directly through a broker and placing a limit order so as to have control over the price paid.

## CORE CEF HOLDINGS

You may be interested in using CEFs to build the core of your portfolio. For this we prefer the older funds since they have long track records and usually stick to a plain vanilla approach. The most basic type of core holdings would consist of one or more selections from each of the following categories:

1. The "classic" equity funds, like Adams Express, Salomon Brothers Fund, or Tri-Continental.

2. Conservative CEBFs. The older investment grade bond funds, like Current Income Shares, 1838 Bond-Debenture Trading Fund, or John Hancock Income Securities Trust are good possibilities. Depending on your tax situation you may wish to select a municipal bond fund.

The relative weights given to each of the two basic categories would depend upon factors such as age, risk tolerance, and liquidity requirements. Young investors with a very long investment period ahead of them may wish to focus mainly or exclusively on the equity funds. Older people who are at or near retirement would place most emphasis on the CEBFs. Whether one invests in tax-exempt or taxable bond funds would depend on one's tax bracket and whether the CEBF is held in a tax sheltered retirement plan, such as an IRA or Keogh plan.

## ADDITIONAL CEF HOLDINGS

After having established a portfolio core, you are ready to consider additional CEF holdings. These would include a few funds selected from various categories like those identified below.

1. Small company funds.
2. Multi-country CEFs.
3. Single-country CEFs.
4. Sector equity funds.
5. High-yield CEBFs.
6. Dual purpose funds.

Younger investors should consider investing in a small company CEF, in addition to one of the classic domestic equity funds. At the minimum, equity investors should hold one multi-country fund. Investors who wish greater exposure to overseas markets should add two or three single-country funds to their portfolios. It's conventional wisdom today that international diversification is important, especially considering the outstanding performances of many of the world's stock markets.

When you invest in a specialized fund you need to consider how that sector is currently being valued. For example, in Chapter 4 we explained that the "relative P/E" is a useful measure for deciding whether to invest in small capitalization stocks. *We feel that you should allocate your assets to those areas where you perceive the greatest value.* If you are looking at a utility fund you would want to know what the composite P/E is for utility stocks—the lower the better.

Bryan Colbert, an investment adviser, likes to use closed-end sector funds in managing client portfolios. He tells why in the Closed-End Insights box.

## FINDING VALUE

A basic thesis of this book is "finding value." Thus, one should be looking for value at all times in terms of an at-

## THE ROLE OF CLOSED-END SECTOR FUNDS IN A PORTFOLIO
### Bryan G. Colbert
### President
### MoneyTrak, Inc.

Closed-end funds can play an important role in the proper management of a portfolio. This is especially true with closed-end sector funds. Once an economic trend is identified, sector funds allow us to focus in on those areas within the economy that we believe will benefit most. This means we can side-step "contamination" from a mutual fund manager who chooses investments in areas we wish to avoid. For example, if inflation heats up again, Petroleum & Resources Corporation, Real Estate Securities Income Fund, and ASA Limited will profit from the subsequent appreciation in the oil and gas, real estate, and precious metals sectors. H&Q Healthcare Investors would benefit under the scenario of the graying of America. There will be a growing demand for health care in all areas as the baby boomers get older.

More times than not, sector funds trade at a discount. But more than that, closed-end funds within those sectors that are "being ignored" by Wall Street can offer exceptional long-term values. Why are they ignored? They are ignored by stockbrokers because they do not offer the commission potential of an open-ended fund, they are ignored by investors who may not feel well enough informed about specific sectors, and they are ignored by investment advisers because certain sectors may be "out-of-favor" with the conventional wisdom of the day.

tractive discount. After all, if you are buying at NAV, or paying a premium, you may as well be considering open-end funds too.

There were times in the 1970s and early 1980s when a number of excellent domestic equity CEFs were trading at fire sale prices, with huge discounts of 25% or 30%, or even more. This is no longer true today, and there appears to be a greater number of sophisticated investors showing an interest. A larger following obviously leads to narrowing discounts. But the closed-end fund universe has grown dramatically, especially the bond fund group. This increased supply tells us that there will still be opportunities to find value, although it will take more effort and the values may not be as great as in past decades. On the other hand, today's closed-end fund investor has more choices than ever and a larger number of funds are managed by well-known investors with outstanding track records. The wider range of choices offers you more options for building your portfolio.

Besides the discount on equity-oriented CEFs, a good guide to decide whether or not to invest in domestic equities would be the valuation measures for the overall stock market, as indicated by the P/E ratios and dividend yields for the Dow Jones Industrial Average and the Standard & Poor's 500. These measures can be tracked weekly in *Barron's* Market Laboratory. In general, the lower the P/E for the market (and the higher its dividend yield) the better the values are. Generally times of low market multiples would be times when CEF discounts are relatively wide. For instance, if the P/E on the Dow Jones Industrial Average is below 10 times and its dividend yield is above 6%, the market would appear to represent excellent value.

The international investor should also track P/E multiples and other valuation indicators in different non-U.S. markets. *Morgan Stanley Capital International Perspective* contains the data needed to do this, as we explain in Chapter 10 (see Figure 10–2). At times when multiples are near their lowest levels and discounts at their widest the CEF investor gets a "double discount," since the undervalued market can be purchased at a discount to NAV through a fund. Opportunities like this may exist during market sell-offs, as we observed beginning in August 1990.

## WHEN TO SELL

We have already said that you should consider selling funds bought at discounts when they go to premiums of 10% or more. There are other times to sell, too. You may want to sell a fund on which you have an unrealized loss so as to obtain your tax write-off. In this case you could invest in another fund immediately, or wait for 31 days (to avoid the "wash sale" rule), and then reinvest in the same fund. You may wish to lighten up on your holdings in equity funds if the market multiple gets to an excessive level (like over 18 or 20 times), especially if you're going to need that money fairly soon, say, for college expenses or retirement.

Sometimes a more volatile fund, such as a specialty or a country fund, may make a sudden upward surge in price, but not necessarily go to a premium. It may be prudent to take a profit at this point. This could be an especially good idea if the fund is held in an IRA, Keogh, or other tax-sheltered account. But, as a general rule, we urge investors to buy and hold their closed-end funds for the long term.

## TAX CONSIDERATIONS

In certain ways, investment companies can simplify your record keeping and facilitate the preparation of your tax returns. On the other hand, they can make life difficult, especially for those who don't keep good records. The tax considerations with closed-end funds are similar to those with open-end funds. We don't intend to give you expert tax advice. For that you should consult a tax adviser. However, we can offer a few general guidelines. For additional information we suggest you turn first to Internal Revenue Service Publication 564 (Mutual Fund Distributions), which covers regulated investment companies.

Investment companies generally make the following kinds of distributions:

1. Ordinary dividends
2. Capital gains distributions
3. Exempt-interest dividends
4. Return of capital (nontaxable) distributions

The amounts of these distributions reported to the IRS on your CEF are itemized on IRS Form 1099-DIV (Statement for Recipients of Dividends and Distributions). In addition, your 1099-DIV will report any foreign tax that you paid. You may be able to claim this amount as a deduction or credit. You will be notified by the fund if this would apply to you. Finally, the amount of any federal income tax withheld is indicated.

Return of capital distributions, as the name implies, are not paid out of earnings and profits but rather represent a return of investment. These distributions reduce your cost basis in the fund. Although, typically, the distribution would not give rise to a tax, circumstances could exist where a portion or all of it could be taxable.

If your fund realizes capital losses, they are not passed along to shareholders, as gains are. Capital losses offset capital gains realized by the fund. Any unused capital loss would be carried forward by the fund to net against future capital gains for up to a maximum of five years.

Prospective CEF investors should time their purchases, especially large ones, so they don't buy their shares just before the fund goes ex-dividend. If the taxable investor buys before the ex-dividend date he would be entitled to the distribution, and thus obligated to pay tax on it (if it is taxable). It is generally best to wait until the fund goes ex-dividend to make the purchase. On the ex-dividend date the NAV and share price fall by approximately the amount of the distribution. Check with your broker or the fund to find out about upcoming distributions.

The investor must pay a tax on taxable income and capital gains distributions, regardless of whether the distributions are reinvested in additional fund shares or taken in cash. You have to keep good records over the years on your reinvested distributions so that you can determine the cost basis when you sell the shares. *Whenever you reinvest a distribution you are effectively buying more fund shares.* Thus, those additional purchases must be added in to your cost basis. If you don't add all the reinvested distributions into the cost basis you will be realizing too large of a profit (or too small of a loss) when you sell your shares.

Your broker is required to report to the IRS the proceeds from securities you have sold. You will receive an IRS Form 1099-B from the broker by January 31 of the year following the calendar year in which the sale occurred. When you sell a portion of your shares in a particular fund you had acquired at different times and different prices, you need to identify the shares sold and determine the basis of those shares. Let's take an example.

In January 1985 you acquired 1000 shares of Fund A at $10.

In March 1987 you acquired 1000 additional shares at $15.

In July 1990 you sell 1000 shares at $16.

For simplicity, assume you took all distributions in cash, reinvesting nothing over the years. Which 1000 shares of Fund A did you sell? According to the IRS, in the absence of specific identification, you sold the 1000 shares acquired in January, 1985. This is known as the first in, first out (or "FIFO") method—the shares acquired earliest are assumed to be sold first. But, in this example, you would benefit from a lower gain if you sold the 1000 shares acquired in March, 1987—your capital gain would be $1,000 instead of $6,000. If you want to realize a smaller gain you should be able to substantiate that the shares sold were the ones acquired in March, 1987. There are two other less commonly used ways of determining basis that use an average cost. These methods, which are

somewhat complex, can be used only if certain requirements are met. They are described in IRS Publication 564.

Finally, some CEFs may retain realized capital gains
as we explained in Chapter 3. This is one of the more complicated tax matters facing the closed-end fund investor.
It is thoroughly explained in Figure 3–3.

## CONCLUSIONS

We have reviewed ideas introduced in earlier chapters and
explained how they could be applied to building your portfolio. One of our major conclusions is that your portfolio
make-up is largely determined by your risk tolerance and
where you are in your life cycle. It is also important to diversify among different fund types—selecting those which
offer the greatest value at the time—so as to achieve the
best long-run results. In the final analysis, only you can
determine the right proportions to allocate to the different
fund types.

### Notes

[1]Dean P. Eberling, Anthony N. Maltese, and Christine D. Rose, *Closed-
End Investment Companies* (New York: Shearson Lehman Hutton,
Inc., May 14, 1990), p. 6.

[2]*Ibid.*

[3]Harry Markowitz, "Portfolio Selection," *The Journal of Finance*,
March 1952, pp. 77–91.

[4]Jeff Madura and John M. Cheney, "Diversifying Among Mutual
Funds," *AAII Journal*, January, 1989, pp. 8–10.

[5]*Ibid.*, p. 10.

[6]Burton G. Malkiel, *A Random Walk Down Wall Street* (New York:
W.W. Norton & Company, Inc., 1990), p. 343.

CHAPTER 18

# *Takeovers and Open-Ending*

When a closed-end fund trades at a discount wider than its normal level, due to market conditions, poor performance or other factors, there is a unique opportunity for outside investor groups to lock in attractive short-term returns if they can open-end it. A few who have a longer-term viewpoint may want to take control of the fund, reorganize it, and manage it themselves. In the 1980s, the "raiders" have been the prominent group with their attempts to profit by closing the gap between price and NAV, so we will take a look at them first.

The raiders aren't really investors at all but are arbitrageurs who purchase a significant number of shares in the target fund on the open market and then attempt to force it to open-end or liquidate. At least some liquidation usually occurs as closed-end fund investors sell out at NAV when the opportunity presents itself. The arbitrageurs, trying to profit from market inefficiencies, usually buy to the limit on margin, and are very short-term oriented, generally expecting to make a profit in less than a year. For the most part this hasn't happened, but a few

381

have succeeded. We think it important that CEF investors be aware of this phenomenon, its advantages and disadvantages, and some of the difficulties. We also present two case studies: one to illustrate how a fund was liquidated, and another that shows how a fund was taken over, reorganized, and turned into a winner by an outstanding long-term investor.

## TAKEOVER BASICS

The arbitrageurs often operate in the form of a limited partnership, as this offers them a vehicle for raising the necessary capital to buy a large position in a fund. As dominant shareholders, they try to influence management and the other shareholders. Recent examples are the Grace brothers (John and Oliver, Jr.) of Sterling Grace Capital Management and T. Boone Pickins III (son of the famous T. Boone Pickins), who in 1987 were successful in initiating the open-ending of The Japan Fund, which was selling at a 27% discount and had $584 million in assets at year-end 1986. The Graces, and others, were also successful in forcing the unitization (open-ending) of the U.K.-based Crescent Japan Fund in 1988. The Graces and Pickins bid for Clemente Global Growth Fund (Chapter 10) in 1989, but were unable to take control of it and the management declined to open-end. Robert Gordon, working through NAV Partners, L.P., attempted to open-end Cypress Fund in 1989 (Chapter 6), but it is taking longer than he would like. Gordon owns 32% of the Cypress stock and is short the portfolio for arbitrage purposes. It looks as though the open-ending will not occur before the June, 1991 annual meeting.

Large shareholders of any publicly held U.S. company are required to disclose their ownership to the Securities and Exchange Commission after they have acquired 5% or more of the company's outstanding shares. They do so by filing a Schedule 13D within 10 days of the transaction. They typically state in the filing that they are unhappy about the fund's performance or that the discount is too large. Sometimes they spell out their plans for remedying the situation.

Timothy Hurley, president of Delta Management Group, has recently become involved in attempts to force CEF managements to take actions to reduce or eliminate their discounts. Prior to 1988 Hurley worked in investment banking. In 1989–90, Hurley's group was involved in attempting to force Counsellors Tandem Securities Fund to reduce the discount by open-ending or liquidating. His group ultimately reached a compromise settlement with Counsellors whereby management agreed to tender for 41% of the fund's shares at 95% of NAV. If more than 50% of the shares were tendered management also agreed to support a vote to liquidate the fund. Ultimately, 45% of the common shares were tendered. The tender at 95% of NAV allowed any shareholder (including Hurley and his group) to realize a price close to the fund's historic high. Hurley and two other large groups were also investors in Schafer Value Trust, which liquidated in 1990.

Hurley feels that large, active shareholders like himself are on the side of all shareholders, because all benefit from an appreciation in the value of their shares. "Our premise is that if we own enough stock we can have influence on management and directors that small shareholders simply can't have," says Hurley. "It's management's job not only to pick stocks and maximize the performance of the fund in terms of NAV, but also to maximize the price of the fund's stock or minimize the discount," he adds. Hurley provides some background on his activities in the Closed-End Insights box.

If a CEF is converted to an open-end fund or liquidated, its discount would disappear, resulting in a sharp gain for those who bought at the discounted price. For instance, if a fund is trading at $7.50 a share when its NAV is $10 and shareholders vote to open-end it, its price should go to $10 on the termination date because, as an open-end fund, its shares will be redeemable at NAV. This may be good for smaller investors who bought shares at a discount and, if it is a newer fund, for original investors who may wish to get even, but it destroys the long-term

## TIMOTHY HURLEY'S VIEWPOINTS
## ON CLOSED-END RESTRUCTURINGS
### Timothy P. Hurley
### President
### Delta Management Group, L.P.

Many of the closed-end funds formed in recent years have not performed up to the expectations of either their creators or their shareholders. Nonetheless, the managers of underperforming funds often refuse the pleas of their shareholders to open-end or liquidate so that shareholders can retrieve their capital with as little a penalty as possible. The directors of poorly performing funds sometimes seem willing to tolerate bad performance for an unlimited amount of time, while shareholders bear the burden of low dividends and sub-par stock performance.

While it is easy to ignore the suggestions of a shareholder with 100 or 1,000 shares, it is difficult to ignore a shareholder with 5%, 10% or 15% of a fund's outstanding shares. Our objectives are no different from those of most shareholders; however, through our ability to acquire a significant percentage of a fund's outstanding shares we are able to have more influence than a small shareholder and to exercise certain shareholder prerogatives that are economically unavailable to small shareholders.

In selecting closed-end funds which we believe would benefit from restructuring we look for two characteristics. First, the fund's investment performance and stock performance must be poor, and there must be clear and indisputable evidence supporting this conclusion. Only then can we feel confident of getting the support we need from other shareholders, who generally have a distinctly pro-management bias. And second, the gap between the fund's market value and its net asset value must be sufficiently large to make the profit potential of the investment commensurate with the risk, both in money and time, of advocating actions which are opposed to management.

> In assessing whether a fund meets the two general tests mentioned above, we evaluate the following data on each fund we consider for investment:
>
> The size of the fund's trading discount, both currently and historically.
>
> The fund's dividend yield.
>
> The fund's investment performance relative to its stated investment objective and relative to the general stock market.
>
> The trading volume in the fund's stock.
>
> The nature of the shareholder body as it is likely to affect (i) the willingness of shareholders to vote for our proposals and (ii) our ability to communicate efficiently and effectively with shareholders.
>
> The provisions of the fund's articles and by-laws as they relate to structural changes in the fund.
>
> The general riskiness and liquidity of the fund's investment portfolio. If the fund holds a portfolio of illiquid, unappealing stocks that we would not want to own directly, we would not want to own the fund's shares either.
>
> In my experience, the directors of closed-end funds tend to be far more tolerant of poor investment and stock price performance than their shareholders. We look for situations where the fund's record is shouting "red alert" and where the directors are willing to give the concept "more time." In such situations shareholders must play an active role in setting the fund's direction simply to protect their investment, or else continue to suffer the consequences of management's resistance to constructive change.

potential of the fund if it is indeed liquidated. This is something for long-term oriented investors to ponder. It's also important to note that shareholders may not be able to get out at NAV just because arbitrageurs are buying shares; few have been successful.

Taking over a fund is somewhat different from taking control of an ordinary company. Perhaps the most important difference is that most funds are run by relatively small organizations so that there will not be a lot of people whose employment and future is at stake. Another difference is that it is easier to value a fund than an operating corporation. Net asset values for funds are available weekly whereas earnings per share or book value figures for operating companies are only available quarterly. Furthermore, the NAV is a much more precise number than the earnings per share or book value of an operating company.

## ADVANTAGES AND DISADVANTAGES
## OF OPEN-ENDING

The major advantage to open-ending is the obvious one— the elimination of the excessive discount. This would benefit shareholders although management is usually opposed to open-ending.

Besides possible liquidation, management's most common argument against open-ending is that an open-end fund has to deal with redemptions of shareholder money at the wrong times—in weak markets when they should be buying rather than selling. Also, mutual fund investors have historically poured money into funds at the top of market cycles rather than at the bottom. With a CEF you don't have to deal with these problems, so you can take a longer-term perspective. Further, an open-end fund manager has to maintain larger cash reserves to meet redemptions and thus would be unable to maintain as fully invested a portfolio. On open-ending the impact of redemptions would be immediate since many investors could redeem their shares at NAV and management would be forced to liquidate positions. This would result in a smaller portfolio with less assets available to generate a management fee. Also, if the fund holds any illiquid assets, such as venture capital or limited partnership positions, they may have to be liquidated at distress sale prices when the fund is open-ended.

The arbitrageurs counter that open-end funds deal

with inflows and outflows of shareholder money all the time. They also point out that management would have more incentive to do their very best by attempting to build more assets on which greater management fees could be earned. We see several problems with this argument. First, if the fund has a good record and the investor wants to remain a long-term holder, the opportunity would be lost to make additional investments over the years at a discount to NAV as well as to reinvest dividends at a price below NAV and thus to achieve a higher yield on those investments. Second, long-term holders who have substantial capital gains may not want to realize those gains and face tax consequences when management is forced into liquidating positions.

Thomas Herzfeld maintains that, because the prices of CEFs fluctuate more widely than NAV, the closed-end form offers frequent trading opportunities for savvy investors. These trading opportunities do not exist with open-end funds. If you can make money trading a CEF it should not matter that it sells at a discount.[1] Herzfeld takes a shorter-term view towards CEFs than we do, but this is another good argument for the closed-end format.

## WHAT ATTRACTS ARBITRAGEURS?

There are at least ten factors arbitrageurs may consider when trying to get control of a CEF. They are identified in Figure 18–1.

Obviously, it would be very difficult, if not impossible, to find funds where all ten factors are favorable for an open-ending. Each case is unique and suitors are attracted to different funds for different reasons. We'll briefly comment on each of these factors.

**The Discount.** Probably the most important factor would be the discount. Discount levels in more recent years have not been as great, on average, as those seen in the 1970s and early 1980s, partly because funds have put in more defenses against raiders. The arbitrageur wants to benefit from the elimination of the "spread" or the dif-

**Figure 18–1. Factors that Attract CEF Arbitrageurs**

1. A wide discount from NAV.
2. A high dividend yield.
3. Poor performance and management.
4. High expense ratios.
5. A liquid fund that trades in sufficient volume.
6. A fund that holds liquid securities.
7. A fund that has fewer, larger shareholders.
8. A fund of sufficient size.
9. Limited defensive provisions.
10. The ability to hedge the fund's portfolio.

ference between NAV and the fund's market price. Discounts of 20% or more would be highly attractive, but even 15% could be sufficient.

**The Dividend Yield.** Arbitrageurs typically buy the stock of the target fund on margin and this necessitates an interest cost. As a consequence, if the fund pays a relatively high dividend it would be an ideal target, since the dividend would offset the interest expense.

**Track Record and Expenses.** If the fund has poor past performance and poor management of expenses there is a good case for a reorganization. Shareholders should favor a change for the better if the opportunity is presented to them.

**Liquidity of Fund.** Since the arbitrageurs generally want to acquire a sufficient amount of stock in a reasonable time the liquidity of the fund is also important. They don't want a fund that "trades by appointment only," or just 100 shares a day. Closed-end funds are generally not that liquid since they usually have relatively small capitalizations. This may limit the raider who wants to accumulate a large number of shares in a short period of time.

**Liquidity of Holdings.** A fund that holds liquid securities is much more attractive than one that holds illiquid securities. If the fund is open-ended or liquidated it would be much easier to sell the liquid securities at prices reasonably close to recent market prices.

**Number of Shareholders.** A fund that has many shareholders with relatively small positions would be difficult to open-end, especially if those shareholders have been with the fund for years and are comfortable with the management and generally pleased with the performance. This would be true even if the fund trades at a relatively wide discount, as many of the older funds do. It is therefore unlikely that Adams Express; Baker, Fentress; General American Investors; Salomon Brothers Fund; or Tri-Continental would be open-ended, as they have good long-term records, many loyal shareholders, and operate with very low expense ratios. Shareholders' natural inclination is to follow management's recommendations unless management can be discredited. Even then, management has certain advantages that a raider will have a tough time overcoming. This is especially true if it is a personality fund or is backed by a brokerage firm, as in the case of Cypress Fund where there was a strong case for open-ending because of poor performance.

**Size of Fund.** Generally, arbitrageurs are interested in open-ending a fund with assets in excess of $50 million. The greater the amount of assets the larger the dollar gains. If a $200 million fund is trading at a 20% discount, there is a $40 million gap between the NAV and the market price. In contrast, if a $20 million fund sells at a 20% discount the gap would be only $4 million. Smaller funds also tend to be less liquid. Someone who wants to run a fund may want to take control of a smaller fund, however.

**Defensive Provisions.** Defenses against predators, like staggered board terms, super majority voting provisions, and, more recently, scheduled tender offers at NAV are effective deterrents. Funds that pay out a fixed percentage of NAV annually (commonly 10%) also tend to be less attractive to raiders. The disadvantage of these provisions is that even though designed to protect shareholder interests they may do more to protect the jobs of managers who should be replaced. Fund managers like Erik

Bergstrom (Bergstrom Capital) and George Michaelis (Source Capital), who have superb long-term records with their CEFs, are left alone by raiders as their premiums or narrow discounts are a deterrent.

**Hedgeability.** Arbitrageurs may want a fund with a portfolio that could be hedged by shorting stock index futures so that the discount could be captured without having to worry about market risk. This will protect them against adverse fluctuations in the fund's NAV. Schafer Value Trust, which was recently liquidated, was very easy to hedge because it held liquid NYSE stocks. If the fund is non-diversified and holds a relatively small number of lesser known stocks the suitor may short the individual stocks in the portfolio as Robert Gordon has done with Cypress Fund.


## ARBITRAGEURS FACE DIFFICULTIES

Closed-end fund specialist Jeffrey Hopson identifies three principal obstacles or deterrents for the prospective arbitrageur to contemplate:

1.  Since discounts rarely exceed 20%, the potential returns are not as attractive as they might be with operating companies that could be found at larger discounts to their underlying values.

2.  The NAV constantly changes making its end value uncertain.

3.  The fund managers will, most likely, bitterly fight any open-ending proposal. Most funds have reasonably effective anti-takeover provisions.[2]

The arbitrageurs do not have that many attractive candidates in the closed-end fund universe. As you already know, equity funds tend to sell at larger discounts than bond funds. Thus, the arbitrageurs would typically be looking for candidates among the equity fund groups. Within these groups only a small number would be attractive at any given time.

Closed-end funds that are relatively easy to open-end tend to trade at narrower discounts than those that would be harder to open-end. The reason is simple: if it is likely that a fund will be open-ended, investors will buy the shares in order to realize an immediate profit when the share price rises to NAV.

Funds with which we are familiar that liquidated or open-ended in the past decade are identified in Figure 18–2.

### Figure 18–2. Funds Liquidated or Open-Ended Since 1980

- Stratton Monthly Dividend Shares (formerly Energy & Utility Shares), began 1972, converted to an open-end fund, 1981.
- Chase Convertible Fund of Boston, began 1972, converted to an open-end fund 1982.
- Precious Metals Holdings, began 1974, changed to an open-end fund 1983.
- U.S. & Foreign Securities, began 1924, the country's first large-scale, leveraged closed-end fund, liquidated in 1984.
- Madison Fund, began 1929, converted to an operating company 1985.
- Nautilus Fund, began 1979, open-ended 1985.
- The Japan Fund, began 1962, the first major closed-end country fund in the U.S., open-ended 1987.
- Progressive Income Equity Fund, began 1987, open-ended 1988.
- Financial News Composite Fund, began 1987, open-ended 1989.
- France Fund, began 1986, open-ended 1989.
- Global Growth and Income Fund, a dual fund, began 1986, liquidated 1989.
- Regional Financial Shares, began 1986, open-ended 1990.
- Schafer Value Trust, began 1986, liquidated 1990.
- Prudential Strategic Income Fund, began 1988, open-ended 1990.

It is a misconception that shareholders inevitably get out at NAV when the first suitor files a Schedule 13D. According to Thomas Herzfeld, in only about two or three of every 10 takeover attempts do they get out at NAV. "It's a low percentage play for investors to jump in on the back of a takeover attempt with the belief that they will realize full value for the shares."[3] Commonly, Herzfeld adds, the insurgents distract management from its duty of running the fund and, in defending itself, the fund runs up the expense ratio. Herzfeld is opposed to takeovers simply for the chance to make a fast buck.[4]

## SCHAFER VALUE TRUST: A CASE STUDY

**Schafer Value Trust** was liquidated in 1990. It was a diversified fund traded on the NYSE with the primary objective of long-term capital appreciation. David Schafer is a value investor who purchased stocks of larger, established companies. This personality fund, which we had planned to profile in Chapter 6, was offered to the public in 1986 with a very low 1% underwriting commission and was sold mainly to institutions. Its total assets were $87 million at year-end 1989. Although it had a good investment record, the fund was forced to liquidate in the summer of 1990 under pressure from three large shareholder groups. The fund had high institutional ownership, which ended up being a disadvantage because institutions have more of a short-term orientation. The discount after the 1987 crash was as wide as 25%; this attracted Tim Hurley as well as Massachusetts-based Jack Rizika of KRR Investors with the idea of open-ending. An 80% super majority vote was necessary to accomplish their aim.

At the 1989 annual meeting the adversaries mustered just over 25% of the 80% vote necessary. The voter turnout was only 60%. David Schafer told us that this low turnout partly resulted from a failure on the part of the transfer agent, Bankers Trust Company, to send proxies to all the shareholders, as 30% of them were therefore unable to vote.

The dominant shareholder groups had more clout for

the 1990 annual meeting and found that to liquidate there was a requirement of only 50% of the vote. By this time a third group, Gateway Investment Advisers, had acquired 13% of the shares and threatened to buy enough additional shares to liquidate the fund. A partnership to do specifically this was organized by Gateway. The directors therefore decided that liquidation would be the best alternative to save the legal costs and in March decided to approve a liquidation plan. Even though the directors felt that the closed-end structure would be in the best long-term interest of shareholders, the difficulties and expenses of fighting to retain it would be too great.[5] Schafer felt that he really needed more time to show that the closed-end format would work well with the fund. Shareholders would have been given the opportunity to vote to open-end in 1992. The arbitrageurs couldn't wait for this date as they were not long-term oriented and had purchased the stock on margin. We see this as a disappointment to a manager with a superior long-term record going back to 1975. The fund's NAV was up 36.1% and 18.3% in 1989 and 1988, respectively. The corresponding figures for the Standard & Poor's 500 Composite Stock Price Index were 31.7% and 16.5%. All returns include dividends which are assumed to be reinvested. Schafer's error was not putting in enough take-over defenses to protect himself.

Schafer has a no-load open-end fund, Schafer Value Fund, and an investment advisory business based in Princeton, New Jersey with $300 million in assets under management. He told us recently that he would like to get back into the closed-end fund business.

## BERGSTROM CAPITAL CORPORATION: A CASE STUDY

We have been focusing on arbitrageurs who have short-term objectives to narrow the spread but have no interest in managing the portfolios of their target funds. Occasionally, a manager does want to take control of a fund and make something of it for shareholders. The history of

Bergstrom Capital is an excellent example. In this case the manager is also the largest shareholder and therefore shares in the benefits of superior performance with all the other shareholders.[6] Although these events occurred in the mid-1970s, their contrast to the take-over activity of today is relevant and striking.

In 1974, at the bottom of the worst bear market since the early 1930s, Erik Bergstrom was looking for an opportunity. He had already achieved an outstanding record as a portfolio manager and private investor and had a lot of cash. He is a value-oriented, risk-adverse, investor who saw in Diebold Venture Capital Corporation, if he could get control, just what he was looking for—an opportunity to make something of a CEF which needed help.

John Diebold, the founder, is a noted international computer consultant but is not a money manager. He had hired a venture capitalist to pick the portfolio and some outstanding choices were made, but the bear market and the resulting poor environment for venture capital start-ups caused many of the portfolio companies to sell at low values. During this period the fund sold at a discount of over 70% due to poor performance and lack of liquidity. This created another asset; the tax losses could be used to offset future capital gains.

Bergstrom therefore began buying shares of the fund, which had declined from $30 million at its offering in 1968 to under $5 million by 1974. He soon had accumulated the five percent required to file with the SEC. At this time, a group of associates joined him and they continued to accumulate shares until they had over 30%. Bergstrom and his family were the largest shareholders. In early 1976, the directors agreed to transfer the fund to Bergstrom's advisory company, but a proxy contest ensued because Charles Steadman, a Washington, D.C. mutual fund manager, wanted to merge the fund into his open-end complex. The Bergstrom group prevailed over the adversaries, however, and in October 1976 the contract was transferred to Erik Bergstrom's control. He reduced the 1% management fees to 0.75%, and to 0.50% on those assets over $50 million. This was because he was more interested in making capital gains as well as cutting the expenses. The name of the fund was changed to Claremont Capital and it was moved to Seattle from New York City.

Bergstrom has succeeded in making the fund, now known as Bergstrom Capital (value $73 million on June 30, 1990), into one of the most outstanding in the United States. It has also been on the *Forbes* honor roll seven years in a row. Although he is an outstanding investor himself, Bergstrom is one of the few fund managers willing to share his management fees with two sub-advisers, who have helped him achieve his superior record. This is something almost unheard of in the business. (See Bergstrom's Closed-End Insights box in Chapter 5.) We see this as part of the take-over activity in CEFs, but we want to stress that Erik Bergstrom has never seen himself as a "raider" as he never intended to open-end or liquidate Diebold Venture Capital Corporation. As a result, he and his shareholders have benefited enormously as he chose to build up the assets over the long-term rather than take the shorter-term objective. We would like to see more long-term investors follow his example.

## KEEPING THE DISCOUNT NARROW

Because of the activities of the raiders and the concerns of fund managers who fear losing investment control of their funds, most of the newer funds have now set dates to put the vote to open-end to shareholders. For example, shareholders of the Templeton Value Fund voted in September 1990 to open-end their fund during the first calendar quarter of 1991. They were given this opportunity to vote on open-ending because the fund had traded at an 8.33% average discount during a 12-week test period from April 12 to June 29, 1990. According to the Templeton Value Fund's prospectus the discount would have to average 5% or more during the designated 12-week test period for the shareholder vote to open-end to be invoked. The prospectus added that the open-ending feature may prevent the fund from going to a wide discount:

The fact that the Fund's Articles of Incorporation provide for the automatic submission to the Fund's shareholders of a proposal to convert the Fund to an open-end investment company may enhance the attractiveness of the Fund's shares to investors, thereby reducing the excess of the net asset value over market price that might otherwise exist. Sellers may be less inclined to accept a significant discount if they have some prospect of being able to receive net asset value if the Fund converted to an open-end investment company.

In an effort to narrow the discount, some funds buy in shares, which if the discount is large enough, does raise the NAV although it reduces the fees paid to the manager (since share repurchases reduce the fund's total assets on which the fees are based). Rights offerings and tender offers, and, particularly, set payouts of from seven to ten percent of NAV are more common to try to keep the discount narrow. Evidence indicates these approaches seem to work. But many investors who are long-term oriented do not want to be forced to pay taxes on capital gains distributions that may otherwise not be realized.

## CONCLUSIONS

You should not simply buy shares in a fund because you feel it will open-end, as some investors do. Nonetheless, this is another attraction of a fund that trades at a large discount. Not only can that fund be an excellent value if it remains closed-ended but your total return will be higher because of your ability to reinvest dividends into shares trading at a discount. No open-end fund investor can do this. If an arbitrageur should become interested, you may receive an unexpected appreciation in your share price. If the restructuring attempt fails, the discount will widen again.

There have been few open-endings relative to the large number of attempts, however. With funds tending to trade at narrower discounts and because takeover defenses are in place, especially with the newer funds, the number of conversions will probably remain a relatively small percentage of the total number of funds. The older domestic equity funds which have many loyal shareholders, low expense ratios, and discounts ranging to 20% are virtually takeover proof and will probably continue to represent some of the best values in the closed-end fund world.

## Notes

[1] Thomas J. Herzfeld, *The Investor's Guide to Closed-End Funds* (New York: McGraw-Hill, Inc., 1980), p. 186.

[2] Jeffrey Hopson, *Closed-End Fund Update* (St. Louis: A.G. Edwards & Sons, Inc., May 4, 1989), p. 3.

[3] Interview with Thomas J. Herzfeld, Chairman and President, Thomas J. Herzfeld & Co., Inc. and Thomas J. Herzfeld Advisors, Inc., *Wiesenberger MUTUAL FUNDS Investment Report*, September 1989, p. 6.

[4] *Ibid.*

[5] "Schafer Value Board Approves Liquidation," *The Wall Street Journal*, March 28, 1990, p. C16.

[6] George Cole Scott has been a member of the Board of Directors of Bergstrom Capital since October 1976.

# CHAPTER 19

# *A Final Word*

Since 1985 the closed-end fund has become a very popular investment vehicle. Although the volume of CEF initial public offerings will probably abate, the closed-end fund will remain important because of its major advantages. After all, the CEF was the original form of investment company and it has met the test of time. In Chapter 11 we traced its early roots to nineteenth century England; The Foreign and Colonial Investment Trust, which began in 1868, is still going strong. As we put the finishing touches on this book, we notice that there is still a continuing flow of closed-end fund IPOs. These include many funds which invest in non-U.S. markets, like European Warrant Fund, Latin America Investment Fund, Mexico Equity & Income Fund, and Singapore Fund.

We feel strongly that closed-end funds are as attractive today as ever. Discounts on better funds may not go to the deep levels of 25 and 30% seen in past decades, but a far wider variety of funds have been created by the industry. A large number of funds can also be found within most categories. This continuing supply could maintain discount opportunities for CEF investors.

## FUNDS VERSUS ORDINARY STOCKS

Our feeling is that most people are better off with funds—open- or closed-end—than with individual stocks. John Templeton pointed out that successful investing is hard work requiring more attention than most investors are willing to devote. This and the value created by buying CEFs at a discount make a convincing argument for closed-end funds. Most investors who recognize the values we've stressed in this book will agree with us. The amount of money they've invested—over $1 trillion in open-end funds alone—is strong evidence of their recognition of the need for diversification and professional management.

We want to emphasize that to have any hope for selecting stocks that will deliver superior performance you need *time* as well as *talent,* since a considerable amount of knowledge, dedication, homework, and emotional discipline are necessary to be successful. *Succeeding with individual stocks is easier said than done—most people who buy individual stocks end up losing money.* Unfortunately, we don't have statistics to substantiate this statement, but our observations over the years lead us to believe that the proportion of losers is alarmingly high. As we stated in our Preface, the mission of this book is to demonstrate what you need to know to become a knowledgeable and successful closed-end fund investor. This will help you to stand among the winners rather than the losers. The advantages of funds today are too great to ignore.

## ADVANTAGES OF OPEN- AND CLOSED-END FUNDS

1. Diversification within the fund's investment area or market(s). Be it equities of companies based in the United States, Singapore, or the rest of the world, junk bonds or a mixture of several different bond market sectors, fund managers spread the risk among different issues within their area of expertise. Fund managers who invest in other parts of the world give you the added di-

mension of international diversification, which most individuals would find exceedingly difficult to achieve on their own.

2. Professional management. The investment world has become highly complex and the services of a competent investment professional are more necessary now than ever. One bond fund manager may switch the portfolio holdings as opportunities arise to achieve a higher total return. An equity fund manager may restructure the portfolio to include greater proportionate holdings in noncyclical stocks to prepare for a possible recession. Another equity fund manager may build up cash for defensive reasons and to prepare for opportunities in weaker markets. In some cases distinguished investors who have achieved exceptional records will be managing your money.

3. Many portfolio choices. More specialized funds are being created all the time to invest in unique groups of securities. Open- and closed-end funds offer the variety necessary to put together an assortment of funds closely tailored to your needs and preferences.

4. Economies of scale. Since the fund deals in larger quantities of stocks or bonds its transaction cost per unit should be much lower than it would be for the individual investor. This is especially important in certain areas like bonds and non-U.S. equities, which may not even be accessible to individuals.

## UNIQUE ADVANTAGES
## OF CLOSED-END FUNDS

In addition to offering you the above advantages of open-end funds, closed-end funds offer some unique advantages:

1. The opportunity buy an *undervalued* fund. This occurs during bear markets, at the end-of-year tax-selling season, when a number of clone funds appear (as in the case of the Germany funds), and when investors are turned off by a particular sector. The large number of closed-end offerings during the 1980s and thus far in the 1990s should saturate the market to such a degree that reason-

ably attractive discounts will result on many funds, as we are now witnessing. Any discount represents value and discounts of 10% or 15% on equity funds should help you to earn better returns on your money over long periods of time. On good bond funds discounts of 5% to 10% can be attractive.

During the 1990 sell-off, which began in August, there were some screaming values in the closed-end fund world—discounts of 20% or more were commonplace. CEFs offer much better values than open-end funds during pessimistic times, since the buyer gets a "double discount"—a depressed market with stocks trading at low multiples and a fund at an extraordinarily wide discount.

Valuations can change rapidly in the specialized equity CEF market. By way of example, the decline in premiums/discounts in single-country funds was quite dramatic between July and August, 1990. Data supplied by Lipper Analytical Services (Table 19–1) report the ten specialized equity funds registering the largest total decline in premium/discount for August 1990—eight of these were single-country funds. The biggest drop occurred in

**Table 19–1. Specialized Equity Funds with Largest Drop in Premium/Discount (July to August 1990)***

|  | July Prem./Disc. | August Prem./Disc. | Change |
|---|---|---|---|
| 1. India Growth Fund | +21.78% | −12.03% | −33.81% |
| 2. Jakarta Growth Fund | +6.08 | −13.34 | −19.42 |
| 3. Portugal Fund | +2.05 | −16.15 | −18.20 |
| 4. Chile Fund | +7.01 | −10.65 | −17.66 |
| 5. Thai Capital Fund | −1.25 | −18.11 | −16.86 |
| 6. Spain Fund | +9.52 | −6.25 | −15.77 |
| 7. Italy Fund | −10.55 | −23.46 | −12.91 |
| 8. Templeton Emerging Markets | +5.06 | −7.46 | −12.52 |
| 9. Alliance Global Environment | −13.09 | −24.84 | −11.75 |
| 10. Brazil Fund | −4.47 | −14.71 | −10.24 |

*Data represent month-end premiums (+) or discounts (−).
Source: Lipper Analytical Services, Inc.

the India Growth Fund which fell from a 21.78% premium to a 12.03% discount at the end of August. (At the end of September the discount on that fund had widened to near 25%.)

2. The opportunity to sell an *overvalued* fund. When you buy at a discount you may have the opportunity some day to sell at a premium. An extreme example of this was the level of premiums reached on some country funds during late 1989 and early 1990.

3. The ability to track intraday price changes and to have greater control over the price at which you buy and sell fund shares through the use of limit orders. Remember that saving an eighth of a point or so on each transaction can improve your long-term performance results significantly.

4. The fund manager should be able to perform better with the closed-end structure than the manager of an otherwise equivalent open-end fund. That individual need not worry about massive inflows of money during a speculative bubble and redemptions by panicky shareholders when things sour. The fact that the manager works with a relatively stable pool of capital means there is no need for a cash buffer to meet redemptions.

**RECIPE FOR SUCCESS**

With people living to older ages, and, in many cases retiring at an earlier age, earning the best return on their savings has become essential. The first and most basic rule is simply: DON'T LOSE MONEY—IT'S A GIANT STEP IN THE WRONG DIRECTION. The following ingredients are the necessary ones to accumulate wealth, through the power of compounding, over the years.

1. *Diversify among closed-end funds and over time.* You must diversify to succeed. A closed-end fund gives you built in diversification within its investment area, but you need to diversify into several funds which invest in different kinds of securities. You also need to practice time diversification, especially with your equity funds, so poor

results in bad markets will be more than offset by superior
results in good markets.

2. *Allocate a portion of your savings to closed-end
equity funds.* This is especially important for younger individuals. In fact, the more time you have to work with,
the larger your allocation to equities can be. Remember
that equities produce superior long-term returns and this
is the key to building substantial wealth.

3. *Act independently and wait patiently for a sound
investment to grow and mature.* These are two of the
most important qualities needed to be a successful value
investor. As John Templeton has said, one must have the
discipline and courage to buy at times when prices are
beaten down to bargain levels and the patience to hold on
for better times.

4. *Give your fund manager a chance.* Don't jump in
and out of funds; trying to time the market can be expensive. One of the reasons for the popularity of mutual funds
is that they allow investors to switch among different fund
family members at little or no charge by simply making a
toll-free phone call. The authors are opposed to hyperac-
tive switching, however, because there is strong evidence
that you cannot consistently time the market correctly.
Switching also leads to taxable gains when you do have
profits, unless your funds are held in a tax-sheltered retirement plan, like an IRA.

## ONE INDIVIDUAL'S SUCCESS STORY

We would like to conclude *Investing in Closed-End Funds*
with the success story of the late Stanislaw Bednarski.[1]
Born in Poland in 1938, Bednarski came to the U.S. in
1965 and held a PhD in systems dynamics from Rensse-
laer Polytechnic Institute. He saw closed-end funds as exceptions to the efficient market theory and, in 1975,
started to invest in them with $16,000. His first invest-
ment was in Highland Capital which was raided by Carl
Icahn in 1975. Bednarski was off to a great start as he tri-
pled his margined investment in Highland in six months.
By 1987, at 48, Bednarski had done so well with closed-

end funds that he retired from his job at General Electric to devote most of his time to managing his portfolio.[2] Bednarski's large positions in recent years have been in Franklin Holding Corporation (Amex: FKL, no longer a CEF), Counsellors Tandem Securities Fund, Quest for Value Dual Purpose Fund income shares, and recently, Convertible Holdings capital shares, and Engex. Bednarski took positions in funds with attractive discounts which he felt have the potential to narrow. He invested in Mexico Fund in 1986 at an average price of a little better than $3 a share, when it was selling at a 45% discount; he sold it about a year later at around 12 when the discount had narrowed to 15%. Bednarski even went to Mexico City when he was accumulating his shares to check on the valuation of the fund's holdings. He also bought shares in Scudder New Asia Fund in early 1988 at a 40% discount and sold them six months later for a 50% gain. He attributed the bargain price of Scudder New Asia to the irrational behavior of large investors.

Bednarski did exceptionally well; he accumulated a margined portfolio of over $10 million, entirely in closed-end funds. He held about a dozen funds and didn't buy anything else. When asked if closed-end funds still offer attractive opportunities to buy at bargain prices, Bednarski responded that in mid-August 1990 he had bought some Capital Southwest (NASDAQ: CSWC), a venture capital investment company, at nearly a 50% discount. "It is still possible to find good buys," he said adding that "The small funds don't attract the professionals because they are not liquid." Bednarski was a patient buyer, accumulating positions gradually with open limit orders when sellers appear. This shows how well an individual investor can do with lots of hard work and a little luck.

## CONCLUSIONS

In conclusion, no one can predict the future. Thus, we don't know what kinds of discounts will be in store for our readers. We do recognize that fund managers and other sophisticated investors are more conscious of the discount today. This means that discounts will probably not widen excessively on good quality funds with low expenses. On the other hand, wide discounts in a severe bear market or in sudden sell-offs, as in October 1987, October 1989, and August–September 1990, are always probable. Like price-earnings ratios on ordinary stocks, discounts, or price/NAV ratios, on closed-end funds will fluctuate in the future and offer value investors the opportunity to buy at bargain prices when others are despondently selling, and to sell at overly inflated prices when others are eagerly buying. Open-end funds do not have this valuation indicator since their prices are tied to NAV. Closed-end funds, on the other hand, have characteristics of stocks as well as investment companies and this creates unique opportunities.

Irrespective of whether you are a large or small investor, or how well or poorly you may have done with your investments in the past, we hope this book has given you some useful ideas for finding value and building wealth. We especially hope that more open-end fund investors—we know there are a lot of them—will see the advantages of moving at least a portion of their wealth into closed-end funds.

## Notes

[1] While we were completing the book we learned of Stanislaw Bednarski's untimely death October 24, 1990.
[2] Jonathan Clements, "The almost-perfect-market thesis," *Forbes*, February 6, 1989, p. 150.

# Glossary

**Administrator** The organization hired by the fund to take care of its administrative duties. These duties would include fund accounting, portfolio pricing, preparing shareholder reports, legal filings, shareholder mailings, and proxy solicitations. The adviser often handles the administrative duties.

**Adviser** (or **Investment Adviser**) A money management unit hired by the fund's board of directors to manage its assets for a fee. The name of the fund's adviser as well as the formula for determining the adviser's compensation is disclosed in its prospectus and in the "notes to financial statements" section of its annual and semi-annual shareholder reports. Some funds also employ one or more sub-advisers.

**All-Or-None Order (AON)** A trading order to be filled in its entirety, usually at a limit price, or not at all. No partial execution is permitted. The AON order is generally used to avoid the higher commissions that would result if the original order were executed piecemeal over several days.

Because they are restrictive and have low priority in the specialist's book, larger AON orders may be difficult to execute.

**American Depositary Receipt (ADR)**  A negotiable receipt for shares of non-U.S. equities which have been deposited in a bank, usually in the issuer's country. ADRs are created by U.S. banks and trade on a securities exchange, like the NYSE or Amex, or over-the-counter (both in NASDAQ and the pink sheets). They trade in the United States in lieu of the actual stock, representing indirect ownership in a foreign company. ADRs are designed to make investing in non-U.S. stocks simpler. There are differences among ADRs; for example, some may have voting rights and others may not.

**American Stock Exchange (Amex)**  An organized stock exchange located in New York City. Its listing requirements are less stringent than those of the New York Stock Exchange. About 30 closed-end funds trade on the Amex.

**Arbitrage**  An attempt to lock in a profit, assuming little or no risk, by undertaking certain transactions. Arbitrage may involve buying and selling the same security in two different markets so as to profit from a price disparity. Today arbitrage commonly involves combinations of different types of securities like stocks and options. The arbitrageur seeking to open-end a closed-end fund hopes to benefit from the elimination of the "spread" or the difference between NAV and the fund's market price.

**Asked Price**  The price at which a dealer is willing to sell a given security. The asked price is always higher than the bid. See Bid Price and Bid-Asked Spread.

**Auction Rate Preferred Stock**  Some closed-end funds issue auction rate preferred to obtain leverage. The preferred stockholders receive varying dividends which are redetermined at relatively short intervals. The dividends would tend to fluctuate with changing short-term interest rates. For the leverage to be favorable, the preferred dividend rate must remain significantly below the rate earned by the fund on its investments.

**Back-End Load**   A redemption charge levied by some open-end funds when you sell your shares. It can be as high as 5% or 6% initially but usually declines as the length of time you have owned the fund increases.

**Basis Point**   One basis point equals one one-hundredth of one percent (1/100 × 1%). Yield spreads between different bond categories are generally expressed in basis points. For example, if Category A yields 9% and Category B yields 8.5% the yield difference or spread would amount to 50 basis points.

**Beta Coefficient**   A measure of the price sensitivity of a security or fund with respect to fluctuations in the overall stock market, as represented by an index like the Standard & Poor's 500. The beta of the overall market is 1.0 and represents average volatility. High beta stocks are more volatile than low beta stocks.

**Bid Price**   The price a dealer is willing to pay for a security. The bid is below the asked price. See Asked Price and Bid-Asked Spread.

**Bid-Asked Spread**   The difference between the bid and asked prices on a security. For example, if XYZ Fund is quoted at 8 bid, 8-1/4 asked, the spread would be 1/4. The spread as a percentage of the bid price tends to be higher on lower priced stocks.

**Board of Directors**   The board members are elected by the shareholders of the fund. The board hires the adviser and approves the renewal of the investment advisory contract. Other duties include approving the fund's portfolio and establishing general corporate policy including the payment of dividends.

**Book Value**   The total assets minus the total liabilities of a company. Book value is often expressed as a per-share number obtained by dividing aggregate book value by the number of outstanding common shares. Book value is also known as net worth and common stockholders' equity.

**Bottom-Up Analysis**   An approach to investment analysis which focuses first on individual companies; next, on industries; and, finally, on the economy. Bottom-up analysts usually place primary emphasis on the company. General American Investors and Tri-Continental are examples of closed-end funds which use the bottom-up approach.

**Call Provision**   An arrangement whereby the issuer of bonds can call them back from investors prior to maturity at a predetermined call price. This is generally done during a period of declining interest rates when the issuer wants to replace a high interest rate debt issue with one bearing a lower interest cost. This is often to the disadvantage of investors who are forced to reinvest at lower interest rates. Most bonds are callable.

**Cannibalizing Assets**   Funds which pay a significant portion of their distributions out of principal cannibalize their assets. This depletes the fund's asset base. Sometimes funds cannibalize assets so as to maintain a dividend and keep unwary shareholders happy.

**Capital Shares**   *See* Dual Purpose Fund

**Cash Purchase Plan**   A plan available with some closed-end funds that allows shareholders to send in cash for investment in fund shares in lieu of the individual buying shares directly through a broker. The plan is usually offered by the fund's transfer agent in conjunction with a dividend reinvestment plan. This is an ideal arrangement for those who wish to dollar cost average by making frequent, small investments as transaction costs are low. Minimum investments may be $25 or $50. Funds offering this plan include Adams Express; Baker, Fentress; Blue Chip Value Fund; Petroleum & Resources; Salomon Brothers Fund; and Tri-Continental.

**Closed-End Fund (CEF; CEBF refers to closed-end bond fund)**   A publicly-traded, managed investment company which has a fixed number of outstanding shares and invests in a portfolio of securities in accordance with its stated investment policy and objectives. The number of outstanding shares may change due to share repurchases, issuances of new shares as dividends, tender offers, rights offerings, and additional public offerings. A CEF does not redeem its shares when investors want to sell—the shares trade on the stock exchange or in NASDAQ. Most CEFs are listed on the New York Stock Exchange. The market price of a CEF is determined by demand and supply and is not directly tied to its net asset value.

**Convertible Security**   A bond or preferred stock which can be exchanged for (converted into) the common stock of the underlying company on specified terms at the holder's option.

**Correlation Coefficient**   A measure of the degree of association between the movements of two variables. Its numerical value ranges between +1.0 and −1.0. A +1.0 would indicate perfect positive correlation, −1.0 perfect negative correlation, and 0.0 would indicate no relationship. For example, if the returns of the stock markets in two different countries have a correlation of 0.0, their price movements would be totally unrelated.

**Credit Risk** (or **Default Risk**)   The risk that the issuer of bonds will default on the payment of interest or principal. Credit risk is judged by the bond issue's agency rating. The higher the quality rating the lower the credit risk.

**Currency Risk**   The risk assumed by one who holds investments denominated in a foreign currency. If the U.S. dollar strengthens or gains in value relative to that currency the investor would be adversely affected.

**Day Order**   A customer trading order to be executed sometime during a given day or canceled.

**Derivative Product**   Securities, such as options, futures, convertibles, and warrants, whose price and value

are tied to a primary security or index of prices that under-
lies the derivative security.

**Direct Placement**   The purchase of an issue of securities directly from the issuer by the investor as opposed to
a public offering where there are many buyers. Also
known as *private placement*.

**Discount**   Refers to a closed-end fund trading at a market price below its net asset value.

**Discretionary Account**   An arrangement between the
broker and customer giving the broker legal authority to
trade the account without consulting the customer. The
authors are against discretionary accounts since they give
the broker too much power over the customer's account.

**Discretionary Order**   A limit order whereby the customer gives the broker the authority to alter the price or
number of shares, depending on market conditions.

**Diversified Investment Company**   An investment
company that invests at least 75% of its assets in a diversified manner. Within the diversified portion of its portfolio
no single security may exceed 5% of the portfolio's total
assets. Additionally, a diversified fund may not own in excess of 10% of the voting shares of any one issuer.

**Dividend Reinvestment Plan**   A program whereby a
third party such as the CEF's custodian bank or transfer
agent will buy the fund's shares in the open market to fill
the demand of shareholders who wish to reinvest their
dividend and capital gains distributions in the form of
shares rather than accept them in cash. The fund will
keep the cost down by buying the shares in large blocks.
We are familiar with a few funds that only issue new
shares to reinvesting shareholders rather than shares that
have been repurchased in the open market. If the company follows the policy of only issuing new shares there
would tend to be more dilution if it typically trades at a
discount. Many funds may issue both shares which have
been purchased in the open market and new shares.

**Do Not Reduce Order (DNR)**    A limit order to buy stock at a specific price which is not to be reduced when the stock goes ex-dividend. Normally, the price on a limit order is reduced by the amount of the dividend when a stock goes ex-dividend. For example, if the limit price is 12, the upcoming dividend 25 cents, and the stock goes ex-dividend, the limit price on an ordinary limit order would be reduced to 11 3/4. If a DNR order is executed on or after the ex-dividend day you would not get the dividend.

**Dollar Cost Averaging**    The investment of a fixed amount of money in a particular security or fund at regular intervals, such as monthly or quarterly. Dollar cost averaging should lead to a lower per share average cost over the long run than buying an equal number of shares each time, since more shares are purchased at lower prices and fewer at higher prices.

**Double Auction**    In a conventional auction you have one auctioneer and many bidders. In the double auction, which takes place on the stock exchange trading floor, the orders of many buyers and many sellers interact at the specialist's post. Price is established by the competitive bidding and offering of buyers and sellers through their brokers. This can result in favorable prices for both buyers and sellers who use limit orders in an effort to buy below the asked price or sell above the bid.

**Double Discount**    Refers to a closed-end fund, selling at an extraordinarily wide discount, that holds securities in a market trading at a depressed multiple. Both the market and the fund are cheap. Double discounts can occur after market sell-offs as in October, 1987 or, more recently, August, 1990. Double discounted closed-end funds represent the best potential values.

**Dual Purpose Fund**    A closed-end fund with a split capital structure consisting of an equal number of *income shares* and *capital shares.* The income shares receive all the income generated by the total portfolio and the capital shares participate in all the gains and losses in market value of the portfolio. The income shares of a dual fund

are retired after a fixed period of time, like 10 or 12 years.
There are many more dual funds in the United Kingdom,
where they are called *split capital trusts*, than in the
United States.

**Duration**   A measure of the average lifetime of a bond.
For a coupon bond the duration would be less than time
to maturity. For a zero coupon bond duration would equal
time to maturity. Duration is the best indicator of the price
sensitivity of a bond (or a bond portfolio) to fluctuations
in interest rates; the longer the duration the greater the
interest rate risk.

**Efficient Market**   In an efficient market assets sell for
prices equal to their true or intrinsic values and prices adjust to new information instantaneously. Bargains and
overpriced assets don't exist in an efficient market.

**Ex-Dividend**   Ex-dividend means simply without the
dividend. On the ex-dividend day the market price and NAV
of a closed-end fund ordinarily decline by the amount of
the dividend since the purchaser is no longer entitled to
receive the upcoming dividend. For example, if Fund A
goes ex-dividend on July 31, the investor purchasing its
stock on or after July 31 would not be entitled to receive
its next dividend. The symbol "x" preceding the volume
figure for a stock (or closed-end fund) in the stock table
indicates that it is ex-dividend.

**Expense Ratio**   The total operating expenses of a fund
divided by an average of monthly net assets. Total expenses include the management fee and various administrative costs. If the fund has incurred significant interest
costs the expense ratio may be computed both with and
without the interest expense. The expense ratio for the
current and prior years can be found in a table of comparative per share data and ratios in the fund's annual and
semi-annual shareholder reports.

**Event Risk**   An unexpected occurrence, like a leveraged
buyout, that reduces the creditworthiness of a company's
debt, causing its bond prices to drop sharply. *See* Leveraged Buyout.

**Front-End Load**   An up-front sales charge levied when an investor buys shares of an open-end fund classified as a "load fund." This charge can be as high as 8.5%.

**Fundamental Analysis**   The analysis of a company's assets, sales, earnings, dividends, growth, management, industry prospects, and so on, in order to determine the intrinsic value of its stock. *See* Technical Analysis.

**Futures** (or **Futures Contract**)   A contract traded on a futures exchange that can be used by portfolio managers and others to hedge their risks or by speculators betting on price changes. Financial futures contracts are available on various stock indexes, interest rate instruments, and foreign currencies. For example, a currency futures contract could be used by a fund manager to hedge against adverse fluctuations in exchange rates between the U.S. dollar and a particular foreign currency, like the Japanese yen.

**Gearing**   A British term which refers to the use of leverage (or borrowed funds) by a portfolio manager.

**Geometric Mean**   A measure of the compound rate of return over time for an asset.

**Good-Till-Canceled Order (GTC)**   An order to remain in effect until either executed by the broker or canceled by the customer. The GTC instruction would commonly be used with limit orders and stop-loss orders. Also known as an *open order.*

**Green Shoe**   An agreement permitting members of an underwriting syndicate to buy additional shares of a publicly underwritten security at the original offering price. This option usually lasts for 30 days.

**Growth Investing**   An investment philosophy which holds that the expected future growth rate in a company's earnings is the most important consideration. Growth investors sometimes pay inflated P/Es for exciting growth situations. They may also pay excessive premiums for "hot" country funds.

**Hedge**   A technique used to insure against loss. A hedge is often implemented by taking a position in a derivative product to offset the risk of loss in a long position in the cash market. For example, if a fund manager is long Treasury bonds, Treasury bond futures contracts could be sold short to protect the long bonds against a rise in interest rates.

**Income Shares**   *See* Dual Purpose Fund.

**Inefficient Market**   In an inefficient market assets may be mispriced. Closed-end funds selling at deep discounts and overly inflated premiums are a good example. *See* Efficient Market.

**Initial Public Offering (IPO)**   An offering of stock by a company in order to gain funds needed to start a business. In the case of a closed-end fund, the money raised would ultimately be invested in a portfolio of securities conforming to the fund's objectives.

**Interest Rate Risk**   Refers to the fact that bond prices and interest rates move inversely. The risk arises from an increase in interest rates which results in a decline in bond prices.

**Internal Management Arrangement**   An arrangement used by some of the older closed-end stock funds whereby the officers and directors attend to all administrative and investment duties. This is in contrast to the vast majority of funds which are managed by an external investment adviser.

**Intrinsic Value (or Investment Value)**   What an investment is really worth independent of its current market price. Intrinsic value is the end product of the fundamental analysis of a company.

**Investment**   A long-term commitment to a sound security that generates a satisfactory income flow and will help the investor preserve capital and build wealth.

**Investment Company Act of 1940**   Federal legislation which serves as the basis for regulating investment companies. The Act requires investment companies to register with the Securities and Exchange Commission and to meet specific disclosure requirements. It also requires extensive SEC oversight of fund activities and their day-to-day operations.

**Investment Company Institute (ICI)** The national association of the U.S. investment company industry. It serves its members and monitors state and federal legislation. It also serves the investing public, news media, and government agencies as a clearinghouse of information on closed-end funds, open-end funds, and unit investment trusts.

**Investment Grade Bond** A bond rated within the top four quality categories by the rating agencies. Bonds rated triple-B or higher are considered investment grade.

**Investment Trust** The British term for closed-end fund. Early closed-end funds in the United States were also called investment trusts.

**Junk Bonds** (or **High-Yield Bonds**) Bonds rated below investment grade by the rating agencies, that is, below triple-B. Junk bonds involve greater credit risk than investment grade bonds.

**Leverage** The use of borrowed money which reduces the amount of the investor's own capital required to purchase an asset. Leverage magnifies gains and losses.

**Leveraged Buyout (LBO)** A takeover of a whole company or a division financed heavily with money borrowed from banks and/or raised through a junk bond issue. The assets of the company or division serve as collateral for the debt. If the whole company is bought out from its shareholders it would go from a public company to a private company. LBOs, which became popular in the 1980s, adversely impact existing bondholders because of the greatly increased debt burden.

**Liquidity** The more shares of a security that can be bought or sold at prices near to those of recent transactions the greater its liquidity. The higher a stock's average daily trading volume the greater its liquidity.

**Limit Order**   A customer trading order to be filled at a predetermined price or better.

**Management Fees**   The fees paid to the fund's adviser for managing the portfolio. The management fee can range between 0.2% to 1.5% of average net assets. In some cases management fees are tied to performance. Detailed information on a fund's management fee arrangement can be found in the "notes to financial statements" section of its annual and semi-annual reports.

**Margin Account**   A brokerage account that allows the customer to buy securities on credit. The amount the customer advances is known as margin; the remainder is borrowed, generally through the broker. The initial margin requirement is presently 50%. Virtually all closed-end funds are marginable; however, most brokers won't margin a stock trading under $5 per share.

**Margin Call**   When the customer's margin falls below the maintenance margin requirement, the broker would call for more equity. To meet the margin call the customer must deposit additional cash or eligible securities in the account. Otherwise, a portion or all of the account must be liquidated to satisfy the obligation. If you buy a stock on margin be sure you fully understand your broker's policy on making margin calls.

**Market Capitalization**   The total market value of a publicly-traded company; it equals the product of its per share price and the number of shares outstanding. For example, a company selling at $10 per share with 10 million shares outstanding would have a market capitalization or total market value of $100 million.

**Market Multiple**   The price-earnings ratio (or P/E) for the overall market as measured, for example, by the P/E for Standard & Poor's 500 index. The market multiple provides an important indicator of the overall level of stock prices. For instance, value investors would be eagerly searching for bargains if the market multiple were 9 times.

**Market Order**  A trading order to be filled as soon as possible at the best obtainable price. With a market order the investor generally buys at the asked price and sells at the bid unless the order is sufficiently large to cause the security's price to change.

**N-SAR Form**  A semi-annual report that funds are required to file with the Securities and Exchange Commission.

**National Association of Securities Dealers Automated Quotation System (NASDAQ)**  A computerized network of brokers and dealers making markets and trading in over-the-counter securities. NASDAQ provides current quotes on stocks in the system. About 10 closed-end funds trade in NASDAQ.

**Net Assets**  The total market value of a fund's security holdings plus its cash and minus its liabilities.

**Net Asset Value (NAV)**  The per share value of a closed- or open-end fund obtained by dividing its net assets by the number of fund shares outstanding. For closed-end funds NAV is computed at least once a week. NAV is used in measuring the fund portfolio manager's performance. *See* Net Assets.

**New York Stock Exchange (NYSE)**  Founded in 1792, the NYSE is the nation's largest stock exchange. Over 200 closed-end funds trade there. Also known as the Big Board.

**No-Load Fund**  An open-end fund which sells its shares at net asset value with no sales charge added.

**Non-Diversified Investment Company**  An investment company that chooses not to adhere to the requirements of the Investment Company Act for being a diversified investment company. Usually a non-diversified company wants to have the flexibility to take bigger positions in certain of its holdings. *See* Diversified Investment Company.

**Odd Lot** A trading order that involves less than 100 shares.

**Open-End Fund** A managed investment company that continuously offers new shares to incoming investors at current net asset value, plus any sales charge, and stands ready to redeem investor shares at NAV, net of any redemption charge.

**Option** An option is a call or a put. Options have limited lives, usually under a year, and generally trade on options exchanges. They sell for a price known as the *premium*. They are used by portfolio managers for purposes of hedging unwanted risk or generating additional income; speculators use them to try to profit from short-term price moves. A *call* gives its holder the right to buy the underlying security at a fixed price before it expires, and a *put* gives its holder the right to sell. Calls increase in value as prices rise and puts gain value as prices decline.

**Option Writing** Selling an option usually for the purpose of generating additional income from the option premiums, which belong to the seller. Option writing is more commonly used by certain of the bond funds, like the U.S. government bond funds, than by equity funds.

**Over-the-Counter Market (OTC)** A decentralized market for securities consisting of a network of brokers and dealers located throughout the country. The dealers (commonly called market makers) make markets in OTC stocks by maintaining inventories of particular stocks. The market makers buy for and sell from their inventories. They profit from the difference in prices at which they buy and sell. The bigger, more active OTC stocks are traded in NASDAQ. *See* NASDAQ and Pink Sheets.

**Pink Sheets** A daily listing of over-the-counter securities and their market makers. The stocks are generally of smaller, more obscure companies that are not part of the

NASDAQ system. The pink sheets are available at broker-age firm offices.

**Political Risk**   A risk faced by those investing in unsta-ble or vulnerable countries. Political risk is defined as un-certainty as to the ability to convert a particular foreign currency into the currency of the investor's country.

**Portfolio Manager**   A financial professional hired by a fund to manage its portfolio. The portfolio manager is em-ployed by the fund's adviser.

**Portfolio Turnover**   A measurement of the amount of trading done by a portfolio manager. Annual turnover is defined as the lesser of the values of a fund's purchases or sales of securities (excluding short-term investments) for a given year divided by an average of monthly net assets. For example, a turnover of 100% would mean that there has been one complete turnover of the securities in a year. The higher the turnover the more active the trading. The turnover ratios for the current and prior years can be found in a table of comparative per share data and ratios in the fund's annual and semi-annual shareholder reports.

**Premium**   A closed-end fund that trades at a market price greater than its NAV sells at a premium.

**Price-Earnings Ratio (P/E)**   The market price of a stock divided by the company's earnings per share. The P/E is also known as the multiple and is a measure of a stock's popularity.

**Price-NAV Ratio (P/NAV)**   The market price of a closed-end fund divided by its NAV. It serves as a valuation indi-cator. Funds selling at a discount will have P/NAV ratios below 100%; those at a premium have P/NAV ratios in ex-cess of 100%.

**Prospectus**   A document accompanying a new issue of securities that provides prospective investors with impor-tant, detailed information about that offering. It contains information on the fund's adviser, its investment objectives and policies, investment restrictions, special considerations/risk factors, and so on. The prospectus is filed by the issuer with the SEC.

**Proxy**   A signed authorization by a shareholder granting a designated party or "proxy" the power of attorney to vote that individual's shares at the shareholders' meeting.

**Proxy Contest** (or **Proxy Fight**)   A contest between opposing fund shareholder groups to obtain votes to support their respective positions. Usually this occurs when a group of adversaries tries to gain control of management and management defends itself. Management's adversaries solicit proxies to vote against the incumbents, often with the objective of open-ending or taking over a CEF. The insurgents flood shareholders with literature, phone calls, and appeals for support. Management, on the other hand, tries to obtain enough votes to prevent the adversaries from gaining control.

**Proxy Statement**   A document mailed to shareholders prior to the annual meeting that contains a discussion of items to be voted on at the meeting as well as detailed information about the company and its principal shareholders, subject to requirements of the SEC.

**Real Estate Investment Trust (REIT)**   A REIT holds a portfolio of income-producing properties like shopping centers and office buildings (equity REIT), or of real estate mortgages (mortgage REIT) or some combination of the two (hybrid REIT). REITs are publicly traded and similar to closed-end funds.

**Reinvestment Risk**   A risk facing holders of fixed income securities during periods of falling interest rates. The risk is that one will be forced to reinvest interest or principal payments at lower interest rates. For example, if you have a maturing CD which had a relatively high interest rate you are forced to reinvest at a lower rate if interest rates have fallen.

**Return on Equity (ROE)** A measure of the profitability of a company calculated by dividing net income available to its common shareholders by the common stockholders' equity.

**Rights Offering** Used by some publicly-traded companies, including closed-end funds, to raise additional capital. Existing shareholders are issued rights that they can use to purchase additional shares at a predetermined subscription price, which would usually be below the fund's market price. Royce Value Trust is an example of a CEF that has used rights offerings. If possible, fund managers like to use rights offerings when their shares trade at a premium to NAV.

**Round Lot** An order to trade 100 shares of stock or a multiple thereof.

**Securities and Exchange Commission (SEC)** A Federal agency established in 1934 under the Securities Exchange Act to regulate the issuance of new securities and the trading of existing securities on the exchanges.

**Settlement Date** The settlement date is generally five business days after the day a security is purchased or sold. The payment for securities purchased or stock certificates for securities sold must arrive at the brokerage firm's office on or before settlement date.

**Short Sale** The sale of stock (or another security) which the short seller does not own, but borrows, for the purpose of selling. If the stock price declines subsequent to the short sale the short seller can repurchase the shares at the lower price and return them to the lender. The difference between the sale price and the lower purchase price would be profit. The short seller is exposed to considerable risk since the stock price may rise.

**Size** The number of shares bid for and offered at the current quote. For example, Fund A is quoted at 10 to 10-1/8, 40 × 60. This means that 4,000 shares are being bid for at 10 and 6,000 offered at 10-1/8. The size is available for funds listed on a stock exchange like the New York Stock Exchange and changes throughout the trading day.

**Specialist**   The specialist is a key player on the floor of the stock exchange and facilitates customer trades by serving both as broker and a dealer in an assigned group of stocks. The specialist's two primary functions are: (1) to maintain a fair and orderly market; and (2) to maintain a book of limit, stop, and stop-limit orders.

**Speculation**   Usually a short-term commitment made with the hope of obtaining extraordinarily high profits. Speculations always involve high risk and speculators may lose considerable amounts of capital.

**Split Capital Trust**   The British name for dual purpose fund.

**Standard Deviation**   A statistical measure of the variability of a random variable, like total return, around its average value.

**Stop-Limit Order**   A hybrid of a stop order and a limit order; it specifies a limit price in addition to a stop price. For example, on a stop-limit order to sell, a stop price of 15 and a limit price of 14 may be stipulated. When the stop price is reached the stop-limit order is activated, becoming an ordinary limit order to be executed at the limit price or better.

**Stop Order** (or **Stop-Loss Order**)   An order to sell a stock if its price touches a predetermined value called the *stop price.* When the stop price is reached the stop-loss order is activated and becomes a market order to be executed as soon as possible at the best obtainable price.

**Street Name**   Refers to securities that are left on deposit for safekeeping with the broker and held in a securities depository, like The Depository Trust Company, in nominee name, with the customer as beneficial owner. This is in contrast to the case where the customer takes delivery and custody of the certificates which would then be registered in the customer's name. Investors who take delivery of securities must recognize that they are assuming the risk of those certificates being misplaced, lost, stolen, or destroyed.

**Technical Analysis**   In contrast to fundamental analysis, technicians use past price and volume data on individual securities or the overall stock market so as to gain insight into the demand and supply situation. They feel that their methods will allow them to predict future prices. *See* Fundamental Analysis.

**Tender Offer**   An offer to buy securities at a specific price. Can be used by a closed-end fund to buy back some of its shares, say, at NAV. Tender offers can also be used by raiders to try to acquire shares of a target company.

**Thin Market**   Securities which trade in thin markets trade inactively (in low average daily volume), are generally illiquid, and have wide bid-asked spreads.

**Time Diversification**   The idea that the longer securities are held the lower their risk, since good market periods are averaged in with bad ones.

**Top-Down Analysis**   An approach to forecasting investment performance which focuses first on the economy; next, on particular industries or sectors; and, finally, on individual companies. America's All Season Fund, The Zweig Fund, and The Zweig Total Return Fund are examples of closed-end funds which employ top-down analysis.

**Total Return**   Total return is a performance measure incorporating an investment's income and capital appreciation (or depreciation) over a specific time period. It is the best measure of an investment's past performance.

**Trades By Appointment Only**   Refers to an inactively traded security.

**Transfer Agent**   Generally a bank appointed by a closed-end fund or other securities issuer. The transfer agent maintains records of the names and addresses of registered security owners and cancels the seller's endorsed stock certificate and issues a new one to the buyer when there has been a change of ownership. The transfer agent also handles dividend reinvestment plans.

**12b-1 Plan**   Used by certain open-end funds, which authorize the management to charge against net assets a portion of the fund's sales, promotion, and distribution costs. The 12b-1 plan may result in a higher expense ratio. Named after a federal government rule, the 12b-1 fee clouds the distinction between load and no-load mutual funds.

**Underwriter**   The underwriter, usually a securities firm, brings new issues public. Generally the underwriter buys the securities from the issuer, thus guaranteeing the issuer the proceeds of sale, and resells them to the public at an offering price that includes a markup. Underwriters generally work together in underwriting syndicates.

**Unit Investment Trust (UIT)**   An unmanaged fund with a diversified portfolio, often consisting of fixed income securities like municipal bonds. Securities in a UIT are usually held till they mature, rather than being traded as they would be in a managed closed- or open-end fund. In the United Kingdom open-end funds are known as unit investment trusts.

**Value Investing**   An investment philosophy that places primary emphasis on price as opposed to forecasted earnings growth. Value investors look for solid companies at bargain prices and closed-end funds at attractive discounts.

**Warrant**   Basically, a long-term call option. Warrants generally have lives of five to ten years and are issued by companies to enable the holders to buy more stock from the company at a predetermined price. The warrant gains in value as the stock increases in price above the warrant's exercise price.

**Yield**   The yield is based on the security's current price and its actual or indicated annual income. A common definition is the dividends or interest paid per share over the last 12 months divided by the security's market price. For example, a stock trading at $20 with total annual dividends of $1 during the past 12 months would have a 5% yield.

**Yield to Maturity**  A total return that would be realized if a bond were purchased at its present price and held to maturity. In order to earn the yield to maturity the investor must also reinvest all interest payments at a rate equal to the yield to maturity. This also assumes that the issuer will make all promised payments on time and in full.

# Appendixes

# Appendix I

# *Directory of Closed-End Funds*

This directory contains 245 funds in existence as of mid-September 1990. Included are all those found in the Investment Company Institute and Lipper Analytical Services lists. Some funds that are not on either list are also included. Addresses and telephone numbers are either for the fund's headquarters office, its administrator, or its transfer agent. The exchange and stock symbol appear for each fund.

**Explanatory Notes**

Amex = American Stock Exchange;

MWST = Midwest Stock Exchange;

NASDAQ = National Association of Securities Dealers Automated Quotation System;

NYSE = New York Stock Exchange;

OTC = over-the-counter;

PR = preferred shares;

TOR = Toronto Stock Exchange.

## EQUITY-ORIENTED FUNDS

### Older Domestic Equity Funds

Adams Express Company                      NYSE
Seven St. Paul Street, Suite 1140          ADX
Baltimore, MD 21202
800-638-2479
301-752-5900


Baker, Fentress & Company                  NYSE
200 West Madison Street, Suite 3510        BKF
Chicago, IL 60606
312-236-9190


Bergstrom Capital Corporation              Amex
505 Madison Street, Suite 220              BEM
Seattle, WA 98104
206-623-7302


Central Securities Corporation             Amex
375 Park Avenue                            CET
New York, NY 10152
212-688-3011


Engex                                      Amex
44 Wall Street                             EGX
New York, NY 10005
212-495-4200


General American Investors Company         NYSE
330 Madison Avenue                         GAM
New York, NY 10017
212-916-8400


Niagara Share Corporation                  NYSE
344 Delaware Avenue                        NGS
Buffalo, NY 14202
716-856-2600

Salomon Brothers Fund                          NYSE
55 Water Street, 34th Floor                    SBF
New York, NY 10041
800-725-6666
212-668-8579

Source Capital                                 NYSE
10301 West Pico Boulevard                       SOR
Los Angeles, CA 90064
213-277-4900

Spectra Fund                                   OTC (Pink
75 Maiden Lane                                   Sheets)
New York, NY 10038
800-223-3810
212-806-8800

Tri-Continental Corporation                    NYSE
130 Liberty Street                             TY
New York, NY 10006
800-221-7844
212-488-0384

---

## The Personality Funds

Blue Chip Value Fund                           NYSE
633 Seventeenth Street, Suite 1800             BLU
Denver, CO 80270
303-293-2020

Cypress Fund                                   Amex
Provident Financial Processing Corp.           WJR
103 Bellevue Parkway, 3rd Floor
Wilmington, DE 19809
800-553-8080/302-791-1047

Gabelli Equity Trust                           NYSE
8 Sound Shore Drive                            GAB
Greenwich, CT 06830
800-422-3554/203-625-0665

Growth Stock Outlook Trust                         NYSE
4405 East-West Highway, Suite 305                  GSO
Bethesda, MD 20814
301-986-5866

Inefficient-Market Fund                            Amex
1345 Avenue of the Americas                        IMF
New York, NY 10105
212-698-3412

Liberty All-Star Equity Fund                       NYSE
Federal Reserve Plaza                              USA
Boston, MA 02210
800-542-3863/617-722-6000

Morgan Grenfell SMALLCap Fund                      NYSE
885 Third Avenue, Suite 1740                       MGC
New York, NY 10022
212-230-2600

Nicholas-Applegate Growth Equity Fund              NYSE
Prudential Mutual Fund Management, Inc.            GEF
One Seaport Plaza
New York, NY 10292
212-214-3332

Royce Value Trust                                  NYSE
1414 Avenue of the Americas                        RVT
New York, NY 10019
800-221-4268
212-355-7311

Z-Seven Fund                                       NASDAQ
2302 West Monterey Circle                          ZSEV
Mesa, AZ 85202
602-897-6214

Zweig Fund                                         NYSE
900 Third Avenue                                   ZF
New York, NY 10022
212-486-7110

## Dual Purpose Funds

| | |
|---|---|
| Convertible Holdings | NYSE |
| Princeton Administrators, Inc. | CNV |
| P.O. Box 9011 | CNV PR |
| Princeton, NJ 08543-9011 | |
| 800-543-6217/609-282-2800 | |

| | |
|---|---|
| Counsellors Tandem Securities Fund | NYSE |
| 466 Lexington Avenue | CTF |
| New York, NY 10017-3147 | CTF PR |
| 800-888-6878 | |
| 212-878-0600 | |

| | |
|---|---|
| Gemini II | NYSE |
| The Vanguard Group, Inc. | GMI |
| Vanguard Financial Center | GMI PR |
| Valley Forge, PA 19482 | |
| 800-662-7447/215-648-6000 | |

| | |
|---|---|
| Hampton Utilities Trust | Amex |
| 777 Mariners Island Boulevard | HU |
| San Mateo, CA 94404 | HU PR |
| 800-342-5236/415-570-3000 | |

| | |
|---|---|
| Quest For Value Dual Purpose Fund | NYSE |
| Oppenheimer Tower | KFV |
| World Financial Center | KFV PR |
| New York, NY 10281 | |
| 800-525-1103/212-667-7486 | |

---

## Sector Equity Funds

| | |
|---|---|
| ASA Limited | NYSE |
| c/o Lyons Associates | ASA |
| P.O. Box 269 | |
| Florham Park, NJ 07932 | |
| 201-377-3535 | |

Alliance Global Environment Fund               NYSE
Alliance Capital                               AEF
1345 Avenue of the Americas
New York, NY 10105
800-227-4618/212-969-1000


BGR Precious Metals                            TOR
The Dynamic Building                           BPT.A
6 Adelaide Street East, 8th Floor
Toronto, Ontario Canada M5C 1H6
416-365-5129


Capital Southwest Corporation                  NASDAQ
12900 Preston Road, Suite 700                  CSWC
Dallas, TX 75230
214-233-8242
(A venture capital investment company)


Central Fund of Canada Limited                 Amex
55 Broadleaf Crescent                          CEF
P.O. Box 7319
Ancaster, Ontario
Canada L9G 3N6
416-648-7878


Dover Regional Financial Shares                NASDAQ
1521 Locust Street, Suite 500                  DVRFS
Philadelphia, PA 19102
800-468-4017/215-735-5001


Duff & Phelps Utilities Income                 NYSE
55 East Monroe Street                          DNP
Chicago, IL 60603
312-368-5510


First Financial Fund                           NYSE
Prudential Mutual Fund Management, Inc.        FF
One Seaport Plaza
New York, NY 10292
212-214-3332

Fund Alabama                                    NASDAQ
1500 AmSouth-Sonat Tower                        FALI
Birmingham, AL 35203
205-252-5900


Global Utility Fund                             NYSE
Prudential Mutual Fund Management, Inc.         GL
One Seaport Plaza
New York, NY 10292
212-214-3332


H&Q Healthcare Investors                        NYSE
50 Rowes Wharf, 4th Floor                       HQH
Boston, MA 02110
617-574-0500


Meeschaert Gold and Currency Trust              MWST
28 Hill Farm Road                               GCT
St. Johnsbury, VT 05819
802-748-2400


Patriot Premium Dividend Fund                   NYSE
211 Congress Street                             PDF
Boston, MA 02110
800-843-0090
617-426-3310


Patriot Premium Dividend Fund II                NYSE
211 Congress Street                             PDT
Boston, MA 02110
800-843-0090
617-426-3310


Patriot Select Dividend Trust                   NYSE
211 Congress Street                             DIV
Boston, MA 02110
800-843-0090
617-426-3310

Petroleum & Resources Corporation            NYSE
Seven St. Paul Street, Suite 1140            PEO
Baltimore, MD 21202
800-638-2479
301-752-5900


Pilgrim Regional Bank Shares                 NYSE
10100 Santa Monica Boulevard                 PBS
Los Angeles, CA 90067
800-331-1080/816-474-8786


Putnam Dividend Income Fund                  NYSE
One Post Office Square                        PDI
Boston, MA 02109
800-634-1587/617-292-1000


Real Estate Securities Income Fund           Amex
757 Third Avenue                             RIF
New York, NY 10017
212-832-3232


Southeastern Savings Institutions Fund       NASDAQ
P.O. Box 1012                                SSIF
Charlotte, NC 28201-1012
704-379-9097


Templeton Global Utilities                   Amex
700 Central Avenue                           TGU
St. Petersburg, FL 33701-3628
800-237-0738
813-823-8712

---

## Single-Country Funds

Austria Fund                                 NYSE
Alliance Capital                             OST
1345 Avenue of the Americas
New York, NY 10105
800-227-4618/212-969-1000

Brazil Fund                                        NYSE
c/o The Scudder Funds                              BEF
P.O. Box 9046
Boston, MA 02205-9046
800-225-2470/617-330-5602


Chile Fund                                         NYSE
One Citicorp Center, 58th Floor                    CH
153 East 53rd Street
New York, NY 10022
212-832-2626


Emerging Germany Fund                              NYSE
One Battery Park Plaza                             FRG
New York, NY 10004
212-363-5100


First Australian Fund                              Amex
Prudential Mutual Fund Management, Inc.            IAF
One Seaport Plaza
New York, NY 10292
212-214-3332


First Iberian Fund                                 Amex
Prudential Mutual Fund Management, Inc.            IBF
One Seaport Plaza
New York, NY 10292
212-214-3332


First Philippine Fund                              NYSE
767 Third Avenue                                   FPF
New York, NY 10017
212-759-3339


France Growth Fund                                 NYSE
Provident Financial Processing Corp.               FRF
103 Bellevue Parkway, 3rd Floor
Wilmington, DE 19809
800-553-8080/302-791-1047

Future Germany Fund                         NYSE
Investors Bank & Trust Co.                  FGF
P.O. Box 1537
Boston, MA 02205-1537
800-642-0144/617-330-6044

Germany Fund                                NYSE
Investors Bank & Trust Co.                  GER
P.O. Box 1537
Boston, MA 02205-1537
800-642-0144/617-330-6044

Growth Fund of Spain                        NYSE
120 South LaSalle Street                    GSP
Chicago, IL 60603
800-422-2848/816-474-8786

India Growth Fund                           NYSE
Provident Financial Processing Corp.        IGF
103 Bellevue Parkway, 3rd Floor
Wilmington, DE 19809
800-553-8080/302-791-1047

Indonesia Fund                              NYSE
One Citicorp Center, 58th Floor             IF
153 East 53rd Street
New York, NY 10022
212-832-2626

Irish Investment Fund                       NYSE
The Vanguard Group, Inc.                    IRL
Vanguard Financial Center
Valley Forge, PA 19482
800-332-5577/215-669-8524

Italy Fund                                  NYSE
c/o Shearson Lehman Hutton                  ITA
31 West 52nd Street, 11th Floor
New York, NY 10019
212-767-3034

Jakarta Growth Fund                           NYSE
180 Maiden Lane, 29th Floor                    JGF
New York, NY 10038
800-833-0018/212-208-2604


Japan OTC Equity Fund                          NYSE
180 Maiden Lane, 29th Floor                    JOF
New York, NY 10038
800-833-0018/212-208-2604


Korea Fund                                     NYSE
c/o The Scudder Funds                           KF
P.O. Box 9046
Boston, MA 02205-9046
800-225-2470/617-330-5602


Malaysia Fund                                  NYSE
The Vanguard Group, Inc.                        MF
Vanguard Financial Center
Valley Forge, PA 19482
800-332-5577/215-669-8513


Mexico Equity & Income Fund                    NYSE
World Financial Center                         MXE
200 Liberty Street, 39th Floor
New York, NY 10281
212-667-5000


Mexico Fund                                    NYSE
342 Madison Avenue, Suite 909                  MXF
New York, NY 10173
212-986-5551


New Germany Fund                               NYSE
Investors Bank & Trust Co.                      GF
P.O. Box 1537
Boston, MA 02205-1537
800-642-0144/617-330-6044

Portugal Fund                                          NYSE
One Citicorp Center, 58th Floor                        PGF
153 East 53rd Street
New York, NY 10022
212-832-2626

ROC Taiwan Fund                                        NYSE
100 East Pratt Street                                  ROC
Baltimore, MD 21202
800-343-9567/301-625-6761

Singapore Fund                                         NYSE
c/o Daiwa Securities Trust Company                     SGF
One Evertrust Plaza
Jersey City, NJ 07302
800-933-3440/201-915-3025

Spain Fund                                             NYSE
Alliance Capital                                       SNF
1345 Avenue of the Americas
New York, NY 10105
800-227-4618/212-969-1000

Swiss Helvetia Fund                                    NYSE
521 Fifth Avenue                                       SWZ
New York, NY 10175
212-867-7660

Taiwan Fund                                            NYSE
c/o Fidelity Investments                               TWN
82 Devonshire Street
Boston, MA 02109
800-544-4774/617-570-6200

Thai Capital Fund                                      NYSE
Princeton Administrators, Inc.                         TC
P.O. Box 9011
Princeton, NJ 08543-9011
800-543-6217/609-282-2800

Thai Fund                                                    NYSE
The Vanguard Group, Inc.                                     TTF
Vanguard Financial Center
Valley Forge, PA 19482
800-332-5577/215-669-8513

Turkish Investment Fund                                      NYSE
The Vanguard Group, Inc.                                     TKF
Vanguard Financial Center
Valley Forge, PA 19482
800-332-5577/215-669-8513

United Kingdom Fund                                          NYSE
245 Park Avenue, 13th Floor                                  UKM
New York, NY 10167
212-272-6404

---

## Multi-Country Funds

Alliance New Europe Fund                                     NYSE
Alliance Capital                                             ANE
1345 Avenue of the Americas
New York, NY 10105
800-227-4618/212-969-1000

Asia Pacific Fund                                            NYSE
Prudential Mutual Fund Management, Inc.                      APB
One Seaport Plaza
New York, NY 10292
212-214-3332

Clemente Global Growth Fund                                  NYSE
767 Third Avenue                                             CLM
New York, NY 10017
212-759-3339

Europe Fund                                                  NYSE
Princeton Administrators, Inc.                               EF
P.O. Box 9011
Princeton, NJ 08543-9011
800-543-6217/609-282-2800

European Warrant Fund                               NYSE
330 Madison Avenue                                  EWF
New York, NY 10017
212-949-9055


G.T. Greater Europe Fund                            NYSE
50 California Street, 27th Floor                     GTF
San Francisco, CA 94111
800-824-1580/415-392-6181


Latin America Investment Fund                       NYSE
One Citicorp Center, 58th Floor                     LAM
153 East 53rd Street
New York, NY 10022
212-832-2626


Pacific-European Growth Fund                        Amex
Piper Capital Management                            PEF
Piper Jaffray Tower
222 South Ninth Street
Minneapolis, MN 55402
800-333-6000 (Ext. 6426)/612-342-6426


Scudder New Asia Fund                               NYSE
c/o The Scudder Funds                               SAF
P.O. Box 9046
Boston, MA 02205-9046
800-225-2470/617-330-5602


Scudder New Europe Fund                             NYSE
c/o The Scudder Funds                               NEF
P.O. Box 9046
Boston, MA 02205-9046
800-225-2470/617-330-5602


Templeton Emerging Markets Fund                     NYSE
700 Central Avenue                                  EMF
St. Petersburg, FL 33701-3628
800-237-0738
813-823-8712

Worldwide Value Fund                     NYSE
P.O. Box 1476                            VLU
111 South Calvert Street
Baltimore, MD 21203
301-539-3400

---

## FIXED-INCOME FUNDS

### Investment Grade Bond Funds

American Capital Bond Fund               NYSE
2800 Post Oak Boulevard                  ACB
Houston, TX 77056
800-421-9696/713-993-0500


AMEV Securities                          NYSE
P.O. Box 64284                           AMV
St. Paul, MN 55164
800-800-2638 (Ext. 4274)
612-872-2638


Bunker Hill Income Securities            NYSE
P.O. Box 70220                           BHL
Pasadena, CA 91117-7220
213-229-1290


Circle Income Shares                     NASDAQ
P.O. Box 44027                           CINS
Indianapolis, IN 46244
317-321-8180


CNA Income Shares                        NYSE
CNA Plaza                                CNN
Chicago, IL 60685
312-822-4181

Current Income Shares                          NYSE
445 South Figueroa Street                      CUR
Los Angeles, CA 90071
213-236-7096


1838 Bond-Debenture Trading Fund               NYSE
One Meridian Plaza, 32nd Floor                 BDF
Philadelphia, PA 19102-2468
215-963-3559


Excelsior Income Shares                        NYSE
114 West 47th Street, 10th Floor               EIS
New York, NY 10036-1532
212-852-3732


First Boston Income Fund                       NYSE
The Vanguard Group, Inc.                       FBF
Vanguard Financial Center
Valley Forge, PA 19482
800-332-5577/215-669-8522


Fort Dearborn Income Securities                NYSE
One North State Street                         FTD
Suite 0123
Chicago, IL 60602
312-346-0676


Hatteras Income Securities                     NYSE
One NCNB Plaza                                 HAT
P.O. Box 30120
Charlotte, NC 28255
704-333-7808


INA Investment Securities                      NYSE
P.O. Box 13856                                 IIS
Philadelphia, PA 19192
413-784-0100

Independence Square Income Securities          NASDAQ
Provident Financial Processing Corp.           ISIS
103 Bellevue Parkway, 3rd Floor
Wilmington, DE 19809
800-553-8080/302-791-1047


InterCapital Income Securities                 NYSE
Dean Witter Reynolds, Inc.                     ICB
InterCapital Division
Two World Trade Center, 72nd Floor
New York, NY 10048
800-869-3863/212-392-2550


John Hancock Income Securities Trust           NYSE
101 Huntington Avenue                          JHS
Boston, MA 02199
617-375-1500


John Hancock Investors Trust                   NYSE
101 Huntington Avenue                          JHI
Boston, MA 02199
617-375-1500


Montgomery Street Income Securities            NYSE
c/o The Scudder Funds                          MTS
P.O. Box 9046
Boston, MA 02205-9046
800-225-2470/617-330-5602


Mutual of Omaha Interest Shares                NYSE
10235 Regency Circle                           MUO
Omaha, NE 68114
402-397-8555


Pacific American Income Shares                  NYSE
P.O. Box 983                                    PAI
Pasadena, CA 91102
818-584-4300

Transamerica Income Shares                  NYSE
P.O. Box 2438                               TAI
Los Angeles, CA 90051
213-742-4141


Vestaur Securities                          NYSE
Center Square, West 11th Floor              VES
P.O. Box 7558
Philadelphia, PA 19101-7558
215-567-3969

---

## Direct Placement Funds

Lincoln National Income Fund                NYSE
1300 South Clinton Street                   LND
Fort Wayne, IN 46801
219-455-2210
(Now focuses more on publicly-traded
issues)


MassMutual Corporate Investors              NYSE
1295 State Street                           MCI
Springfield, MA 01111
413-788-8411


MassMutual Participation Investors          NYSE
1295 State Street                           MPV
Springfield, MA 01111
413-788-8411


Revere Fund                                 NASDAQ
575 Fifth Avenue, 17th Floor                PREV
New York, NY 10017
212-808-9090

---

## High-Yield Corporate Bond Funds

CIGNA High Income Shares                    NYSE
1350 Main Street                            HIS
Springfield, MA 01103
413-784-0100

CIM High Yield Securities                          Amex
Shareholder Services Group                         CIM
P.O. Box 1376
Boston, MA 02104
(Attn: Corporate securities)
800-331-1710

Colonial Intermediate High Income Fund             NYSE
One Financial Center                               CIF
Boston, MA 02111
800-248-2828/617-426-3750

High Income Advantage Trust                        NYSE
Dean Witter Reynolds, Inc.                         YLD
InterCapital Division
Two World Trade Center, 72nd Floor
New York, NY 10048
800-869-3863/212-392-2550

High Income Advantage Trust II                     NYSE
Dean Witter Reynolds, Inc.                         YLT
InterCapital Division
Two World Trade Center, 72nd Floor
New York, NY 10048
800-869-3863/212-392-2550

High Income Advantage Trust III                    NYSE
Dean Witter Reynolds, Inc.                         YLH
InterCapital Division
Two World Trade Center, 72nd Floor
New York, NY 10048
800-869-3863/212-392-2550

High Yield Income Fund                             NYSE
Prudential Mutual Fund Management, Inc.            HYI
One Seaport Plaza
New York, NY 10292
212-214-3332

High Yield Plus Fund                               NYSE
Prudential Mutual Fund Management, Inc.            HYP
One Seaport Plaza
New York, NY 10292
212-214-3332

Kemper High Income Trust                    NYSE
120 South LaSalle Street                    KHI
Chicago, IL 60603
800-422-2848/816-474-8786


New America High Income Fund                NYSE
10 Liberty Square                           HYB
Boston, MA 02109
617-426-0182


Prospect Street High Income Portfolio       NYSE
One Financial Center, 37th Floor            PHY
Boston, MA 02111
617-350-5718


USF&G Pacholder Fund                        NYSE
The Spectrum Office Tower                   PHF
11260 Chester Road
Cincinnati, OH 45246
513-771-5150


Van Kampen Merritt Intermediate Term        NYSE
    High Income Trust                       VIT
1001 Warrenville Road
Lisle, IL 60532
800-341-2929/708-719-1000


Van Kampen Merritt Limited Term High         NYSE
    Income Trust                            VLT
1001 Warrenville Road                       VLT PR
Lisle, IL 60532
800-341-2929/708-719-1000


Zenix Income Fund                           NYSE
c/o Shearson Lehman Advisors                ZIF
Two World Trade Center, 101st Floor
New York, NY 10048
212-298-7350

## U.S. Government Bond Funds

| | |
|---|---|
| ACM Government Income Fund | NYSE |
| Alliance Capital | ACG |
| 1345 Avenue of the Americas | |
| New York, NY 10105 | |
| 800-227-4618/212-969-1000 | |

| | |
|---|---|
| ACM Government Opportunity Fund | NYSE |
| Alliance Capital | AOF |
| 1345 Avenue of the Americas | |
| New York, NY 10105 | |
| 800-227-4618/212-969-1000 | |

| | |
|---|---|
| ACM Government Securities Fund | NYSE |
| Alliance Capital | GSF |
| 1345 Avenue of the Americas | |
| New York, NY 10105 | |
| 800-227-4618/212-969-1000 | |

| | |
|---|---|
| ACM Government Spectrum Fund | NYSE |
| Alliance Capital | SI |
| 1345 Avenue of the Americas | |
| New York, NY 10105 | |
| 800-227-4618/212-969-1000 | |

| | |
|---|---|
| ACM Managed Income Fund | NYSE |
| Alliance Capital | AMF |
| 1345 Avenue of the Americas | |
| New York, NY 10105 | |
| 800-227-4618/212-969-1000 | |

| | |
|---|---|
| American Government Income Fund | NYSE |
| Piper Capital Management | AGF |
| Piper Jaffray Tower | |
| 222 South Ninth Street | |
| Minneapolis, MN 55402 | |
| 800-333-6000 (Ext. 6426)/612-342-6426 | |

American Government Income Portfolio      NYSE
Piper Capital Management                   AAF
Piper Jaffray Tower
222 South Ninth Street
Minneapolis, MN 55402
800-333-6000 (Ext. 6426)/612-342-6426

American Opportunity Income Fund          NYSE
Piper Capital Management                   OIF
Piper Jaffray Tower
222 South Ninth Street
Minneapolis, MN 55402
800-333-6000 (Ext. 6426)/612-342-6426

Dean Witter Government Income Trust        NYSE
Dean Witter Reynolds, Inc.                 GVT
InterCapital Division
Two World Trade Center, 72nd Floor
New York, NY 10048
800-869-3863/212-392-2550

Dreyfus Strategic Government Income        NYSE
144 Glenn Curtiss Boulevard                DSI
Uniondale, NY 11556-0144
800-334-6899/718-895-1396
(Broker inquiries only)

Kemper Intermediate Government Trust       NYSE
120 South LaSalle Street                   KGT
Chicago, IL 60603
800-422-2848/816-474-8786

MFS Government Markets Income Trust        NYSE
500 Boylston Street                        MGF
Boston, MA 02116
800-225-2606/617-954-5000

Putnam Intermediate Government Income      NYSE
   Trust                                   PGT
One Post Office Square
Boston, MA 02109
800-634-1587/617-292-1000

## Mortgage-Backed Securities Funds

| | |
|---|---|
| American Adjustable Rate Term Trust-<br>1995<br>Piper Capital Management<br>Piper Jaffray Tower<br>222 South Ninth Street<br>Minneapolis, MN 55402<br>800-333-6000 (Ext. 6426)/612-342-6426 | NYSE<br>ADJ |
| American Adjustable Rate Term Trust-<br>1996<br>Piper Capital Management<br>Piper Jaffray Tower<br>222 South Ninth Street<br>Minneapolis, MN 55402<br>800-333-6000 (Ext. 6426)/612-342-6426 | NYSE<br>BDJ |
| American Government Term Trust<br>Piper Capital Management<br>Piper Jaffray Tower<br>222 South Ninth Street<br>Minneapolis, MN 55402<br>800-333-6000 (Ext. 6426)/612-342-6426 | NYSE<br>AGT |
| Blackstone Advantage Term Trust<br>Prudential Mutual Fund Management, Inc.<br>One Seaport Plaza<br>New York, NY 10292<br>212-214-3332 | NYSE<br>BAT |
| Blackstone Income Trust<br>Prudential Mutual Fund Management, Inc.<br>One Seaport Plaza<br>New York, NY 10292<br>212-214-3332 | NYSE<br>BKT |
| Blackstone Target Term Trust<br>Prudential Mutual Fund Management, Inc.<br>One Seaport Plaza<br>New York, NY 10292<br>212-214-3332 | NYSE<br>BTT |

Franklin Principal Maturity Trust          NYSE
777 Mariners Island Boulevard              FPT
San Mateo, CA 94404
800-342-5236/415-570-3000

Hyperion Total Return Fund                 NYSE
Princeton Administrators, Inc.             HTR
P.O. Box 9011
Princeton, NJ 08543-9011
800-543-6217/609-282-2800

Lomas Mortgage Securities Fund             NYSE
Princeton Administrators, Inc.             LSF
P.O. Box 9011
Princeton, NJ 08543-9011
800-543-6217/609-282-2800

RAC Income Fund                            NYSE
10221 Wincopin Circle                      RMF
Columbia, MD 21044
301-730-6851

---

**Global and International Bond Funds**

ACM Managed Multi-Market Fund             NYSE
Alliance Capital                          MMF
1345 Avenue of the Americas
New York, NY 10105
800-227-4618/212-969-1000

First Australia Prime Income Fund         Amex
Prudential Mutual Fund Management, Inc.   FAX
One Seaport Plaza
New York, NY 10292
212-214-3332

Global Government Plus Fund               NYSE
Prudential Mutual Fund Management, Inc.   GOV
One Seaport Plaza
New York, NY 10292
212-214-3332

Global Income Plus Fund                                 NYSE
Provident Financial Processing Corp.                    GLI
103 Bellevue Parkway, 3rd Floor
Wilmington, DE 19809
800-553-8080/302-791-1047


Global Yield Fund                                       NYSE
Prudential Mutual Fund Management, Inc.                 PGY
One Seaport Plaza
New York, NY 10292
212-214-3332


Kleinwort Benson Australian Income Fund                 NYSE
200 Park Avenue, 24th Floor                             KBA
New York, NY 10166
800-237-4218
212-687-2515


Templeton Global Governments Income                     NYSE
    Trust                                               TGG
700 Central Avenue
St. Petersburg, FL 33701-3628
800-237-0738
813-823-8712


Templeton Global Income Trust                           NYSE
700 Central Avenue                                      GIM
St. Petersburg, FL 33701-3628
800-237-0738
813-823-8712


World Income Fund                                       Amex
Princeton Administrators, Inc.                          WOI
P.O. Box 9011
Princeton, NJ 08543-9011
800-543-6217/609-282-2800

## Multi-Sector Bond Funds

American Capital Income Trust                NYSE
2800 Post Oak Boulevard                      ACD
Houston, TX 77056
800-421-9696/713-993-0500


Colonial Intermarket Income Trust I          NYSE
One Financial Center                         CMK
Boston, MA 02111
800-248-2828/617-426-3750


First Boston Strategic Income Fund           NYSE
The Vanguard Group, Inc.                     FBI
Vanguard Financial Center
Valley Forge, PA 19482
800-332-5577/215-669-8522


Kemper Multi-Market Income Trust             NYSE
120 South LaSalle Street                     KMM
Chicago, IL 60603
800-422-2848/816-474-8786


MFS Charter Income Trust                     NYSE
500 Boyslton Street                          MCR
Boston, MA 02116
800-225-2606/617-954-5000


MFS Intermediate Income Trust                NYSE
500 Boylston Street                          MIN
Boston, MA 02116
800-225-2606/617-954-5000


MFS Multimarket Income Trust                 NYSE
500 Boylston Street                          MMT
Boston, MA 02116
800-225-2606/617-954-5000

MFS Multimarket Total Return Trust          NYSE
500 Boylston Street                          MFT
Boston, MA 02116
800-225-2606/617-954-5000


Oppenheimer Multi-Government Trust          NYSE
Two World Trade Center                       OGT
New York, NY 10048-0669
800-525-7048/212-323-0200


Oppenheimer Multi-Sector Income Trust       NYSE
Two World Trade Center                       OMS
New York, NY 10048-0669
800-525-7048/212-323-0200


Prudential Intermediate Income Fund         NYSE
Prudential Mutual Fund Management, Inc.      PIF
One Seaport Plaza
New York, NY 10292
212-214-3332


Putnam Diversified Premium Income Trust     NYSE
One Post Office Square                       PDN
Boston, MA 02109
800-634-1587/617-292-1000


Putnam Master Income Trust                  NYSE
One Post Office Square                       PMT
Boston, MA 02109
800-634-1587/617-292-1000


Putnam Master Intermediate Income Trust     NYSE
One Post Office Square                       PIM
Boston, MA 02109
800-634-1587/617-292-1000


Putnam Premier Income Trust                 NYSE
One Post Office Square                       PPT
Boston, MA 02109
800-634-1587/617-292-1000

State Mutual Securities Trust                  NYSE
440 Lincoln Street                            SMS
Worcester, MA 01605
508-852-1000 (Ext. 2299)


USLIFE Income Fund                            NYSE
NYSE 125 Maiden Lane                          UIF
New York, NY 10038-4985
212-709-6000

---

## Flexible Portfolio Funds

America's All Season Fund                     NASDAQ
422 West Fairbanks Avenue, Suite 300          FUND
Winter Park, FL 32789
800-333-4222
407-629-1400


Comstock Partners Strategy Fund               NYSE
Princeton Administrators, Inc.                CPF
P.O. Box 9011
Princeton, NJ 08543-9011
800-543-6217/609-282-2800


Flexible Bond Trust                           Amex
Provident Financial Processing Corp.          FLX
103 Bellevue Parkway, 3rd Floor
Wilmington, DE 19809
800-553-8080/302-791-1047


Franklin Multi Income Trust                   NYSE
777 Mariners Island Boulevard                 FMI
San Mateo, CA 94404
800-342-5236/415-570-3000


Franklin Universal Trust                      NYSE
777 Mariners Island Boulevard                 FT
San Mateo, CA 94404
800-342-5236/415-570-3000

MFS Income & Opportunity Trust     NYSE
500 Boylston Street     MFO
Boston, MA 02116
800-225-2606/617-954-5000

MFS Special Value Trust     NYSE
500 Boylston Street     MFV
Boston, MA 02116
800-225-2606/617-954-5000

Zweig Total Return Fund     NYSE
900 Third Avenue     ZTR
New York, NY 10022
212-486-7110

**Municipal Bond Funds**

Allstate Municipal Income Opportunities     NYSE
  Trust     AMO
Dean Witter Reynolds, Inc.
InterCapital Division
Two World Trade Center, 72nd Floor
New York, NY 10048
800-869-3863/212-392-2550

Allstate Municipal Income Opportunities     NYSE
  Trust II     AOT
Dean Witter Reynolds, Inc.
InterCapital Division
Two World Trade Center, 72nd Floor
New York, NY 10048
800-869-3863/212-392-2550

Allstate Municipal Income Opportunities     NYSE
  Trust III     AIO
Dean Witter Reynolds, Inc.
InterCapital Division
Two World Trade Center, 72nd Floor
New York, NY 10048
800-869-3863/212-392-2550

Allstate Municipal Income Trust                      NYSE
Dean Witter Reynolds, Inc.                           ALM
InterCapital Division
Two World Trade Center, 72nd Floor
New York, NY 10048
800-869-3863/212-392-2550

Allstate Municipal Income Trust II                   NYSE
Dean Witter Reynolds, Inc.                           ALT
InterCapital Division
Two World Trade Center, 72nd Floor
New York, NY 10048
800-869-3863/212-392-2550

Allstate Municipal Income Trust III                  NYSE
Dean Witter Reynolds, Inc.                           ALL
InterCapital Division
Two World Trade Center, 72nd Floor
New York, NY 10048
800-869-3863/212-392-2550

Allstate Municipal Premium Income Trust              NYSE
Dean Witter Reynolds, Inc.                           ALI
InterCapital Division
Two World Trade Center, 72nd Floor
New York, NY 10048
800-869-3863/212-392-2550

Apex Municipal Fund                                  NYSE
Princeton Administrators, Inc.                       APX
P.O. Box 9011
Princeton, NJ 08543–9011
800-543-6217/609-282-2800

Colonial High Income Municipal Trust                 NYSE
One Financial Center                                 CXE
Boston, MA 02111
800-248-2828/617-426-3750

Colonial Investment Grade Municipal Trust            NYSE
One Financial Center                                 CXH
Boston, MA 02111
800-248-2828/617-426-3750

Colonial Municipal Income Trust                    NYSE
One Financial Center                               CMU
Boston, MA 02111
800-248-2828/617-426-3750


Dreyfus California Municipal Income                Amex
144 Glenn Curtiss Boulevard                        DCM
Uniondale, NY 11556-0144
800-334-6899/718-895-1396
(Broker inquiries only)


Dreyfus Municipal Income                           Amex
144 Glenn Curtiss Boulevard                        DMF
Uniondalc, NY 11556-0144
800-334-6899/718-895-1396
(Broker inquiries only)


Dreyfus New York Municipal Income                  Amex
144 Glenn Curtiss Boulevard                        DNM
Uniondale, NY 11556-0144
800-334-6899/718-895-1396
(Broker inquiries only)


Dreyfus Strategic Municipal Bond Fund              NYSE
144 Glenn Curtiss Boulevard                        DSM
Uniondale, NY 11556-0144
800-334-6899/718-895-1396
(Broker inquiries only)


Dreyfus Strategic Municipals                       NYSE
144 Glenn Curtiss Boulevard                        LEO
Uniondale, NY 11556-0144
800-334-6899/718-895-1396
(Broker inquiries only)


Kemper Municipal Income Trust                      NYSE
120 South LaSalle Street                           KTF
Chicago, IL 60603
800-422-2848/816-474-8786

Kemper Strategic Municipal Income Trust    NYSE
120 South LaSalle Street                   KSM
Chicago, IL 60603
800-422-2848/816-474-8786


MFS Municipal Income Trust                 NYSE
500 Boylston Street                        MFM
Boston, MA 02116
800-225-2606/617-954-5000


MuniEnhanced Fund                          NYSE
Princeton Administrators, Inc.             MEN
P.O. Box 9011
Princeton, NJ 08543-9011
800-543-6217/609-282-2800


Municipal High Income Fund                 NYSE
c/o Shearson Lehman Advisors               MHF
Two World Trade Center, 101st Floor
New York, NY 10048
212-298-7350


MuniInsured Fund                           Amex
Princeton Administrators, Inc.             MIF
P.O. Box 9011
Princeton, NJ 08543-9011
800-543-6217/609-282-2800


MuniVest Fund                              Amex
Princeton Administrators, Inc.             MVF
P.O. Box 9011
Princeton, NJ 08543-9011
800-543-6217/609-282-2800


New York Tax-Exempt Income Fund            Amex
Oppenheimer Fund Management, Inc.          XTX
Two World Trade Center, 34th Floor
New York, NY 10048-0669
800-255-2750/212-323-0200

Nuveen California Municipal Income Fund          NYSE
333 West Wacker Drive                            NCM
Chicago, IL 60606-1286
312-917-7810


Nuveen Municipal Market Opportunity              NYSE
  Fund                                           NCO
333 West Wacker Drive
Chicago, IL 60606-1286
312-917-7810


Nuveen California Municipal Value Fund           NYSE
333 West Wacker Drive                            NCA
Chicago, IL 60606-1286
312-917-7810


Nuveen California Performance Plus               NYSE
  Municipal Fund                                 NCP
333 West Wacker Drive
Chicago, IL 60606-1286
312-917-7810


Nuveen Investment Quality Municipal              NYSE
  Fund                                           NQM
333 West Wacker Drive
Chicago, IL 60606-1286
312-917-7810


Nuveen Municipal Advantage Fund                  NYSE
333 West Wacker Drive                            NMA
Chicago, IL 60606-1286
312-917-7810


Nuveen Municipal Income Fund                     NYSE
333 West Wacker Drive                            NMI
Chicago, IL 60606-1286
312-917-7810

Nuveen Municipal Market Opportunity          NYSE
    Fund                                     NMO
333 West Wacker Drive
Chicago, IL 60606-1286
312-917-7810

Nuveen Municipal Value Fund                  NYSE
333 West Wacker Drive                        NUV
Chicago, IL 60606-1286
312-917-7810

Nuveen New York Municipal Value Fund         NYSE
333 West Wacker Drive                        NNY
Chicago, IL 60606-1286
312-917-7810

Nuveen New York Municipal Income Fund        Amex
333 West Wacker Drive                        NNM
Chicago, IL 60606-1286
312-917-7810

Nuveen New York Municipal Market             NYSE
    Opportunity Fund                         NCP
333 West Wacker Drive
Chicago, IL 60606-1286
312-917-7810

Nuveen New York Performance Plus             NYSE
    Municipal Fund                           NNP
333 West Wacker Drive
Chicago, IL 60606-1286
312-917-7810

Nuveen Performance Plus Municipal Fund       NYSE
333 West Wacker Drive                        NPP
Chicago, IL 60606-1286
312-917-7810

Nuveen Premium Income Municipal Fund         NYSE
333 West Wacker Drive                        NPI
Chicago, IL 60606-1286
312-917-7810

Putnam High Yield Municipal Trust     NYSE
One Post Office Square     PYM
Boston, MA 02109
800-634-1587/617-292-1000


Putnam Investment Grade Municipal Trust     NYSE
One Post Office Square     PGM
Boston, MA 02109
800-634-1587/617-292-1000


Putnam Managed Municipal Income Trust     NYSE
One Post Office Square     PMM
Boston, MA 02109
800-634-1587/617-292-1000


Seligman Select Municipal Fund     NYSE
130 Liberty Street     SEL
New York, NY 10006
800-221-7844
212-488-0384


Taurus MuniCalifornia Holdings     NYSE
Princeton Administrators, Inc.     MCF
P.O. Box 9011
Princeton, NJ 08543-9011
800-543-6217/609-282-2800


Taurus Municipal New York     NYSE
Princeton Administrators, Inc.     MNY
P.O. Box 9011
Princeton, NJ 08543-9011
800-543-6217/609-282-2800


Van Kampen Merritt California Municipal     Amex
    Trust     VKC
1001 Warrenville Road
Lisle, IL 60532
800-341-2929/708-719-1000

Van Kampen Merritt Investment Grade          NYSE
  Municipal Trust                          VIG
1001 Warrenville Road
Lisle, IL 60532
800-341-2929/708-719-1000

Van Kampen Merritt Municipal Income          NYSE
  Trust                                    VMT
1001 Warrenville Road
Lisle, IL 60532
800-341-2929/708-719-1000

---

## Convertible Funds

AIM Strategic Income Fund                    Amex
11 Greenway Plaza, Suite 1919                AST
Houston, TX 77046
800-347-1919/713-626-1919

American Capital Convertible Securities      NYSE
2800 Post Oak Boulevard                      ACS
Houston, TX 77056
800-421-9696/713-993-0500

Bancroft Convertible Fund                    Amex
56 Pine Street, Suite 1310                   BCV
New York, NY 10005-1515
212-269-9236

Castle Convertible Fund                      Amex
75 Maiden Lane                               CVF
New York, NY 10038
800-223-3810
212-806-8800

Ellsworth Convertible Growth & Income        Amex
  Fund                                     ECT
56 Pine St., Suite 1310
New York, NY 10005-1515
212-269-9236

Lincoln National Convertible Securities          NYSE
    Fund                                         LNV
1300 South Clinton Street
Fort Wayne, IN 46801
219-455-2210

Putnam High Income Convertible and              NYSE
    Bond Fund                                    PCF
One Post Office Square
Boston, MA 02109
800-634-1587/617-292-1000

TCW Convertible Securities Fund                 NYSE
400 South Hope Street                            CVT
Los Angeles, CA 90071
213-683-4000

# APPENDIX II

# *Directory of Closed-End Fund Information Sources and Services*

## SELECTED INFORMATION SOURCES

*The American Association of Individual Investors*
625 North Michigan Avenue
Chicago, IL 60611
312-280-0170

An independent, non-profit association founded in 1979 with over 40 chapters throughout the U.S. and over 110,000 members, it is dedicated to assisting individual investors through educational and information programs. Membership includes the *AAII Journal* published monthly except June and December. Reading the *AAII Journal* is a good way to keep up with the field of investing in general.

*International Fund Monitor*
P.O. Box 5754
Washington, D.C. 20016
202-363-3097
Publisher: Jon Woronoff

A monthly publication covering closed- and open-end funds investing in non-U.S. equities as well as general issues facing international investors.

Investment Company Institute
1600 M Street, NW Suite 600
Washington, D.C. 20036
202-293-7700

The trade association of the U.S. investment company industry.

*LIPPER Closed-End Bond Funds Analysis*
*LIPPER Closed-End Equity Funds Analysis*
Lipper Analytical Services, Inc.
1380 Lawrence Street, Suite 950
Denver, CO 80204
303-534-3472

Contains extensive data on closed-end funds prepared for professional investors.

*Mutual Fund Forecaster*
The Institute of Econometric Research
3471 North Federal Highway
Fort Lauderdale, FL 33306
800-327-6720
305-563-9000

Contains data on nearly 60 closed-end funds in addition to its coverage of open-end funds. Sample issue free.

*Standard & Poor's Stock Reports*
Standard & Poor's Corporation
25 Broadway
New York, NY 10004
212-208-8000

The most complete source of detailed data on individual closed-end funds. It is available in libraries and brokerage firm offices. Copies of individual S&P's Stock Reports are available from Standard & Poor's Corporation, 345 Hudson Street, New York, NY 10014; telephone 212-924-6825.

*The Value Line Investment Survey*
711 Third Avenue
New York, NY 10017
212-687-3965

Contains general commentary on closed-end funds and thorough profiles of over 40 closed-end funds.

## CLOSED-END FUND ADVISORY SERVICES AND NEWSLETTERS

*Closed-End Fund Analyst*
Worden Brothers, Inc.
111 Cloister Court, Suite 104
Chapel Hill, NC 27514
919-490-5250

*Frank Cappiello's Closed-End Fund Digest*
1280 Coast Village Circle, Suite C
Santa Barbara, CA 93108
800-282-2335
805-565-1112

*The Investor's Guide to Closed-End Funds*
Thomas J. Herzfeld Advisors, Inc.
P.O. Box 161465, Miami, FL 33116
305-271-1900

*The Scott Letter: Closed-End Fund Report*
Box 17800
Richmond, VA 23226
800-356-3508
804-741-8707
Sample issue free

Each of the above services is described in Chapter 3.

## FINANCIAL PLANNERS, INVESTMENT ADVISERS AND STOCKBROKERS SPECIALIZING IN U.S.-BASED CLOSED-END FUNDS

### Financial Planners and Investment Advisers

Bryan G. Colbert, CFP
MoneyTrak, Inc.
5100 California Avenue, Suite 110
Bakersfield, CA 93309
805-327-1155

Robert E. Frey, CFP
KMS Financial Services, Inc.
2 Nickerson Street, Suite 300
Seattle, WA 98109
800-262-3739
206-285-1730
(also stockbroker)

Thomas J. Herzfeld
Thomas J. Herzfeld Advisors, Inc.
The Herzfeld Building
P.O. Box 161465, Miami, FL 33116
305-271-1900
(also stockbroker)

Theodore E. Loud, CFP
TEL Advisors, Inc. of Virginia
2333 Old Ivy Road
Charlottesville, VA 22901
804-977-4407

Ronald Olin
Olin Asset Management
6022 Stones Throw
Houston, TX 77057
713-780-8501

Steven Samuels
Samuels Asset Management
13749 Riverside Drive
Sherman Oaks, CA 91413
818-981-1900
(also stockbroker)

George Cole Scott
Anderson & Strudwick
318 William Street
Fredericksburg, VA 22401
800-800-1821
703-373-1821
(also stockbroker)

## Stockbrokers

Bill Chapman
Rauscher Pierce Refsnes, Inc.
300 Convent, Suite 1600
San Antonio, TX 78205
800-777-7289
512-225-6611

Pete Daly
Interstate/Johnson Lane
Charlotte, NC 28280
704-379-9208

Tal Fletcher
Bear Stearns & Co., Inc.
Citicorp Center
1 Sansome Street
San Francisco, CA 94104
800-688-2327 (Ext. 2975)
415-772-2975

Robert A. Hays, Jr.
Shearson Lehman Brothers Inc.
101 E. Kennedy Boulevard, 34th Floor
Tampa, FL 33602
800-767-2525
813-222-7602

Peter Poletti
Dean Witter Reynolds
4582 S. Ulster Parkway, Suite 300
Denver, CO 80237
800-347-5099
303-771-0808


Bradley A. Roberts
Lynch & Mayer, Inc.
650 Fifth Avenue, 22nd Floor
New York, NY 10019
212-246-7760


Eric Walton
Dean Witter Reynolds Inc.
111 Mission Street
Santa Cruz, CA 95060
408-426-4500
800-433-3436


**BROKERS AND ADVISERS SPECIALIZING
IN NON-U.S. CLOSED-END FUNDS**

**British Funds**

Roger Adams
S.G. Warburg Securities
1 Finsbury Avenue
London EC2M 2PA
011-071-606-1066


George Foot
Newgate Management Associates
126 Main Street
P.O. Box 628
Northampton, MA 01061
413-586-6520

## Canadian Funds

Douglas W. Hitchlock
Midland Walwyn Capital Inc.
7030 Woodbine Ave., Suite 100
Markham, Ontario, Canada L3R 1A2
416-474-4374

# Closed-End Funds Followed by The Value Line Investment Survey

**Domestic Equity Funds**

ASA Limited
Adams Express Company
Gabelli Equity Trust
General American Investors
H&Q Healthcare Investors
Liberty All-Star Equity Fund
Morgan Grenfell SMALLCap Fund
Niagara Share Corporation
Petroleum & Resources Corp.
Royce Value Trust
Salomon Brothers Fund
Tri-Continental Corp.
Zweig Total Return Fund

## Foreign Funds

Austria Fund
Brazil Fund
First Australia Fund
Germany Fund
Italy Fund
Korea Fund
Malaysia Fund
Mexico Fund
Scudder New Asia Fund
Spain Fund
Swiss Halvetia Fund
Taiwan Fund
Templeton Emerging Markets Fund
Thai Fund
United Kingdom Fund

## Income Funds

ACM Government Income Fund
American Capital Bond Fund
Duff & Phelps Utilities Income
1838 Bond-Debenture Trading Fund
Global Yield Fund
John Hancock Investors Trust
Kemper High Income Trust
MFS Multimarket Income Trust
Montgomery Street Income Securities
Mutual of Omaha Interest Shares
Nuveen Municipal Value Fund
Patriot Premium Dividend Fund
TCW Convertible Securities Fund

# Index

## A

A. G. Edwards & Sons, 71
Abtrust New Thai, 257
ACM government bond funds, 308
Adams, Roger, 253–57
Adams Express, 12, 19, 36, 38, 82, 121, 368–70
  distributions, analyzing, 80–83
  expense ratio, 75–78, 79
  profile, 122
ADRs (American Depositary Receipts), 220
Advantages, of all funds, 20–22
  stock funds, 100–106
Adviser role, in closed-end fund, 9, 121
  sub-advisers, 134
Advisory letters, 70–71
Age, and investment plan, 365–66
AIM Advisors, 336

AIM Strategic Income Fund, 336
Alger, David, 137, 339
Alliance Capital Management, 303
Alliance New Europe Fund, 226, 241–42
Alliance Trust of Dundee, 256, 259
Allmon, Charles, 4, 16, 100, 107, 121, 146–48, 248
All-or-None Orders, 355
American Capital Asset Management, 337
American Capital Bond Fund, 281–83, 288
American Capital Convertible Securities, 337
American Depositary Receipts (ADRs), 220
American Stock Exchange, 6
America's All Season Fund, 317–18
Analyzing a fund, 61–91

Analyzing a fund (*cont.*)
  authors' philosophy, 61–63
  brokers who specialize,
    71–72
  data, 73–91
  dual purpose funds, 174–77
  standard sources, 63–70
Anderson, Seth Copeland, 55
AON orders, 355
Applegate, Fred, 151
Arbitrageurs, 382, 387–92
Arendt, Nina, 138
Aronstein, Michael, 318
ASA Limited, 47, 187–89,
  368–69
Asia Pacific Fund, 226, 237,
  238, 241, 242
Asset allocation, and interna-
  tional diversification,
  211–13
Asset allocation funds, 316–20
Asset plays, 107–8
Association of Investment Trust
  Companies, 258
Austria Fund, 238
Authors' philosophy, 364–65
Average daily trading volume,
  349–50
Averaging down, 25–26


**B**


Baillie Gifford Shin Nippon
  Trust, 254
Baker, Fentress & Co., 19, 36,
  38, 54, 110, 121
  distributions, analysis of, 80
  profile, 132–33
Baldwin, William, 172
Bancroft Convertible Fund,
  337–38
*Barron's*, 44, 64, 69
  bond indexes, 320, 324
  computation of discounts,
    34–36
Baughman, Bruce C., 180–81

BEA Associates, Inc., 230
Bednarski, Stanislaw, 4, 135,
  404–5
Behrmann, James, 337
Bergstrom, Erik, 4, 107, 121,
  134, 394–95
Bergstrom Capital Corporation,
  4, 80, 90, 117, 120, 239
  case study, 393–95
  profile, 133–34
Berkshire Hathaway, 3
BGR Precious Metals, 189–90
Bid-asked spread, 350–51
Blackstone trusts, 309, 310–11
Blue Chip Value Fund, 19, 44,
  54
  profile, 144, 145
Board of directors, 9
  directors' ownership of
    funds, 65
Bond funds, 17–18
  year-end average discounts,
    50
  *See also* Closed-end bond
    funds
Bond value of a convertible,
  328–29
Boston Personal Property
  Trust, 10
"Bottom-up" approach, 106
Bourque, Thomas, 71
Branson, Frank, 133
Brazil Fund, 226, 238
BRE Properties, 201
British funds, 251
  funds trading on NYSE, 258
  history of, 10, 252, 255, 259
  London investment trusts,
    252–59
  Scottish funds, 259–60
Broker, dealing with, 347–62
  broker advice, 359–61
  cash versus margin, 356–58
  entering orders, 351–56
  NAV syndrome, 356
  stock certificate consider-
    ations, 358
  trading basics, 348–51

Brokerage commissions, 7, 27, 74
Brokers specializing in closed-end funds, 71–72
Brunette, David, 210–11
Buffett, Warren, 3, 108, 121, 146, 147, 155
Bull market of 1980s, 14
Bunker Hill Income Securities, 281–83

C

Canadian Fund, 225, 261–62
Canadian funds, 261–62
  history of, 10
Canadian General Investments, 262
Capital, stability of, 23–24
Capital gains
  distribution of, 18–19, 78, 80
  retaining of, 80
Capital shares, 166–67, 168–69, 171–72, 174–76
Carr, Alan, 52
Carr, Fred, 135
Carr Securities, 137
Cash accounts, 356
Cash purchase plan, 373
Castle Convertible Fund, 339
Central Fund of Canada Limited, 190–91
Central Securities, 12, 38, 121, 122–24
Cheney, John, 371
Chicago Tribune, 34, 35
Chile Fund, 238
Claremont Capital, 133, 395
Classic funds, profiles, 122–32
Clemente Global Growth Fund, 241, 242, 382
Clements, Jonathan, 273
Closed-end bond funds
  active management in, 296–97
  analyzing, 280–81

basics, 271–86
categories, 304–5
closed- and open-end bond funds compared, 272–74
fund types and characteristics, 303–26
older bond funds, 287–301
ratios, 281–84
risks, 275–78
selection guidelines, 325–26
types, 274–75
See also Convertible bond funds
Closed-end equity funds, history of, 14
Closed-End Fund Analyst, 70
Closed-end funds
  advantages, 20–22, 22–25, 401–3
  analyzing, 61–91
  bond fund universe, 18
  brokers who specialize in, 71–72
  disadvantages of, 26–28
  and dollar cost averaging, 203–5
  equity and bond funds compared, 101–2
  history of, 10–14
  initial public offerings, 1980s, 14–15
  and open-end funds compared, 5–7, 92–94
  organizational structure, 7–10
  and REITs, 202–3
  selection guidelines, 159–61
  small cap closed-end funds, 112–15
  specialized equity and convertible fund universe, 1985–89, 17
  trading advantage, 24–25, 43–44
  types of, 28–29
  universe, 15
  Wall Street coverage of, 71–72

Closed-end funds (*cont.*)
  *See also* Closed-end bond
    funds; Stock funds, in-
    vesting in
"Closed-end mutual funds", 6
Closed-end stock funds, 28
"Closed-up funds", 7
CMOs, 310
Coburn, Gary, 312–14
Cohen & Steers Capital Manage-
  ment, 201
Colbert, Bryan G., 374, 375
Collateralized mortgage obliga-
  tions, 310
College funds, 105
Commission discount, 360
Common shares. *See* Capital
  shares
Common stock funds. *See* Do-
  mestic equity funds
Compounding interest, 103–5
Computer sources of informa-
  tion, 93
*Comstock Investment Strategy
  Commentary*, 318
*Comstock Investment Strategy
  Review*, 318
Comstock Partners Strategy
  Fund, 2, 318–19
Conversion value, 329
Convertible bond funds, 16–17,
  275, 327–42
  basics of, 327–32
  convertible strategies,
    332–34
  price of, and common stock
    price compared, 331
  profiles of funds, 336–42
Convertible funds. *See* Conver-
  ible bond funds
Convertible Holdings, 172–73,
  178, 179–80
  profile, 339
Cooke & Bieler, 148
Core holdings, 373
Cormey, John, 144, 145
Corporate bonds, 274–75, 312

*Corporation Records* (Standard
  & Poor's), 65, 68
Counsellors Tandem Securities
  Fund, 178, 180, 182,
  183n, 192, 383
Country funds, 28, 47, 213,
  216–17, 221
  attraction of, 227–28
  expense ratios, 74–75
  as growth stocks, 233
  historic evolution in U.S.,
    225–26
  multi-country funds, 240–48
  NAV total return vs. market
    price performance,
    234–35
  1989 performance, 233–35
  1990 performance, 235–36
  single-country funds,
    223–40
  valuation, 232–40
  *See also* British funds; Cana-
    dian funds; Global in-
    vesting
Crash of 1929, 12
Crash of October, 1987, 12, 34
Credit risk, 277
Crescent Japan Fund, 256, 382
Currency fluctuations, 217
  effect on international invest-
    ment returns, 218
Currency risk, 278
Current Income Shares, 289,
  290, 292–93
Cycle of stability strategy,
  313–15
Cypress Fund, 144, 145, 390

**D**

Davis, Andrew, 71
Davis, J. Morton, 135
Davis, John, 258
Davis-Dinsmore Management
  Company, 337
Dean Witter, 71

Deep Discount Advisors, 4, 161, 173
Default (credit) risk, 277
Defensive provisions, 389–90
de Montebello, Georges, 231–32
Derivative products, 90–91
Deutsche Bank AG, 150
Diebold, John, 133, 394
Diebold Venture Capital Corp., 4, 133, 394
Dimensional Fund Advisors Small Company Fund, 100
Dinsmore, Ronald, 337
Dinsmore, Thomas, 332–33, 337, 338
Directors. See Board of directors
Direct Placement Funds, 299–301
Discounts, 22, 31–58, 162–63
  advantages of, 39–40
  attraction of for arbitrageurs, 387–88
  availability of, long term, 55–56
  computing, 34–37
  and country funds, 236–37
  dual purpose funds, 172
  fund specific factors for, 45–46
  fund type, and effect on discount, 49–51
  general factors for, 47–49
  narrower discounts, strategies for, 51–54, 395–96
  and price-earnings ratio analogy, 58
  price/NAV ratio, 35
  risk factor, 37–39, 40–41
  sector specific factors for, 46–47
  stock funds and bond funds compared, 105–6
  tracking, 85–87
  year-end average discounts,

closed-end funds, 32–34, 38
Discretionary orders, 355–56
Distributions, 46, 78–83
Diversification
  of funds, 20, 46, 109, 370–71, 403–4
  in international investing, 208–13
Diversified stock funds, 99–100, 177–79
Dividend payments, 78, 388
Dividend reinvestment plan, 18–19
DNR orders, 354–55
Dodd, David, 107
Dollar cost averaging, 203–5, 372–73
Domestic equity funds, 117–40
  basic data, 118, 119
  classic funds, 117, 122–32
  fund profiles, 121–22
  management arrangement, 121
  other older funds, 132–37
  performance measurement, 138–39
  performance records, 118, 120
  See also Personality funds
Do Not Reduce Orders, 354–55
Dover Regional Financial Shares, 195–96
Dow Jones Capital Markets Wire, 35
Dragon Trust, 260
Drayton Japan, 256
Dual purpose funds, 14, 165–83, 334
  analysis of, 172–77
  basics of, 166–71
  diversified common stock funds, 177–79
  gauging discounts and premiums, 172
  potential pitfalls, 171–72
  specialized dual funds, 179–80

Dual purpose funds (cont.)
utilities, 181–82
Duff & Phelps Utilities Income,
16, 192–94
Dunn, Stephen, 289, 292
Duration, of closed-end bond
funds, 276, 279

**E**

Eberling, Dean, 71
Eberstadt, Walter, 253
Ebright, Thomas, 114
Economic Investment Trust,
262
Economies of scale, 21
Edinburgh Investment Trust,
257
1838 Bond-Debenture Trading
Fund, 273, 290, 292
profile, 293–94
1838 Investment Advisors,
L.P., 293–94
Ellsworth Convertible Growth
& Income Fund, 16–17,
337, 338
Emerging Germany Fund, 226,
238
EMF Java, 257
Engex, 78, 134–35
Europe, Australia, and Far East
(EAFE) Index, 210
Europe, unification of markets,
208, 214
European Warrant Fund, 226,
243
Europe Fund, 54, 226, 241,
242–43
Europe Index, 210, 211
Europe 1992 Fund, 248
Evans, Barry, 295–97
Event risk, 277
Excelsior Income Shares, 290,
292, 294–95
Ex-dividend, 355

Expense analysis, 73–78,
283–84

**F**

Fidelity Magellan Fund, 24
Financial company funds,
195–98
First Australia Fund, 16, 225,
238
First Australia Prime Income
Fund, 261, 312
First Boston Asset Management
Corporation, 166
First Financial Fund, 196
First Iberian Fund, 226, 238
First in, first out method, 379
First Mercantile Currency Fund
Inc., 261
First Philippine Fund, 237, 238
First Spanish Investment Trust,
257
Fixed-income funds, 28–29,
267–69
Flexible portfolio funds, 316–20
Foot, George, 263
Forbes, 13, 64, 84–85, 160
Forcing conversion, 330–32
Foreign bonds, 275
Foreign and Colonial Invest-
ment Trust, 10, 252, 255
Foreign & Colonial Manage-
ment Limited, 253
Foreign government bonds, 312
Form N-SAR, 64
France Fund, 226
France Growth Fund, 226, 238
Frank Cappiello's Closed-End
Fund Digest, 70
Franklin Balance Sheet Invest-
ment Fund, 7, 8
Franklin Group, 8
Frank Russell Company, 210,
222
Fraser, Don R., 54–55

Fred Alger Management, Inc.,
    137, 339
Fund basics, 5–10
    open-end and closed-end
        compared, 5–7
    organizational structure,
        7–10
Funds versus ordinary stocks,
    400–401
Fund switching, 27–28
Future Germany Fund, 16, 226,
    238
Futures, 5, 143


**G**

Gabelli, Mario, 4, 106, 107, 146
Gabelli Equity Trust, 16, 35,
    54, 107, 146
    distributions, analysis of, 80
    profile, 146
"Gearing", 253
Gedale, William, 124
Gemini Fund, 14
Gemini II, 166, 172–73, 177–79
General American Investors,
    10, 12, 38, 110, 121,
    126–27
    expense ratios, 78, 79
    profile, 124–25
German Smaller Companies In-
    vestment Trust, 254–55
Germany Fund, 6, 226, 234,
    237, 238
    profile, 228–29
Germany Fund of Canada, 261
Global Advisors, 317
Global bond funds, 311–12
Global equity funds, 28, 221.
    See also Global investing
Global Growth and Income
    Fund, 166
Global investing, 207–22
    advantages, 208–17
    annualized total returns, se-
        lected world markets,
        216
    diversification, 208–12
    factors affecting return,
        220–20
    investment company route,
        219–20
    risks, 217–19
    types of funds, 221
    See also Multi-country
        funds; Single-country
        funds
Global Utility Fund, 192
Globe Investment Trust, 256
Gold-oriented funds, 187–91
Gordon, Robert, 146, 382, 390
Grace, John and Oliver, Jr., 382
Graham, Benjamin, 31, 107,
    108, 146
Grayson, Richard, 289
Groth, John C., 54–55
Growth Fund of Spain, 226, 238
Growth investing, 106, 109–10
Growth Investment Corpora-
    tion of Toronto, 261
Growth Stock Outlook Trust,
    16, 100, 112, 248
    profile, 146–48
G.T. Greater Europe Fund, 226,
    241, 243–44
Guaranteed annual distribu-
    tions, 46


**H**

Hammond-Chambers, Alex,
    259–60
Hampton Utilities Trust, 29n,
    178, 180–82, 192
Healthcare funds, 198–200
Heard, Edwin, 294
Hedging, 279, 390
Helvetia Capital Corporation,
    231
Herzfeld, Thomas J., 3, 43, 64,
    171, 236, 263, 392

Herzfeld, Thomas J. & Co., Inc.,
71
*Herzfeld, Thomas J., Encyclo-
pedia of Closed-End
Funds*, 70, 262
Herzfeld Closed-End Average,
36, 44
High-yield corporate funds,
305–7
Hitchlock, Douglas, 261–62
Ho, James, 295–97
Hopson, Jeffrey, 71, 323, 390
Hottinger family, 231
H&Q Healthcare Investors, 16,
35, 51–52, 198–200
*Hulbert Financial Digest*, 155
Hurley, Timothy, 383, 384–85
Hyperion Total Return Fund,
309, 311

**I**

Ibbotson, Roger G., 100–101
Icahn, Carl, 404
Illiquid holdings, 45
Illustrative weekly closed-end
fund data, diversified
funds, 36
Incentive fee arrangement, 9
Income dividends vs. income,
281–83
Income and earning potential,
and investment plan, 366
Income shares, 166, 168–71,
174–76
India Growth Fund, 226, 238,
402, 403
Indonesia Fund, 16, 226, 238
profile, 229–30
Inefficiency of market, 48
Inefficient-Market Fund, 54,
148
Initial public offering (IPO), 6
disadvantages to buying
funds at, 26–27
in 1980s, 14–15

Institutional holdings, 68, 118
*Intelligent Investor*, 31
Interest rate risk, 276
Intermediate term government
funds, 308
Internal Revenue Service, 21,
80
International bond funds,
311–12
International equity funds, 28,
221. *See also* Global in-
vesting
International Financial Society,
10
*International Fund Monitor*,
214, 237
International investing. *See*
Global investing
Investing overview, 3–29
investment, definition, 4–5
Investment companies, and
global investing, 219–20
Investment Company Act of
1940, 13, 51, 116n
Investment Company Institute,
13, 23, 35, 36
as information source, 64, 68
Investment grade bond funds,
287–88
Investment plan, developing,
365–67
*Investment Trusts*, 258
Investment (bond) value,
328–29
*Investor's Guide to Closed-End
Funds*, 70
Irish Investment Fund, 226,
236, 238
profile, 240
Irwin, Robert J.A., 125, 138
Israel Development Corp., 225
Italy Fund, 225–26, 238
Ivory & Sime, 259

**J**

Jakarta Growth Fund, 226,
230, 238

Japanese market, 215
Japan Fund, 13, 225, 382
Japan OTC Equity Fund, 226,
    238
Jessell, Kenneth, 210
John Hancock Income Securi-
    ties Trust, 291, 292, 295
John Hancock Investors Trust,
    291, 292, 295
John Levin & Co., 144
Johnson, C.A., 123
Junk bonds and bond funds,
    278, 305-7, 312


**K**

Kapito, Robert S., 309, 310-11
Kern, Robert, 150
Kidd, Wilmot, 123-24
Kidder, Peabody, 71
Kleinwort Benson Australian
    Income Fund, 312
Koger Equity, 201
Korea Fund, 6, 16, 41, 42, 217,
    225, 234, 236, 238


**L**

Latin America Investment
    Fund, 226, 241, 244
Lazard Freres, 10
Lehman Brothers, 10
Lehman Corporation, 128
Leverage, 39, 40, 143-44, 279,
    357
    and municipal bond funds,
    323
Leveraged buy-outs, 277
Leveraged investment of trusts,
    creation of, 11
Leveraged Opportunities Trust,
    254, 257
Leverage factor, 167-68
Liberty All-Star Equity Fund,
    16, 29n, 54

profile, 148-50
Library sources of fund infor-
    mation, 65-69
Limited partnerships, 382
Limit order, 352-54, 359
Lincoln National Convertible
    Securities, 17, 339-40
Lincoln National Income Fund,
    291, 299
Lincoln National Investment
    Management Company,
    300, 339
Lipper, A. Michael, 267-68,
    271, 293
Lipper Analytical Services, Inc.,
    17, 35-36, 69-70
*Lipper Annuity & Closed-End
    Survey,* 70
*Lipper Closed-End Bond Funds
    Analysis,* 69, 160
*Lipper Closed-End Equity
    Funds Analysis,* 69, 160
Lippman, William, 7, 8, 180-81
Liquidated or open-ended funds
    since 1980, 391
Liquidity, 348-49, 388-89
    liquidity risk, 278
    requirements, and invest-
    ment plan, 366
Loan participation funds,
    324-25
London American Ventures
    Trust, 254
London Financial Association,
    10
Long-term discount patterns,
    86-87
Long-term performance,
    100-102
Lynch, Peter, 24
Lynch & Mayer, 339-40
Lyski, Wayne, 276, 308


**M**

McGowan, Joseph, 71
Madura, Jeff, 210, 371

Malaysia Fund, 226, 238
Malkiel, Burton G., 32, 372
Maltese, Anthony, 71
Management, of funds, 20–21
  of closed-end bond funds,
    273
  growth and value investing
    compared, 106–10
  multi-management, 149–50
  of older domestic equity
    funds, 121
  of personality funds, 143,
    160
Management fees, 9, 143
  for country funds, 228
Margin accounts, 356–58
Market price, determining, 6–7
Market sentiment, 48, 157
Market timing, 157
Markowitz, Harry, 370
Marks, Howard, 341
Massachusetts Financial Ser-
  vices funds, 29n, 303
Massachusetts Investors Trust,
  303
MassMutual Corporate Inves-
  tors, 288, 291, 299, 300
Mass Mutual Participation In-
  vestors, 300–301
Maturity date, dual income
  funds, 168–69
Meeschaert Gold and Currency
  Trust, 191
Mercury Asset Management,
  258
Merrill Lynch Asset Manage-
  ment, 180, 339
Mexico Equity & Income Fund,
  16, 226, 231
Mexico Fund, 16, 217, 225,
  230–31, 238
Mezzanine Capital and Income
  Trust, 254
MFS Intermediate Income
  Trust, 18
MFS Municipal Income Trust,
  271

MFS Special Value Trust, 316,
  319
Michaelis, George, 3, 4, 52, 53,
  82, 107, 108, 121,
  135–37
Minter, Charles, 318
Mitchell Hutchins Asset Man-
  agement, 144
Mobius, Dr. J. Mark, 108,
  245–47
Modern Portfolio Theory, 367,
  370
Modern Value Investing Ap-
  proach, 144
Money management unit, 9
Monthly distributions, 46
Moody's, 63
Morgan Grenfell SMALLCap
  Fund, 110, 112, 150
Morgan Stanley Asset Manage-
  ment Inc., 232
Morgan Stanley Capital Inter-
  national Perspective,
  234, 376
Mortgage-backed securities,
  275, 308–11
Mortgage strips, 310
Multi-country funds, 240–48
Multi-sector funds, 312–16
Munger, Charles, 3
Municipal bond funds, 17–18,
  271, 275, 320–24
  choosing, 322–23, 324
Mutual funds, 6
Mutual Fund Forecaster, 70
"Mutual Fund Scorecard", 69


**N**

National Association of Securi-
  ties Dealers Automated
  Quotation System
  (NASDAQ), 6–7
Near-term discount patterns, 87
Neff, John, 4, 7, 107, 171, 177
Net asset value, 6, 371

of dual purpose funds, 174
New America High Income
    Fund, 279, 307
Newbold's Asset Management,
    148
New Germany Fund, 226, 229,
    238
New Horizons Fund, 111–13
New issues, effect on supply
    and demand, 47
New Money Masters, 137, 177
New York Stock Exchange, 6
New York Times, 34, 35
Niagara Share Corporation, 12,
    38, 121, 125–28, 248
Nicholas, Arthur, 151
Nicholas-Applegate Growth Eq-
    uity Fund, 9, 16, 35, 51,
    110, 150–51
Nikkei Index, 236
Nikko Securities Co., 166
Non-diversified funds, 99–100
Norwitz, Steven, 111–12
Nuveen Advisory Corp., 303
Nuveen funds, 321–22
Nuveen investment Quality Mu-
    nicipal Fund, 322
Nuveen Municipal Value Fund,
    18, 321–22


O

Officers' ownership of funds, 65
Olin, Ron, 3–4, 161, 173–74
Old-line stock funds, 28
Open-end funds
    and closed-end funds com-
        pared, 5–7
    development of, 13
Open-ending, advantages and
    disadvantages, 386–87
Open-ending stipulations, 46
Oppenheimer Capital, 148, 179
Oppenheimer Multi-Sector In-
    come Trust, 315–16
Options, 5, 143

closed-end bond funds,
    279–80
Option theory, 174–75
Organizational structure,
    closed-end funds, 7–10
Our First 50 Years, 12
Overhead, and discounts, 45


P

Pacholder & Co., 307
Pacific American Income
    Shares, 291, 292, 298
Pacific Assets Trust, 260
Pacific Basin Index, 210, 211
Pacific-European Growth Fund,
    226, 241, 244–45
PaineWebber, 71
Panic on Wall Street, 11
Parity, 329
Participation certificates, 275
Pass-through securities, 275
Patriot Premium Dividend
    Fund(s), 194–95
Patterns, 86–87
Performance, 100–102, 140n
    and arbitrageurs, 388
    and discounts, 45
    domestic equity funds,
        118–21
    examining, 83–85
    long-term, of older stock
        funds, 120
    projecting, 162
    studies, 54–55
Perkins Smith, Inc., 137
Personality funds, 16, 141–64
    fund features, 143–44
    selection guidelines, 159–63
Petroleum and natural re-
    sources funds, 200–201
Petroleum & Resources Corp.,
    12, 19, 121, 122,
    200–201
Phoenix Investment Counsel,
    148

Pickins, T. Boone III, 382
Pilgrim Prime Rate Trust, 325
Pilgrim Regional Bank Shares,
    16, 54, 196–98
Political risk, and international
    investment, 219
Porter, Michael, 71
Portfolio
    building, 363–80
    choices, 21
    composition, of closed-end
        bond funds, 278
    turnover, 87–89, 151, 161,
        279, 285
Portfolio manager, in closed-
    end fund, 9–10, 20–21
Portugal Fund, 238
Preferred shares. See Income
    shares
Premiums, 31–32, 34, 58
    computing, 34–37
    and convertibles, 329–30
    and country funds, 237–39
    dual purpose funds, 172
    price/NAV ratio, 35
    risks, 40–42
    tracking, 85–86
Present value analysis, 175–76
Price, T. Rowe, 109
Prospect Street High Income
    Portfolio, 279, 307
Provident Investment Counsel,
    148
Proxy statements, 64–65
Prudential-Bache, 71
Prudential Mutual Fund Man-
    agement, 9
Purchasing power risk, 278
Putnam Duo-Fund, 14
Putnam funds, 29n
Putnam High Income Convert-
    ible and Bond Fund, 17,
    340
Putnam Management Com-
    pany, 303, 312–13
Putnam Premier Income Trust,
    18

Q

Quest Advisory, 83, 114–15,
    151
Quest for Value Dual Purpose
    Fund, 172–73, 177, 178,
    179

R

Railway and Light Securities
    Fund, 10
Random Walk Down Wall
    Street, 32, 372
Ranieri, Lewis, 311
Ratios, and analysis of closed-
    end bond funds, 281–84
Real estate funds, 201–3
Real Estate Investment Trusts
    (REITs), 201–3
Real estate mortgage invest-
    ment conduits (REMICs),
    310
Real Estate Securities Income
    Fund, 16, 201
Record keeping, 21–22
Regional funds, 221, 224, 226,
    237. See also Global in-
    vesting
Regulated investment com-
    pany, 80
Reik, William J., Jr., 144
Reilly, Richard M., 179
Reinvestment, shareholder,
    18–19, 160
Reinvestment rate risk, 276,
    277
REMICs, 310
Restructuring, 384–85
Revere Fund, 288, 291, 299,
    301
Richards, R. Malcolm, 54–55
Risk, 5
    case study, 368–70
    closed-end bond funds,
        275–78

credit risk, 277
currency risk, 278
discounts, 37–39, 40–41
dual purpose funds, 171–72
event risk, 277
global investing, 217–19
interest rate risk, 276
and overseas investments,
    217–19
premiums, 40–42
purchasing power and liquid-
    ity risk, 278
reinvestment rate risk, 276
sector, 186–87
Risk-return trade-off, 367–68
Risk tolerance, and investment
    plan, 366
Roberts, Richard, 148
Royce, Charles, 4, 83, 107, 114,
    151–52
Royce Value Trust, 16, 73, 83,
    90, 112, 114, 151–53
Russell 3000 Index, 210


                      S

Salomon Asset Management,
    240
Salomon Brothers Fund, 12, 19,
    38, 90, 128–30
    expense ratios, 78, 79
Salvigsen, Stanley, 318
Samuels, Steven, 56–58,
    359–61
Schafer, David, 392
Schafer Value Trust, 16, 383,
    390, 392
Schieferdecker, G. Peter,
    211–12
Schwertfeger, Timothy, 322
Scott, George Cole, 140n
Scottish funds, 259–60
Scottish Investment Trust, 259
Scott Letter, 48, 70
Scudder Duo-Vest, 14

Scudder New Asia Fund, 226,
    237, 238, 241, 245
Scudder New Europe Fund,
    226, 241, 245
Second Market Investment
    Company, 248
Second General American In-
    vestors, 10
Second Market Investment
    Company, 255
Sector equity funds, 185–206
    dollar cost averaging, 203–5
    financial company funds,
        195–98
    gold-oriented funds, 187–91
    healthcare, 198–200
    petroleum and natural re-
        sources, 200–201
    real estate, 201–3
    role in portfolio, 375
    sector risk, 186–87
    selection, 203
    utility funds, 192–95
Securities Act of 1933, 12
Securities Exchange Act of
    1934, 12
Securities and Exchange Com-
    mission, 12–13, 64
Security Analysis, 107
Security lending, 280
Security Owner's Stock Guide
    (Standard & Poor's), 65,
    68, 349
Seligman group, J. & W., 130
Selling, timing of, 377
Sentiment indicators, 48,
    157–58
Shareholder record keeping, 21
Shareholder reinvestment,
    18–19
Shareholder reports, 64–65
Shareholders, and difficulty of
    open-ending, 389
Shearson Lehman Hutton, 71
Shin Nippon, 260
Singapore Fund, 226
Single country funds. See
    Country funds

Sinquefield, Rex A., 100–101
Size quotes, 351
Smaller Markets Trust, 260
Small stocks, investing in,
110–15
Smith Barney, 71, 148
Sobel, Robert, 11
Solomon, Anthony, 258
Source Capital, 3, 38, 52, 53,
54, 90, 108, 117, 120,
135–37, 237, 239
Sources, for analyzing funds,
63–70
advisory letters, 70
library, 65–69
Lipper data, 69–70
media coverage, 63–64
shareholder reports, 64–65
Southeastern Savings Institu-
tions Fund, 198
Spain Fund, 41, 42, 226, 233,
237, 238
Spaulding, Thomas, 322
Specialized equity funds, 16–17
with largest drop in pre-
mium/discount, 402
Specialty funds, 185. *See also*
Single country funds
Spectra Fund, 78, 79, 89, 137
illiquidity of, 349
Stability of capital, 23–24
Standard & Poor's, 63, 65
Steadman, Charles, 394
Steers, Robert, 201–2
Sterling Grace Capital Management, 382
Stock certificate considerations, 358–59
Stock funds, investing in,
97–116
advantages of, 100–106
differences, 98
diversified vs. non-diversified, 99–100
growth vs. value, 106–10
selection guidelines, 159–61
small stocks, 110–15

*See also* Domestic equity
funds; Personality funds
*Stock Reports* (Standard &
Poor's), 9, 65
Stock(s)
funds, year-end average dis-
counts, 50
volatility of, 26
*See also* Stock funds, invest-
ing in
Stone, Douglas, 210–11
Stone, Mary, 128–29
Stop orders, 354
Straight corporate bonds,
274–75
"Superstar funds", 16
"Superstar managers", 106
Suckow, Paul, 315–16
Sun Life Assurance of Canada,
319
Swiss Helvetia Fund, 226, 231–
32, 238

T

T. Rowe Price New Horizons
Fund, 111, 112, 113
Taiwan Fund, 237, 226, 238
Takeover basics, 382–86
Taxation, and funds, 21–22,
45, 48, 80–81, 377–80
Tax bracket, and investment
plan, 367
Tax Reform Act of 1986, 181
TCW Convertible Securities
Fund, 17, 54, 340–41
Templeton, John, 4, 107, 108–
9, 246
Templeton Emerging Markets
Fund, 109, 224, 226, 237,
238,
241, 245–46
Templeton Global Govern-
ments Income Trust,
311–12

Templeton Global Income
Fund, 311–12
Templeton Global Utilities, 16
Templeton Growth Fund, 108
Templeton International,
108–9
Tepper, Norman, 69
Thai Capital Fund, 226
Thai Fund, 226, 238
Third Canadian General Investments, 262
*Thomas J. Herzfeld Encyclopedia of Closed-End Funds*,
70
Thompson, Rex, 54
Time diversification and risk reduction, 102–3, 372
Timing of investment, 111–12
entering orders, 351–56
"Top-down" analysis, 316
*Toronto Globe and Mail*, 261
Total return
calculation of for multi-year holding period, closed-versus open-end fund,
92–94
and closed-end bond funds,
284–85, 303
computing, 84–85
defined, 272
examining, 83–85
investment for, 24
Total return funds, 316–20
Trading advantages, 24–25,
43–44
Trading basics, 348–51
Train, John, 137, 177
Transaction costs, controlling,
359–61, 372–73
Transamerica Income Shares,
291, 292, 298–99
Transamerica Investment Services, Inc., 299
*Treasury-Junk Yield Spread*,
306
Tri-Continental Corporation,
12, 19, 24, 38, 110

operating expenses of, 75,
78, 79
profile, 130–32
*Stock Report*, 66–67
Turkish Investment Fund, 16,
226, 232, 236, 238
Turnover, portfolio, 87–89,
151, 161, 279, 285
12b-1 plan, 27

**U**

Uniform Gifts to Minors Act,
105
United Corporations, 262
United Kingdom Fund, 226,
238, 258–59
*See also* British funds
United States & Foreign Securities, 11, 12
United States Trust Company
of New York, 295
Universal Health Realty Income
Trust, 201
Unrealized capital appreciation,
45, 89–90
U.S. government bond funds,
17, 307–8, 312
U.S. Treasury securities, 275
USF&G Pacholder Fund, Inc.,
307
Utilities, 181–82
Utility funds, 192–95

**V**

Valuation in the market, 158
Value, finding, 374, 376–77
Value investing, 106–9
*Value Line Investment Survey*,
63, 69
Vanguard Group, 177
Veitia, Diego, 317–18
Vitale, Robert, 273, 284, 293
Volatile securities, 23, 224

**W**

*Wall Street Journal,* 34, 35,
     63–64, 69
Walsh, Ted, 71
Weirick, Glenn, 341
Weiss, Kathleen, 26–27
Wellington Management Co.,
     177
Western Asset Management
     Co., 298
Wiesenberger's Diversified In-
     vestment Company Aver-
     age, 37–38
*Wiesenberger Investment
     Companies Service,* 34,
     68–69, 85
Wilkinson & Hottinger, 231
William I, King of Netherlands,
     10, 208
Williamson, J. Peter, 149
Windsor Fund, 7, 177, 179
Worldwide Value Fund, 54,
     246, 248
Woronoff, Jon, 214, 237

**Y**

Yale University, 150
Yield, 39–40, 272–73

**Z**

Z-Seven Fund, 16, 24, 25, 73,
     74, 143, 153–55, 248
  distribution, analysis of,
     80–81
  expense ratios, 78, 79
Zero-coupon bonds, 274
ZICO Investment Holdings,
     337–38
Ziskin, Barry, 16, 24, 25, 153,
     154
Zweig, Dr. Martin, 4, 52, 54,
     106, 121, 155–157, 320
Zweig Fund, 16, 36, 47, 54,
     155–58
Zweig Total Return Fund, 54,
     155–56, 319–20